A TREASURY OF SCANDINAVIAN DESIGN

A TREASURY OF
SCANDINAVIAN DESIGN

Edited by

ERIK ZAHLE

Director of the Museum of Industrial Art, Copenhagen

GOLDEN PRESS, NEW YORK

For the different parts of Scandinavia, the following editors wrote the general articles, picture captions, and biographies, and also selected the illustrative material.

Denmark

ARNE KARLSEN, Architect, M.A.A.
ANKER TIEDEMANN, Architect and Editor

Finland

H. O. GUMMERUS, Director,
Finnish Society of Crafts and Design, Helsinki
BENEDICT ZILLIACUS, Editor,
Hufvudstadsbladet, Helsinki

Norway

FERDINAND AARS, Director,
Norwegian Society for Industrial Arts and Design, Oslo

Sweden

SVEN ERIK SKAWONIUS, formerly Director,
Swedish Society for Industrial Design, Stockholm

Erik Hansen, photographer, Copenhagen, took the great majority of the photographs for the illustration section.
Advice on the English text was given by Hugh Wakefield of the Victoria and Albert Museum.

Published by Golden Press, Inc., New York, New York.

CONTENTS

UNITY AND DIVERSITY
IN SCANDINAVIA

Frantz Wendt

We live in a period of international co-operation. Culturally and in economics, in defence and communications, and in many other fields, national frontiers are losing their significance and gradually becoming no more than coloured lines on the map. States are coming together in groups presenting more and more of a unity to the outside world, and their social functions are becoming increasingly integrated. Even so, it is still somewhat exceptional for the representatives of four countries, as in this book, to collaborate closely in portraying an important element in the cultural life of their nations.

For the outsider this may appear less unusual, in that he has been accustomed to think of the Northern lands as a unit called Scandinavia. This comprehensive term, with its suggestion of Vikings on the seas and 'Vikings' in the air, nevertheless covers five completely sovereign states (since Iceland is also one), each with its separate Head of State, parliament, government, and all the other actual and nominal attributes of national independence, and each with a long and glorious history, a distinctive culture, and differing traits of national character.

But the name 'Scandinavia' is no mere geographical term: it expresses a tangible reality and a community of ideas which have inspired this book, and covers an increasing integration of social and economic policies, law and justice, transport, and intercourse in all spheres of human activity. Above all, the word 'Scandinavia' stands for a many-sided common culture, which gives a solid foundation for more material activities. This stems from three main roots–affinity in religion, law, and language–together with a common racial origin and consequent similarities of temperament.

The peoples of the North were simultaneously converted from the heathen worship of the Vikings to Catholicism, and again to the Lutheran form of Protestantism at the Reformation. A common legal system has also had a culturally unifying effect: from the earliest known times the Northern peoples have had the same ideas of right and wrong, of good and evil, and their laws are founded on the same basic concepts.

The strongest of all binding forces has been the very close affinity between the Northern languages. In the early Middle Ages the differences between them were slight, and even today Danes, Norwegians, and Swedes can speak and write their own tongue and be mutually understood without much difficulty. This is true not only of a cultured few and the academically educated, but to a very considerable extent of the man in the street. In addition to this Danish-Norwegian-Swedish similarity of language, many Icelanders speak Danish, and a culturally influential (though numerically very limited) group of Finns have Swedish as their mother-tongue, while a growing number of Finnish-speakers learn Swedish as a second language. Icelanders and Finns are therefore also active members of the Scandinavian language-community.

The importance of this affinity of language can hardly be exaggerated. Because of it, one can speak of a common Scandinavian cultural life which could never have developed if the various languages were completely foreign to the great majority. Newspapers, books, and periodicals written in Danish, Norwegian, or Swedish can be read without translation anywhere in Scandinavia, except for certain parts of Finland.

For the purposes of scholarship, this language affinity allows the publication of common periodicals and textbooks in Danish, Norwegian, or Swedish, according to the tongue of the author. In this way the handicap to the cultural life of the separate nations which would be imposed by the smallness of their language-area is overcome. Furthermore, it permits the exchange of teachers and students between Universities, Grammar Schools, and even Modern Schools. Theatre companies frequently perform in each other's countries. Most valuable co-operation has been established between the State Broadcasting and (especially) Television services, which in time will bear particular fruit in the latter sphere, organised under the common name of Nordvision.

The fact that Scandinavians (apart from a majority in Finland) can talk to and write for each other without interpreter or translation, has of course made personal contacts across the national frontiers much easier. During the last thirty years this association has been vastly enhanced by many-sided contacts between like-minded societies and institutions in the different countries, covering the most diverse aspects of community life. These links have been formed both as the result of a spontaneous desire among colleagues to meet and collaborate, and from the wish to further particular common interests by concerted action. State support for this cultural co-operation, which now covers all the Scandinavian lands with a close network, has recently been directly or indirectly forthcoming.

One considerable and vigorous aspect of this has been collaboration in the realm of art, with constant exhibitions, frequent visits by critics and lecturers, conferences, and even conjoint demonstrations to the outside world. As we have already said, this book is itself an example of this kind of Scandinavian co-operation.

But though there are so many similarities and parallels in the Northern peoples and their historical development, this has in no way prevented each of them from evolving an art and poetry peculiarly its own. One reason for this has been the great variety of natural scene in the wide area of Scandinavia, including as it does the Greenland icefields, the lava-flows and volcanoes of Iceland, the storm-beaten basalt cliffs of the Faroes, the deep narrow fiords of Norway, Sweden's endless forests, the great barrens of the Far North, Finland's myriad lakes, and the gentle plains and idyllic beechwoods which are the special characteristic of the Danish landscape. While the spiritual and artistic life of each people has been indelibly moulded by its national origins, it has through the centuries been fertilised and inspired by constant contacts with the great centres of civilisation and continual mutual influences from the other Scandinavian peoples.

Thanks to affinity of language, and cross-frontier links between individuals and organisations, the finest works of their art and literature belong not only to the separate nations but to all Scandinavia. It is also highly significant that a common racial origin and attitude to life's vital problems allow us Scandinavians, in the words of the Swedish art historian Axel L. Romdahl, to love and understand each other's art, poetry, and music better than we can that of the outside world.

Romdahl also points out as a peculiarity in the art of the Scandinavian peoples, that right from the earliest known times there were developments in each country which are not simultaneously found to the same degree or extent in the others. This diversity has given the art of Scandinavia a many-sidedness and vigour within its unity, which is a common enrichment and inspiration.

DENMARK

Arne Karlsen and Anker Tiedemann

The term 'applied art' implies that the objects which it embraces have properties which make them practically useful, and, equally, values which give us an artistic experience. They have a dual nature, and the most vital problems of every industrial artist or artist-craftsman lie in this duality. His work involves the fulfilment and mutual balance of these two main purposes. If he neglects one or the other he ceases to be an industrial artist: on the one hand he becomes a technician, or on the other produces art for art's sake.

It is thus the fate of the industrial artist to be a split personality: within him the practician struggles with the artist, and from this dualism comes the inner tension of his work. When we make a critical appreciation of an industrial artist and his work, much of the judgement will be concerned with how far his thought has been dominated by concern for utility or for aesthetics. The same applies if we are dealing with schools of industrial artists, or, from a greater distance in time, if we are considering periods in the history of applied art.

At the outset of the period we are here concerned with—the years 1930 to 1960—we were in the midst of developments which for a while made the demand for *fitness for purpose* uppermost in the minds of the leading artists. Throughout the Western World, artists felt the need to break free not only from the lifeless copying of earlier styles but also from conscious desire to produce a 'style' which marked the Art Nouveau period. Though this aspiration was formulated and practised in many different ways, the objective was the same: a defined and valid programme with principles naturally related to the increasing industrialisation and social levelling of the new age. The conclusion reached was *functionalism*—that the method of production and the practical purpose of the object should be emphasised and used to an aesthetic end.

During the last hundred years the rise of new ideas has often been emphasised by large exhibitions. For Scandinavians it is natural to connect the break-through of functionalism with the great Stockholm Exhibition of 1930, in which Northern designers—after two decades of hesitation—decisively adopted the line pioneered by such men as Walter Gropius, Mies van der Rohe, and Le Corbusier. It is of course dubious to connect a change of style with one particular event and date, but the Stockholm Exhibition presented for the first time a clearly defined programme of functionalism. Its extent and high artistic standards gave weight to the new ideas, not only as against those artists who still concealed their objectives in the garb of classicism but also in the eyes of the general public.

The exhibition gave a tangible demonstration of the great breadth of scope in functionalist architecture. Its organiser, the Swede Gunnar Asplund (1885–1940), and his collaborators, expressed in their buildings the theorist's dream of using industrialised production methods to replace the old social order with a new one having new social and cultural values.

It would often seem that Danish artists are not naturally given to the formulation of aesthetic systems. The Danish groups which were working their way towards functionalism in the Twenties did not follow the same track as, for example, the internationally famous pioneers of the Bauhaus school. They were certainly influenced by some of the currents which emanated from Bauhaus-Dessau, but did not allow themselves to be bowled over by them. By international standards they thus produced nothing of particular ideological significance, but they regarded the new ideas critically and attempted to bring theory into closer relationship with social reality. For this reason, the practical results they achieved often showed greater maturity than those of thorough-going theorists.

Even those artists who welcomed the new ideas most readily were not genuine artistic revolutionaries. For example, those concerned with the avant-garde periodical *Kritisk Revy* (1926–28) were above all else socially-conscious, and not—like the Bauhaus people—committed to a programme with an aesthetic basis. They did indeed carry on an aggressive propaganda, which attacked the classicist fantasies of the period without respect of persons, but for them the fundamental point was to establish reality as the foundation of all work in the arts.

Kritisk Revy (Critical Review) was founded by architects, and architecture remained its principal subject, but in the few years of its existence the criticism of art as applied to objects of everyday use became an important sideline of its propaganda. The editor, the architect Poul Henningsen, realised that a change in the ideological

Chair for Faaborg Museum: designed 1914 by Kaare Klint and made in oak by N. M. Rasmussen. The furniture for Faaborg Museum, which Klint assisted the architect Carl Petersen in building, was Klint's first important work.

status of industrial art would gradually have a moral and didactic influence on every aspect of the home, and thereby also on house-building. A change of emphasis within the industries concerned, towards increased regard for good standards in articles of everyday use, was therefore one of the planks in the paper's platform.

With this in mind, Poul Henningsen incessantly attacked the pottery and furniture industries for their neglect of democratic obligations, and he flayed their designers for deliberately keeping them behind the times. He pointed out, for example, how inexcusable it was that the perfected techniques achieved in the two great Danish porcelain works over the whole previous period had never been employed to produce wares for the general public. Refusing to let aesthetic theories blind his social vision, he addressed to those in the industries concerned such appeals as this:

"Dear craftsmen friends! How can you expect us to go on respecting you, while this swindle continues in the name of art, and while you ignore all your obligations to the modern world? We have no proper tumblers, plates, water-sets, spoons, knives, or forks, while richer homes are flooded with trash and rubbish at fantastic prices! Think a little, and consider your obligations to make things for the delight of your fellow-men in their daily life! Throw away your artists' berets and bow-ties and get into overalls. Down with artistic pretentiousness! Simply make things which are fit for use: that is enough to keep you busy, and you will sell vast quantities and make lots of money!"

In their informal methods, and in their direct propaganda, Poul Henningsen and the group connected with *Kritisk Revy* were far removed from another school of Danish artists with a common background of training at the Academy of Art Department of Furniture, who played a decisive part in developing Danish design towards functionalism. In their attitude towards the ethics of applied art, however, and in many matters of principle, the two groups were often nearer to each other than those concerned realised at the time. Their attitude to tradition was broadly the same.

Poul Henningsen repeatedly emphasised that *Kritisk Revy* desired no change of form unless dictated by function: and here he was in direct opposition to Bauhaus, which held that to create forms appropriate to the present it was essential to thrust from the mind everything traditional and begin anew. In this way Bauhaus rejected not only traditional forms based on association with the idiom of earlier times: the German school also dismissed the functional tradition, which is type-forming. But the further improvement of traditional types of furniture was precisely the chief purpose of the Department of Furniture. This section of the Danish Academy of Art was founded in 1924, and from the beginning it was dominated by one man – the architect and designer Kaare Klint.

Klint was no agitator, seldom lectured, and wrote still less. For this reason he has not been generally acknowledged – like the men of *Kritisk Revy* – as a founder of functionalism. Nevertheless, the ideals on which he based his teaching were closely allied to those in early functionalism which survived the break-through. Today the attitude towards the construction of furniture which he built up through his own work and through his teaching is a common heritage which every Danish furniture-designer – and every practical artist – carries with him whether he knows it or not.

Kaare Klint created the modern Danish tradition, not by dictating a particular form-idiom but by teaching his pupils strict working principles based on knowledge of materials and thorough investigation of the function of different pieces of furniture and their scaling in conformity with the dimensions and movements of the human body.

As early as 1917 Klint produced a series of studies of proportion based on the inter-relationship of people and furniture, in connection with an abortive project for mass-produced furnishing. Contemporary designers did not realise the scope of the material thereby presented to them, but Klint was on the right road, and he never subsequently left it. Based on his own peculiarly developed feeling for economy of space, Klint evolved a simplified method of calculation which helped him to lay out his pieces of furniture on scales which were easy to grasp and derived their meaning from their purpose alone. In his own productions this drive against the indefinable residue resulted in shrewdly proportioned and succinct storage units. For example, in connection with the 1917 project he began to plan out the appropriate dimensions for types of furniture whose design depends on the size of sheets of paper, such as writing desks, bookcases and shelving, and filing cabinets. Attempts at standardisation proceeded from the sheet of paper to include three-dimensional objects. The starting point here was simply the desire to provide suitable accommodation for articles in common use, based on analysis of the needs of an average family.

In this connection Klint–and in due course his pupils– measured a large range of Danish and foreign table-ware of all kinds–plates, cups, jugs, knives, spoons, forks, etc. From this they found that differences of height and diameter, or length and breadth, were quite small, and that a simple series of dimensions could be laid down by which shelves and drawers could be scaled without limiting their potential use for different purposes. Furthermore, it was found that the various heights could without difficulty be co-ordinated to the same scales laid down for plan dimensions. Thus, in connection with the natural height of articles in use, a scientifically based foundation was worked out for the design of a large range of storage units.

Klint regarded this material as more valuable in teaching than subjective ideas of aesthetic finesse, and it was with pardonable pride that he could state, in an article in the periodical *Arkitekten* in 1930, that the researches then published in Germany had already been carried out by himself five years before. Moreover, he could establish that the standardisation work of the Department of Furniture was based on more thorough research than that of the Germans.

In English furniture of the Eighteenth Century Klint found an echo of his own perception that suitability for purpose should be the most vital consideration in aesthetic principles. A thorough study of that period came to set its stamp on many pieces of his own and of his pupils. He saw nothing derogatory in learning from the experience of others, whether with regard to function or to form. In his view the Bauhaus school, in their aversion from everything ancient, sacrificed width of vision and shut themselves off from the benefits of being able to build on the accumulated experience of centuries. While Bauhaus pupils sought aid and inspiration only from contemporary abstract art in painting and sculpture, Klint's were made to study existing types of furniture, to seek for functional elements in surviving material, analyse methodically

Interior from the Kaare Klint memorial exhibition, held in the Danish Museum of Industrial Art in 1956. Bookcase designed 1933 and made in mahogany by Rud. Rasmussen: table and chairs designed 1930 for Thorvaldsen's Museum, made in mahogany with ebony inlay by N. C. Jensen Kjær.

what they found, examine their results theoretically, and only then work out their own version of the type. Rough sketches and preconceived notions of the outward appearance of the final product played virtually no part in the work.

Klint did not draw his inspiration from Eighteenth Century England alone. He used appropriate elements from many lands and periods, though always excluding stylistic traits which had no functional content. In this way he worked out a range of well-known examples of uncommitted and timeless character, simply structured pieces, whose static construction could be immediately grasped. Through types such as the safari-chair, the deck-chair, and the chair for Grundtvig's church, he laid the foundation for our contemporary idea of a piece of furniture as an unpretentious useful object, convenient for everyday use.

At this point, in the years immediately before 1930, the Cabinetmakers' Guild of Copenhagen took a decisive hand in developments. This was not because the furniture craftsmen themselves had formed any artistic or social programme, but because events made them an instrument for the new movement of the time. Unemployment in their trade, resulting from a falling-off of home demand and increasing competition from furniture factories, forced the Cabinetmakers to make an active bid to convince the public of the value of old-time craftsmanship.

Their method was to hold annual exhibitions, together

Danish version of Viennese chair: frame in steam-bent beech, seat and back in Cuba mahogany. Designed 1930 by Fritz Scheegel and made by Fritz Hansen Ltd.

with competitions for suggestions for new types of furniture. The Guild held its first exhibition in 1927, and has stoutly continued ever since in spite of German occupation and trade fluctuations. The Master-Cabinetmakers of Copenhagen are an obstinate lot, touchy and self-conceited, but for that very reason possessed of an exceptionally tough determination to survive as a craft.

The first year's exhibition was quite simply a sales-drive, but they very soon acquired a second and more cultural object. It was necessary to take to heart promptly the attacks on imitative style made by socially committed critics and designers, and to seek co-operation from the younger designers who had a social programme to further. Paradoxically enough, it was thus the hand-craftsmen and their designers–and not the furniture mass-producers–who set out to produce clean-lined and simple pieces for use in small homes. As an illustration of this we may mention that the principal exhibit of the 1930 exhibition was a furnished two-room apartment, designed by the architects Hans Hansen (1899–1958) and Viggo Sten Møller (b. 1897).

In the nature of things the pieces shown in the Cabinet-makers' Guild's exhibition were generally too expensive for the man in the street, but these displays played a large part in changing the time-honoured popular idea of furniture as a prestige symbol. In this way the Guild prepared the way for a contemporary furniture industry with a programme similar to its own.

The Cabinetmakers' Guild recruited its designers in the first two decades from two groups, partly from Klint's school and partly from architects who had sought in vain for factory-made furniture designed to the same ideals as socially-conscious apartment-building, and therefore turned to this exclusive channel. For most architects, furniture-designing was no more than an interlude in their major interest of building dwellings; and when the furniture industry was eventually obliged to follow up the development they had helped to initiate at the Guild exhibitions, most of them again passed out of the picture, leaving factory-made furniture also to those who had been trained in the craft.

Amongst these building architects may be mentioned Kaj Gottlob (b. 1887), Arne Jacobsen (b. 1902), Hans Christian Hansen (b. 1901), and Viggo S. Jørgensen (b. 1902), Flemming and Mogens Lassen (b. 1902 and 1901), Fritz Schlegel (b. 1896), and Magnus Stephensen. Klint's pupils included Ole Wanscher, Rigmor Andersen, and O. Mølgaard-Nielsen, who made their mark in the first year of the exhibition.

The revolutionary changes in Danish furniture round about 1930 naturally also had their effect on other branches of practical art. And just as Klint was responsible for the most important developments in furniture, so there appeared in other crafts individuals with the will and talent to carry their development forward. In silverware Kay Bojesen was an outstanding pioneer of new forms, in ceramics Nathalie Krebs, and in textiles Marie Gudme Leth.

Kay Bojesen was brought up in the period of elaborate and stylised craftsmanship at the beginning of the century. He was trained by the internationally famous Danish silversmith Georg Jensen (1866–1935), and as a young craftsman he worked–in accordance with the period's ideas on the importance of decoration–in close contact with pure artists such as the sculptors Kai Nielsen (1882–1924) and Gerhard Henning (b. 1880). In the First World War years, however, he began to abandon restless and over-decorated forms, and, after a short neo-classicist period, went over completely to the principles of early functionalism. In spite of the expensiveness of his material, he was one of the first to understand that the future function of industrial art lay primarily in producing rational and useful articles at a reasonable price.

With his usual impulsiveness, in 1928 he vigorously attacked the florid current style in silverware, based on Georg Jensen's much admired work, in an article in *Nyt Tidskrift for Kunstindustri* entitled *Hammerslag* ('hammerstroke'), following this up with a campaign in the daily Press. He particularly attacked the overdone treatment of surfaces with hammering and oxidisation, and the excessive combination of materials–silver, amber, semi-precious stones, ivory, wood, etc. At the same time he criticised silverware makers for the bogus appearance of hand-craftsmanship which they gave their products. In this campaign he was completely at one with the line taken by *Kritisk Revy*, the main point of which was that modern designers should break away from handicraft principles and instead express their own inner convictions in forms appropriate to the natural qualities of the material.

In the work which he himself produced, Kay Bojesen showed much the same basic principles as Kaare Klint. His purpose was to refine *types*, and here he drew on tradition without allowing his style to smack of anti-quarianism. He was first and foremost concerned with objects having a practical use, and thus his favourite line of work was quickly determined.

In 1929 he produced, in collaboration with the designer Gunnar Biilmann Petersen (b. 1897), a set of cutlery ornamented only with a grooved edge; and in the same year he brought out by himself a set with a slight ridge along the mid-line of the handles. Both were based on earlier models, but each point was critically worked over, and the traditional form altered where it was found wanting. For example, the handles were made slightly shorter than had previously been usual; and in a later set from 1938 the edge of the knife-blade was also made more curved, so that one could use more of it than formerly for cutting. Most subsequent Danish cutlery sets show this functional change in proportion.

Bojesen's container-pieces have also had a significance beyond their intrinsic value. His tea- and coffee-pots, covered dishes, and cooking-pots are completely simple in form, but not (like, for example, the corresponding products of the Bauhaus workshops) pure cylinders, spheres, or cones determined by mathematical formulae. They are not sharp edged, but pleasantly rounded. Bojesen himself said: "Lines should be friendly. The things we make should have life and heart in them, and be a joy to hold. They must be human, vital, and warm."

With his tautly functional silverware, cleansed of all ornament but enriched with simplicity of line, Bojesen established the basic principles for a whole generation's work in a complete range of subjects. His contemporaries Inger Møller, a silversmith trained like himself in Georg Jensen's workshops, and the architect Magnus Stephensen, who made designs for him for many years, carried out his ideas most clearly and consistently.

Kay Bojesen showed through his work that there was no necessary opposition between distinction and simplicity. In this he was in agreement with the efforts being made in those branches of craftsmanship whose materials alone, by their costliness, made it impossible for their products to meet the social ideas of the period.

This interest in products of an everyday nature but of

Silver table-ware, designed and made by Kay Bojesen, 1929. Cotton fabric designed 1960 by Vibeke Klint for the Cotil collection of C. Olesen Ltd.

the highest technical quality – first-class mass-production – was for example expressed in an exhibition of British craftsmanship organised at the Danish Museum of Industrial Art by the architect Steen Eiler Rasmussen (b. 1898) in 1932. The exhibits were chosen in England by Danes, and therefore give a good idea of contemporary criteria of quality. No unique or purely decorative pieces were shown, but only those forms of practical craftsmanship which the English had for a couple of centuries produced better than anyone else – sports equipment (rackets, and balls for all types of games), leather goods (saddlery, footwear, trunks and bags), men's clothing, china and earthenware, household stoneware, silver teapots and canisters, fine aluminium cooking utensils, etc.

Exclusive craftsmanship began to think in terms of *output*. While the high quality of distinctive craftwork was maintained, it was realised that indifference about price was ethically untenable, since – to quote the later words of the architect Jacob E. Bang – it 'detracted from that honest frugality which should be the hall-mark of Danish products'.

At the end of the Twenties the Royal Copenhagen Porcelain Manufactory used stoneware almost exclusively for sculptural purposes. Knud Kyhn (b. 1880) produced animal forms, and Jais Nielsen (b. 1885) human figures and large vessels ornamented with relief. At the beginning of the Thirties Axel Salto joined the factory, and this artist's designs are still the basis of its current output of stoneware. At Bing & Grøndahl were Cathinca Olsen (1868–1947), whose ideas of form belonged to the Age of Elegance: Jean Gauguin (1881–1961), whose work was entirely sculptural: and Ebbe Sadolin, who was in charge of practical stoneware.

Both factories, in spite of the large output of the Royal Porcelain Manufactory, virtually confined themselves to producing collectors' pieces. In opposition to this, the Swede Gunnar Nylund (b. 1904) and Nathalie Krebs set up in 1929 the workshop 'Nylund & Krebs', where they collaborated in an effort to produce stoneware on the scale necessary for individual pieces to sell at a reasonable price. Nylund left the firm in the following year, and Nathalie Krebs carried on alone, changing the name to 'Saxbo'.

Axel Salto and Nathalie Krebs were the leading lights of the period in stoneware: but while Salto remained a lonely figure in Danish ceramics, the products of Nathalie Krebs soon became an important element in the contemporary scene. Salto's style was too personal, and his dynamic force was so at odds with functionalist rationality, that his perception of decoration as a function of effects arising from the material found fertile soil only in a much later generation of potters.

In 1932 the young ceramic artist Eva Stæhr-Nielsen joined Saxbo, and it was through her years of collaboration with Nathalie Krebs that the firm's regular output assumed the form now often called 'the classic Saxbo style'. Saxbo's products were mainly monochrome, and quite free from decoration, with their simple shapes proportioned in a thin body. The bowls with their open well-defined forms, and the slender jugs and vases tapering in at the top to a slim, often incurved, neck, are almost anonymous in design, their smooth taut surfaces bearing only Nathalie Krebs' semi-matt glazes. The qualities of the glaze are thus given more prominence than those of the form, and in the glazing colour is more important than structure.

Nathalie Krebs left nothing to chance, and though she could never bring herself to replace her coke-fired kiln with an electric one, her ideal was a perfect product. Every process must be based on thorough and systematic research, and be capable of repetition with unfailing certainty. Her object was to make pottery comparable in technical quality with classic Chinese work, but modern and Danish in its artistic character.

Similar ideals lay behind the fabric-printing of Marie Gudme Leth. After experiments with block-printing in the late Twenties, she soon realised that this time-honoured technique would not satisfy her in the long run. Its printing process was too slow and inexact for her taste. Like so many others of her generation, she felt the need to take her work further than block-printing would allow. She wanted her fabrics used not only by a few wealthy individuals but in ordinary homes. She wished

'Split jug': stoneware with brown glaze. Designed by Eva Stæhr-Nielsen, glazed by Nathalie Krebs: Saxbo, 1932.

to demonstrate that an artistic and a commercial purpose could well be combined, and that it was possible to work as an artist-craftsman without being reduced to living on a pittance.

In 1934 Marie Gudme Leth was allowed to visit a German textile works, and here for the first time she encountered the process of *screen-printing* – a technique hitherto quite unknown in Denmark. When she returned she at once set to work to develop an efficient technique out of the slender amount of material she had managed to acquire, and a year later her workshop was already capable of printing faultless lengths of material in great quantities. For the first time Danish printed fabrics appeared in ordinary Danish homes, which had previously used only imported material.

There is one important difference between Nathalie Krebs and Marie Gudme Leth. While the former concerned herself exclusively with glazing and material, and never personally fashioned stoneware, Marie Gudme Leth mastered all the artistic work in her craft. At Saxbo, under Nathalie Krebs' direction, a staff of potters each worked independently; but in Marie Gudme Leth's workshop she was herself the driving artistic force in all fields. Just as her technical pioneer-work had a decisive influence on the development of Danish domestic printed fabrics, so did her large stock of patterns powerfully affect the design of the period. This was particularly noticeable amongst her pupils after she became in 1930 the head of the textile-printing department at the Copenhagen School of Arts and Crafts.

The patterns which Marie Gudme Leth designed for screen-printing in the Thirties were finically-drawn sil-

Printed fabrics by Marie Gudme Leth. Left, 'Mexico', in brown on partly bleached English linen, 1935: height of composition 72 cm. Right, 'Village', in two shades of blue on partly bleached English linen, 1936: height of composition 50 cm.

PH lampshade, designed by Poul Henningsen for Louis Poulsen & Co. Ltd., 1927. Shade constructed in three sections, designed to cover the bulb and throw light on the table surface without its being more than once reflected.

houettes and restricted ornamental motifs which merely adopted the basic forms of block-printing. The large areas of design permitted by screen-printing were simply cut up into patterns of block size. The separate elements in the design stood clearly separate from each other, printed in only one colour on a natural-coloured ground which was often half-bleached linen with a strongly marked structure. Colour areas were homogeneous and intense.

A tour in the East had a great influence on Marie Gudme Leth's choice of motifs: she introduced the whole oriental world of flora and fauna into Danish textile art. But despite this outlandishness of motif her prints were thoroughly Danish in character, and completely in accordance with their period. Her clear-cut compositions with their simplified colour and calm arrangement of figures had no element of oriental mysticism; and there is no vital difference of expression between her representation of an exotic landscape, as in the print 'Mexico' of 1935, and that of the Danish countryside in the design 'Village' of 1936. Brightness, homeliness, and humour characterise her prints, whether chameleons, frogs, cobras, or figures from Hans Andersen occupy the scene.

If we now, before leaving the period around and after 1930, look for a single work whose principles of art and construction sum up the most vital endeavours of those years of struggle, we cannot do better than the PH lamp-shade. One of Poul Henningsen's allies, the architect Jacob E. Bang, who himself sought to express functionalism in glass, has this to say about this symbol of the period:

"We wanted a *synthesis*, a pure, genuine, clarified type: for example, not simply *a* lamp-shade but *the* lamp-shade, not just *a* beer-glass but *the* beer-glass. We were convinced that the pure objective functional form was beautiful, *because* it was no more than objective, self-effacing, neutral, and anonymous. Looking back, one thinks of the PH lamp-shade, that ingeniously contrived gospel of light, a precise and almost scientific systemisation, marvellously based on its own inward logic. Somehow it set free something within us, and there was a *religious* element in the joy and veneration which greeted its appearance. To hang it on one's light-fitting was to affirm that one was an intellectual and of the avant-garde."

With this summary of the chief characteristics of the ideals and endeavours of the Thirties we leave this decade, in which the great break with the past took place, and whose doctrines—in spite of their narrowness—form the ideological basis of Danish applied art to this day.

In 1939 came the war, and in 1940 the German occupation of Denmark: the frontiers were closed, imports were restricted, and prices rose. This being so, one might have expected that efforts would be concentrated on making goods cheaper. Far from it. The existing labour force had to be kept busy with the available material. Production in quantity therefore again made way for exclusive work, since expensive wares, taking many hours of labour to produce, became the only means whereby hand-craftsmanship could survive.

Quite obviously, the social-political tendencies of the

'Peter's room': interior from the Cabinetmakers' Guild exhibition of 1943. Pieces designed by Børge Mogensen for Erhard Rasmussen.

Thirties had little scope for further development in these circumstances. The furniture exhibitions of the Cabinetmakers' Guild did not completely abandon their social objective, but the two-room apartment of 1930 was replaced by larger types of home, and the pieces shown took a more exclusive form. Børge Mogensen and Hans J. Wegner in 1945 and 1946 therefore undertook the fitting-out of a three-room apartment, where the object was mainly to show handsome furniture of good workmanship.

In Børge Mogensen's works there was still an emphasis on usefulness. He had kept everyday furniture in the exhibition with types designed for children's rooms, shown in 1940 under the title 'Hanne's attic' and in 1943 'Peter's room'. Meanwhile, as chairman of the Association of Danish Co-operative Societies' department of furniture design, he made a broadly-based effort to carry the theoretical work of the Klint school over into the production of unpretentious everyday pieces. From 1942 to 1950 he worked out a large range of mass-produced furniture, which was sold all over the country through the Co-operative stores found in every Danish village. Inspired by Swedish 'stick' furniture, English windsor and American 'Shaker' types, and other similar popular examples, he produced furniture for all obvious everyday purposes. In this connection he worked out, on the basis of his own and Klint's researches, the first Danish series of fitted unit furniture, carefully designed to meet storage requirements and scaled to fit the normal size of rooms in Danish homes.

The products of the Danish C.W.S. were to a great extent made in light-coloured woods, principally beech, and therefore had difficulty in overcoming the ordinary man's deep-rooted preference for highly polished imitation mahogany. Nevertheless, the inexpensive and good-quality pieces found their public. The middle-class intellectuals, who had ten years previously been enthusiasts for the garden-city idea, and were now taking over modest terrace-houses in Copenhagen built for working-class families, took advantage of the new opportunity for informal modern furniture. Through this connection with circles which traditionally set the fashion, the pioneer products of the C.W.S. helped to encourage private furniture-makers to see that there was profit in a change of policy.

Børge Mogensen and Hans Wegner represented a type of designer new to the Cabinetmakers' Guild. While the most prominent furniture-designers of the Thirties were mainly architects, who designed furniture as a side-line simply because they were interested, Mogensen and Wegner were qualified furniture craftsmen, who were specially trained in furniture-design and devoted themselves entirely to it. Moreover, while the architects of the Thirties only exhibited for a few years, Mogensen and Wegner established a standing collaboration with particular cabinetmakers and exhibited for years on end. Again, while architects such as the aforementioned Hans Christian Hansen, Flemming Lassen and Mogens Lassen in the years around 1940 made unconventional experiments with massive, dramatic upholstered pieces, the 'cabinetmaker-architects' were concerned with wood, and with their intimate knowledge of the craft they made the most of its possibilities.

Gradually the Cabinetmakers' Guild's permanent staff of craftsmen-designers grew with the appearance of Ejner Larsen and A. Bender Madsen, and the group soon became a stabilising influence in the exhibition and produced the continuity of work which was necessary if the experiments of years were to be applied in settled types. This process of thought tended to concentrate on the handicraft and functional sides of furniture design – which, because of the war, went on without distracting commercial pressure. Thus was built up a fund of knowledge which later on gave a sure basis for the massive expansion and development of the Danish art of furniture in the Fifties.

The fanciful upholstered pieces already represented a reaction against early functionalist cubism and against the Klint school's domination of form. Unadorned functionalism no longer satisfied, and in all branches of applied art in these years a new demand for decorativeness found expression. The furniture-designers Tove and Edvard Kindt-Larsen, for example, broke away from the ideas of the Klint school, not only with heavier and more plastic proportions but also by substituting for its cult of uncoloured natural materials the contrast effects obtained by combining untreated wood with strongly coloured surfaces of smooth lacquer. In addition, they often used veneer inlays on their larger pieces as a decorative device. Similar surface ornament can also be seen on the silverware produced by the Kindt-Larsens – and many other Danish designers – in these years. This delight in colour as an escape from the cold rationality of functionalism may well be, to some extent, a natural expression of the desire to get away from the grey glumness of the war years.

This desire found expression everywhere in the realm of art-handicrafts. In textiles, Marie Gudme Leth produced a series of prints in which the riches of the sea unfold in naturalistic representation, and Arne Jacobsen as a refugee in Stockholm let the wild flowers of field and hedgerow luxuriate over his drawing-board and on to brightly coloured lengths of material. In furniture, the dream of a peaceful existence in close contact with nature resulted in exhibition interiors inspired by the life of hunting lodges and sports huts. In this connection Wegner and Mogensen produced sturdy pieces, matter-of-fact in form and construction but romantic in spirit.

This urge for contact with something fundamental, primitive, and ordinarily human, also showed itself in another manner. Study of the artifacts of primitive tribes influenced many craftsmen: a corresponding tendency also asserted itself in the preserves of the fine arts, and on the borderline between pure and applied art appeared yet another significant figure in Finn Juhl.

Right from his first year as a furniture-designer, Finn Juhl established himself as one outside the circle of those who, though they had developed differently, all had a common background in Klint's school. While Klint and his pupils aimed to draw on the experience of centuries of craftsmen in construction, strength, and ability to stand up to daily wear, as elements in the establishment of a type, Juhl strove to give his pieces an artistic value of their own, not closely bound up with functional form but asserting itself in a special sculptural quality. He modelled his wood up to the limit of its capacity, and balanced the attached upholstery according to elaborate structural rules emphasising the *bearing* and the *borne*. For the form of individual wooden elements he sought inspiration in, for example, the tools and weapons of African negroes: for the static structural whole in a study of modern sculptors' experiments with bodies in repose and in restrained movement.

Juhl was not the only one to cultivate the sculptural element in furniture and to model legs and struts in

Chair in ash with teak arm-rests: designed by Hans J. Wegner for Johannes Hansen, 1947.

dimensions varying according to the need for strength. Nor certainly was he alone in smoothing out and concealing the joints within an organically unified form. The master-cabinetmaker Peder Moos, who designed his own pieces, did the same thing. Nor were those designers working on more traditional lines unaffected by interest in the sculptural possibilities of wood. Wegner, for example, produced at the end of the Forties the first of the chair-types which were to make him world-famous. Wegner's pieces showed massiveness and sculptural force. In his chairs he still used an under-frame of traditional construction, but above this he set upper parts with a special sculptural quality and treatment of the wood which were fully in line with the work of abstract sculptors using wood as a medium of artistic expression.

Interest in sculptural effects was a general characteristic of work in the applied arts in the later Forties. Juhl designed wooden bowls for Kay Bojesen with full and elegant curves, very different from Bojesen's own work based on simple geometrical lathe-turned shapes. Inger Møller produced tea- and coffee-services with a boldly curved outline, and Erik Herløw and Ibi Trier Mørch designed silverware with wavy fillets and sharp edges in a rococo spirit, producing mirror-like reflections on the plain surface. This interest in the sculptural culminated in 1949 in silver jewellery pieces of pure abstract form, modelled by the sculptor Henning Koppel. It seemed as if a new Art Nouveau period was on the way, in which function would be only a nominal, and no longer a real, basis for the artistic endeavours of the applied artist. But in fact the developments of the Fifties were to follow quite a different line.

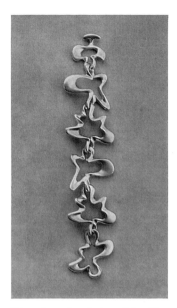

Silver bangle: designed by Henning Koppel for Georg Jensen Ltd., 1948.

Open frontiers, and the general increasing prosperity of the West, enabled Scandinavian applied art to spread beyond the narrow confines of the home market within a few years of the end of the Second World War. The outside world became conscious of Scandinavians' living standards, and learned to value the care which they gave to furnishing their homes. As a result of their climate, the peoples of the North had always been more concerned with their homes and the life inside them than those of more southerly regions, where family life can to a great extent be lived in the street, the bistro, and the trattoria. The war, with its insecurity and manifold restrictions, had accentuated this love of home, and turned people's interests still more indoors. When the war was over, therefore, Scandinavian craftsmen had resources to draw upon: there was sufficient technical and artistic raw material in the modern Northern art of living to form the basis for a large-scale production.

For the Danes, this larger market meant not only increased prosperity for hand-craftsmen but also the chance for industry to adopt the ideas which the former had laboriously pioneered since 1930. A sound basis for mass-production of quality goods was assured. Once more, the furniture trade took the lead. Up to 1950 Danish furniture output, by foreign standards, may be regarded as 'rationalised handicraft', but from this point onwards new materials and processes played a decisive part in developments. Not only was the unchallenged supremacy of wood ended by the increasing use of other materials such as steel, glass, and plastic, but wood itself through new methods of industrial processing became a quite different material. By slicing into plywood, steam bending, and various pressing techniques, wood becomes plastic.

The Finn Alvar Aalto and the Swede Bruno Mathsson both worked before the war with laminated plywood, but this medium was first fully used in Denmark in the 'Ax' pieces designed by Peter Hvidt and O. Mølgaard-Nielsen for Fritz Hansen Ltd. With their laminated seats and sides, and backs in moulded plywood, the chairs of this series are the first Danish industrial furniture to make consistent use of the new technical possibilities of mass-production. At the same time, they were among the first mass-produced pieces designed with a rational solution of the transport problem in mind. Exporting was already such a vital consideration for Danish furniture-makers that ease of dispatch had an obvious bearing on construction. To be fully up-to-date, furniture must be capable of being taken apart and sent off in easily handled packages.

Three years after 'Ax' furniture appeared, Fritz Hansen Ltd. made further advances; and at the same time a new and characterful figure appeared amongst those Danish furniture-designers who were gradually becoming world-famous. Arne Jacobsen, whose architecture is amongst the most outstanding in the country, had from time to time taken a hand at furniture-design since the Thirties, but it was only with the three-legged moulded plywood chair of 1952 that he found the material, technique, and form which were to be his speciality. This elegant little chair, inexpensive, easy to move around and to stack, marked a turning point in modern Danish furniture. With it, industry found a form of its own, based on its own assumptions and completely divorced from earlier methods of production and models.

A corresponding development occurred simultaneously in other branches of industrial art. Industrial artists, in the modern sense of the word, at last began to make headway with Danish manufacturers. Leading industrialists came to realise the extent of the designer's potentialities, and acknowledged that his task was not to inflate sales by giving products a sensational appearance but—in accordance with the times—to co-ordinate the efforts of technicians, craftsmen, and salesmen within a planned scheme. He must have a hand in the production process from first to last, and must therefore not only have the analytic and artistic flair of the artist-craftsman but also business sense, readiness to collaborate, and talent for organisation. These fresh and various demands gradually called forth a type of artist new to Danish applied art—the *industrial designer*. Naturally there had already been such individuals in Denmark, but they had been isolated figures. Now a whole series of them appeared with the same end in view.

Kay Bojesen was one of the first trained hand-craftsmen to establish a permanent link with industry. As designer for the Universal Steel Co. he produced, in the first year of the firm, a series of kitchen- and table-knives which soon became a model for similar factories. Later on Erik Herløw was in charge of the firm's production, and with him the designer found a regular place in Danish industry. *Industrial Design* became a profession.

Herløw, as already mentioned, had previously worked in silver, but with this change to everyday articles his distinctive mental powers found full scope. His talent was not confined to analysing the work in hand and the technical production possibilities of the firm in question: he had the faculty of grasping the many different factors involved, combining them in ways hitherto unknown, and producing quite simple solutions. He understood how to reconcile the technical capacity of plant and the qualities of the material with practical and aesthetic requirements. This flair for simplification gave his earliest designs for industry a wholesome simplicity of form, and through their number and variety they set a new standard of quality in Danish industrial art. At the same time, his well-thought-out designs gave an artistic fillip to inexpensive materials such as plastic and nylon, and lifted these synthetic substances high above the level of ordinary hardware.

Erik Herløw showed that quite cheap and expendable goods were still worth an artist's time. In spite of continual replacement, this remains a permanent and important factor in the modern domestic scene.

New modes of living, with less formal dining habits and residence divided between a town apartment and a summer chalet, the whole change in the popular way of life which attended rising living standards in the years after the war, encouraged this development and hastened on pioneer work in industrial art. Not only were many new fields opened to new producers, but also many businesses which had carried on in apparently changeless conservatism for decades were obliged to recognise the new demands. Among these last were the great porcelain factories.

The lack of domestic servants, and the spread of the kitchen-dining room, brought with them a need for simpler methods of serving meals. In Finland and Sweden this need called forth at the beginning of the Fifties a range of multicoloured table-wares which were not – like the ordinary Danish ones – made as complete sets. Attention was thus directed more towards the usefulness of the individual piece than towards the completeness of a set, and it was possible to get away from the traditional demand that all parts of a set should have a common pattern. Further, efforts were made to meet the wish of the housewife that bowls and covered dishes should be equally usable for preparing the meal in the kitchen and serving it on the table. Various parts of the service were therefore first made oven-proof and then also flame-proof.

The first Danish attempt to meet the changed demand was made at the Royal Copenhagen Porcelain Manufactory in 1957, when Magnus Stephensen produced a range of oven-proof covered dishes, serving ware, and soup plates, in close collaboration with the factory's outstanding technicians. This new series, which began a change of attitude throughout the whole Danish porcelain industry towards practical wares, was later followed up with a robust and bluff-shaped set in earthenware. The unchallenged dominance of the Danish market by white – generally decorated – porcelain was finished.

At Bing and Grøndahl's porcelain works a corresponding task was later undertaken by Richard Kjærgaard (b. 1920), while Axel Brüel took charge of the production of practical wares at the 'Danmark' factory. Of this last, the coffee-set 'Thermodan' deserves special mention, since with its insulating cavities in cups and jugs it is a technical innovation.

The pottery industry was not the only one to meet the new demands. Interest in articles which could be used both in the kitchen and in the living-room set in motion a whole new line of developments, and brought a large range of everyday objects within the scope of the designer. Jens H. Quistgaard (b. 1919), Henning Seidelin (b. 1904), Jørgen Ditzel, Erik Herløw, and Tormod Olesen worked out series of enamelled serving ware; and Erik Herløw and Magnus Stephensen (amongst others) did corresponding work in stainless steel and aluminium. Per Lütken and Jacob E. Bang produced glassware to suit the new way of living. Kitchen utensils were no longer neglected by Danish industrial art.

Textiles, which had hitherto been the Cinderella of industrial art in Denmark, also flourished in the Fifties. Though Denmark had indeed had textile artists of standing throughout the whole period in question, there were few of them, and their production – which as far as weaving was concerned was confined to handlooms – was small in quantity and accessible only to a limited circle. The aforementioned fabric-printer, Marie Gudme Leth, was an exception.

Inspired by developments in furniture, and impressed by the possibilities of increased exports, textile manufacturers now became interested in giving their wares a peculiarly Danish stamp. Previously they had almost without exception bought their patterns from foreign studios, and their connection with Danish textile artists was therefore slow to form.

One of the most important of those who were able to

adapt for industrial production their experience of weaving was Lis Ahlmann. Her work for the Cotil collection of C. Olesen Ltd. became the moral backbone of the modern Danish textile industry, through its extent, its artistic consistency, and its high technical quality. In the Thirties she worked in close collaboration with Kaare Klint, and like him relied on tradition—not only in Danish folk-weaving but in similar popular and timeless textiles drawn from folk-cultures all over the world. In the same way that Klint and his pupils made use of the peculiar material properties of wood, she exploited the material qualities of yarn in her cloth, seeking simple effects through working with the structure of the material and using simple traditional weaves. Her use of colour was correspondingly direct, but powerful in its conscious restraint. Often she used only the tones which wool has on the sheep's back: white, grey, brown, and black.

When she became connected with industry, she began a collaboration with the furniture-designer Børge Mogensen. Encouraged by his masculine talent, she learned how to use the massive machinery and was soon able to adapt the material qualities of handicraft to mass-production, without at any point imitating handwork. Her colour-schemes became richer and her contrasts bolder, her patterns larger in size and more bluff. In spite of her age, she brought new life to Danish textile art, and showed that a fresh outlook does not necessarily come only from the young. Great forward steps are often made by people with the professional experience of a long life behind them.

Rapid and vigorous developments in one sphere always produce a prompt reaction in others: the balance is maintained. The rising artistic standards in mass-production, and its conquest of new fields which had been in part the preserve of the hand-craftsman, meant that practical work in the years up to 1960 increasingly slipped out of the craftsman's hands. Naturally enough, therefore, he looked closer to the realm of the pure artist for occupation.

The material perfection and intellectual design of industrial products brought a cold tone into the household, which soon gave rise to a demand for personalised developments in the few things which were still hand-made. The wheel had gone full-circle, and once more the hand-craftsman was reduced to working on ornamental objects. Nor was the situation comparable with that in the Twenties; before 1930 there was no socially-conscious industry to attend to practical demand, but now there was. Hand-craftsmen could therefore work for the individual without compromising their moral principles.

At the present time the situation is therefore that Den-

Armchair with frame of matt chromed steel and upper part of laminated ash: upholstered seat covered with leather. Designed by Poul Kjærholm for E. Kold Christensen Ltd., 1958. The same type as Klint's Faaborg chair shown on p. 10. Both are dominated by aesthetic considerations, while in the interval between them functionalism was in the ascendant.

mark has both a level-headed, practical-minded art-industry, in which technical quality, artistic form, and price have found a balance, and highly personalised handicrafts using a rich variety of media, pushful and sometimes aggressive, but still maintaining their original standards of craftsmanship. The two spheres complement each other in the applied arts, and are both equally active in the present-day context.

Reaction against industrial regularity and precise design appeared first amongst the potters. Many small new potteries mushroomed alongside those already extant, and together they had an influence which the few earlier ones had not been able to achieve. Though furniture and silver had previously been the first to show new tendencies, it was now the potters who set the pace, closely followed by the textile experts.

Simple earthenware is not naturally suited for mass-production, because of the peculiarities of the material, and nearly all of its products come from tiny workshops. Mass-produced wares are therefore (in Denmark) rare. Clay is one of the handcraftsman's most compliant materials, and thus readily serves the purposes of the individualist. Without needing to sink much capital he can, in pottery, have at his disposal a great variety of material effects: glazes, ranging from the lightest to the darkest, from subdued tones to loud colours, and surface structures varying from the smooth and shiny to the matt and rustic.

The fundamental work in Danish ceramics was done by a handful of women potters, who with their instinctive flair and delight in colour developed further the tradition of unsophisticated pottery and used simple time-honoured techniques in their individual ways. Lisbeth Munch-Petersen, Lisa Engqvist, Gudrun Meedom Bæch, and Gutte Eriksen (b. 1918) are some of those who started from a traditional basis and from practical forms and developed their pottery with a natural grace, frankly decorating it with slip, incised lines, and stamped impressions.

To these must be added several new names, for whom decoration has become the most important element. Grethe Lindblad, for example, covers her very simple – often moulded – bowls and dishes with paintings carried out in opaque and transparent coloured glazes. Marianne Herlufsdatter and Lars Thirslund combine primitive glaze decoration with representative relief. But while animals, birds, and flowers form the mainstay of most modern potters' ornamental schemes, Marianne Herlufsdatter and her husband Thirslund also introduce human forms. So does Birte Weggerby, who plays freely with the human figure in the same way as modern abstract painters, transforming it into mysterious creatures and magic symbols. Under her hands even the body of the pot takes on human shape.

In stoneware too the flight from the aesthetic refinement of the Thirties and Forties made its mark. Already in the late Thirties Christian Poulsen stood out against the time-honoured view that stoneware was an exclusive material which permitted only subdued effects. By working with contrasts between bare stoneware body and glaze, and using smooth, glossy, and brittle glazes in clear colours, he transferred to stoneware some of the colour and simple material effects of earthenware. But Poulsen was always an isolated figure, going his own way independently of the general trend.

Now, however, a whole group of young ceramic artists (Peter Rasmussen, Finn Lynggaard, etc.) exploded stoneware's solemnity, and set out to experiment with coarser material effects and a more robust use of glaze than that based on Chinese influence. The larger workshops, too, did not remain indifferent. At Bing & Grøndahl the prominent ceramic artist Gertrud Vasegaard bided her time and continued the bland character of her products with her graceful painting and quiet patterns in light relief over calm functional forms. But at Saxbo the new urge found early expression while Lisa Engqvist was working there in the early Thirties. With the young Kirsten Weeke, who joined Saxbo in 1955, the new style made a decisive break-through. The fine-drawn smooth stone characteristic of the 'classic Saxbo style' gave way to a vigorous grained finish. In the 'classic' style the form served principally to bear the glaze, but now with its weight and monumentality it acquired an independent value of its own.

Saxbo's faithful supporters, Eva Stæhr-Nielsen and Edith Sonne Bruun, provided a sounding-board for the new ideas and broke completely with the old. The former, for example, has in recent years produced a number of large jars which in their monumental force have revealed a new and impressive aspect of her talents. Like Christian Poulsen, who abandoned wheel-turned forms in favour of modelled vessels with large simple shapes, Eva Stæhr Nielsen has cast aside cold precision in her regular output of wheel-pottery and works on the pot as a sculptural form. Each piece from her hand now has its own individuality.

In the field of textiles the urge to employ a more rustic-natured material was expressed in Paula Trock's work in making new curtain yarns in coarse-spun wool; and Franka Rasmussen sought new possibilities of artistic expression by combining different weaving techniques and yarns of different structure in her tapestries. Apart from this, textile artists of the late Fifties were chiefly interested in *colour*, and sought to enhance the coloristic potentialities of the material. Both in weaving and in printing, therefore, pattern design gave way to colour composition. Weavers worked with freely-related stripes and mixtures, with adjoining colours often in close tones. Printers designed simple geometrical patterns for their lengths, in which repeated overprinting produced an immense number of shades besides the actual colours used. Marie Gudme Leth's and Arne Jacobsen's domestic textiles of these years, which represent a decided break with their earlier products, illustrate this general change of style. Rolf Middelboe's curtains, with their patterns formed by overprinting uniform regular surfaces, are a similar example taken from mass-production.

In unique weaves, especially rugs and mats, graphic composition was similarly displaced by colour; and in unique fabric-prints and decorative hangings the preferred method was direct painting with a brush. In Ruth Hull's and Ruth Christensen's fabrics, painting is combined with traditional printing; and in Tusta Wefring's works it is the sole technique. As in avant-garde ceramics, the frontiers of pure art were crossed. The artistic message of the object was vigorously and directly proclaimed, unmuffled by commonsense demands for practical usefulness.

Three decades may appear a short period, but in the course of the last thirty years the applied arts have undergone what seems to us a fundamental development. Perhaps the many variations of artistic purpose, which we have regarded as epochal, will later on seem only slight oscillations in a long gradual process of evolution. In the foregoing sketch much has been over-simplified: it does not claim to be either exhaustive or systematic, but only to give such explanation as seems necessary for the subsequent illustrations to give a satisfactory (if only approximate) picture of Danish practical arts in the present flourishing period. Much else could have been included, and other artists might have been chosen to illustrate developments. Several finer points have been left for explanation in the text accompanying the illustrations.

FINLAND

Benedict Zilliacus

When Finland's industrial art blossomed out of the grey poverty of the post-war years like a magnificent gay tulip, the outside world probably regarded the phenomenon as a flower without stem, roots, or prospect of growth. It was a sudden outburst of unrestrained imagination and unrestricted experiment, marked by a combination of robust vigour, brashness, and sensitivity. Elsewhere it was received certainly with amusement and wonder, possibly with anxiety and shock, in countries where traditional forms were strong and deeply entrenched and therefore had a moderating and restraining influence.

The Finnish public themselves, it must be admitted, felt similarly taken aback. Where did all this come from? It was some time before official Finland took notice, laughed, and put the gay flower in the buttonhole of its plain and threadbare suit. It seems, too, that not only the uninitiated public but also a large section of practising artists felt the flower had been picked out of empty air. The circumstances of the previous decade had been so grim, and the break-through—marked by the great Zürich exhibition and the Milan Triennale of 1951—so sudden. If ever the Devil set himself to tempt an entire profession to the sin of pride, he chose the Finnish artist-craftsmen of the Fifties. But if so, he thereby did them no direct harm: it was a fructifying pride, a stimulus which continually brought forth new and notable achievements, a fillip for industry, and eventually also an inducement to the State to open its coffers and assist this hitherto neglected branch of culture. The only thing missing was a general sense of perspective.

Gradually this perspective begins to emerge, and it becomes increasingly clear that there were roots and potentialities for growth, that the abundant creative energy of the Fifties was not rootless but had its own groundwork and traditions to build upon. It was realised that this was one episode amongst others in Finland's cultural history; and furthermore, in some circles it is now regarded as finished or nearing its end.

To return once more to the flower analogy: we Finns had happily put the flower in our buttonhole, and now we have begun to regard it as an essential ornament—to the point at which our public would be highly offended if ever our industrial art came back from Milan without a Grand Prix. It is quite possible this may happen next time, but if it does it need not indicate any decline. On the contrary, it would mean the beginning of a new period: a consolidation of the ground so far gained, a further extension of good quality in everyday wares (which is a healthy development, even at the expense of the very best), more emphasis on the useful and sensible and human, and a retreat from the over-aesthetic and over-sophisticated.

This does not, on the other hand, mean the renunciation of the past joyous decade, which was just as essential to development as it is now necessary to adopt a fresh approach. It blazed the trail, and opened doors. Some of the Fifties' brilliance and extravagance in art for art's sake will, we hope, survive—at least to the extent that our activities remain flood-lit, and the rest of the world does not forget us ... In the words of Cole Porter: "It was great fun ... painting the town".

Foreign critics have attached many kindly-meant labels to Finnish art-handicrafts: charming, artless, primitive, honest, derived from the Far North, marked by intuitive appreciation of material, free from burdensome tradition. Symbolism has also run riot. When a Finnish exhibition toured Europe early in the Fifties we learnt that our white glazes were obviously inspired by our endless snowfields, that a black glaze mirrored our unbroken winter darkness. Much of what was written was fanciful romanticism, but even the crudest generalisations may contain a grain of truth.

It is understandable that the outside world should wonder how such extravagant products, unrestrained by considerations of usefulness and economy, should burgeon amongst a people known for their sober and simple way of life, and, indeed, their poverty—a people somewhat sluggish and gloomy. Like many other clichés, those concerning the folk-character of the Finns are far too sweeping. We have also a faintly oriental weakness for the extravagant, for luxury for its own sake, which sometimes amazes casual visitors. With cheerful insouciance a man will waste a fortnight's hard-earned pay on one riotous night, without regrets the next morning, or buy some coveted and far too expensive work of art for a simple home with the most modest living standards. This peculiarity, for better or worse, distinguishes Finns from the common-sense regularity of other Scandinavians. To some extent this generous and devil-may-care attitude is a legacy from earlier Russian boyars, and in a negative sense it also derives from Finland's political geography, which has placed her in a position where thought for the morrow has frequently been unavailing. Whatever the reason, the result is that Finns to some extent can see beyond the 'more beautiful useful things' of the rest of Scandinavia to the enjoyment of irresponsible 'more beautiful things for pleasure'.

This being so, one may wonder why this defiant reaction against the poverty and greyness of our environment, these carefree fanfares and gay flashes of colour, are so little found outside the field of art-handicrafts. Another odd fact is that these luxury articles are stamped with such sophisticated artistry: the kindest judgement of our people must admit that in most other manifestations of their way of life they are far from sophisticated.

Fortunately we are able to say that artistry has been kept within reasonable bounds, and not allowed to run to excess. This is perhaps explained by that element of national character which at its worst is expressed in a certain sluggishness, and at its best in considered wisdom. It is certainly also a legacy from Finnish folk-culture, with its sense of moderation dictated by so many serious and practical considerations. Finally, we have one vital characteristic—a feeling for the material we work with. This is not the same thing as appreciation of good craftsmanship, which came sadly near being ruined by some of the inevitably botched work of the years of war and crisis. Feeling for the material goes deeper. Possibly it is connected with the fact that in Finland industrialisation never managed to destroy the genuine traditions of craftsmanship before handwork was again revived and valued; and in addition, Finnish art is such a recent development that it has not lost contact with the popular background of handicrafts.

In this connection we may perhaps also wonder why it was precisely in two particular fields, architecture and art-handicrafts, that Finland achieved international importance in such a striking fashion. It would be wrong to underestimate activity in other cultural spheres, and Finland has certainly produced a number of composers, authors, scientists, and painters who have won recognition outside her frontiers: perhaps as many as one could expect from a population of four millions, perhaps rather fewer because of unfavourable circumstances and a grim history, and because cultural achievements are not proportional to population but result from intangible stimuli. But in the two fields mentioned it cannot be denied that Finland holds a place in the present-day world quite remarkable in relation to her resources, history, and geographical position.

As far as architecture is concerned it can be, and often has been, explained by a paradox: lack of traditions, and of surviving buildings of historical significance, geographical remoteness from the sources of our civilisation, together with the country's precarious position and increased Russian repression in the last years of the previous century, were all negative factors which gave positive stimuli to those who laid the foundations of our new and national architecture in the last decades of the Nineteenth Century.

No traditions: no hampering ties. The Kalevala-world of awakened national romanticism inspired art and literature, but could provide no architectural patterns: the new inspiration had to be expressed in creating a national architecture. Finland was 'the remotest part of Europe': there were no dominant stylistic influences to break away from, when the time was ripe for a new creation.

Finally, political repression: this was a stimulus to still greater freedom in those spheres where national sentiment was really at liberty to make itself felt. All this meant that one could draw strength from the spirit of the past, while at the same time being without prejudices and open to the technical and rationalist currents of the period in realising one's dreams. The architects and artists of poor and oppressed Finland thus found themselves freer, and with wider opportunities, than most of their European colleagues.

What we have said of architecture is also true, *mutatis mutandis*, of decorative and applied art, not least because architecture and industrial art had already by that time begun to collaborate in the spirit of the Art Nouveau style, which ignored frontiers. This symbiosis was emphasised by architects like Eliel Saarinen and Valter Jung, and is realised to this day in the talented work of Alvar Aalto.

This connection between two environment-forming branches of art was heavily underlined by the retrospective exhibition arranged in the autumn of 1959 within the framework of Scandinavian Design Cavalcade by the Finnish Society of Crafts and Design and the association of industrial designers, Ornamo. It included the whole working life of the former, 1875–1959, and was of great assistance to the public in dispersing the fog concealing the continuous tradition which our art-handicrafts can still claim in spite of everything. This tradition is continuous from the national renaissance through the structural expression of Art Nouveau, the classicism of the Twenties, the form-idiom and social consciousness of functionalism, and the comparative vacuum of the Forties, to the aesthetic outlook of recent years.

In tracing and recording earlier influences which have led up to today's industrial production, we find that the date 1875 (or rather, its decade) is a milestone. Some particular strands can be traced further back to folk-culture, and this is so in the three branches of craftwork which we commonly regard as most typically Finnish, in textiles, ceramics, and glassware. The links are by no means continuous, but it is obvious that ethnographic and historical material has had much influence as a source of inspiration in these spheres.

Rugs demand to be mentioned first, since they are particularly typical of Finland. This is not to say that their technique or traditional use is peculiar to this country: on the contrary, we clearly have here a mediaeval borrowing from Sweden. But rug-weaving has been through the ages one of the most genuine and vigorous expressions of a vernacular need for aesthetic achievement. Much ancient work, moreover, has survived right down to the present day, since inherited rugs have been prized and treated with great care in the ordinary home. These facts together have made rugs an important influence on the consciously artistic textile production of modern times.

The earliest definite evidence for rugs in Finland dates back to the Fifteenth Century. These were for use, had a thick pile, and were employed to give warmth in bed, or in boats during winter sealing and fishing trips. In the Eighteenth Century patterned and coloured decorative rugs came in, akin to English turkey-work. The modern art-rug takes its inspiration from the often wonderfully chosen values in the folk-production of the Eighteenth and Nineteenth Centuries, while its long pile derives from the original practical rug.

With regard to ceramics, we can if we like talk of influences from finds of the New Stone Age. Far more important are those from ordinary household utensils of red clay, wholly or partly glazed pots with supple decoration in white or black-and-white. This type of ornamentation has reappeared as a trend in the artistic (or semi-artistic) ceramics of the present day.

Finnish art-glassware goes back to the 1680's, when the first real glassworks opened up in Nystad. At the end of the Eighteenth Century several others followed, of which the eighth, Notsjö, founded in 1793, is the oldest now surviving and the only one to go back to the period of Swedish rule. The old art-glassware made for the wealthy has left little trace in modern products, but the green and brown bubble-glass and apothecary's glass of the Eighteenth Century has certainly influenced present-day artists.

Possibly the reflection in folk-furniture of Duke Johan's renaissance decoration of Åbo Castle has some connection with the classicism of the Twenties, just as the Gustavian style spread over the whole country via the officers'

quarters at Sveaborg. But in 1870 it was hardly possible to speak of a living style in Finland. It was a room echoing confusedly with styles (and lack of style) from every source which the national pioneers began to sweep out and refurnish. Their spirit was marked on the one hand by a backward-looking romantic patriotism, and on the other by international rationalism's faith in the future.

The 1870's saw three institutions founded, each of which has from then onwards played a particularly vital part in the fields with which we are here concerned. In 1871, on the initiative of the well known professor of aesthetics C. G. Estlander, was founded the so-called Craft School, which later, as the Central School of Arts and Crafts, and, since 1949, as the Institute of Industrial Design, has provided continuously for the training of the country's artist-craftsmen. In 1875 the Society of Crafts and Design was founded, and took over the management of the school. Teaching facilities have on the whole been meagre, and lack of space and the primitiveness of technical equipment have been (and are now particularly) conspicuous. But a succession of highly gifted teachers, inspiring with their enthusiasm, have managed to surmount the difficulties in a way which compels respect.

The work of the Society of Crafts and Design was thus partly the management of the school, partly the care of collections of art-handicraft material which had already made a modest start some years before through private donations, and the encouragement of industrial art activity in general. Right from the start exhibitions, which in time became annual, played a large part in its programme. Its lotteries, too, are an institution, serving not only to support its funds but making an important contribution to popularising art-handwork, presenting its products to the public, and improving taste in general.

Industrial art gained a third powerful supporter in the 'Friends of Finnish Handicraft'. This society was founded in 1879 and ever since has had a great influence on textiles, both by the members' own work and by the patterns distributed.

While Estlander as a teacher and organiser founded instruction in arts-and-crafts, he must share the place of honour as the originator of Finnish industrial art with Axel Gallen-Kallela (1865–1931), the artist who provided practical examples. On a journey in Outer Karelia he was much impressed by the Kalevala saga-cycle, and indefatigably transposed its themes into the most diverse spheres. His villa in the barrens set the style for the new national architecture: his graphic art and posters, like his textile patterns, furniture, jewellery, bookbinding, and stained glass, all helped to form style in industrial art.

Gallen-Kallela was a man of many parts, even in his

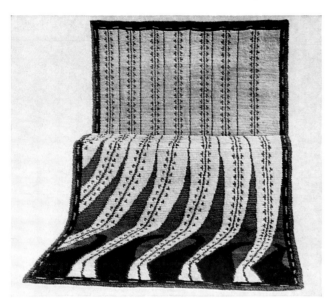

The painter and grand seigneur Axel Gallen-Kallela, with his comprehensive activity, gave a stimulus to virtually all branches of applied art. His own bench-rug 'Flame' was woven in 1913 by the Friends of Finnish Handicraft.

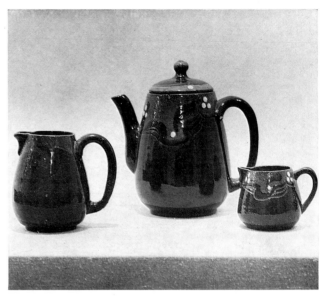

'Iris' pottery by A. W. Finch, c. 1900. The output of his modest workshop even at that period aimed at 'more beautiful everyday things', and Finch was the pioneer of modern Finnish ceramics.

personal character: inhabitant of the Finnish wilds, African big-game hunter, highly successful one-man exhibitor at San Francisco, man of the people and grand seigneur. He was also a salutary phenomenon: at that time Finland badly needed someone who showed that a Finn could hold his own all over the outside world. Today Finland would do well to remember that to be outward-looking need not mean to be any the less Finnish.

Indirectly, Gallen-Kallela contributed to Finland's sharing the ideas of Ruskin and William Morris on the blessedness of craft traditions as opposed to the degradation of taste produced by industrialism. It happened that he brought the Swede Louis Sparre (b. 1863) to Finland, and Sparre in turn introduced the Anglo-Belgian painter and potter A. W. Finch (1854–1930). These two set up in the little town of Borgå a factory, 'Iris', to make Sparre's furniture and Finch's ceramics. The former were stamped with the best in Anglo-Saxon ideas of design, practicality, quality of craftsmanship, and honest attitude to the material. The spirit of Van de Velde hovered over Finch's pottery, which was made in restrained forms with rhythmic linear decoration. In his practical ware he anticipated the later slogan 'more beautiful everyday things'. The example so well presented by both of them had a much greater effect than sprang from the limited and short-lived output of their little workshop alone. As a teacher at the Central School, Finch continued his positive influence on Finnish industrial art right up to the end of the Twenties.

Foreign influences had also been important; but at the turn of the century came a move in the opposite direction, heralded by a fanfare–the World Exhibition at Paris in 1900. Finland's representation there was largely due to Gallen-Kallela and the (later world-famous) architect Eliel Saarinen (1873–1955). As so often later, there was a real harmony between architecture and furnishings in our national pavillion, and the effect was most fortunate. Here for the first time was an example of a phenomenon to prove helpful again in the Fifties: success abroad was a great stimulus to interest at home. For the first time, too, that significant union of architect and interior designer in one man was manifested in the person of Saarinen. Examples of his furniture and glass have held their own from that day to this.

It thus became characteristic of the leading architects in the years ahead that they did not confine themselves to designing buildings but also took an interest in the smallest details of the interior. Here at last one could see an 'art of environment', concerned with a complete solution to the problems of the interior and of the atmosphere-creating elements in colour-schemes, as well as with the adaptation of external architecture to internal needs.

As we have already said, national romanticism had on the whole no real form-patterns: but on the other hand later classicism (or rather, the synthesis of German classicism and Russian imperialism) left us a series of examples of buildings by the German-born architect Carl Ludvig Engel, who built the monumental centre of Helsinki between 1818 and 1840. The Biedermeier

By his work as a teacher, Arttu Brummer set his mark on creativeness in Finnish applied arts for several decades. His own taste for the gay and splendid is well expressed in the vase 'Finlandia' of 1945.

style, which for example took root and flourished in Denmark, made little impression on Finland.

This legacy from Engel, and, perhaps, renaissance traces in folk-furniture, gave a certain cultural anchorage, which admittedly came to mean much to those who up to the Twenties endeavoured to get away from the somewhat turbid sources and emotional mistiness of Kalevala romanticism to less questionable classical models. This purifying tendency was especially influential in the architecture and furniture of the inter-war years. Two of the outstanding works of this school were the Parliament House and the new wing to Engel's university buildings, both designed by J. S. Sirén (1889–1961) and furnished in collaboration with the versatile artist Arttu Brummer. (Sirén was president of the Society of Crafts and Design from 1931 to 1949, and from 1955 till his death the chairman of its Board of Governors).

The link with classical ideas also shows itself in a material such as glass. The man who may be called the founder of Finland's modern art of glassware is Henry Ericsson (1898–1933). This is chiefly on account of his fine engraved vases for the Riihimäki glassworks, but the rest of his very varied output also kept to the classical line.

In textiles the Twenties were a revolutionary period. While the folklorism of the turn of the century survived in a subdued form, the many new banners and church fabrics which were made after the country achieved independence were subject to the strict rules of heraldry and tradition. Work of this kind was especially done by

the Friends of Finnish Handicraft, and there rug-weaving was also revived on Brummer's initiative, competitions etc. being held. In rug-design the national motifs took at first a stylised cubist form, followed for example by Impi Sotavalta (1885–1943) until she took to a more free and painter-like style.

Ceramic artists worked more independently of classical influence, following Finch's principles of dependence only on the wheel-thrown form and the studied play of colour in the glazes. So did the metal-workers, amongst whom O. W. Ehrström (1881–1934) did pioneer work as artist-smith and engraver. His activity was many-sided, and amongst other things he wrote a handbook, *Art-Craftsmanship*, which is one of the outstanding publications in Finland's sparse professional literature on this subject.

A central and very colourful individual, inspiring teacher as well as productive artist, was Arttu Brummer (1891–1951), who is gradually becoming something of a legendary figure in Finnish applied arts. In his designs he brought out more than anyone else the gay and the splendid. His youth coincided with the period in which the interest of the Central School was transferred from natural forms to a freer artistic field, and the great inspiration of his adulthood was the first head-on clash between cubism and the classicism of the Twenties. He expressed his always highly personal ideas in furniture and glassware. His interest in these two lines was shared by J. S. Sirén, and this led to an unusually fruitful collaboration over the interiors of Sirén's Parliament House and the new wing to the University. Brummer's love of the grand manner never led him to overdo things: his ambition expressed itself in a mixture of sensitiveness and austerity. This trait is found for example in his heavy works in glass, such as the famous Sibelius Vase.

Perhaps even more important than his output of work was his contribution as a teacher and inspirer. He had a compelling personal charm, rare amongst us and almost latin, which appealed particularly to the young. He had an eye for the talented, and gave them the freedom they needed, while leading others by the hand. The success-struck present generation of artist-craftsmen cannot thank him enough.

Brummer worked from 1919 as a teacher at the Central School of Arts and Crafts, and from 1944 as its artistic director. He was also chairman of the association of industrial designers, Ornamo, an active member of the Friends of Finnish Handicraft, and in charge of the Industrial Art Museum – the collections previously mentioned, which were housed first in the Athenaeum and later in Villa Hagasund. The exhibits are at present in store, awaiting a decision about their ultimate home.

Brummer's work as a teacher of the productive artists

The expert furniture-designer Werner West continued to serve the art of furniture in Finland for many years, while the versatile Henry Ericsson died young. This cupboard, made for the World Exhibition in Barcelona, is a result of their collaboration. Ericsson did the marquetry, with Helsinki motifs.

of the Fifties was shared by Rafael Blomstedt (1885–1950), who was at that time Rector of the Central School. Blomstedt was the humanist of Finnish industrial art, a very farsighted man with an unusually thorough training. He represented the many-sided enlightened cultured man, almost a Renaissance type, at a time when professional specialisation was increasing. He also did important work in aesthetic and industrial-art circles as an author.

Collaboration between the reserved and placid Blomstedt and the dynamic and colourful Brummer must have been full of frictions, but it was fruitful. The high level of craft training in Finland, in spite of almost intolerable external circumstances and very poor technical facilities, is largely due to these two.

The nearer we approach the Fifties, the more numerous are the working artists who demand our attention. Some names can hardly be omitted, if we are to be in a position to evaluate current production. One is the furniture-designer Werner West (1890–1959), who brought sound knowledge and sure judgement to his neglected and ill-regulated craft. He was a pioneer in modern mass-production, and the fact that he worked for the large Stockmann store gave his efforts a still wider influence in forming taste. West also furnished a large number of public and private interiors. Another furniture artist, equally attached to Scandinavian tradition and quality but following a more exclusive line requiring crafts-

manship of an almost Danish standard, is Runar Engblom. His output is now less abundant, but remains of the same distinguished standard.

There is the group of artists who decisively captured textile art for the distaff side: Margareta Ahlstedt-Willandt, Maija Kansanen (whose tapestries have won international fame through her several Grand Prix), Eva Anttila (a tapestry-weaver who achieves almost as colourful effects with purely textile media as others with brush and paint), Laila Karttunen (an expert at double-weaving) and the rug-weavers for the Friends of Handicraft playing a new Finnish trump card at the Paris Exhibition of 1937 with rugs after patterns by Gunvor Grönvik, Eva Brummer, Viola Gråsten, Uhra Simberg-Ehrström, and Eva Eklöf-Olsoni.

In the field of ceramics the legacy of Finch has been carried further by Elsa Elenius, Toini Muona, and Kurt Ekholm. Porcelain of high quality is made by Aune Siimes and Friedl Kjellberg, while Michael Schilkin (1900–1962) worked primarily as a naturalistic ceramic sculptor.

Gunilla Jung (1905–1939) produced fine compositions in silver and light-fittings. Gunnel Nyman (1909–1948) was a particularly clear shining light, an artist in glass whose life, like those of Henry Ericsson and Gunilla Jung, was untimely cut short. At the aforementioned retrospective exhibition of 1959 Gunnel Nyman's works stood almost alone in representing the Forties. This was a well-deserved tribute to one of the most talented pioneers in Finnish industrial art who has become something of a symbol: the shining figure of a leader at the opening of

The artistic level of Finnish furniture was formerly quite modest. One of the few who made a real contribution in this field was Werner West, designer for Stockmann. He designed this armchair in 1948.

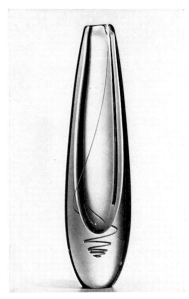

Gunnel Nyman's crystal vases, in their purity, restraint, and consciousness of the material, are among the most outstanding products of Finnish design. This vase, 'Serpentine', dates from 1946 and is typical in its economy of line.

The sanatorium in Pemar is regarded as one of the best of Alvar Aalto's early architectural works. In its interior (1930) he first introduced his later world-famous furniture in laminated wood.

a great era. Her works represented the Forties, since her output culminated in that period; but they have the same validity a decade after her death, and will have in fifty years' time.

Gunnel Nyman was originally a furniture-designer, and was awarded prizes for her well-balanced and comfortable chairs, before she found her final medium. Perhaps it is truer to say that it found her. In her earliest works she still allowed decoration to play a certain part, but soon she was completely fascinated by the life and essence in the flowing glass-metal. At times the most simplified forms can take on character, as through the refraction effects in a faceted rim, which is shown in as early a work as 'Facet I' of 1941, bought by the National Museum in Stockholm, or in the cut-crystal dishes in the collections of the King of Sweden and the Industrial Art Museum in Oslo.

In some of her works she has drawn inspiration from nature, as in 'Lily', 'Snail' and 'Roseleaf' with its glittering opal flash. The last of these is in the Nordenfjeld Industrial Art Museum at Trondheim. In spite of her love for clean taut forms, she was also quite ready to play with technical effects in the metal, like the gas-bubbles in the tulle-like transparent 'Veil', the spiral in 'Serpentine', and the veil of living smoke between layers of glass in her last works. But though her work varied in rhythm, forms, and technique, her imagination was always fast anchored to her medium: this was her starting-point, set the norm, and also provided her principal source of inspiration.

After her last exhibition, at Oslo in 1948, she wrote in the Norwegian periodical *Bonytt* an inspired tribute to glass as a material. She called this article her testament; and it undoubtedly has been, and will be, read with fascination and respect by artists in glass and others who have a feeling for the material which Gunnel Nyman herself used with such mastery. Her significance for Finnish art-glass was all the greater in that she actually came to work for all three of the leading glassworks.

Before Gunnel Nyman, the house-furnishing and industrial-art firm Artek made an important contribution. It was founded in 1935 by Nils Gustav Hahl and Alvar and Aino Aalto, in collaboration with Maire Gullichsen. This is the right place to mention this firm, since it is still producing and inspiring, and forming a living link between the Thirties and the present day–one might almost say, between the functionalism of the Thirties and that of tomorrow.

Artek was founded to make and sell Alvar Aalto's well-known furniture, which translated the steel tubing of the functional style into Finnish pressed wood and combined a large degree of standardisation with pure and simple beauty. Artek introduced these pieces to the outside world. In addition, the firm's exhibitions (which, for example, introduced good Swedish industrial art to Finland) gave valuable and fertilising contacts. In general, during its existence of more than a quarter-century, Artek has been an exceptionally stimulating centre for good design, and most influential in forming taste through the quality of its own products and those it has imported.

This organically designed glassware was made by Alvar Aalto in 1937 and, like his Artek chairs, has in no way become dated in the subsequent quarter-century.

"The young imagine the world was made the day they were born: they would do better to realise we gave it them as a christening-gift." These words of Goethe, frequently quoted with emphasis by Arttu Brummer, were the slogan of the 1959 retrospective exhibition in honour of those who gave the christening-gift of opportunity to craftsmen and designers. In the same way this article has so far tried to point out a line of development, and to emphasise the sometimes rather obscure connecting links between the practising artists of today and yesterday and those of earlier years.

Today's craftsmanship and industrial art are products both of the artists' own creative genius and of their heritage. At the same time, two other important stimuli must be mentioned–public support and public demand, both now far greater than ever before. These can be illustrated by considering two different exhibitions. In the autumn of 1949 the furniture trade held a giant exhibition in the Trade Fair Hall at Helsinki. The exhibits could well have formed two separate shows: a very small but select one of responsible design, and a large and representative one of degenerate craftsmanship. The artistic, intellectual, and technical quality of most of the furniture shown was so atrociously bad that part of the Press reacted very sharply. The bitter criticism, and the consequent reaction against it, gave rise to a controversy which had wholesome results. While the phrase 'more beautiful everyday things' had long been well-known and accepted in Sweden, it now for the first time made its impact on the Finnish man in the street. The daily and weekly Press took it up in earnest, and the public

was soon sufficiently aware to formulate demands which furniture-manufacturers could not in the long run ignore. A general slum-clearance in this field resulted, led not only by the always responsible-minded producers such as Artek but also, and more important, by a popular firm like Asko, with a sales organisation covering the whole country.

At the furniture fair of ten years later we may say that there was hardly a single horror exhibited. The cultivated and socially-conscious line of thought had in fact caused such a levelling-out that the overall picture was again almost depressing – and the ungrateful critics took the opportunity to complain that more room was not found for the footloose and fanciful amongst so much austere worthiness. However that may be, this was one of the stimuli that ten years ago awakened critical opinion, not only as concerned furniture but over the whole field of art-handicraft.

An almost simultaneous and equally important phenomenon was the positive interest which the public now began to show in designers and their work. This interest came in a round-about way from Milan, and, as previously mentioned, it was the marked success at the 1951 Triennale which provided the spark. The credit for the Finnish contribution here being so weighty, together with the consequences at home and abroad which followed, is largely due to the Arabia porcelain-works in the Wärtsilä combine and to the Ahlström firm's Iittala glassworks. At this period the State was not at all prepared to give financial support to industrial art, and the Society of Crafts and Design had not yet developed its important and helpful activities to the full. But these two great private firms assumed most of the burden of finance, and they certainly have had no cause to regret it.

The harvest of prizes at Milan in 1951 – six Grands Prix, seven gold and eight silver medals – gave our craftsmanship excellent publicity: both abroad (where, for example, the Italian periodical *Domus* gave fourteen illustrated pages to the Finnish section) and at home, where our artist-craftsmen suddenly found themselves in the same limelight of popularity as film-stars and the aces of sport.

This general awakening of interest first and foremost reanimated the Society of Crafts and Design, which up to now, apart from its traditional annual exhibitions, had passed a somewhat ruminative existence. Its consultants, typically, had only given two hours work twice a week. Now it took on a permanent consultant, whose work soon became that of a managing director. It appointed Olof Gummerus, a well-proven power in the service both of education and industrial art (Arabia), and an uncommonly forceful personality. Not surprisingly the Society's activities now took a new line, more publicity-conscious and interested in international co-operation. Gummerus trimmed the sails cleverly to catch the favourable wind that was blowing, and the bark of industrial art, under the blue and white flag, sailed ever more frequently to the rest of Europe and as regularly came back loaded with commendation. Finland began to take an active part in the movement towards Scandinavian, and later European, collaboration in this field.

All this by no means took place with general agreement –how often is this seen in the world of art, or in Finnish cultural policies as a whole? The 'foreign' or 'commercial traveller' line met strong resistance, both within and without the Society of Crafts and Design. Partly this resulted from the general Finnish abhorrence of publicity-mongering and foreign peculiarities–a negative outlook– and partly from the positive and wholesome view that the applied arts at home should first be put on a firm foundation, before we made a show with the gloss on the perhaps incidental top. It was urged that the basis should be widened, that the home market should be patiently cultivated through travelling exhibitions and lecture-tours in the country districts. Both education and the means of production needed improvement, to meet the new demands, and interest should be transferred from shop-window specialities to articles of practical use.

There was much to be said for this attitude, and it is perhaps even more valid today than ten years ago. But it may also be claimed that it was better policy to seize the offered opportunities. It was soon clear that digressions abroad influenced the home public, industry, and above all the government, in a way which could hardly have been more effective. The experience from the Paris Exhibition of 1900 was repeated.

Influenced by a barrage of flattering attention from abroad, and increasingly well-informed and therefore demanding opinion at home, firms began gradually to employ trained artist-designers. Industrial design became an established profession. The State too, whose interest in applied art had up to now been decidedly lukewarm, could not remain indifferent to the first-class propaganda value of art-craftsmanship, which was probably Finland's finest good-will ambassador. Education, information, and exhibition activities at last began to receive notable financial support. The State subsidy to the Society of Crafts and Design increased by fifteen times in ten years, and direct co-operation was established between the Society and the Ministries of Education and Foreign Affairs.

Finnish industrial art has been consistently exhibited abroad with the direct intention of attracting notice. This began when Tapio Wirkkala at the Triennale of 1951 'hypnotised the Press of the world with a display at once sybaritic and hard as iron', to quote a Swedish observer. Three years later Wirkkala followed up this success with an equally strictly selected Finnish section at the Triennale, restrained in content but striking in effect. In 1957 Timo Sarpaneva achieved a masterstroke by repeating the success in his own personal style. Finally, in 1960, it was the turn of Antti Nurmesniemi to attract the world's camera-lenses onto a studied and photogenic Finnish exhibition. At all four Triennali Finland won a Grand Prix for the layout of her display. This line has been cultivated for the last decade, and for virtually all that time the dispute about its justification has continued. The debate flared up particularly in connection with the much-discussed Hälsingborg Exhibition of 1955. The form in which Timo Sarpaneva presented Finnish handicrafts on this occasion was both beautiful and succinct. "Every day I go first to the Finnish pavilion, for mattins", wrote one of the more eminent English correspondents. "Congratulations for slaying the rest of us so completely", called Arne Jacobsen from the Danish section; and *Domus*' photographer spent twelve hours work on the Finnish exhibits. Aesthetically they were above all criticism; but the selection, and the policy behind it, was all the more freely questioned on grounds of principle.

One ground of criticism lay in the other Scandinavian sections, which were indeed less striking and photogenic but on the other hand aimed to illustrate what those countries had to offer, and so were closer to the human-centred theme of the Exhibition. There was, for example, a wide presentation of practical everyday articles, which were almost completely lacking in the Finnish display.

One school of thought in Finland was demanding precisely this kind of production, as well as a more honest exhibition policy. It pointed out that while other countries, at Hälsingborg and elsewhere, displayed their ordinary standards and average quality at any given time, Finland continued to show only her very best, in a selection dominated by considerations of aesthetic unity. The other school replied that each country showed what it had, and Finland could not demonstrate a breadth of production which in fact she did not possess. The forte of her industrial art was precisely the high quality of her quantitatively limited best, and the most had to be made of this if we were to compete in national publicity. From this viewpoint the aesthetic line was not an end in itself: moreover, it was possible to defend aestheticism on principle, on the ground that Wirkkala's 'unpractical' vases and Dora Jung's 'useless' tapestries fulfilled a need –a need for beauty. Part of the English and Danish Press in fact took the same line, and criticised the Hälsingborg Exhibition for producing nothing new and for marching on in the functionalist woollen stockings of the Thirties.

The counter-argument was of course that this line was sterile and dangerous, so long as the programme of the Thirties remained unfulfilled in Finland. So much was still lacking in understanding and education, in public demand for fitness for purpose combined with beauty, in the willingness of producers to meet this demand, and in the output of good everyday wares and good design in useful articles.

On one point there was general agreement: in exhibitions at home the need for a greater supply of everyday products must not be ignored. The Finnish public must be given a chance to see what was available in the way of things which could make their daily life easier and more satisfying. This was regarded as one necessary condition on which outward-directed display could continue as before, the other being that the exclusive top-ranking artists must not let themselves become tied to particular types and thereby exhaust the existing favourable state of affairs.

Have these conditions been fulfilled? Yes and no. In many fields one might say that over-aesthetic forms are more marked than ever. A keen observer has already detected annoyance amongst the home public with tricks of design: they have had enough of them. It is open to question whether Finland, at and after the 1960 Triennale, has missed the bus. Certainly, thanks to brilliant display, it managed once more to 'hypnotise'; but, considering how far the exhibits were out of line with the general theme at Milan, we might have expected a more negative reaction.

On the other hand, there is clearly now a completely new interest in production for use. As a symptom of this, the sophisticated draftsman and glass-artist Timo Sarpaneva (probably the most outré and fantastical of all) has lately turned with enthusiasm to working on cast-iron ware for a large industrial firm in Björneborg, and on colour-schemes and patterns for the standard products of a large cotton-mill in the same town. It is perhaps significant, too, that in these fields he has in fact produced work both more distinguished and more popular than his latest pieces in glass.

It is of course of great importance that industrial firms have at last come to terms with the designer. New spheres of work are continually opening up, and in Finland there is gradually coming to be an artist behind the design of the better household articles and machines, scooters and motorboats, tools, and packaging. But there are still large fields of activity for him to conquer.

The Finnish art industry has seen marked centralisation. This begins with teaching, which is the exclusive concern of the Institute of Industrial Design (the former Central School). If we skim through the biographical pages at the end of this book, we shall find very few Finnish artists working in the applied arts who were not trained at this school. This may be a source of strength, but also of weakness. As long as the school remains in active contact with the times it is a strength, in that it can disseminate up-to-date ideas throughout the corps of artistcraftsmen. The moment this contact is lost, centralisation becomes a danger. Up to now there has been no reason to complain of the results the school has achieved. With the present method of selecting teachers–most of them from amongst the most currently productive and personally lively artists–and with the interest both industry and artists take in the Society of Crafts and Design and thereby in the school, there is certainly no immediate threatening danger. The instruction seems to have had no levelling effect on young talents: in the spirit of Brummer, ability has been respected and given a free hand.

Centralisation also applies to production. In contrast with the rest of Scandinavia, Finland has no fair garland of flourishing private workshops; and this is distinctly a pity. One thinks, for example, of the masterly way in which Danish cabinetmakers carry out the ideas of furniture-designers, and of the small silversmith and pottery workshops which enrich that country's production. In Finland Marita Lybeck, the only single-handed ceramic artist of significance, recently had to close down her studio near Helsinki after a score of years of partly pioneering activity. Her individual feminine works in faience and her finely modelled fire-proof ware could not in the long run compete with mass-production. It is hard to say what differences of economic structure allow one form of activity to flourish in one part of Scandinavia and not in another. But undoubtedly a land without small potteries lacks some variety in its production.

Technically, factory conditions give the artist great opportunities. The availability of a variety of materials and different kiln temperatures frees him from much time-wasting and tedious preparatory work, as well as from financial insecurity. But, as Tyra Lundgren says, 'he all too easily gets a sliver in his eye from the magic mirror of technology'. It is a dangerous environment. Moreover, we cannot ignore the fact that with kilns monopolised in this fashion there is no guarantee that it is always the most anxious to work and the most artistically productive who actually have the chance to create. It would be much better if we could offer a living to 'studio potters' who could carry on the work of Finch and Elsa Elenius.

This must not be taken as a criticism of Wärtsilä-Arabia, our major producer of ceramics. This would be most ungrateful to a firm which, at the instance of its former head, the famous industrialist Carl Gustaf Herlitz, has done so much for Finland's industrial art. Alongside a preponderant output of sanitary ware, technical porcelain, and ordinary practical products (in some lines perhaps the largest in the world), the firm has given a number of individual artists the opportunity to let their creative imagination and technical experiments have free scope. At the same time it has guaranteed them a living regardless of their immediate inspiration and productivity. Many of Finland's laurels have been won with their assistance, and nearly all the ceramic artists considered worthy of a place in this book's illustration section in fact belong to the Arabia group.

One consideration may be set off against the lack of private potteries. In many countries the ceramic-designer and the glaze artist are two different persons: sometimes even three – the drawing-board designer, the wheel-potter, and the chemist in the glaze laboratory. Arabia's artists work with both wheel and glaze-bath: they are responsible for each successive process, from the first conception of the design, and its realisation in clay, right to the moment when the last layer of glaze is in place and the article has been put in the kiln.

Amongst the most genuine potters in Arabia's artists' quarters high above the rushes in the old city bay of Helsinki, we must first mention Toini Muona and Kyllikki Salmenhaara who are both equally expert in throwing and glazing. Toini Muona was a pupil of Finch, in the days when he had abandoned his Van de Velde-like decoration and his inexpensive earthenware in favour of richer materials and a more difficult technique stressing pure wheel-thrown form and varied glazes. If Finch established the principles of cultivated design in modern Finnish pottery, it was Toini Muona who first carried them to perfection. Her range of stoneware design includes robust strength and delicate sensitiveness. The oft-repeated cliché that Finns find their inspiration in nature is in her case unusually true; and one may also to a great extent speak of her intuitive creations, though the good technical quality of her products is equally the fruit of long experience.

With Kyllikki Salmenhaara it is more a matter of conscious study. She is a careful and expert chemist, who leaves nothing to chance. Her exactitude, coupled with lively imagination, has resulted in an output outstanding in Finnish art. Her stoneware also mirrors the Finnish landscape in a quite unlaboured and natural fashion, which makes her art both national in expression and international in acceptability. Her glazes, especially those of

the early Fifties, suggest to the mind birchbark, the ancient hills, or autumn leaves, and the subtle timeless form harmonises with the surface glaze to make a rare and complete ceramic unity. After a travelling scholarship in America, where she studied primitive Indian art and clearly derived new impulses from it, she abandoned her earlier delicate lines and instead worked with stronger and more strictly geometrical forms, and with more robust and dramatic glazes.

A third important force in the same line of work is Raija Tuumi, who allows traces of throwing to remain on her stoneware bowls and dishes as a vivid symbol of the process of creation. Her carefully prepared glazes are generally in brown earthen shades. In direct contrast with this type of ceramics stands Rut Bryk, who creates a most charming and personal art on plaques with romantic motifs in deep glaze. Previously she used an incised technique, with closely matched and rather sugary pastel shades. At the beginning of the Fifties she went over to strong deep glowing glazes, which she poured over the surfaces between the slightly raised contours of the figures. The subjects of these large or small ceramic paintings are generally birds, butterflies, fish, madonna motifs, and palace façades, all in an unsophisticated style; and, in conjunction with her individual technique and unusual choice of colour, the result is both unique and most harmonious.

Rut Bryk's earlier works showed a close affinity with those of Birger Kaipiainen of the Forties and early Fifties. This artist worked principally on large earthenware surfaces in dishes and bowls, which he decorated in a highly artistic and sometimes rather morbid fashion in incised technique – often figures in Florentine profile amongst dark butterflies and flowers. While in such work Kaipiainen was almost a painter, his products gradually took on more sculptural forms. At first these were stylised human figures with broad heads, a theme which he repeated and modified indefinitely. Later he adopted surrealistic motifs based on inanimate objects, in which a bizarre humour replaced pensive gloom. The bird motif has always interested Kaipiainen, and its latest version is a sculpture made of rows of pottery beads stretched on a steel frame. This won him his Grand Prix at Milan in 1960.

The most outstanding sculptural artist attached to Arabia was Michael Schilkin, who is often dramatic and often humorous in his powerful lines and strong glazes. From purely naturalistic animal and human figures, his work with the years became increasingly stylised. It is often a play with forms which he could equally well have expressed in other media than clay: but he had shown, both in the surface glaze of his sculptures and in some wall-plaques, that he also had a remarkable instinct for ceramics. His monumental works–partly massive reliefs for interior- as well as exterior-decoration –have won him a special place amongst Finnish ceramic artists. One of these can be seen on an outside wall of the Arabia porcelain works, and another on the façade of the Finnish Commercial College in Helsinki.

Once more to go from one extreme to another, thin porcelain is a particular speciality of Aune Siimes and Friedl Kjellberg. The latter has attracted attention with her bowls and coffee-sets in the difficult Chinese rice-grain style, but her undecorated services in bone-china with their simple and restrained design are really finer. She has also worked with celadon and sang de boeuf glazes. Aune Siimes' most important works are her bowls with relief patterns, which give varying transparency to the thin white, cobalt, or pink porcelain. In the same recherché material and the same spirit she has made personal ornaments, especially necklaces, with 'pearls' in the form of mussels or leaves.

One more distinctive member of Arabia's band of artists is the German-born Schultz-Köln, who expresses a painter's temperament both in the decoration of his geometrically-shaped vases and in larger works like a wall-ornament at Helsinki Air Terminal.

The young and gifted Richard Lindh and his wife Francesca have attracted attention at many exhibitions with their sensitive ceramics, and he was for some time in charge of Arabia's industrial art department.

A contribution which can hardly be overvalued is Kaj Franck's designing of Arabia's modern standard production, especially table services. In that field he has managed to revolutionise public taste in Finland–and in much of the outside world. He soon declared war on complete uniform services, and instead made a large number of practical and attractive separate pieces which complemented each other and could be had in various well-chosen colours in an endless variety of possible combinations. He planned on a large scale, while also taking care of small well-thought-out and pleasing details, to meet the housewife's need for everyday wares which would be easy to wash up, did not take much space, and were both economical and beautiful. Franck's work has an unlaboured and unpretentious element particularly welcome in Finland, where pointless artiness sometimes has too free a rein. In his task of clearance and fresh creation Franck had invaluable assistance from Kaarina Aho and Ulla Procopé, two skilful ceramic artists who have both become known for their elegant work.

One other large industrial firm, Kuppi's factory in Åbo, has achieved good artistic results. Its artists Mar-jukka Paasivirta, Orvokki Laine, and Linnea Lehtonen, have also won prizes at Milan for their unaffected and genuine work on the borderline between decorative and useful art. In Kuppi's output the traditional Finnish red clay once more holds an honoured position.

Art-glass in Finland is produced by three firms, which have all, like Arabia, given scope to artistic talent and have co-operated in giving industrial art a worthy representation in exhibitions abroad. They are the Iittala glassworks, Wärtsilä-Notsjö, and Riihimäki. In each case their major output is in technical wares, but they have also shown a remarkable and valuable interest in art-glass and have given its designers a free hand.

Most Finnish glass-artists are versatile, and this is not to be wondered at. They are designers, and a man with paper before him and a pen in a trained hand may well come to design other things besides glass. Likewise, it is natural that a man designing other things may one day sketch the lines of a glass vessel on his paper. Once he has become involved in the fascinating process of making works of art in glass, he is easily captured by the glass-house and becomes primarily a glass-artist. Examples can be given of development in either direction. Franck, who began as a textile-artist, designs practical ware for Arabia and art-glass for Notsjö. Timo Sarpaneva of Iittala first became known for his imaginative embroidery, and is a really top-ranking draftsman. The same applies to Tapio Wirkkala, who besides his work for Iittala also designs in plywood, silver, and ceramics.

Wirkkala's versatility also appears in his glass. He is quite exceptional in using so many different techniques at the same time; paper-thin chanterelle vases and crude massive crystal: sand-blasting and etched decoration: vigorous as well as delicate and sensitive forms. Which one prefers must be a matter of taste. Chanterelle glasses have sold well to the general public, but Wirkkala is most at home with more dynamic forms of expression. Some of his crystal, for example, has the effect of a petrified explosion, and some on the other hand is peaceful in its simple and natural lines. Some small objects gather light and the reflections of their surroundings in a composite play in their tensely curved forms. Amongst his coloured glassware one remembers especially a series of small pieces with orchid shades in brown and green under a top layer of clear glass.

The two Iittala artists Wirkkala and Sarpaneva have a lot in common, not only in competing as talented and expert exhibition designers and draftsmen but also in their glassware. But there is an obvious and important difference: while Wirkkala's work shows intuitive natural force, Sarpaneva's gives a more considered and intellectual impression. The most fitting term is perhaps brilliant. His undoubtedly best work, his tall, lancet-like, plain vases, has a cold clarity like the logic of a mathematical equation or the beauty of a mathematical curve. This may not sound encouraging, but it is not intended as derogatory: the form is certainly not dead – on the contrary, it is intensely alive and changes with each fresh viewpoint, just as a curved lens mirrors the surroundings and breaks them up into ever different pictures as one turns it round. Moreover, one has a strong feeling that Sarpaneva's work was created in the immediate vicinity of the glasshouse fire, where, through technical processes in part new and independent, he has managed to bring out fresh effects from the glass material.

Göran Hongell has been working for the same firm for many years, and producing service glass of an unusually pure and even standard which early embodied ideas of 'more beautiful everyday things'. His forms are so unsensational that he has never been widely acclaimed, but nevertheless he has given a valuable stimulus to many of today's well-known glass-artists.

For the Notsjö glassworks (which, as we have said, now belongs to the same combine as the Arabia factory), Kaj Franck produces both art glass and useful wares in his typical unpretentious but brilliant style. He has most happily combined spirit with functional considerations in the best historical tradition of the old glassworks. This can be seen for example in his bottle-green glass and the soda-bubbles which freely imitate the air-bubbles in the glass of early times. His shapes are extremely simple – cylinders, parts of cones and spheres, and ovoid vases thin as soap-bubbles – when he is not giving his fancy free rein in cunning little figures which seem intended chiefly to amuse.

Franck had another talented colleague at Notsjö in Saara Hopea, who made excellent useful glassware both in the form of stacking tumblers and in more festive pieces such as her white-wine glasses in elongated hour-glass form. Later on she went over to work in silver, and now through marriage has left for the United States and there become a new force in American industrial art.

All three of the important glassworks have kept their individual character. At Riihimäki, where Henry Ericsson founded modern Finnish glass-art, Helena Tynell and Nanny Still have in recent years been chiefly responsible for design. Tynell's new mother-of-pearl-like crystal, holding all the colours of the rainbow, bears comparison with the best products of the other glassworks. Nanny Still works mainly in polychrome and other strongly coloured glass, and her enterprising experiments with different techniques and forms have produced striking results. Both have also worked on useful glassware.

To some extent there has also been centralisation in the field of textiles. On the one hand the Friends of Finnish Handicraft have long attracted the best rug-artists, and on the other the large factories have in recent years increasingly employed artists as pattern-designers. One firm which has led in this direction has been Björneborg Cotton, and it is worth noting that this was a direct result of a controversy over principles in the Press. The protagonists were the head of Artek, Maire Gullichsen, who herself is both an artist and a patron, and the then head of Björneborg, Runar Hernberg. The debate was about the need for, value of, and responsibility for employing artists in industrial production. Hernberg's answer to Maire Gullichsen's temperamental but well-meant outburst against industry was to set up a department of artist-designers in his own firm, and to put Timo Sarpaneva in charge. Many other textile businesses shook their heads and declared that to bring the artist into industry was to invite the devil into the boat. But it was not long before one after the other followed this example; and Hernberg, who is now head of the Villayhtymä woollen combine, has now also let him loose in woollens.

Designers have long been associated with woollen handicraft production, especially with rug-weaving under the aegis of the Friends of Handicraft. The original inspiration, as mentioned above, was the refined colours of the folk-weaves of the late Eighteenth and early Nineteenth Centuries. The technique goes right back to the Middle Ages: the yarn is attached to the warp (with the same Smyrna-knots used in making oriental carpets) in such a way that the 3–6 cm. pile completely or partly covers the ground-weave. But the pattern is freely 'painted', and though similar in form, size, and material, the rugs each have a definite individuality typical of different artists. Amongst the foremost of these are Eva Brummer, Kirsti Ilvessalo, Uhra Simberg-Ehrström, Maria Boije, Toini Nyström, and – since 1960 – Ritva Puotila. In Kirsti Ilvessalo's work, for example, one can trace a freely interpreted echo of traditional national decorative motifs, while Uhra Simberg is a pure colourist with her own harmonious scale in earthy tones of brown, green, grey, and lilac. The same colour-scale is repeated in her compositions for mass-produced woollens, scarves, plaids, and shawls. Kirsti Ilvessalo also works for industry with subdued and well-considered furnishing-fabrics, besides personally weaving at her own loom.

The most famous name in Finnish textiles, Dora Jung, also makes her distinctive damask in her own workshop. She combines to an unusual degree the absolute mastery of her media with a fine artistic insight. She has herself developed the equipment and technique behind her damask-weaving, and is thus able to achieve hitherto unsuspected effects. The colouring is controlled and restrained, with occasional bursts of brightness against the dominant grey, and her composition is economical and sure-handed. Dora Jung's products mark the absolute zenith of Finnish art-craftsmanship.

Marjatta Metsovaara-Nyström on her own premises weaves tapestries and furnishing-fabrics in a well-balanced combination of traditional and unconventional materials. She likes to use natural-coloured fibres with a gay weft of metal- or plastic-thread, giving her fabrics and tapestries a modern and almost American note. Laila Karttunen and the tapestry-weaver Eva Anttila also have their own workshops. The latter, in her unique weaving technique, 'paints' pictures almost as sensitive and finely shaded as if she were using a brush on canvas. She has produced a number of exhibition pieces of distinguished monumentality, but most of her works are delicate 'sketches' on a smaller scale. Laila Karttunen on the other hand works with the typical Finnish double-weave, 'täkänä', in which the pattern appears on both sides. She mostly builds her compositions on decorative folk-motifs, simple, solid, and in subdued colours–often grey in a variety of fine shades.

An efficient and unconventional new firm, Printex, under the direction of Armi Ratia, has succeeded in gaining for Finnish printed fabrics a foothold in America and elsewhere. It employs a number of expert pattern designers, such as Vuokko Eskolin, Maija Isola, and Liisa Suvanto. Printex prints the fabrics, and its daughter concern Marimekko makes them up into fashionable dress-models. Since Mrs. Kennedy bought nine Marimekko models, the unconventional and colourful Finnish cottons have received much Press publicity in the United States.

Furniture has already been mentioned in connection with the famous exhibition of 1949, and since then development has been positive and remarkable, if perhaps rather limited in breadth. Individual designers like Alvar Aalto have their pieces made up in small workshops; but for the most part it is the large firms who have, in this field as well, carried out the designer's ideas. This was to be expected, once interest began to turn from unique show-pieces and semi-sculptural works towards the line which is the forte of Danish designers and furniture-makers–socially-conscious furniture, designed for the all too few and too small rooms of Finnish housing standards. After a period of frightful experiments with all types of abortive combination-pieces, the social policy has at last produced acceptable results–even though the high level of wages and business overheads has kept prices undesirably high.

One speciality is pieces which can be stacked and

Detail of tapestry woven by Dora Jung in 1961 for a room in the newly restored renaissance wing of the otherwise mediaeval Åbo Castle. This is now one of the finest historical settings in Finland and in all Scandinavia.

dismantled, designed for export. Ilmari Tapiovaara in particular has been engaged in solving technical difficulties and packaging problems, and his small structural chairs in wood and steel tubing, unassuming as they are, may be considered as among the best products of Finnish furniture. All show the same cool, logical, and clean stamp as his interiors. Not for nothing has Tapiovaara, in his rôle as teacher and author, stressed the importance of structural ideas.

Even in forested Finland, such materials as steel and plastic are becoming steadily more important alongside timber and plywood. They are expertly employed by interior-designers like Antti Nurmesniemi and Olli Borg, who both, like Tapiovaara, have their private studios. Other prominent designers of overseas reputation work for the furniture departments of large firms, for example Olavi Hänninen, Lasse Ollinkari, Olof Ottelin, and Reino Ruokolainen.

Foreigners sometimes wonder why mahogany and teak have been apparently favoured at the expense of native woods. But deal and birch have lately made something of a come-back, partly because a new method of treatment with plastic allows birchwood to keep its characteristic white surface without yellowing. Artek, moreover, has for many years used birch regularly and on a large scale. Furniture has become an important item in Finnish exports–first to the United States, and later to West Germany and the Soviet Union. In Germany it is in part sold directly from the producers' own showrooms.

At the beginning of the Fifties, Bertel Gardberg

originated a great boom in art-metalware from a small and primitive cellar-workshop. His works in silver and brass, and in combinations of metal and wood, won acclaim from the first; and as a teacher on his own premises and at the Institute of Industrial Design he proved a great inspiration for young craftsmen. Large industrial firms also became interested in this field. Hackman & Co. were the first to commission designs from him for tableware in steel and silver, and soon other firms employed other artists. This was mostly a matter of cutlery and personal ornaments, and less of silver vessels. The large goldsmith firms discovered that modern jewellery in gold, silver, and native precious stones, was in great demand. Our national anthem says that 'our land is poor, and will always be, for him who longs for gold': but in fact Finland is now almost self-sufficient in this respect. Over 800 kg. of gold is mined annually, all for use at home, and nearly 80 % of this is made into fashionable articles.

Amongst our expert and talented jewellery-designers are Gardberg's pupil Börje Rajalin, a very distinctive artist, and Eero Rislakki, Björn Weckström, and Elis Kauppi. Wirkkala has designed silver vessels for various firms, but in this sphere he has not been quite so successful as with his glass.

It is fair to say that Gardberg alone deserves to represent the classical art of the silversmith. He has an intuitive appreciation of silver and the materials he uses in combination with it. His vessels are simple and balanced in their lines, made with exceptional care, and functionally thought-out in every detail. Amongst them we may note a series of silver articles for church use. His interest in combinations of wood and metal is shared by the talented and self-taught Olof Bäckström, who first won recognition with his fine works in wood and now designs tableware for Fiskar's factory. The glass-artist Nanny Still has also achieved remarkable results as a wood-carver, and Tapio Wirkkala's original dishes in laminated plywood, from the early Fifties, attracted world-wide attention.

If silversmithing still remains a somewhat undeveloped field of Finnish form-refinement, light-fittings already have a long tradition. Paavo Tynell's shades of brass and glass have long won respect, not least in America, where, for example, he has designed the fittings for the U.N. building. The leading designer in this sphere is now Lisa Johansson-Pape, who shows economy of form and well-thought-out solutions to technical lighting problems. Her shades in glass or perspex are entirely undecorated, but though their basis is purely functional they are not without life and imagination. She has done most valuable work in planning the lighting of many restored mediaeval churches.

Another equally expert designer of light-fittings is Yki Nummi, a very versatile artist who amongst other things may be regarded as Finland's leading authority on colour combinations, and as such he is frequently employed both by industry and house-furnishing firms. One branch of industry most intimately associated with the designer's work, is that of wallpaper manufacture. In this a congenial field of work has opened up for artists both in textiles and house-furnishing. A completely fresh start was needed, and has been made. Wallpapers, previously so neglected, are now definitely a prominent and accepted part of Finnish industrial art.

The coming together of artist-designers and industry is naturally a result of the times: the need, and examples from abroad, became so plain that they could not be ignored. The influence of the Press also played a large part. The vigorous propaganda campaign of the newspapers and the Society of Crafts and Design – often mutually inspired – has been one of the most decisive developments of the previous decade. On average, the Finnish Press has produced every day three articles or controversial notices directly concerned with the country's industrial art. Very important too have been the annual exhibitions in Helsinki, travelling displays in the provinces, and trade fairs, organised by the Society. It is a pity that the valuable collections of the Industrial Art Museum are still packed away because they yet have no permanent home of their own. On the other hand, an impressive number of overseas exhibitions has been organised partly or wholly by the Society – nearly a hundred in ten years. Some of the most important of these are worth mentioning.

The series began in 1951 with the collection which was shown first in Zürich and later at the ninth Triennale in Milan. The following year a large exhibition of both industrial and fine art was shown in thirteen North American cities, and then in Glasgow, London, Leeds, Brighton, and Dublin. In 1954 followed the tenth Triennale, and in December an industrial art show was the main event of a Finnish Week in Brussels. There was also that year an exhibition in Oslo. In 1954–57 Finland shared in the triumphal progress of 'Design in Scandinavia' through 24 cities in the United States and Canada. 1955 saw the turn of Hälsingborg, and the same year a representative show of the three leading artists Franck, Gardberg, and Jung was given in Gothenburg and in Copenhagen. In 1956 rugs, historical and modern, were displayed in Oslo, Bergen, and Trondheim; and further shows were held in Augsburg, Faenza, and New York. A large industrial art exhibition visited a dozen West German cities in 1956–57.

The eleventh Triennale came in 1957, as well as rug-exhibitions in Copenhagen, Stockholm, Gothenburg, the Hague, and Brunswick. The industrial art section was a major element of the Finnish display at the Brussels Exhibition of 1958, and the same collection was later shown in Stuttgart. In collaboration with the Artists' Guild fine and applied arts were shown in Athens, and Finland was well represented at the international art exhibition at Syracuse N.Y. A rug display visited London and six German cities in 1958–59, 'Formes Scandinaves' was shown in Paris, and Sarpaneva demonstrated Finnish glass and fabrics in Rio de Janeiro, São Paulo, Buenos Aires, and Montevideo. The following year came another Triennale, and in 1961 a show in Moscow and the greatest Finnish industrial art exhibition of all time in Zürich – the place in which all this started. Since then travelling exhibitions have been shown in Amsterdam, London, Vienna, Madrid, Copenhagen, Warsaw, Paris and Stockholm.

Finland has now at last also begun to open permanent 'shop-windows' in the outside world, both in the form of sales-rooms belonging to individual firms and in that of design-centres such as those in Finland House, London, and 'Formes Finlandaises', Place de la Madeleine, Paris.

This external propaganda activity, equally with the direct results garnered for example from the Triennali – 21 Grands Prix, 32 gold medals and 27 silver medals – has put Finland on the world map as a country to be reckoned with in industrial art. But our satisfaction at this should not blind us to the fact that this success in exclusive work does not reflect a corresponding general level. What has been shown abroad is not simply the best of a broad and soundly-based production. This must be obvious to foreigners, since it was nearly always the same artists who were represented in the exhibitions of the Fifties, and a very limited number at that.

More disturbing than the small number of our creative forces, and the somewhat arbitrary manner in which these few have been exploited, is the lack of correspondence between their work and Finland's actual average level of design. Anyone who attempts to build up a picture of the ordinary man's standard from Finnish show-pieces makes the same mistake as one who judges the standards of Italian homes from the pages of *Domus*.

Beside the brilliance and intuitive creativity of Finnish artists of the Fifties, the exhibits of other Scandinavian countries may at times have appeared somewhat colourless and matter-of-fact – at least in the opinion of Swedish and Danish critics. But it is important that Finns themselves should realise that this is largely due to different principles of selection and methods of display, and is not true when we compare actual national standards. The solid bourgeois and handicraft traditions of the Danes, and their balanced culture-philosophy, or the thorough democracy and social-security principles of Swedish everyday life, do not lend themselves readily to exhibition display but are realities of lasting value.

We proudly assume that the rest of Scandinavia can learn something from our fresh and untrammelled creativeness in alliance with Nature, but at the same time we must admit that there is a new test before us. We need to think how to guide our art-craftsmanship away from the ill-considered, the over-aesthetic, the dehumanised, towards something less productive of limelight and gold medals but much more representative of our actual capacity.

In the above pages it has been accepted as right and proper that we seized the opportunities of the past decade for such effective national publicity, with its consequent propaganda effects at home. But now we must look for a renaissance in other directions. This is not to be taken simply as the subjective opinion of the present author: one will find in talking to some of our most significant and clear-thinking artists that they feel the same. This arises from the enhanced interest in the applied arts and the design of standard industrial products. Perhaps more important still, it appears to be the prevalent belief among the generation who are now learning and will shortly be our creative artists.

NORWAY

Ferdinand Aars

The Norwegian landscape is one of great distances, narrow valleys, and deep fiords, and only in recent times have cities of any size developed. In earlier times the towns were too small to transmit changing foreign fashions effectively, and outside influence therefore did not make much impact upon the conservative Norwegian peasantry. The result was that national traits had full scope for development in peasant culture, and considerable talent was no rarity in Norwegian craftsmanship. It would seem that the natural scene, with its strong contrasts and extreme differences between summer and winter, made its mark on the people and developed the Norwegian feeling for colour and form.

The town environment was poorer than in other countries. When in the Nineteenth Century style-confusion spread over the world and industrialisation was making its first bid to replace handicraft, in Norway it was natural to look to the countryside for new developments. People came to recognise the fresh and direct beauty in village weaving, wood-carving, and floral painting, and the reacceptance of these values resulted in folk-art dominating contemporary efforts to create a new and artistically satisfying style.

But it soon became clear that conditions no longer allowed a renaissance on a purely folk-art basis. Industrialisation had changed the country's economic structure, and the towns had become larger and richer. Eventually a distinct urban culture developed. Communications constantly improved, technical advances were made daily, and all contributed to a complete change in Norway's economic, social, and cultural make-up. Contacts between the countryside and the town, and with the outside world, became much closer, and general living standards and philosophy of life completely changed. Industrialisation, with its particular potentialities and problems of factory mass-production, could not expand on the old handicraft basis. An attempt was indeed made to transfer folk-crafts to machinery, but this proved impossible. Instead, foreign examples were copied without regard to the laws of mental copyright. Meanwhile Norwegian businessmen began to import foreign goods which were generally the surplus from the cheapest mass-production. As a result, uncertainty and style-confusion were generally and surely made worse. Those firms which recognised the importance of making goods suitable for mass-production had the greatest difficulty in finding people to help in carrying out the artistic side of their programme. Schools of craftsmanship and industrial art produced at that time many excellent handcraftsmen; but they had no idea of what was required if their training was also to serve industry. At first firms employed 'fine' artists–they at least had a name: but the results of this co-operation left much to be desired, since they often proved to lack a grasp of practical matters.

The one definite attempt to develop a modern style in the field of applied arts was the annual lotteries which the Norwegian Craftsmen's League arranged in the three largest towns–Oslo, Bergen, and Trondheim. Competitions were held between the best designers of furniture, textiles, and tableware, and the winning entries were exhibited in connection with the lotteries. These exhibitions had a special influence on furniture-design, but one of their important functions was to bring designers into direct contact with craftwork and industry.

This was the general situation in Norway up to 1918, but that year was in several ways memorable. The word 'Brukskunst' was coined, and the Brukskunst (or Applied Art) Association was founded. I must point out that 'Brukskunst' is a wholly Norwegian word, though it has since found its way into the other Scandinavian languages because it is so convenient and comprehensive. It has become an idea, including art-craftsmanship, industrial art, and industrial design. It has only one fault–it is hard to translate into any non-Scandinavian tongue.

As we have said, there were no unifying principles in Norwegian artistic crafts and industry before 1918. The style-confusion of the Nineteenth Century was still much in evidence, and the patriotic copying of ornamental motifs from the Viking period was oddly married to the Art Nouveau of the early Twentieth Century. Products were often marked by casualness and a sad lack of quality. Market analysis and market research were, generally speaking, almost unheard of. At the same time there was a group of culturally conscious people much concerned with the various problems in this field, and willing to make an effort towards improvement. It was because of this that a few designers, museum folk, craftsmen, and artists founded the Applied Art Association.

Since the Association has on the whole worked on consistent lines from that day to this, it is worth noting how the new body's statement of aims was framed:

"The object of the Association is to encourage Norwegian craftsmanship and industry in an artistic direction by:

(a) Procuring good rational pattern-types and thereby creating a direct and effective connection between crafts, industry, and art.

(b) Maintaining as far as possible standing exhibitions.

(c) Issuing a periodical with a modern, practical, and progressive programme."

These were the large tasks which the new Association set itself. In brief, the realisation of this programme demanded that everything needed for everyday life should be practically fit for its purpose and artistically beautiful. The Association began its work from scratch; it was far from easy simultaneously to think out new, rational, and artistically valid forms of expression for craft and industry and to educate the public to understand and value them and thereby align themselves with the Association.

This was no Columbus' egg which the Association's founders had discovered. In several other countries people were working towards the same goal and from the same fundamental ideas. But conditions were perhaps more difficult in Norway, since it was a small country lying on the edge of things, with a limited scale of production and a sparse population. Eager spirits like Jakob Prytz, Thor Kielland, Henrik Sørensen, and Harald Aars felt impelled to tackle everything, since they saw possibilities of raising the standard of living of the Norwegian people, and making them happier, through the creation of homes and everyday things which were both more practical and more beautiful than those they had had to be content with before.

Right from the start the Applied Art Association made it clear that its aims were social in character. Artists and industrial firms must be helped in various ways, and the public must be persuaded to make demands in design, quality, and colour. A market had to be built up for articles of both technical and aesthetic value. From the very first the Association worked to educate the public to understand the difference between good things and bad–to learn what had quality and what only claimed to have it. One of the Association's goals was that the general population should come to live according to the well-known words of William Morris: 'Have nothing in your houses that you do not know to be useful, or believe to be beautiful'.

As regards producers, the Association tried to make it clear that time had now brought developments to a decisive point. It was no longer enough for firms to commission drawings and proposals for design and decoration from artists who sat in their offices or studios in solitary meditation. If artists were to make a contribution of real significance, it was absolutely necessary for them to share in the work at the place of manufacture. They must know every process in detail, and they must understand what machines and craftsmen could do. Only then would they have the necessary basis to work effectively towards a worthwhile change. Every new model must be carefully followed through, to achieve the organic relationship between design and realisation which is the hallmark of any product at once practical and beautiful.

It was from this standpoint that the Association addressed itself to industry, and it was soon clear that the argument was not falling on deaf ears. Firms realised how true it was that artists working for industry could achieve quite different results by being directly attached to the works than by merely sending in drawings from a distance. It was established that artists must have a thorough knowledge of production techniques, and work in close collaboration with the factory's technical staff. In the years after 1918 a series of artists were appointed by industrial firms, and it was soon plain that Norwegian applied-art products were assuming a characteristic stamp of their own.

But the Applied Art Association did not confine itself to seeking contacts with industry. It also established a connection with artist-craftsmen working in their own small premises without any thought of mass-production. Contact groups were set up for the various trades, so that artist-craftsmen could the more easily further their interests, and the Association supported them to the best of its ability with deed and word. Anyone who wished to try his luck in industry was also put in contact with firms.

A whole series of artists soon took advantage of this, thinking that they could make a contribution in industry in accordance with the principles of the Association. One good example is Sverre Pettersen, originally a very talented book-artist and decorative painter, who with the Association's help found a niche at Hadeland glassworks and worked there till after the Second World War. His contribution was the basis for the renaissance in the Norwegian glass industry. Another was Nora Guldbrandsen, who came to play a similar rôle in the porcelain industry after her appointment to Porsgrund porcelain-works. Jakob Prytz was the great reviver of Norwegian work in silver. In the textile field several designers appeared who made a great improvement in quality, both in patterns and in choice of material.

As previously mentioned, individual artists had designed furniture for the lotteries of the Craftsmen's League. Now more of them began to take an interest in creating rational and beautiful forms; and a new professional group, interior-designers, joined in. Today hardly a single Norwegian furniture factory does not employ a designer for its output.

The effect of the Applied Art Association's efforts was soon to be seen in the exhibitions it arranged, and these became the object of steadily increasing public interest. Displays were held of glass, ceramics, furniture, stoves, textiles, book-production, and silverware, besides large general exhibitions of Norwegian applied art. The Association also repeatedly staged shows of the products of foreign firms and artists. All exhibitions had this in common, that they had a central theme, and that nothing was shown to the public without first being examined and accepted by the Association's jury.

For many years the Association had no fixed exhibition site, and used whatever facilities were available. It might be a newly built property, in which the Association furnished apartments according to its own principles. Room was also found in industrial art museums, or on ordinary business premises. The Association's leaders fully realised that it would be more satisfactory to have their exhibitions in one definite place: it would, for example, give the public a clearer idea of what they were really aiming at. When the artists of Norway eventually built their own premises, the Association was able to rent the main hall as its permanent site for exhibitions. Here, from 1930 up to the last war, were held continually changing displays illustrating every aspect and problem of applied art in Norway. The number of foreign exhibitions was also much increased, since they gave useful stimuli to our artists and manufacturers. What was equally important, the Norwegian public had a chance to learn of current tendencies, and one had a good opportunity to make comparisons with corresponding home products.

Between 1918 and the Second World War, international taste and ideas of style went through a clearly marked change. It can of course be asserted that this development would have reached Norway even without the activities of the Association: modern forms of expression would in any case have broken through. Changes in fashion will always spread, and be generally copied and imitated. But we cannot deny that it was the Association which took up these questions for consideration and action. It was Norway's sounding-board for the new ideas and opinions, since they coincided with its own principles. We did not engage in slavish copying, but instead adapted the new and valuable ideas which were in the air to fit Norwegian conditions. New forms and styles are completely satisfactory only in their place of origin: to suit other surroundings they must be adapted and changed. Throughout its existence, the Applied Art Association has led developments along a line which has allowed the expression of Norwegian individuality and temperament.

The Second World War interrupted development in Norway. The country became impoverished during the five years it lasted; and it took several more to restore what the war had ruined, both materially and culturally. The shortage of goods, which was very serious both during and after the war, gradually weakened the Norwegian taste for quality; and inferior materials slowly forced their way in everywhere. To meet the great demand which arose as soon as the war was over, producers succumbed to the temptation to put something on sale irrespective of quality. Anything would find a buyer.

During the war years, interest in the home and in everything to do with its furnishing and equipment greatly increased. Travel was impossible, and Norwegians were reduced to living behind closed blinds. The home consequently became a more important element in one's existence, and this again increased interest in the applied arts. One association for applied art was no longer enough: new ones were founded all over the country, which were federated in the Norwegian Society for Industrial Arts and Design. This meant no change in the movement itself, but only a very necessary development in organisation. The work has since been carried on according to the same programme adopted by the Association's founders in 1918.

Not only in Norway had there been changes: all over the civilised world by the end of the war a complete alteration in social structure had taken place. This development still continues, and we cannot escape the fact that economic, social, and cultural changes are now in process of altering men's standards and attitude to life at an ever faster rate.

It is several centuries since there was an aristocracy in Norway, but even without this there were marked differences between the various classes of the population. Now this is no longer the case, and Norway has become a classless society. Most people earn roughly the same, whether they work with hands or brain. Social classes which formerly lived in straitened conditions and could afford only the bare necessities of life can now set their sights much higher. They have incomes which would have been unthinkable one or two generations ago. A new public with purchasing power has come into the picture, and this has had the effect of greatly extending the home market for the products of industrial art.

Changed living conditions have brought with them new demands. Today many of the things which previous generations used are no longer wanted, but on the other hand developments have brought us to a point where we can no longer manage without much that our predecessors never had. This is a quite new situation. It is not only the people who are to live in the new housing and use the new equipment suitable for it who have had to adjust themselves: it is industry as well. In Norway the art-industry has been painfully slow to recognise this, and for that reason it is only in recent years that Norway has become internationally competitive in this field.

As we have already mentioned, there were even before the war a number of firms with an output of artistic quality. But the war stopped all determination to make an effort in this direction, and generally speaking it is only now that Norwegian industrial art firms are waking up to the fact that it is not enough merely to produce goods. Recently they have come to realise that production based on both technical and artistic quality is urgently needed, and that without it they will be unable to face foreign competition or make satisfactory sales at home or abroad. A steadily increasing number of artists has been taken on by industrial firms, and as time goes by it is becoming plainer that co-operation between them and the firms' technical staff and sales organisation is bearing fruit. Norway is now equipped to play her part equally with the other Scandinavian countries in contributing to the concept known to the outside world as 'Scandinavian Design'.

Developments in the higher technical institutes have also assisted progress. Previously the State School of Crafts and Industrial Art, the State Industrial School for Women, and the Bergen School of Arts and Crafts concentrated rather one-sidedly on teaching art-handicrafts, without considering that the pupils might also be trained to make themselves useful in industry with a knowledge and understanding of its special needs. Now the case is altered, and artists are trained both as independent craftsmen and as designers for artistic quality products.

At this point the question arises—how do the Norwegian applied arts stand today? To answer it we must survey their separate fields.

Norway has an ancient weaving tradition. Examples of cloth are found right back to the Fifth Century A.D., and Viking burials from as early as the Ninth have also yielded many rich finds of everyday fabrics and woven tapestries. From the Middle Ages up to our own era handweaving has been common all over the country, and on the whole Norway has been self-sufficient both in ordinary cloths and those for special occasions. Norwegians have always loved bright and gay colours, and present-day artists build both instinctively and consciously on the colour-effects and colour-sense of earlier times. It is as if our artistic temperament has found its natural and obvious outlet in the realm of textiles.

During the last thirty years, many great decorative schemes have been carried out by textile-artists or by 'fine' artists in collaboration with expert weavers. Such work makes great demands on both parties. The artist must have a thorough knowledge of the possibilities and limitations of various weaving techniques, before he tackles his sketches; and there is a similar heavy responsibility on the weaver, who must work out which colours and materials will best realise the artist's intentions. Else Halling's name will always be connected with modern Norwegian pictorial weaving. In collaboration with various artists, she and her assistants in Norwegian Tapestries Ltd. have produced a great number of monumental pieces for public buildings. The largest of her tapestries covers 27 square metres.

Norwegian artists who design for tapestry-weaving consciously strive for the greatest possible simplicity consistent with the best traditions of the art in Norway. Else Halling also employs the same technique that our weavers have used as far back as we have knowledge. The yarn she uses is hand-spun outer wool of the 'Old Norwegian' sheep. This has such a rich effect that it seems to become animated in the light.

Annelise Knudtzon is another weaver who has achieved great results in collaboration with an artist. Her rugs, based on sketches by the painter Knut Rumohr, show a new development in an old Norwegian technique. They are bright with gay colours, and made with a clear eye to any possibilities of bringing new textile values to the artist's lay-out. In recent years she has begun a promising collaboration with Røros Tweed, a firm which makes woollen curtains and furnishing fabrics from patterns which she has developed by experiments in her workshop.

Sigrun Berg is an outstanding example of collaboration with industry. She has had her own looms since 1947, and has produced on them many richly coloured rugs as well as furnishing fabrics and curtains for churches, public buildings, and private homes. She was awarded a diplôme d'honneur at the Milan Triennale of 1954. Besides directing her own workshop, she has for the last four years served as art-consultant for United Woollen Mills, which also produces her fabrics on an industrial scale. Both she and the firm achieved gold medals at the Triennale of 1960.

Elise Jakhelln has a large establishment by Norwegian standards, where a dozen weavers execute the patterns and fabrics she designs—probably the most typically Norwegian of any now produced.

In a general article like this it is impossible to name

all those weavers who have played a part in the development of Norwegian art-textiles in recent years. Their great number alone shows how well-established the country now is in this field. Meanwhile, it is most encouraging that new small workshops are continually being set up, with expert and purposeful weavers making fabrics of high quality. A considerable number of textile-artists have taken up embroidery, for example Fanny Mørch and Eli Marie Johnsen, both of whom have shown a talent for adapting old embroidery traditions to suit modern forms of expression.

It is perhaps especially in textiles that the advanced craft-schools have made their greatest contribution, not only through individual pupils but to Norwegian crafts and industry in general. The State Industrial School for Women runs an experimental workshop, where, amongst other things, systematic work is done to discover the best possible and most appropriate types of yarn from home sources. The State School of Crafts and Industrial Art can also claim effective results from its training in textile crafts.

In this section on textiles I have deliberately postponed mention of Norway's greatest textile artist, and for a definite reason. She herself declares that she is not an 'applied' but a 'fine' artist, and therefore she is not represented in the illustrations. Hannah Ryggen is a unique genius, in a class by herself. We cannot write about Norwegian textiles without mentioning her name, which we do with great admiration. Her tapestries generally take their motifs from the current political situation, and are full of powerful feeling, with their effect accentuated by vivid colour-contrasts. Unlike most other artists she composes direct on the loom, without sketches or other preparation. She denies being an 'applied' artist: but the great thing is that she exists, to the joy and benefit of Norwegian textile-artists and applied art.

Glassmaking in Norway is of comparatively recent origin, the first glassworks having been founded about 1740. From then onwards till the beginning of the Nineteenth Century several others opened up in various parts of eastern Norway, where there were sufficient easily accessible materials for producing window-glass, bottles, and other simple articles. But only one of them made fine glass and glass of high artistic quality – Nøstetangen, founded near Drammen in 1744. Later on this production was moved to Hurdalen. Quite a number of glass objects of that period are to be found in museums, and it is remarkable how advanced the technique then was. In particular many chandeliers survive, which give an impressive idea of the artistic standards of the period.

Only one glassworks has survived the vicissitudes of time – Hadeland, which can now look back over more

Detail of tapestry, now in Oslo Town Hall, made by Else Halling at Norsk Billedvev (Norwegian Tapestries) in 1948, to a design by Kåre M. Jonsborg. 360 × 720 cm.

than two centuries of unbroken activity with continual progress and renewal. Today it is much the largest glassworks in Norway. The renown it has won during the last thirty years is primarily due to a single artist, Sverre Pettersen, whom we have already mentioned. He took over the artistic direction in 1928, and immediately a new aesthetic sensitiveness appeared in its products. Technically Hadeland was well-equipped, and – perhaps still more important – it had a staff of expert craftsmen, with a loyalty to the firm based on the fact that their forefathers had worked there for generations.

Until 1928 table glassware formed the major part of the output, and in that field Hadeland had won international recognition with extensive exports, especially to England. Sverre Pettersen possessed a marked sense for form. In the early years of his appointment he designed a large number of new table-services, which had something of old tradition in them but at the same time a charm and refinement of line that was peculiar to himself. He also took up the production of art-glass, and after a few years this side of his activities became very important. He managed to develop art-glass to a level which gave Hadeland a second international reputation, and in Norway it became the fashionable thing to give art-glass from Hadeland on all occasions which called for an unusually fine present.

But the Second World War stopped all art-glass production. The world situation abruptly cut off foreign imports, and like all the other Norwegian industrial firms Hadeland was compelled to go over to articles of necessity. During the war years the demand for table-

Ornamental glass goblet, designed by Sverre Pettersen for Hadeland glassworks, 1928: a typical example of his work of that period. Height c. 25 cm.

Table-glasses, designed by Sverre Pettersen for Hadeland glassworks, 1927. This set is still in production, but is the only one of Pettersen's to remain so.

glass grew steadily, and to meet it the production programme had to be rationalised and simplified. Nevertheless, Pettersen did not give up: he continued to experiment with new techniques and forms. The war was bound to stop some day, and meanwhile the vital fact was that he trained a large body of highly skilled craftsmen who, when the time came, showed themselves capable of the most difficult work. When it was once more possible to resume art-glass production, fresh young artists were taken on by Hadeland and learned much from Pettersen.

Willy Johansson showed brilliant promise as an artist in glass. His father was the most skilled craftsman in the works, and under his tuition the son learned every branch of glassmaking. It was soon clear that he was fulfilling every expectation. The thorough knowledge he had acquired of the craft of glassmaking and its various techniques allowed him to tackle every form of production, from moulded glass to costly work in crystal. Results followed rapidly, for Johansson had great artistic talent. Simple and natural forms, in which he showed a remarkable sense of line and proportion, soon made his name known outside Norway. In 1954 he was awarded a diplôme d'honneur at Milan, and at the following Triennali of 1957 and 1960 he won both gold and silver medals.

Hermann Bongard was another artist who was attached to Hadeland for a long period after the war. Bongard, who later received the Frederik Lunning Prize, produced a series of works in glass for Hadeland, and in particular created elegant and refined specimens of art-glass. Arne Jon Jutrem joined Hadeland in 1950, after

finishing his training at the State School of Crafts and Industrial Art with distinction. He is an artist to his fingertips, and has enriched Hadeland's output with many models, all with something characteristic about them which expresses his sensitive temperament. In 1955 he received the Frederik Lunning Prize, and in addition both he and Bongard have won gold medals at Milan.

For many years Hadeland stood alone in producing artist-designed glassware in Norway. Then shortly before the Second World War a new company, Norwegian Glassworks, was started at Magnor. This firm made little impression before the war, and was burnt out during hostilities. After the war the works was at once rebuilt, and the firm gave employment to young artists. Gradually its output attracted attention. Artists like Eystein Sandnes, Arne Lindaas, and Axel Mørch set their stamp on its products, and the firm has made its impact in exhibitions in various parts of the world. In recent years most of its models have been created by Axel Mørch, who also won a silver medal for his glass at Milan in 1960. There can be no doubt that Norway has gained by having two glassworks. Competition impels each firm to further effort, and stimulates the artists to do their utmost. Today glassmaking in Norway has a promising future.

The art of the silversmith is again one of those fields of applied art in which development in Norway can be traced right back to the Viking period. In the old burial mounds has been found work in gold and silver which shows that even in ancient times Norwegians could express in these metals a well-developed appreciation of ornament and an artist's mastery of the materials. It is true that much jewellery of foreign origin has been discovered, which shows that the old Vikings were men of violence who plundered wherever they went: but it also shows their well-developed love of beauty. Most gold and silver work in the burials is in any case of native origin. The jewellery and ornaments which survive from the Middle Ages also indicate a notable delight in craftsmanship and a feeling for decorative embellishment. Unhappily, it is known that great quantities of gold and silver work have been melted down during the various economic crises which Norway has undergone, so that the precious metals could buy for their owners the necessities of life.

Developments have come in waves, and there have been long periods when the art of the silversmith has been at the ebb. Today, however, Norway has many skilful silversmiths, and few other countries use as much silver per head. The craft has kept up with technical progress. Extensive use has been made of machines, but silverwork remains a combination of handicraft and industry which makes great demands on the craftsman's expertise and understanding of his material.

No-one has made a greater contribution to the prestige and quality of Norwegian silverwork than Jakob Prytz. He was the grand old man among silversmiths, and as an artist he showed himself to possess very great technical and aesthetic understanding. His greatest impact, however, was undoubtedly in his inspiring influence as head of the State School of Crafts and Industrial Art. He knew how to communicate his own appreciation of the values to be found in beautiful and expert craftsmanship in metal. He died in 1962.

One of the artists who was trained by Jakob Prytz and went further on his own account was Thorbjørn Lie-Jørgensen, who died in 1961. His vessels are among the best products of Norwegian silverwork, and his creations show a sensitive understanding of the potentialities of silver and a simple and natural form of expression which gives full scope to the character of the material.

There are fashions in silverware, as in every other branch of applied art: but there are also objects which rise superior to changes of fashion and have such great intrinsic values that they are valid for all time. Many of Lie-Jørgensen's works appeal quite as strongly to our sense of beauty today as they did when they first appeared many years ago. At the annual applied art exhibition at Oslo in 1960 he showed a range of silverware in which he had still further simplified his media, and once again confirmed his position in the art in Norway.

There is no sign of a forthcoming recession in the artistic quality of Norwegian silverware. New names of promise are continually emerging. The all-round artist Tias Eckhoff won an inter-Scandinavian competition (organised by the Georg Jensen firm in Denmark) for a set of cutlery; and his winning entry sells all over the world, because of, or perhaps despite, its high artistic quality. Steinar Flatheim is a young silversmith who has opened his own workshop in Stavanger, and who has already had a one-man-show in the Nordenfjeld Industrial Art Museum at Trondheim. He too shows a certain simplicity of line and form which indicates a genuine and original perception of beauty.

Enamel has become a Norwegian speciality, and we know of no other country which uses it so freely in connection with precious metals. Enamel-work demands craftsmanlike methods. In applying enamel to gold and silver, the object is to leave the metal visible through the enamel so that its form and surface treatment give the enamel depth and colour-tone. The interplay between metal and enamel creates a new and exciting composite effect. The reason why enamelling has become so popular here is perhaps that Norwegians recognise something of the country's own natural scene in the material. The strong pure enamel colours show a significant likeness to those of the landscape. They are in fact the same colours which we find also in Norwegian textiles and painting.

Grete Prytz Korsmo, a daughter of Jakob Prytz, has taken the lead in the development of modern Norwegian enamelling. She has worked out her own technique in this field, and has overcome the greatest difficulties in a craftsmanlike fashion. But it is the artistic element in her work which has won her international recognition, and led to her being awarded a Fulbright Scholarship, the Frederik Lunning Prize, a Grand Prix at Milan, and many other distinctions.

Sigurd Alf Eriksen is another prominent Norwegian artist in enamel. He originally based the design of his jewellery on mediaeval examples, but has since found his own personal form, abstract in motif and with a complete mastery of technical processes.

There is a direct connection between the vigorous filigree work of earlier Norwegian folk-artists and the jewellery made by young artist-craftsmen of today. It has led to the slight but sensitively designed compositions generally made in silver-wire, of which Tone Vigeland has recently produced examples. Other silversmiths have taken up the heavy and massive ornamental work of the Viking period, but treat its motifs from a modern angle. Else and Paul Hughes produce work of this type, modelling their rings, brooches, and bangles in wax before casting. These artists in cire-perdu use a technique by which no two articles can ever be identical. They have already achieved impressive results, both through their marked feeling for the sculptural and through managing to make the material itself co-operate with a charm of its own in their compositions.

In early times Norwegian churches were richly adorned, but from the time of the Reformation their furnishings grew steadily more spartan. Puritanism was triumphant, and anything of a joyous nature was regarded as sinful. Only in our own times have ideas become more liberal, allowing colours, church fabrics, and artistically-made altar silver to find a foothold. The State Industrial School for Women has played a leading part in ecclesiastical textiles, and many splendid vestments have been produced here, designed by artists attached to the school.

One young artist who has made a speciality of Church fabrics is Grete Lein. She has shown particular talent for carrying out this work in a modern manner but with complete understanding of the Church's special needs. Thorbjørn Lie-Jørgensen, already mentioned, is undoubtedly the Norwegian silversmith who has been most successful in giving his altar-silver a consistently sacred character. In this particular field his works are simple and natural, but with a most effective religious element. Fortunately it no longer happens that ecclesiastical fabrics are embroidered by well-meaning and worthy but untrained ladies. Applied art and its exponents have set their stamp on Church adornments in ever increasing degree, and the Norwegian Church is in process of acquiring a character of its own.

In recent years two international expressions have appeared which have also won a foothold in Norway –'Industrial Design' and 'Industrial Designer'. They mean that industry realises the importance of design, and that there are designers working specially for industry. There is, in fact, nothing new in these ideas. Since the Norwegian Society for Industrial Arts and Design first came into being, its member organisations have had artists designing for industry. The question arises–what is an 'artist' in this context? The answer must be, a suitably trained man or woman who works with the set purpose of raising the aesthetic and practical quality of handicraft and industrial products. It matters little, therefore, whether the person concerned calls himself 'industrial designer' or 'artist'.

In Norway the expression 'Industrial Design' appeared first and foremost in connection with industrial products in metal. In this field Arne and Grete Korsmo, in collaboration with the Cathrineholm concern, launched stainless steel with enamel overlay in simple clean forms, using Grete Korsmo's extensive knowledge of the properties of enamel. The result has been dishes and bowls

'Moonsilver' cutlery, designed by Jacob Prytz for J. Tostrup, 1930. This set has proved its vitality, and sells as readily today as thirty years ago.

in which the steel plays a striking part in the total effect and gives the product a quite independent character. These wares are notably different from work in enamelled silver, not only in price but in appearance.

Bjørn Engø, on behalf of Emalox, has after much research produced aluminium bowls in an anodised finish with a delicate surface treatment and tranquil lines. Bjørn A. Larsen and Tias Eckhoff have modelled doorhandles, fittings, and catches in metal, with results that give more an appearance of handwork than of industry; paradoxical as it sounds, designers working for industry can hardly go much further than this.

Cutlery and all kinds of kitchen equipment in stainless steel are made in Norway, as in most other countries. But Norwegian industrial plants are small by foreign standards: there are limits to what they can produce, and what the home market can absorb. With new international agreements, export possibilities are being considered: we shall have to wait and see what this may mean in the future. Technically and in design Norwegian products hold their own with what has appeared in world markets from other sources, as examples of 'Industrial Design'.

Norwegian furniture in the modern sense is almost confined to the period since the Second World War. Many worthy efforts were indeed made to encourage the production of furniture of value, ever since the Applied Art Association began its activities in 1918, but for the most part without effect. Neither competitions nor exhibitions produced results. Most Norwegian pieces were copies or imitations of foreign models, produced on licence. There was also an extensive import of furniture, especially from the large factories of Germany and Sweden, and the small Norwegian firms could hardly compete. The few home products which could stand comparison with those from abroad were generally designed by architects as a side-line, and had no chance of reaching the general public. The price of individually made articles must anyhow be in a quite different range from that of those mass-produced. The change came when the technical colleges began seriously to train furniture specialists –interior designers– and when alert industrialists began to employ these designers in their factories.

Alf Sture is one of the few Norwegian furniture-designers who have managed to make a considerable mark on Scandinavian production. He studied anatomy to discover the essential principles by which a chair's design could fully satisfy its functions. In 1940 he displayed a model in which he had taken care to make the line of the back anatomically correct. It is worth mentioning that no other Scandinavian designer had at that time thought out a similar form. This chair was the forerunner of a long series of corresponding models, all based on Alf Sture's solution.

To a greater extent than most Norwegian furniture-designers, Sture invests his products with a national quality plainly inspired by old Norse peasant furniture and carried out in native woods. Aage Schou, employed by the Norwegian Domestic Crafts Association, has also made himself a spokesman for the same policy. But home-crafts in Norway are still firmly anchored in national tradition, and it has been difficult for Aage Schou to break away from this. However, some of his models show a clear understanding of modern developments and a sureness and worth which, it is to be hoped, may lead the way to a complete renaissance in domestically produced Norwegian furniture.

Since the term 'Scandinavian Design' became a hallmark of quality, Norwegian industrialists have become aware of the possibilities in the export of quality furniture. A larger market would mean larger mass-production, with correspondingly rationalised organisation and reduction of overheads, and export could thereby help to make things easier for the home market. Norwegian industrial circles have certainly been impressed by Danish furniture exports, which are on a fantastic scale by Norwegian standards. This has undoubtedly had a stimulating effect, and Norwegian furniture manufacturers have made increasing use of interior-designers to transform their production. It would now seem that our furniture is winning itself a place in the sun, not least because of its high standard of technical quality. It actually needs an

Silver-plated cutlery, designed by Arne Korsmo for J. Tostrup 1947. Its appearance has marked a new phase in the development of cutlery, and it has since been copied in many countries.

expert to tell whether a chair was made industrially or by hand-craftsmen.

Honesty is the best policy, and it must be admitted that many Norwegian furniture-designers are still glancing sideways to see what their Danish colleagues are up to. But there is no longer any need for this, for in fact Norwegian furniture production has now reached a stage where it can stand on its own feet. Bendt Winge is one of our designers who prefer to do just this, and not to be swayed by outside influences. Without any doubt he has made a great contribution to the development of an independent Norwegian quality output. He has, for example, transformed an old Norse chair-type, 'Jaederstolen', into a logical and simple modern chair, well-adapted for industrial production.

Rolf Rastad and Adolf Relling have worked together for many years, and design in collaboration for several large firms. Their models are strongly influenced by 'Scandinavian Design', and so are not particularly Norwegian. We cannot escape the fact that there is a Scandinavian language of form, but Rastad and Relling fortunately speak it with their own dialect. The young designers Sven Ivar Dysthe and Arne Halvorsen both work on an international basis, but have shown exceptional understanding of line and proportion, and have the talent to give their models a definite individual stamp.

In general, Norwegian furniture-making is rapidly improving. But–and it is a big but–it is sad to have to admit how large a part is played by the whims of fashion. We can't get away from them. Norway is rich in timber

Chair designed by Alf Sture, 1940, and made by Hiorth & Østlyngen. This was the forerunner of a series of similar models by various Scandinavian designers, and is based on thorough anatomical study.

–pine, spruce, oak, birch, elm, and others are common. But we still make our furniture chiefly of imported woods. The international fashion demands teak, mahogany, and palisander, and we plainly can't ignore that.

Conditions for ceramics in Norway are ideal. The land has great electric power resources, and electricity gives clean heat. Electric firing in our kilns causes no discoloration, which is particularly important in making white porcelain. Besides this, with electricity the firing temperature can be continuously controlled. To a great extent the country is also self-sufficient in ceramic raw-materials.

It is perhaps superfluous to remark that Norway has a small population in relation to its area, and for this reason it has never had more than one porcelain factory. The market has not been large enough to absorb more than this one works could produce; and, as already stated, export in the applied-art field was unknown here till very recent years. The Porsgrund porcelain factory has meanwhile completely met all demands. From its foundation 75 years ago it has aimed at quality products, and from a technical angle it is today equipped to meet any foreign competition. Its management has also employed artists throughout this period, with happy results. From the start Porsgrund followed the line already established by European porcelain works; but from the middle of the Twenties it began to strike out on its own, after the artist Nora Guldbrandsen was appointed as art director.

After the First World War there was a great reaction in Europe against the stylistic confusion of the Victorian period, and against naturalistic decoration and the rhythmic curvilinearity of Art Nouveau. Nora Guldbrandsen took this youthful and enthusiastic revolt with her to Porsgrund. Like other young Norwegian artists, she also reacted against Vikingism and folk-romanticism. She went to work for Porsgrund with the brisk courage of her convictions, and the management supported her very sympathetically in her struggle on behalf of pure colours, new and restrained forms, and simple and restricted ornament. In this revolutionary period, the era of functionalism, Nora Guldbrandsen made an important artistic contribution at Porsgrund over a number of years, establishing the policy which the factory has followed ever since. After the Second World War Porsgrund developed steadily; and a series of artists have helped to build up the position it holds today, in which it not only supplies porcelain to the home market but also exports to many other countries.

Tias Eckhoff, Konrad Galaaen, Eystein Sandnes, and others have done their best work for Porsgrund, and have thereby contributed to giving its products a definite stamp and character. Its output is marked by simple forms with sure lines, and the factory's high technical standards enter as a matter of course into every article made. One proof of this is that Porsgrund has won a gold medal at each of the Triennali in which it has been represented.

There are three Norwegian firms producing earthenware, and two of them in particular–Figgjo Faience and Stavangerflint–have taken on artists to improve their production and have shown anxiety to achieve the best possible technical and aesthetic results. In Norway, as in other countries and in all lines of business, industry is often compelled to compromise. It is an unfortunate fact that our pottery works cannot survive on an output entirely of artistic quality. Many people have still not got used to, or have refused to accept, modern forms of expression. This is not the fault of industry: it cannot educate the buying public without assistance. This is one field where the Norwegian Society for Industrial Arts and Design can do much: public enlightenment must be carried on through exhibitions and through speech and writing. Moreover, this must be addressed not only to the adults who are the buyers of today but also to school children who will be the homemakers and buyers of the next generation.

As already mentioned, there are few pottery factories in Norway; but there are, on the other hand, many private potteries. After the Second World War, when clay was almost the only material one could get hold of in Norway, and when ceramics were the only things one could buy as presents, over five hundred small potteries were working. The number is now far smaller, since in many of them production was of a poor standard. They could not survive in normal times, and thank God for that: for there was hardly any limit to the ceramic monstrosities which flooded Norway at that time. Today the position is quite different. Most small potteries work to a definite artistic standard, with the result that they have found a market not only at home but in other European countries and in America.

Erik Pløen is in the first rank of Norwegian ceramic artists. In his little pottery, where moreover he works quite unaided, he has experimented continually and patiently with clay and glazes; and today he produces stoneware in which form, manipulation, material, and glaze are all of the highest standard. It is not given to every artist to achieve this much, and there are years of hard work and almost superhuman will-power behind Pløen's output of stoneware. These have enabled him to produce results which no other Norwegian ceramic artist can match.

Dagny and Finn Hald are two other artists working in stoneware, and their work is so similar that they may be regarded as one. This couple's products are characterised by an unusual interplay between glaze and decoration, and in this line they have achieved highly interesting results.

Margrethe and Jens von der Lippe are another married couple who have taken up ceramics, but in this case we have two artists each with an individual form expression. Margrethe's simple dishes and bowls are of marked by powerful and painterlike ornamentation, while Jens' products, mainly earthenware, show a direct interest in utility and form and are often decorated in slip technique.

Rolf Hansen lives in the small town of Kongsberg, and makes pots and jars in chamotte which show a fertile imagination. He can be quite restrained in his form of expression, as is shown by his part-glazed vases and bowls. Here he keeps to austere shapes and sketches the ornament with a line technique in the white glaze. At the same time, he can strike out with figures or dishes and bowls with burlesque imagery in their decoration. If Askeladden (a Norwegian folk-tale figure who wins the princess by always being more cunning than the rest) had been a potter, he would no doubt have done much the same.

Woodworking has always been a common spare-time occupation for Norwegian country folk. They either made everyday implements, kitchen-utensils, and other household articles, or did decorative carving–a medium for the artistic urge from early times. Then the wood-

Table-ware and vase, designed by Nora Guldbrandsen, 1932, for Porsgrund porcelain factory.

work was done by hand. Today they have no time for that sort of thing. They can earn more money in other ways; and besides that, machines now do such good work in this field that domestic handwork no longer pays. It is sad to have to admit this, but it is an unfortunate result of modern technical development. Woodcarving as a craft is therefore gradually dying out. Society, and the modern world, find less and less use for it. What is still done today is nearly all pure copying, and therefore lacking in interest.

On a quite different basis, and in harmony with what is afoot elsewhere in the applied arts, a few craftsmen have again taken up woodworking. On a Vestland island Hanna Christie Abrahamsen turns and carves elegant bowls, massive bowls, bowls thick and bowls leaf-thin, all according to the different types of wood she works with and the form she thinks will make the best of each separate piece. Her rare sympathy and respect for the material has here created something new in applied art. But these things can neither be made by the home craftsman nor by machines: it needs an artist of her stature to make works in wood of lasting value.

There are some glass-designers whom we have not so far mentioned, simply because they do not design glassware–or at any rate glass in the forms described above. Jonas Hidle designs glass light-fittings, especially chandeliers for churches, public buildings, assembly-rooms, and the like. These do not appear in exhibitions of applied art: to start with they take too much room, and they are difficult to photograph because they generally hang so high that pictures do not do them full justice. But Jonas

Part-glazed dish and jar, made by Ragnar Grimsrud, 1937. These were shown in the Norwegian section of the World Exhibition at Paris in the same year, and were bought by the Sèvres Museum.

Embroidered cushion, designed and made by the Norwegian textile-artist Fanny Natvig, 1958. 35 × 30 cm. The ground is dark-blue linen, and the figures are sewn with linen thread in various shades of red.

Hidle has made a very considerable contribution, and it is true to say that there is nothing better in Norwegian applied art today.

Arnulf Bjørshol also designs glass light-fittings, but these are intended more for large-scale production to meet ordinary demand. In this line of work form is closely tied to technical requirements, but Bjørshol works in a restrained convincing style with a sure appreciation of quality. Birger Dahl has designed a long series of light-fittings for all purposes, and simply-formed lampshades, all characterised by his knowledge of his craft and his artist's eye for values. Besides this he is head of the State School of Crafts and Industrial Art, with design as his speciality.

It is hard to believe that a violinist can play the piano just as well as he plays the violin, and still more difficult to conceive that he could also be an outstanding painter. But there is nothing unusual in the same artist designing glassware, porcelain, silverware, books, and fabrics. Naturally there are specialists amongst them, but many play a part in the most varied fields without their versatility lowering the quality of their achievement in each separate sphere. Arne Lindaas is an artist who has with equal success turned his hand to glass, porcelain, and work in both wood and metal. He has also won fabric competitions. He is one of those who make it exciting to follow the development of Norwegian applied art, and who give us reason to hope that Norway will continue to maintain her place in 'Scandinavian Design'.

If there is a final conclusion to be drawn from what has here been said of the applied arts in Norway, it must be something like this: The level thay have now reached is due to several different factors. The achievement of our artists, the willingness of industrial firms to co-operate, and the public's steadily growing understanding of modern styles, have made the development possible. But without the Norwegian Society for Industrial Arts and Design and the idealism which has marked all its activities, this development could hardly have gone as far as it has. The Society has been the necessary co-ordinating link and nerve-centre in all the work which has been done in this sphere for over forty years.

SWEDEN

Sven Erik Skawonius

In the brief time man has lived on earth, he has managed to make a host of things to meet his primary needs for clothing, food, shelter, and domestic life. Revolutionary in turn were the art of making fire, the construction of the wheel (essential to any industry), the arts of weaving fabrics from fibres, of shaping, firing, and glazing clay into useful articles, and of making glass. But man could not be content with the simplest solutions, and even primitive tools and utensils show a conscious desire to enrich goods and environment with aesthetic values. We take great care over whatever can be perceived by the sense of touch, but the other senses are also catered for: the smell of different kinds of wood or leather, the ring of thin stoneware or crystal glass, and perhaps even taste in the sense that our utensils must not taste of anything. We want our possessions and surroundings to be efficient, to be made of materials appropriate to their purpose, and to produce a pleasing impression – an aesthetic quality.

This last depends to a great extent on time and place. Our grandfathers had, generally speaking, a different way of looking at things, and primitive peoples have different ideas again. Nevertheless, there are certain fixed criteria for a good environment and the appropriate construction of useful articles. Someone has said that these are found where aesthetic and practical considerations combine. The requirements of production and consumption join those of aesthetics, giving rise to a type of product which has quality both in material and form. These can then be made singly, by hand, or in great quantity by the use of machines. Sometimes one method gives the best results, sometimes the other. In Scandinavia we have largely accepted industrial products, but still can appreciate the qualities derived from a tradition of craftsmanship which has never been completely broken. Industrial products are therefore not regarded as the only solution: there is still room for semi-industrial and hand production, and for domestic industry. Thanks to this there are exciting alternatives in production, which must certainly be considered as an impetus.

If we look to the people behind the objects, we have on the one hand craftsmen working manually, by themselves or perhaps with one or two assistants for purely routine work. Such artists are represented in Sweden by, for example, Edgar Böckman, Forse Gnista, Hertha Hillfon, and Ulla Schumacher-Percy. On the other hand we have the designer, controlling the output of mass-produced goods by drawings or models without himself taking part in their manufacture. He may be permanently employed by one firm, or a free-lance working for several. Artists of this type are here represented by Folke Arström, Sigvard Bernadotte, Acton Björn, and Carl-Arne Breger. Finally there is a middle group, who both work as craftsmen in workshops, often on the verge of 'fine' art, and at the same time model wares which are entirely or partly produced industrially, in long or short runs. Amongst these may be mentioned Viola Gråsten, Alice Lund, Stig Lindberg, and Sigurd Persson. It is typical of Sweden, and of Scandinavia in general, that these form the largest category. There will be occasion to refer again to this situation, which is to some extent due to the fact that the Scandinavian countries are not large enough to support mass-production on the American scale. Inherited popular tradition also plays its part. In country districts in particular there are still many women who weave, and men who carpenter for domestic purposes – or at least have seen their elders do so. Manual training is still part of the school timetable, and in industrial art training much emphasis is still laid on proficiency in manual skills.

Handicraft and domestic industry are thus forms of production still to be reckoned with. Furniture is made not only in factories but also by craftsmen in small workshops, with the help of power-driven saws and planing and polishing machines. Glass factories are a collection of workshops under one roof, and production is to the highest degree a matter of hand-craftsmanship. Fabrics and floor-coverings are woven, knotted, or inlaid by hand; silver is hammered with the smith's tools, and pottery is thrown on the wheel, even if this is now generally driven by electricity. Manual production is admittedly expensive, but when it is well done it often has aesthetic – and some would say ethical – qualities.

Do handwork and industry necessarily stand opposed? "Developments point to the steady growth of large-scale impersonal organisation, to forms of production and social life and amusements in which anonymous conformity eclipses personal contacts. Only a life which has work and aspiration can be happy, but mechanised work is benighted boredom." (Carl Malmsten). They may still have thought this in the Twenties, but now things are different. In 1958 we hear from the same source: "Before 1930 people largely based their work on accepted patterns of style. Functionalism broke this dependence on tradition, and led to investigation of the form of our everyday things regardless of all previous assumptions, and to a synthesis of function, construction, material, and the expressive value of the form."

The expressive value of the form: we naturally think of handmade stoneware or earthenware, but an ordinary plate is rightly made mechanically. To make it by hand would give it no extra value beyond that of a curiosity. It sometimes happens, too, that potentialities in materials and production methods give rise to new types of ware. Stainless steel combined with modern pressing techniques has given us excellent stainless cutlery. It is thanks to machines that this and porcelain plates are within the reach of everyone. Some things are industrially made because they are better so, and not only for the sake of mass-production and cheapness. There are industrial products too which can be 'a synthesis of function, construction, and material', and possess 'the expressive value of the form' to quite as great a degree as hand-made wares.

There must be someone to ensure that this synthesis is achieved, and him we call the designer or industrial artist. It is apparent that he is often a practised craftsman, and it has therefore been said that handicraft is the laboratory of industry. In one way this is indeed the case: patterns from domestic and workshop products are transferred to miles of machine-woven fabrics. That does not mean that they are transposed direct to the machines, but that they act as sources of inspiration and that the artist translates his aesthetic experience to suit the machine's possibilities. We are not here commending the assimilation of different kinds of creative work: we certainly have no desire to see stainless steel cutlery made to imitate silver, however artistic, or moulded glass imitating crystal glass. When we heard that Scandinavian Airways planned to furnish its DC6 machines in 'the Scandinavian style', we wondered why the exteriors too were not to follow the same theme, with a casing of northern shingles or southern half-timber.

The industrial designer has a wider field of work than the artist-craftsman. He is not, like the latter, tied to 'his material', even though one can specialise in metal, another in plastic, and others perhaps in means of transport or office machines. Nevertheless he learns to know the material's properties, he collaborates with technicians, researches into function, and eventually produces something which works well, is well-adapted for manufacture, and looks attractive. From the consumer's angle there is a demand for goods of different values: on the one hand the unobtrusive everyday things, silent servants which alter in appearance, change with our habits, and may quickly be replaced with something more useful; and on the other, things we want to keep for a lifetime, which have personality and intrinsic value. Some may hate plastic but fall into ecstasies over a stoneware vase, while others think it a waste of effort to produce stoneware and think plastic a splendid material. How far it is beautiful or otherwise is a minor consideration.

Nowadays there is a hitherto undreamed-of wealth of consumer goods. In Sweden much effort has been made, and much pressure brought to bear, to achieve a 'synthesis of function, construction, material, and expressive value of form'. The Swedish Society for Industrial Design has in particular led the struggle to achieve good design of articles and interiors. In 1846 the old guild regulations were abolished in Sweden, and everyone was then free to practise any trade. But it was feared that the feeling for quality and good craftsmanship would be obliterated by advancing industrialisation. This Society was therefore founded, principally to run a school of design intended to give craftsmen an aesthetic training. The school was later taken over by the State, and has grown into the present School of Arts, Crafts and Design in Stockholm. A branch of the Society was founded in Gothenburg, Sweden's second city, and though it did not long survive it managed to establish the country's other industrial art school, which is now run as a municipal institution.

The Swedish Society for Industrial Design arranged in 1909 an industrial art exhibition in Stockholm, in 1917 one of furnishings for small apartments, in 1930 it co-operated in the Stockholm Exhibition, and in 1955 organised that in Hälsingborg. It has arranged, or assisted with, various large and small displays, both at home and abroad, and taken part in the Milan Triennali, 'Design in Scandinavia' in the United States (1954–57), 'Interbau' in Berlin (1957), Zürich 1957, 'Formes Scandinaves' in Paris in 1958, Amsterdam 1959, and the Hague 1960. The Society includes craftsmen and artists, manufacturers, and consumers, and is therefore unique as a common forum for all who are concerned with good design in articles and interiors. Its most important regular publication is its periodical, first published in 1905, and since 1932 entitled *Form*. Since 1950 it has also published the annual *Kontur*, specially addressed to the outside world, as well as various publications dealing particularly with the various aspects of home-furnishing.

In this complex existence it is not sufficient merely to

St. Thomas' Cross, for St. Thomas' day, December 21st. A timeless ornament, without practical function but with powerful symbolic content: a unique work, made of wood with a single tool–a sharp knife. A contemporary product of the Swedish Domestic Crafts Association, full of feeling, even for those not familiar with the tradition.

Typewriter, designed by Sigvard Bernadotte and Acton Björn in 1958 and made by Åtvidaberg Industries Ltd. A modern product for a modern function, the result of team-work. A machine with many integral parts of various (including synthetic) materials, practical, and attractively designed after a thorough study of every point.

have convictions about the design of our surroundings: we must also have knowledge. The Swedish Society for Industrial Design and the National Association of Swedish Architects carried out in the Forties and Fifties a massive research into living conditions under the direction of Gotthard Johansson. This was published in 1958 as *Living Habits and Standards*. This investigation was the first step towards an analysis of space requirements in the home, and of its most practical furnishing. One result was the first set of standards for the universally admired Swedish kitchen. The logical extreme was the coining in the Forties of the phrase 'from cutlery to town-planning', implying that all the separate detailed aspects of habitation are interdependent. The cutlery in the kitchen drawer, for example, determines the size and placing of other units, and along with a mass of other details governs the house as a whole and eventually the general town plan.

The Society for Industrial Design has done research in other directions, for example on bedsteads, tables, and cupboards, published respectively in 1950, 1957, and 1960. The director of these investigations was the furniture-designer Erik Berglund, and we are happy to say that both public and manufacturers recognise the importance of these enquiries and give them the necessary financial support. One publication of 1961 analyses the dimensions and requirements of table-services, another deals with questions of lighting, and yet another with problems of colour. In this way a basis is gradually being built up with the help of which designers and manufacturers can produce not only more beautiful but also more efficient everyday things–two aspects which we consider indissolubly linked. In a popular form the published results of these researches give valuable advice to the consumer (i. e. to everyone) on what to demand from objects of use.

The Friends of Handicraft Association was founded in 1874 with the object of broadening craftwork in textiles. It produces fabrics, carries out decorative work, and trains teachers of weaving. The Swedish Domestic Crafts Association, which supports domestic craftwork, was founded in 1894. The National League of Domestic Crafts Associations is a federation of the country's various domestic crafts associations, dating from 1913.

When the craftsmen's guilds were abolished in the 1840's, craft and industrial associations were founded to take care of the interest of handicrafts. 'Hantverket' in Stockholm organises exhibitions and the sale of craft products of an everyday nature, such as furniture, textiles, and silver. In Stockholm there is also the Guild of Artist-Craftsmen, which likewise sells craftwork; and in Gothenburg a similar guild does the same.

The School of Arts, Crafts and Design (Konstfackskolan) is the State school for artist-craftsmen and designers. It goes back to 1844, and in 1959 it took over an excellent new building. It has classes at two levels, and gives instruction in textiles, decorative painting, sculpture, ceramics, furniture and interior-decoration, metal work, book crafts, and advertising. It also has a department for training drawing-teachers for schools. In Gothenburg is the corresponding School for Art and Design already mentioned.

Gothenburg also has Sweden's only independent industrial art museum, the Röhsska Konstslöjdmuseum, which frequently holds exhibitions. The National Museum in Stockholm has representative collections of earlier and modern craftsmanship, and arranges topical displays. The Nordiska museum has large collections of everyday things, popular domestic craftwork, practical ware and interiors, and similar collections are found in provincial museums. Malmö and Lund have two of the largest, and the Småland museum in Växjö has specialised in glass and wood.

In Stockholm there is a permanent exhibition of modern industrial art and design, the Swedish Form Design Centre, in the Konstfackskolan building. The large stores in Stockholm, Gothenburg, Malmö, and several other towns often have representative displays of industrial art. Great efforts are thus being made in Sweden to improve consumer goods and home furnishing. Public interest has increased remarkably, which is certainly connected with rising standards of living, and the Press devotes much attention to industrial art. Naturally the goal is never reached, simply because it is not fixed but continually moving. Beyond today's horizon lie fresh and unexplored fields. Nevertheless, one can now find good things, and even the fastidious buyer can discover what he seeks.

This endeavour to create better articles and a better setting for everyday life, and also to persuade the public to take an interest in them, has in part had a social aim since the end of the Nineteenth Century. It has not been a matter only of making fine and exclusive products for the few, but of allowing all to share in things of good technical and aesthetic quality. Artists have not been simply concerned to win personal praise with pure bravura pieces, but have tried to raise the general level through the common efforts of many. "The propaganda work with lectures, exhibitions, etc., now addressed to consumers, can raise ideas of living standards amongst those steadily growing sections of the population which we may expect in future to exercise a decisive influence in public life. Their standards are thus more important than those of the middle class, which up to now have been dominant in society."

Up to the end of the Nineteenth Century, Sweden was an agricultural country: and at that period it was going through a, by local standards, revolutionary change with difficult social readjustments. Large sections of the population emigrated to America, and others were adapting themselves to the transition from agriculture to industrialisation. When an Industrial Exhibition was held at Stockholm in 1897, one had the impression that the ordinary Swede was bewildered to find that his country was becoming a modern industrial state, had woken up to her natural resources, and had started to build factories, saw-mills, and railways.

Even so, industrialisation came late to Scandinavia. Efforts to protect and preserve the aesthetic and creative qualities of domestic folk-crafts had already started. From England came aesthetic impulses via the South Kensington Movement and the Preraphaelites – John Ruskin, William Morris, Charles F. A. Voysey, and Charles R. Mackintosh – whose ideas were disseminated through the much read and appreciated *Studio*. From France came Art Nouveau and contemporary painting; and from Germany the Jugend style, championed by personalities such as Peter Behrens and Henry van de Velde, as well as the very active Deutscher Werkbund, which influenced the work of the Swedish Society for Industrial Design.

All this was received with enthusiasm in many quarters. "The object of this movement is well-known: emancipation from historical styles, the universal slavish imitation of which made the Nineteenth Century a painful period in the realm of taste. Instead was established an independent and individual creativeness, both in handicrafts and decorative art." Amongst the independent forces in industry were, for example, Gunnar Wennerberg, attached to Gustavsberg porcelain works, and Alf Wallander at Rörstrand. Wallander also worked in textiles, glass, and other fields. An artist of the calibre of Carl Larsson furnished his home in the new spirit, and depicted it in water-colours which were reproduced in popular illustrated books and created an ideal for the Swedish home which has remained valid right down to the present day.

The social side of the movement was always strong. Ellen Key, the well-known writer on social ethics, published in 1897 in a small and cheap popular education series four articles written in the Nineties, under the common title 'Beauty for All'. There we read: "... always, when we buy something for our homes, we should ask ourselves if it fulfils the most vital requirement – namely, that everything should answer the purpose it is intended for. A chair should be comfortable to sit on, a table comfortable to work or eat at, a bed good to sleep in. Uncomfortable chairs, ricketty tables, and narrow beds are therefore automatically ugly. But it does not follow that comfortable chairs, steady tables, and broad beds are beautiful. Things must, as everywhere in Nature, fulfil their purpose in a simple and expressive manner, and without this they do not achieve beauty even if they satisfy practical requirements."

Interior from the home in Dalarna of the painter Carl Larsson (1853–1919), from his own water-colour for the illustrated book *Ett Hem* (a home) – contemporary with late-Victorian clutter. His water-colours were shown at the Industrial Exhibition, Stockholm 1897, published in book form, 1899, and established the ideal of the Swedish home – light, practical, comfortable, and also creating taste. National Museum, Stockholm.

'Summer fairy-tale – the white city'; by the architect Ferdinand Boberg, who also designed various craft products. The architecture at the exhibition of art-craftsmanship and industrial art at Stockholm in 1909 was a Swedish version of Art Nouveau or the Jugend style; a protest of the new century against the imitative styles of its predecessor, which in Sweden took a positive national form.

Previously Sweden, on account of her remote position, had received rather than exported influences. In the Eighteenth Century it was French culture which made a deep impression on the country's cultural ideas. But imported styles were modified and acclimatised. Because of straitened financial resources they were simplified and cleansed of extravagance, and the result was often beautiful, humanised, and inelaborate. Something similar occurred with continental influences at the turn of the last century. They proved an impulse from which grew a Swedish variant with strong national characteristics and links with the beauty of the Eighteenth Century in Sweden, especially in the choice of materials and colours. The Swedish version of the Jugend style, with native flower-patterns and motifs from the Swedish summer, found expression in the Industrial Art Exhibition of 1909 in Stockholm organised by the Society for Industrial Design, the first of its kind in the country. This was not simply a bright midsummer night's dream: as arranged by the architect Ferdinand Boberg, under the plain influence of the Americans Henry Richardson and Louis Sullivan, it also embodied the social programme for one-family houses, small farmers' homes, and working-class apartments. This was, of course, of the greatest importance at this time of expanding population, when, for example, Stockholm was beginning to overflow its ancient boundaries and become a great city. One

of the family houses in this exhibition was in fact later moved to a new housing district outside the city centre, where it is still standing and in use.

In this exhibition, where industrial art and handicrafts were, of course, well represented, we find the names of Gunnar Wennerberg, Alf Wallander, and Märta Måås-Fjetterström, the first Swedish industrial artists and artist-craftsmen in the modern sense. Popular domestic textile-production had not died out, as so many in the Nineteenth Century had feared. The home-crafts movement was now in full swing. In the provinces local associations were working, and in Stockholm were the Swedish Domestic Crafts Association and the Friends of Handicraft, whose object was not only to preserve the textile tradition but also to adapt it to modern needs. All this was taking place in a period of social and political changes and frictions, but also in general one of optimism and confidence in the future. It was the time between the Boer War and the First World War. Great social reforms were in progress, and those who created modern home- and housing-conditions did not stand aside from these but were themselves gripped by the prevailing spirit and made an important contribution to its developments.

Five years later the First World War broke out. That summer the Baltic Exhibition had been held in Malmö, with all countries around the Baltic Sea taking part. The Russian and German pavilions closed prematurely – war

"The pursuit of comfort and beauty in the home–the demand for good and inexpensive products with a simplified service-able form." Living-room in a two-room and kitchen apartment, furnished by Carl Malmsten at the Society for Industrial Design's exhibition of small home furnishing at Stockholm in 1917.

was a certainty. As far as the Swedish exhibits were concerned, the Society for Industrial Design's periodical was somewhat critical. In the section on furniture and interiors we read: "Since the 1909 exhibition our furni-ture manufacturers have marked time. This summer's display in Malmö has plainly shown up the the flaw in our artistic culture which still characterises Swedish furniture: simple and inexpensive pieces for the industrial and farm worker still do not exist, and our more modest town homes still lack furniture specially designed to meet their needs. Generally speaking we have made pro-gress only with exclusive and individual de luxe pieces."

Silver and metalware were similarly condemned by another expert; and the same was the case with glass and ceramics, concerning which the Society's secretary Erik Wettergren concluded by expressing the hope that "in the long run this mixture of good and bad may prove more fruitful than a momentary success, and that from this soil of well-intentioned self-knowledge may grow a new determination and strength of purpose". The re-sponsibility of large manufacturers to the consumer was particularly emphasised. Luxury wares, and hand-made show-pieces, were famous, but where were good everyday things, within the reach of the man in the street–tools and articles with their 'purpose expressed in the form' in accordance with the already current formula?

Inspired by the activities of the Deutsche Werkbund, the response to this soon became apparent when the Society arranged an exhibition of fittings and furni-

ture for small homes in the newly built Liljevalch Art Gallery, Stockholm, in 1917. This featured the results of competitions organised by the Society for the fitting out of one- and two-room apartments (this was during the wartime housing shortage), for heating stoves, fire-places, and kitchen ranges (the fuel shortage was serious), and for various practical articles such as lampshades, carpets, hangings, and wash-stand sets (bathrooms were not yet common). "It has long been recognised in theory that beauty is not only a luxury for the well-to-do. Con-vinced that the taste of the Swedish public is better than is generally admitted, and that bad taste in nine cases out of ten is the result of lack of opportunity to satisfy a bet-ter one, the leading lights of the Society for Industrial Design have endeavoured through this exhibition to stim-ulate the production of types and models suited to mass-production and therefore inexpensive, yet in good taste. It is no less vital that during our present period of isolation (1917) Swedish industry should prepare to compete more successfully by meanwhile giving its products systematic, refined, and independent design. In other words, the collaboration of industry with art is now more important than ever."

After this came a call on the Society to act as intermediary in finding models and designs for industry, and in putting it in touch with artists, a facility of which the large porcelain and glass firms have made particular use. Like Van de Velde, Behrens, and later on Le Cor-busier, several of these artists were originally painters. We may mention Edgar Böckman of Höganäs-Billesholm potteries and later of Rörstrand porcelain factory, Simon Gate and Edward Hald of Orrefors glassworks (Hald was also connected with Rörstrand, and later with Karls-krona porcelain works), Elsa Gullberg of Nordiska and other textile firms, Wilhelm Kåge of Gustavsberg porce-lain works, Carl Malmsten with his own furniture work-shop, Edwin Ollers of Kosta glassworks, and Jacob Äng-man of Guldsmedsbolaget, Stockholm. Young architects working on domestic fittings, furniture, and equipment included Hakon Ahlberg, Erik Gunnar Asplund, Paul Hedquist, Sigurd Lewerentz, Ivar Tengbom, and Uno Åhren.

The 1917 exhibition was a great success, and is re-garded as marking the breakthrough of modern practical arts in Sweden. The exhibits must have been a new and refreshing experience for the public, completely different from those shown at the Baltic Exhibition. They indicate the final acceptance of the artist-designer into the facto-ries' teams of producers. In 1919 Gregor Paulsson, then director of the Society for Industrial Design, published his paper 'More Beautiful Everyday Things'. "In principle it is thus obvious that the designing of everyday wares as well must be left to the community's specialists in design, the artists." The author acknowledged that difficulties might arise in practice, but expressed the hope that the next generation would give more beauty to everything. Naturally this hope has not been completely fulfilled, but most large and many small Swedish consumer-goods factories have now appointed one or more specialists in design. Today many businesses have one director who is specially responsible for the design of the products.

Just as the Napoleonic Wars were followed by the Romantic Movement, so there developed in Scandinavia after the peace of 1918 a somewhat imitative neo-classical style which was certainly inspired by the unpretentious charm which characterised the much admired style of the late Eighteenth and early Nineteenth Centuries, before the 'fancy-dress ball' period set in. An amalgam of Eighteenth Century classicism and Nineteenth Century romanticism has often been remarked on as a prominent trait of later style development in Sweden, a conservative influence, sometimes positive and sometimes negative in its effects.

It was in this classicist form that modern Swedish industrial art first showed itself to the outside world in the Paris Exhibition of modern decorative arts in 1925. It was in connection with this that Erik Wettergren published a handsome and comprehensive book, *L'Art Décoratif Moderne en Suède*, and the decorative art was honoured with many grands prix, diplomes d'honneur, and medals. The English critic Morton Shand, in connection with later developments, coined the expression 'Swedish Grace'. Of the display as a whole the architect Uno Åhren says: "Forms, forms, forms . . ." and continues: "The real hall-mark of modernity is to give practical things an artistic form without the 'artistic' being obtrusive. For me the highlight of this exhibition was the building erected by the periodical *L'Esprit Nouveau*, with Le Corbusier and Pierre Jeanneret as architects. Here there was room to move, to talk seriously or to crack a joke; here there was plenty of fresh air and light, space on the walls to hang works of art, and space on the floors to arrange furniture just as one pleased."

The ideas which *L'Esprit Nouveau*, edited by Le Corbusier, Paul Demée, and Amédée Ozenfant, first publicised in its pavilion, proved very fertile. They were shown fully embodied as early as 1927 in the Deutscher Werkbund's exhibition, 'Die Wohnung', in Stuttgart. Here Weissenhof-Siedlung entered houses designed by, amongst others, Peter Behrens, Walter Gropius, Mies van der Rohe, Le Corbusier, and Paul Jeanneret, as well as the Viennese Josef Frank who will appear again in these pages.

Functionalism was an accomplished fact, and under

Goblet with lid and bowl of crystal glass, richly cut and engraved, designed by Simon Gate and made at Orrefors glass works: 85 cm. high. One of the prestige pieces at the Paris Industrial Art Exhibition, 1925, typical of the elaborate decorative style of that decade. Given to the city of Paris by the city of Stockholm.

strong influence from Stuttgart the Stockholm Exhibition of 1930 was organised with Gregor Paulsson as general director and E. G. Asplund as chief architect. This introduced functionalism to Sweden. One had previously talked of 'purpose expressed in form', but now this was to be seen in the concrete many were shocked. The cultural world was divided into two camps, and the clash between them was something of which we had not seen the like for a long time. The programme soon took a radical form: "The fundamental changes which have taken place in the technical and social structure of our society are in process of creating a zeitgeist, philosophy of life, or whatever we like to call it, which objective observers regard as quite as different from that of the previous era as, for example, the zeitgeist of the renaissance was from that of the Middle Ages. The new style of building, the much-discussed functionalism, is—unconsciously—an essential part of this new attitude to life.

Since an explanation of my personal view of this new trend is perhaps called for, I will state plainly that I greeted it with joy and positive approval. It involves an intellectually and morally sound approach to artistic questions, which I find doubly refreshing after our late worship of strange gods with the outward appearance of national tradition or classical beauty but with misleading labels. The belief that a modern culture of building and living can be established in direct connection with, and as a reanimation of, earlier styles and ways of life, shows

"The Stockholm Exhibition of 1930 covers three equally vital aspects of the environment in which modern man lives. Architecture, especially house-design, provides the main framework: means of transport and the equipment of street and garden the setting for life outside the home: and finally household equipment, the separate things with which we make our homes."

"Swedish Modern–a movement towards sanity in design." Rural interior in the Swedish pavilion at the New York World's Fair of 1939. Functionalism has become less uncompromising. Wood in natural shades, pair of red-lacquered chairs, textiles in bright colours. Furniture and light fitting designed by Elias Svedberg, fabrics by Astrid Sampe for Nordiska Co. Ltd.

a lack of insight into the major values of artistic creativeness. If we allow a fixed, mechanical symbolism to replace the spontaneous, free experience and development of a culture's vital spirit, real sensitivity will disappear along with its power to stimulate vigorous and genuine creative work." (Gregor Paulsson).

The ideology of the exhibition was summed up in 1931 in a propaganda paper published by E. G. Asplund, Wolter Gahn, Sven Markelius, Gregor Paulsson, Eskil Sundahl, and Uno Åhrén. All these were architects who had exhibited there, except Paulsson who, as we have said, was general director.

When we look at photographs of the Stockholm Exhibition of 1930, it is remarkable how purist the trend was. Together with 'forms, forms, forms . . .' there was a natural reaction, a salutary purge, a recognition of the interdependence of form and function and of social and technical elements in town-planning, transport, and housing and house-furnishing, at a time when it was understood that the home would take on increasing functions and greater importance. Functionalism never completely swept the board, but it was a cleansing force and provided reliable criteria. Traditionalism was strong, the public taste was, as we have said, rooted in the Eighteenth Century, the time of the admired 'flower-king' Linnaeus. Was it through him that Swedes acquired their great affection for flora? Flower patterns again began to flourish: at the New York World's Fair in 1939 one of

the carpets shown bore the characteristic name 'Flora Suecica'. On the site where the Stockholm Exhibition stood is now a maritime museum, designed by Ragnar Östberg in the style of Eighteenth Century classicism.

Developments in the decade following the Stockholm Exhibition have been summarised by Åke H. Huldt, later director of the Society for Industrial Design in *Arts and Crafts and Domestic Crafts in Sweden 1930–1940*. This period up to the Second World War brought a perhaps natural reaction, or, as it was called, 'humanisation'. On the Continent the radical and progressive forces were suppressed. One centre of rationalism, the Bauhausschule at Dessau, was closed and its chief personalities driven into exile. The Swedish household interiors and articles shown at the New York World's Fair in 1939 in a pavilion designed by Sven Markelius were called 'Swedish Modern', and on their own showing were 'a movement towards sanity in design'. They were still functional, as well as attractive, and were very popular, but were not given long to enjoy their success. The next year the world had something else to think about, and with the Second World War came cultural isolation: such contacts as were maintained were of a different kind. Sweden managed to keep out of hostilities, but we were unhappily cut off from our Scandinavian neighbours and from more distant centres of culture. When the war was at last over, it was with great expectations that we again renewed ties with the outside world. In the years that followed, our hopes

Volvo Amazon, with body designed by Jan Wilsgaard, 1958. The home is a fixed point, but the desire to travel and extend one's horizons is strong. Sweden is one of the countries with most cars in proportion to population, and home-produced cars were in 1960 27°/₀ of the total. In January 1961 a 5-6 seater was produced.

were remarkably fulfilled. New ideas spread like lightning through much intensified travel, exhibitions, and a flood of periodicals; and a universal style developed to a point where one needs to be an expert to tell whether an article or a view of a glass-and-metal city comes from Milan, Tokyo, New York – or Stockholm: whether cameras, typewriters, or for that matter chairs or cupboards, are Scandinavian, German, English, or Japanese. A popular catchword a few years ago was 'streamline', and there seems to be something of this in the ease with which one falls into an international groove in design, whether as a result of loss of individuality or in the hope of achieving economic success in a world market of rising living standards.

The Bauhaus principles which Europe rejected in the Thirties – partly because their exponents were forced to emigrate to America, for example, Gropius in Boston and Moholy-Nagy in Chicago – have now been reimported. A metal chair by Mies van der Rohe, exhibited in Barcelona in 1929, arrived from New York as a best-seller in 1961. A new exoticism, derived especially from Japan and similar to that which influenced craftwork and painting at the end of the Nineteenth Century, is another ingredient which has reached us by way of the United States. Some of our younger artist-craftsmen have become fascinated by Latin American primitivism, but Scandinavia can offer them an alternative. Much of the success of Scandinavian ideas on housing is certainly

due to their having kept their individuality, which is itself founded on the traditional home-culture of the Northern peoples. In our climate the house is naturally of special importance, and is designed not merely as a place to lodge in but as a home.

The exceptionally high living standards of the Twentieth Century have brought growing opportunities for everybody to live better and to acquire ever more things for use and comfort. Increasingly automated production methods increase leisure, which is spent in the home or the summer chalet, in travel, or in the countryside. Thus new occupations, fresh arrangements for the interior, and new articles find a place in our lives. The Swede likes to spend the short summer, when it is light all round the clock, in the country: he wants a place to go out to for holidays and weekends. Someone has said that every Swede dreams of owning a house he can walk round. Alternatively, he wants to get out in a boat or take his fishing-tackle and enjoy life somewhere along the 5000 miles of coast or on one of the 96,000 lakes. He wants to walk in the woods and open country, or in winter to go skiing or skating. In rural surroundings he prefers countrified things, and so a considerable proportion of Swedish products have a rustic character. He needs an open air equipment, and a travelling outfit, and such things are well-designed in Sweden. The two native makes of four-seater car are also good and attractive to look at.

Democratic culture involves a concern that good quality, material and immaterial, should be accessible to all, and not simply that fine luxury products should be made for a small social group. We have already mentioned the work of educating taste which originated from several sources. In the mass-production of consumer goods it is vital to preserve a high standard of craftsmanship and the creativeness of the individual artist: it has been said that luxury is the highest degree of quality. A craft tradition still survives in Sweden from pre-industrial times, for example in glassworks where skills are generally passed on from father to son through generations. It is also found, as the biographical section will show, with the silversmiths, who in a remarkable number of cases have learnt their craft in their father's workshop, and with furniture craftsmen and other handicraft trades. In domestic production we find a corresponding taste and skilled craftsmanship, as well as that feeling for quality which makes the housewife as consumer what might be called an independent buyer. Exclusive products thus serve not as direct models but as examples of quality for the things we need for work and for practical use, which can then generally be mechanically made to keep down costs and to satisfy the demand which has vastly in-

"The chairs and writing-tables he won first and second prize for seemed very modern at the time, while at the same time conveying a remarkable sense of security. Perhaps then we did not recognise as fully as we do now how Swedish they were." Carl Malmsten won first prize in 1916 for this chair in ash with cane plait seat in a competition for certain types of furniture for Stockholm Town Hall. This building is in its entirety a monument of the Twenties.

creased with rising living standards. The artist therefore has a definite place in manufacture, either in his own small workshop or as one of a team under the production director in a large mass-producing industrial enterprise. The industrial art and art-craftsmanship of the Forties has been described by Arthur Hald and Sven Erik Skawonius in the book *Nyttokonst – Contemporary Swedish Design* of 1951.

Several of the generation of artists, craftsmen, and industrial designers who have had a share in developments since the years before 1920 are still alive and working, or recently retired. Amongst these are Edgar Böckman, Elsa Gullberg, Edward Hald, and Carl Malmsten. Wilhelm Kåge has died since work on this book was started. Amongst the architects already mentioned, Hakon Ahlberg, Paul Hedquist, Sigfrid Lewerentz, Sven Markelius, Ivar Tengbom, and Uno Åhrén are still active. In giving a general survey of practical artists now flourishing, there are several possible methods of classification: by generation, by type of work, or by the material they work with. It would be easy to classify them by age, and youth often has, or is supposed to have, fresher ideas than the older generation. But this difference is overshadowed by temperament, means of expression, and material or materials. In the field of furniture, for

example, we have two artists born in the Eighties with only three years between them – Carl Malmsten and Josef Frank. They came from different cultural backgrounds, had different careers, and so achieved different results in their work: but both have had a great influence on contemporary Swedish furniture-design. Carl Malmsten attracted attention as early as 1916, when he won the highest prizes in the Society for Industrial Design's competition for furniture for Stockholm Town Hall, (designed by Ragnar Östberg). Erik Wettergren wrote of Malmsten in another connection in 1956: "His object is to achieve a combination of the functional and the completely pleasing, which he does with the simplest means. A virtuoso in work with exotic woods, he showed himself equally at home with Swedish pine and birch. In the form of his pieces one could see connections with Swedish folk-furniture, peasant-rococo, the Gustavian period, and the late Empire. Malmsten had so assimilated impressions from earlier interiors that they came naturally to him, and therefore we were struck with what was new in his work – we were surprised how Swedish he was." Malmsten has also designed patterns for wall-hangings and printed fabrics which match his furniture. He has also had great influence through his work as a teacher and his patient propaganda activity.

Josef Frank is from Vienna and a pupil of Josef Hoffmann. He has designed houses in Vienna, and constructed the Viennese Café at the Paris Exhibition of 1925 and a house at the Werkbund exhibition at Stuttgart in 1927. The well-known critic Gotthard Johansson wrote of him in 1952: "One may wonder if anyone has had a greater influence than the Austrian Josef Frank on the design of modern Swedish furniture and household equipment which was called 'Swedish Modern' in America back in the Thirties, and which preserves its distinctive character in the international context by its at once austere, charming, simple, and lovable character. In any case his appointment from 1932 as assistant at the house-furnishing firm of Svenskt Tenn, controlled by Estrid Ericson, marked the beginning of a new phase in the development of – and in some ways departure from – the functionalism of the early Thirties. Without advertising himself and his ideas, Josef Frank has had an artistic influence in his adopted country which it is still too early to assess but which has undoubtedly been of great importance. And without himself having any ambitions as a creator of style, he has certainly to a large degree had the effect of one." Josef Frank prefers to work with exclusive and exotic materials and combinations of material. He has designed almost everything imaginable in the fields of interior-design, furniture, printed fabrics, wallpapers, carpets, light-fittings, glass, silver, tin, and precious materials, always with good taste and attractive appearance.

The furniture-designers of the middle generation also differ from each other in temperament. The best-known outside Sweden is Bruno Mathsson. Full of doggedness and self-confidence, he has worked his way through from his first experiments in his father's carpenter's shop via his own studies to his constructions in laminated and moulded wood. He has worked on the same principles for nearly three decades, refining, improving, and perfecting, and his products bear his unmistakable signature. At the 'Interbau' exhibition at Berlin in 1957 they were still amongst the most modern things shown. Mathsson has also produced interesting building constructions following the same principles.

Axel Larsson is a quiet sincere furniture-artist, and since the Stockholm Exhibition of 1930 has made finely balanced practical pieces which have, precisely on account of these qualities, been an example to others. For many years he designed for Swedish Furniture-works Ltd. both mass-production pieces and bespoke interiors and exclusive furniture. The National Museum in Stockholm has a pinewood cupboard which shows his talent for analysis, his sense of proportion, and his feeling for the material. Larsson has also made various designs for handicraft production by cabinetmakers, to be sold through Hantverket in Stockholm.

Carl-Axel Acking works as a free-lance, and he too has designed both factory-made serial furniture and individual pieces for hand-craftsmen. Acking has been equally active as an architect, which is noticeable in his interest in the structure of furniture. He has taken on large commissions as interior-designer, especially in hotels and ships. As principal teacher in the furniture and interior-decoration department of the School of Arts, Crafts and Design during the first decade of the new régime, and teacher in design and materials for the student-architects of the College of Technology, he has naturally exerted a great influence through his far-sightedness, his talent for functional analysis, and his understanding of materials.

Karl Erik Ekselius works exclusively for the firm J. O. Carlsson. After a period when he was much influenced by the English Eighteenth Century (which is by no means the worst influence) he has, through constant contact with his factory, developed into an individual and modern furniture-designer with a thorough knowledge of his craft.

Nils Strinning, Sven Kai-Larsen, Alf Svensson, and Björn Hultén are a few of the younger furniture-designers. Nils Strinning is particularly known for his 'String' series, in which he has combined bearing parts in plastic-covered metal wire with supported parts in wood. The idea is brilliant in its simplicity, and has resulted in various attempts at imitation. Alf Svensson has worked chiefly for the Dux mattress-factory, the country's largest producer of upholstered furniture, which has an awe-inspiring production programme and a fully considered design policy. He also works on light-fittings. Sven Kai-Larsen on the other hand confines himself to interior-arrangement, with specially-made pieces designed by himself. Björn Hultén, who is one of our youngest furniture-artists, has designed sound and straightforward pieces for mass-production. He shows a new line in Swedish style, with a clear distinction between bearing and borne parts, and a preference for right-angles and the combination of surface elements. These do not allow the wood sculptural forms with smooth curves and a massiveness in the separate parts. We can thus distinguish trends within Swedish furniture, which at the same time do not imply any contradiction between its various segments. First and last it is a matter of personalities, which stand out as fixed points above the waves in the contemporary current. Different ideas can thrive alongside each other, complement each other, and give a wider choice to the consumer.

One important factor in every room is lighting, both natural and artificial. But this is a field in which men are still working on doubtful assumptions, and with many preconceived notions of showy forms of lighting such as chandeliers. Many modern fittings are therefore intended to fulfil a decorative rather than a practical function, and much is ephemeral. Certain types, on the other hand, are based on such sound ideas that they survive independently of passing fashion: this applies to Tore Ahlsén's simple spheres of wire covered with fabric, to Carl Fagerberg's compositions in glass from Orrefors, and to B. J. Gullberg's shades of wire trimmed with plastic.

For colour and decorativeness, textiles play the most important part in our interiors: carpets, furnishing fabrics, and curtains, or purely decorative weaves such as hangings and tapestries. Weaving is in principle allowing the threads to cross alternately over and under each other, and it is a very ancient craft. Countless variations have developed in the course of thousands of years. Each weaver chooses the technique and material with which she can best realise her intentions. Sweden has a strong textile tradition, as we have already said, and this has undoubtedly had a decisive influence on our products; but important also is the purchaser's active appreciation of quality. As is well-known, it was in England that textile manufacture was first industrialised,

Märta Måås-Fjetterström (1873–1941) began with completely traditional handicrafts and developed into a textile artist with a highly individual approach and with a strong influence on Swedish hand-made fabrics. She was not, however, interested in the industrial production of useful textiles. Rug, with a voided pile, in white and grey c. 1925.

in the later Eighteenth Century. When Richard Arkwright made his water-frame for spinning, the workers drove him from his home because they thought their living was in danger. The Reverend Edmund Cartwright suffered similarly when in 1787 he demonstrated his power-loom, which was a development from James Hargreaves' Spinning Jenny – the first effective spinning machine, patented in 1770. In the end Cartwright was given a government grant of £10,000. Joseph Maria Jacquard, who invented the loom which bears his name, was also a victim of persecution: his machines were smashed – but later on he was given a pension by the city of Lyons, and machine-made cloth became an accomplished fact. Everywhere mechanisation soon followed. The machines were long used mainly for copying style patterns, and they were efficient implements for the extensive style-imitation – often of poor quality – of the Nineteenth Century.

This was the sort of thing that the founders of the Swedish Society for Industrial Design were afraid of; but it was not till the end of the century that it was generally realised that the native wealth of design and textile tradition contained values which it was important to preserve. On the self-sufficient farms there were still home-woven materials of many kinds – carpets, wall-hangings for special occasions, rugs for benches and floors and beds, pillows and mattresses, and of course bed- and table-linen, and towels both for use and for ornament. The

material was native wool and flax, and sometimes cattlehair. What we now know as the domestic crafts movement gained ground, and in the provinces shops were set up exclusively for home-made products. In 1872 the famous folklorist Arthur Hazelius began his collections, which in course of time grew very large and are now in the Nordiska Museum and the Skansen open-air museum in Stockholm. The Friends of Handicraft Association was founded in 1874 for 'the artistic development of Swedish women's handicrafts'; and the Swedish Domestic Crafts Association was started in 1899 'to protect and disseminate the output of Swedish domestic crafts, and to advance the good taste of the workers and the quality of their products by advisory activities and the provision of good models and patterns'. Local homecrafts associations were established in the provinces, often affiliated to the homestead movement, and in 1913 these were federated in the National Federation of Swedish Domestic Crafts Associations.

At this time there were strong national influences in literature, painting, sculpture, and music. Even August Strindberg in the final scene of his *Serious Comedy for Midsummer* of 1901, has persons in the dress of the Vasa period as well as in national dress assembled around Gustav Vasa's bust at the aforementioned Skansen, singing a national song which opens with the words: "I know a land far up in the distant North, not warm nor rich as countries of the South . . ."

Amongst those who have had a particularly great artistic influence on our period, Märta Måås-Fjetterström is outstanding both for her long working life and her strong personality. She was active from the beginning of the century to her death in 1941. As early as 1909 she took part in the exhibition of that year, and later on had her own workshop at Båstad in West Sweden. She worked in various techniques, and used all of them with unfailing certainty. Her workshop in Båstad is still in operation, making partly her own products and partly new ones. Barbro Nilsson has been in charge since 1942, and amongst her assistants have been Marianne Richter and Ann-Mari Forsberg. Barbro Nilsson has adopted Märta Måås-Fjetterström's principles in a natural but quite personal manner, and is expert in all the various weaving techniques, though she prefers tapestry. She has a monumental vein, which gives clarity of composition to her smaller fabrics, carpets, and tapestries, while making her large works for public buildings (such as concert-halls, administrative offices, and business premises, besides ship-interiors) finely balanced with bold lines and colour-schemes originally bright and intense but now increasingly subdued. She is a typical artist-craftsman, and machine production has failed to attract her. She has taught at several textile schools, finally for ten years as head of the textile department of the State School of Arts, Crafts and Design.

In 1942 Marianne Richter also began work at Båstad. She is a fine colorist, and works chiefly in the colourful and interesting rug-technique in which the pieces of yarn are fixed with a special knot to a simultaneously woven foundation. This makes the surface alive and continually changing. She shows a vigorous ingenuity in decorative effects.

Ann-Mari Forsberg also has a rich decorative imagination. She has done embroideries, and for the Båstad workshop she has made woven tapestries and rugs in cooler colour-schemes and more delicate design. Elsa Gullberg, a central figure in Swedish textile art for several decades, has a quite different temperament. She began her work in connection with the domestic crafts movement at the beginning of the century, and was one of the pioneers in the period before 1920, when in charge of the Society for Industrial Design office which placed many later well-known artists in industry and found artists commissions. This work, as we have said, produced important results. As a practising artist, and a director of several firms until she began production in her own workshop, she carried out many large commissions such as the fabrics for the Stockholm Concert Hall. She has also had a considerable hand in mass-production, especially furnishing and curtain fabrics in cotton and wool and table-cloths. Her work as organiser and administrator has attracted much attention. Now she has retired to well-earned leisure, and works only occasionally. Around the two personalities of Märta Måås-Fjetterström and Elsa Gullberg one can, without making general artistic comparisons, assemble textile designers into two groups: those who devote themselves exclusively to hand-made fabrics, and the more versatile ones who also work for industry or are exclusively industrial.

It is plain from its title that the afore-mentioned Friends of Handicraft Association belongs to the former group. This organisation makes decorative fabrics, and also hand-woven practical cloths in wool and linen. It has its own store in Stockholm, as well as running a school there and in Dalarna. Since 1951 its chief has been Edna Martin, a versatile artist, who has produced miniature-like representational embroideries and has designed printed fabrics, decorative floor-coverings, and mass-produced linens. She is also head of the textile department of the School of Arts, Crafts and Design. Alf Munthe, who is properly a painter, has long been working with textiles. In 1923 he attracted attention with a decorative embroidered frieze in the Scandia Cinema in Stockholm, designed by E. G. Asplund. In the years 1935–50 he worked for the Friends of Handicraft, particularly with large decorative pieces in double-weaving–an interesting technique in which there are actually two weaves, partly woven together and partly separate, with the pattern positive on one side and negative on the other. He now, with Greta Gahn, has his own workshop in Dalarna. The younger Kaisa Melanton, who has her own workshop as well as teaching at the Friends of Handicraft school and the School of Arts, Crafts, and Design also does double-weaving, especially in black and white. She is an interesting artist with strict ideas on decoration, well acquainted with the technical possibilities in embroidery, and also a designer of industrial fabrics. The Friends of Handicraft often carry out work by Sten Kauppi, both in embroidery and weaving, and this artist also does both on his own account. He was born north of the Arctic Circle, and this seems to have a definite bearing on his original and imaginative mode of expression in both textiles and painting.

There is not much doubt that the Swedish character varies somewhat from province to province. Sweden is a large country, and a thousand miles stretch between its northern extremity about 69 deg. N. and its southern about 55 deg., equivalent to the distance between Copenhagen and Naples. The country's topography varies greatly, from the mountainous North, barren but so rich in natural resources, over the extensive forest so important to the national economy, to the fertile southern plains; from the cliffs of the North Sea shore to the fragmented skerrygard coast of the Baltic. The characteristics of the population vary likewise: at any rate, there are plain differences in folk-art which may be attributed to different sources of inspiration. In the rich southern farming districts there is much continental influence, e.g. from Flemish weaving, giving fabrics deep colours and rich patterns. In the adjoining province of Blekinge colour-schemes are lighter, pale blue and pink in ingenious striped designs. In the district around Siljan in Dalarna, where folk-costume and domestic crafts have survived longest, the colours are stronger and purer and the patterns larger. Here a splendid imaginary flora flourishes in folk-painting, which is different in character from that found in Småland and Halland to the south. Northwards, things change again: the colours become intense and often dark, before once more brightening in the blue and red colour-schemes of the Lapps in the far North.

Many cloth dyes were derived locally from a variety of plants, a skill which in many places survives. The homecraft associations of the different provinces endeavour to preserve local peculiarities. They do important work, partly in encouraging the use as patterns of old and valued prototypes which are often surprisingly timeless and remarkably suited to the modern environment; and partly by adapting tradition and technique to modern demands, for example in clothing materials which are now required to be much lighter, and in knitting and table-cloths. The material is generally native wool, linen, or in certain cases 'cottonin' – originally an ersatz material produced as a by-product of flax and hemp, which showed such remarkable properties that it is still used. Besides these, use is also of course made of imported cotton. The domestic craft associations have both an inspirational and advisory function and a sales organisation. For the former purpose they are all federated in the National Federation of Swedish Domestic Crafts Associations, which also includes the older Swedish Domestic Crafts Association. This and other bodies have their own sales arrangements, but most associations belong to that run by the Domestic Crafts League. Naturally the quality of their products depends to a great extent on their respective chiefs, and here we must mention particularly the directors of the Domestic Crafts League (Gull Lilliecrona), of the Domestic Crafts Association (Marianne von Münchow), and of the local associations of Malmöhus (Gertrud Ingers) and of Borås (Boel Sällfors). They give advice and inspiration, and have a great responsibility for preserving a heritage and keeping traditions in contact with the modern world.

A shining example of how this can be done is Bohus-Stickning, an organisation built up by the wife of a former governor of Gothenburg and Bohus counties, Emma Jacobsson. This was originally a social institution intended to help the families of workers in the granite quarries of the area. Facilities were provided for domestic work in the form of knitting, and for the sale of the products. With its strict standards of quality and its artistic designs and colour-schemes, the output has become an excellent example of Swedish folk-craftwork. Emma Jacobsson's assistants were Anna-Lisa Lunn and Annika Malmström.

Several artists work, as Märta Måås-Fjetterström did in her time, in their own workshops. A good example of this group is Alice Lund, who produces individual decorative compositions for churches, schools, libraries, and restaurants, regularly makes furnishing fabrics, and in addition arranges patterns and types of weave for industry. Her fabrics are simple and restrained in colour, but have interesting interweaving techniques and genuine textile effects. In recent years she collaborated with Sofia Widén, who died while this book was in preparation. Sofia Widén was an enthusiastic and productive artist, especially in church fabrics, and it has been claimed that works of hers can be found in over a thousand Swedish churches. For over twenty years she was director of the Licium textile firm, which specialised in ecclesiastical fabrics and is now incorporated with the Friends of Handicraft. She was a skilful designer, and her works distinguished themselves with their bold and firm composition. She treated her colours in a flat manner, even in embroidery, a technique which allows transitions, gradations and nuances. It is therefore not surprising that in her later years she began to allow freer rein to her disciplined decorative imagination in appliqué work, often in close colours-chemes such as white-grey-black or a series in shades of blue.

Ingrid Skerfe-Nilsson, Ulla Schumacher-Percy, and the young Birgitta Graf and Inga Brand may be taken as examples of the different trends in this group of artist-craftsmen. Ingrid Skerfe-Nilsson has her own workshop at Uppsala, where she weaves floor-coverings and fabrics, as well as producing her characteristic shawls and knotted rugs in deep colours. Ulla Schumacher-Percy does completely painting-like work in rug-making. The old Swedish and Finnish rugs either had only slight patterns or none at all, and were used as coverings in the same way as skins, or they were purely decorative with striking patterns and adorned walls or made-up beds. Ulla Schumacher-Percy's rugs are of the latter type, both in their size and their vigorous abstract motifs.

One of the assistants in Elsa Gullberg's firm, now controlled by her daughter Elsa-Maria Gullberg, is Birgitta Graf, who is still young but has none the less shown distinct personality. She makes patterns for printed fabrics, decorative rugs, and 'rölakan' carpets. 'Rölakan' is a technique using a linen warp with inlaid yarn. Where the colours meet, the yarn is crossed or tied with characteristic knots. Birgitta Graf was trained at the Crafts Association school in Gothenburg, and comes from the West Coast. The same applies to Inga Brand, who in her own workshop makes boldly designed weaves which are often in a technique similar to that used for 'rölakan'.

In value of output the textile industry in Sweden comes fourth after metals, food, and timber, and on a level with the paper industry. It includes the excellent Swedish ready-made clothing. Though furnishing- and curtain-fabrics account for only a small proportion of the total, this branch of the industry is very thriving and attracts much attention. This is connected with the Swedish interest in home-furnishing, and perhaps also with a need for comfort and colour in a climate where the winter is long and, though invigorating, monotonously monochrome. The textile industry therefore employs various qualified artists, and an outstanding example of these is Astrid Sampe. Since 1936 she has worked for the Nordiska Company in Stockholm, the well-known large store which takes a line of its own in textiles and also produces furniture. At the Paris Exhibition of 1937 she organised the firm's textile-manufacture section, which acquired the name of 'NK's Textilkammare'. For this firm she has made floor-coverings, furnishing fabrics, prints, and other textiles for the home; and in co-operation with others, such as Kasthall carpet works and Almedahl-Dalsjöfors, she has arranged and co-ordinated textile production programmes. Astrid Sampe is an elegant and ingenious designer, and in particular an organiser and co-ordinator.

Edna Martin, previously mentioned in connection with the Friends of Handicraft, has also worked as industrial designer, for example with printed fabrics for Mölnlycke Textiles Ltd. and with practical linens for Oskarström linen-works. Age Faith-Ell began in the domestic crafts movement, but has now put her technical knowledge and her wealth of ideas at the service of industry. She prefers effects based on purely textile media, whether in linen or woollen curtains, furnishing fabrics, or clothing materials. Her textiles for Eriksberg weaving-mills are particularly interesting.

Viola Gråsten, who now works chiefly on prints for Mölnlycke, has a quite different temperament, and her cloths are principally decorative. For over ten years she worked with NK's Textilkammare, and had a splendid output of expressionistic rugs with intense colour-effects. She has also done factory-woven carpets for Kasthall, and like Faith-Ell has designed bedspreads for Tidstrand woollen mills. Her printed fabrics for clothes and curtains are unusually decorative, and have proved very popular. She uses surprising combinations in her colour-schemes, but also works with graphic effects in white-grey-black.

Ingrid Dessau is primarily a carpet weaver, and works both for handicraft and for industry. She designs hand-woven carpets for the Domestic Crafts Associations of Malmö, Kristianstad, and Borås, and machine-woven ones for Kasthall. She uses geometrical and linear motifs, always employing them in a fresh and decorative fashion. She supervises the production of work she has planned, knowing that it is not enough simply to deliver a design but that the process must be followed through to the end product. Göta Trägårdh is production director for the Stobo cotton firm. With her unusual insight into the world of fashion, she assembles her elegant collections with patterns from designers such as Faith-Ell, Ulla Ericsson, and Al Eklund as well as her own. Other important aspects of her activity have been her work as a teacher and as a fashion consultant.

We can thus assert that the efforts made since before 1920 to bring the artist into industry have really borne fruit in the field of textiles, where factories employ a large number of distinguished experts to shape and co-ordinate their production and to give it good patterns to work from. These artists also in many cases produce textiles in their own workshops, or design patterns for hand-craftsmen and home workers.

By domestic crafts we do not mean only weaving and other handwork in textiles; the term also includes work in wood, iron and other metals such as copper and tin, pottery, bone, and horn. Such work originated in earlier rural self-sufficiency, but there were some 'domestic industry areas', districts where the return from the land and stock was so scanty that people earned a much-needed extra income from making things at home and selling them elsewhere. Dalarna was one such district, from which young men and girls went as itinerant hand-workers. From here came the 'prefabricated house', which was put together, each piece marked, then dismantled and re-erected for a distant buyer. From the poverty-stricken districts of southern Västergötland pedlars tramped with home-woven and knitted goods, and it was on this basis of tradition that the centre of the Swedish textile industry later developed. The highlands of Småland were poor in arable and cattle but rich in timber, ideas, and energy. There wooden furniture and tools and decorative articles were made, and pedlars wandered with their stock from the glassworks on their backs. In that area today we find most of the furniture factories and all but one or two of the glassworks.

Domestic crafts in wood and similar materials were naturally for the most part men's work, but women made basketry of chips, withies, bark, and rushes. Their tools were simple, often only a knife, and they depended on the skill of their hands. Such popular manual dexterity and sense of form can produce works of real artistic quality, as for example those of Johnny Mattsson – wooden bowls, implements and carvings with fine design and expert use of the material. Mattsson is completely self-taught, and in his own fashion has arrived at a completely modern form. In recent years wood has been increasingly used for articles such as salad-bowls and serving implements, and in combination with other materials.

Sweden has a number of skilful wood-carvers. Co Derr is indeed Dutch by birth, but a naturalised Swede: he selects his exotic woods with fine taste, and treats them in such a manner as to bring out as much as possible of their colour-tones and structure. Forse Gnista in a way represents a different type; he too has an open mind for his material, but appears to approach it more from fixed principles of function and form. His products always have a use, whether as candlesticks or candelabra, table bowls, or stands for fruit-knives.

Leather is a natural material with properties of its

Bottle-case of natural coloured calf-leather by Mårten Palmgren, Stockholm. Handwork as a form of production is becoming more and more rare. When it is well done, in a 'genuine' material and with appreciation of form, material, and process, it makes an unusual aesthetic impression.

own. An English proverb says: 'There's nothing like leather'. But its use is now limited because the horse as a draught-animal has become a rarity, and new and less noble materials have taken its place. The Court saddlery firm of Palmgren still carries on the craft as art-handwork, with Mårten Palmgren as expert designer and controller of production.

Glassworks, as already mentioned, are concentrated in Småland around the oldest surviving art-glass manufactory, Kosta, founded in 1742. Both in years and in activity, Edward Hald is the senior Swedish glass-artist now at work. He also belongs to the generation which made its breakthrough shortly before 1920. Since 1917 he has been attached to Orrefors, where, together with Simon Gate, who died in 1945, he led the artistic advance which brought this glassworks its triumphs at home and abroad. In his everyday wares, simple moulded bowls and table-services, and in his show-piece cut-glass sets and engraved crystal goblets, we see his depth of experience, his active intellect, and his artistic talent. He has worked with and developed the factory's *Graal* and *Ariel* techniques, by which, respectively, glass is ornamented by colour or air within the glass material. Sven Palmqvist and Nils Landberg belong to the middle generation at Orrefors. They grew up working at the factory, are familiar with glass techniques, and work out new production methods – Palmqvist for example in his Fuga series, which are produced in a moment of creation

and are supple in form and inexpensive. Nils Landberg designs both decorative and table glass, in exclusive crystal or of attractive everyday quality. Both work with coloured glass, in which by different methods they achieve fine decorative effects.

Ingeborg Lundin and Gunnar Cyrén are two of the younger experts. The former has an extremely personal style, beautifully expressed in closed forms which are mostly undecorated and untinted. Cyrén is a newcomer, but has worked successfully with the engraving technique which Orrefors employs with masterly expertise. Carl Fagerlund, as previously mentioned, is in charge of the firm's light-fittings.

The leading spirit at the over two centuries old Kosta works is Vicke Lindstrand, with his imaginative mobile decoration and his great technical skill. He has an insatiable appetite for work, and a buoyant delight in experiments with colour and form, expressed in purely decorative objects, in ornamental and table glassware, and in mosaic. For some years Monica Schildt has also worked at Kosta. She has a preference for coloured glass, superimposed in several layers, which can yield fine colour-effects. The Kosta works makes both useful and ornamental ware, and its artist assistants have the task of designing both.

At Gullaskruf work Arthur C:son Percy and Kjell Blomberg. Percy is a painter, and has worked chiefly in ceramics. Blomberg belongs to the younger generation, and works on this firm's attractive output of hand-made glassware, frequently with coloured glass, and on uncoloured moulded products. Glass is transparent, light-refracting, and easy to shape. Its various properties can be exploited by blowing it into a thin and almost immaterial bubble, or forming it into a heavy lump. It can be cut and polished into glittering sharp-edged polyhedra, or opened out at the furnace into a massive bowl, clear as water or intensely coloured. Amongst these various forms the artist chooses whichever he thinks will best answer his purpose.

Hugo Gehlin worked at Gullaskruf till his death in 1953, and used the glass material as a smooth coloured plastic mass. Erik Höglund at Boda goes still further. He aims at completely bluff effects with powerfully modelled forms in a coloured glass full of air bubbles. When he uses cutting it is coarse and unconventional. All his work is the opposite of elegant and precise. A similar primitivism can be seen in several of the younger craftsmen, probably as a reaction against the well-groomed forms, precise lines, and polished surfaces of industrial design. Bengt Edenfalk at Skruf also works with the glass in a heavy lump with many irregular bubbles, which nevertheless arrange themselves into decorative figures. Since Skruf's most important output is tableware, Edenfalk also designs products of that sort.

Glassworks naturally vary in size, but since there is a definite minimum for economic working, the differences are not as great as in ceramics, which are quantitatively dominated by three great undertakings providing service-ware and porcelain. After these come several medium-sized firms, producing earthenware and various types of stoneware with some degree of specialisation, and finally we have potters working by themselves, or studios with two to four workers. In each of these types of production there are artist experts, in the large ones as leaders and members of a team. In this case most have a double function: partly to give good form and decoration to mass-produced ware, and partly to make articles of an exclusive or experimental nature on a studio basis.

The doyen of ceramic artists was Wilhelm Kåge. In 1917 he joined Gustavsberg porcelain works in connection with the movement for more beautiful everyday things, and there he produced various well-thought-out and surely designed practical wares, table-services, and household pottery, besides a big output of particularly individual stoneware. Though he continued to work at Gustavsberg till his death, he resigned control of the works in 1949 and was succeeded by Stig Lindberg, who had already for twelve years been one of the firm's artists. He is an exceptionally versatile and vigorous personality, who works with utility wares and with studio products in the various materials the factory has at its

The phrase 'more beautiful everyday things', coined in 1919, which strikingly typifies the aspirations of that period, is excellently illustrated in this earthenware service with blue copper-printed ornament designed by Wilhelm Kåge for Gustavsberg as part of the jubilee exhibition at Gothenburg in 1923. The form is clear and practical, and suited to the period's ideas of style which derived from the end of the Eighteenth and the beginning of the bourgeois Nineteenth Century.

disposal—earthenware, bone china (which Gustavsberg alone makes in Sweden) and stoneware. He also finds time to be the head of the School of Arts, Crafts and Design's ceramics department; and in addition he provides designs for printing on paper and textiles, and concerns himself with industrial design. When Lindberg became a teacher the artistic direction of the factory was handed over to Arthur Hald, son of Edward Hald and known as a writer and as editor for many years of the Crafts Association's periodicals *Form* and *Kontur*. Berndt Friberg is the direct opposite of Lindberg. He keeps exclusively to individually-made pieces of stoneware, which he throws and to which he gives vital form and fine glazing—the only media he allows himself. Younger experts are Karin Björqvist and Lisa Larson, the former, who makes both useful and decorative pieces, representing serious-minded aspiration, and the latter gaiety and fun.

The oldest ceramic works in Sweden is the Rörstrand porcelain factory, founded in 1726, which produces earthenware, faience, felspar-porcelain, 'vitreous china', and stoneware. Carl-Harry Stålhane is now the firm's senior artist, having been appointed in 1939. He has developed into a sure designer of table wares and an interesting stoneware artist, who after earlier work with more traditional slender forms and contrasting glazes has now evolved a massive enclosed form with an intense opaque glaze. Hertha Bengtson has produced two of the firm's best-known services, modelled in a solid manner which inspires confidence and showing a clear preference for one of the most ancient ceramic colours—cobalt blue—which she often uses in contrast with the white or pale blue-grey clay. She also makes charming things in stoneware, pots and bowls with matt or glossy coloured glazes. Marianne Westman, the youngest of the group, is responsible for both the form and the decorative colouring of a series of serving dishes, cooking vessels, and casseroles.

The third large ceramic firm is Upsala-Ekeby, which also includes potteries in Gävle and Karlskrona. Arthur C:son Percy has made a long and important contribution here since he was appointed to Gävle in 1923. In 1925 he aroused interest with table services and richly modelled and coloured earthenware. Later he developed a more restrained style, and made a series of services and lightly-fired stoneware with his own typical charm. The Gävle factory makes earthenware and 'vitreous china'. At the Karlskrona works he has made excellent services in felspar-porcelain. He is also a fine painter, with exuberant gay colours, and has designed fabric-prints as well as glass for Gullaskruf. Ingrid Atterberg and Mari Simmulson work at the mother-factory, which chiefly produces wall-tiles but also has a considerable output of useful and ornamental earthenware. The former has a taut and restrained style, principally in chamotte ware and with geometrical decoration, while the latter is more imaginative and colourful. For a time in the Fifties, and again since 1961, Sven Erik Skawonius has been in charge of the factory's design department and personally designs useful ware for the firm.

Amongst firms of medium size is Andersson & Johansson, with John Andersson as designer; this is in a class by itself with its sound and attractive output of household wares and colour-glazed ornamental stoneware in pure forms. A traditional type of Scanian pottery, salt-glazed brown stoneware, is made at Wallåkra stoneware-works under the direction of Arthur Andersson, who is a craftsman himself and has evolved his own sense of form. These products have a simple balanced shape with a lightly-incised geometrical decoration.

In the same part of Scania as these factories Edgar Böckman—one of our most outstanding independent ceramic artists—began his work in the second decade of the century as co-operator with Höganäs-Billesholm Ltd., which in those days also produced household stoneware. His products have bold pure lines, and the material is given full scope, though decoration is slight. For the first ten years after the School of Arts, Crafts and Design was reorganised he was head of its ceramics department. Erich Triller and his wife Ingrid have had their own studio north of Stockholm since 1935, making select and individual stoneware. In Stockholm itself Tom and Grete Möller make charming useful earthenware and stoneware, teapots, jugs, bowls, and dishes, pleasingly designed and sometimes lightly decorated. Tyra Lundgren on the other hand is a purely decorative-minded artist: she occasionally uses functional forms like bowls and dishes, but always gives them a markedly ornamental appearance. She is known for her figures and reliefs with flower, bird, or fish motifs, and has exploited ceramic materials in a masterly fashion in large ornamental works. Signe Persson-Melin of Malmö is satisfied with a simple range of forms, monumental in character even when small in size, and with colour- and glazing-schemes closely related to the material, whether she is making simple and attractive useful articles or ornamental compositions for walls. Hertha Hillfon is temperamentally quite different, and is another exponent of the policy of encouraging primitive effects based on the material, emotional rather than precise. Her dishes are primarily decorative, and she also makes fanciful abstract ceramic sculptures. Hans Hedberg works in France, after training in Italy, and represents a continental element in Swedish ceramics. He uses large complete vessel-forms, but his chief object seems to be to achieve ornamental effects with opaque coloured glazes, which are sometimes extravagant.

Sweden's wealth of good practical wares in textiles, glass, wood, and ceramics offers great opportunities in table-setting. This can be varied in accordance with the time of year, with Easter, light summer meals, late summer crayfish-parties, and the great Christmas festival marking the rhythm. On special occasions we have a regular table lay-out on a linen cloth. For everyday purposes we can be less ceremonious, but not therefore less well served, with dishes which can be brought direct from the kitchen stove to the table and with a pleasing cloth of plastic. We can still have a pair of lighted candles on the table, a vase of flowers from the fields or the flower-market in summer, a colourful tulip in winter, or in spring twigs which have been encouraged to blossom.

Amongst the materials used for table-ware, metals appear both as cutlery and serving dishes, jugs, coffee- and tea-services, and other things made of silver, electroplate, or steel. The last is new to our tables: it requires mechanical processing, and has of course a different character from silver. Silver, with its softer structure and lustre, can be worked in various ways, and different periods have found different styles of form. Compare, for example, a Swedish coffee-service of the rococo period, with its bulging lines and flower-decoration, with a corresponding set in the Empire style, with its smooth level surfaces and rigid ornament à la grecque. Similarly, one can see different conceptions of the nature of the metal in modern Swedish silversmith's work. Wiwen-Nilsson is one of our most interesting artists in this field, and since the end of the Twenties he has with strict consistency developed a style of his own. He works with large entire plane surfaces, joined with sharp edges, and manages with inflexible geometrical forms—polyhedra, cones, pyramids, and spheres—used in a variety of ways to produce ever fresh reflecting and reflected forms in accurate and craftsmanlike construction.

A younger generation is represented by Sven-Arne Gillgren, Sigurd Persson, and Åke Strömdahl, of the same age but none the less different in character and in work. Gillgren has since 1942 been art-director for the large Guldsmedsbolaget, Stockholm, and during this time has done various kinds of work. The Church in Sweden nowadays frequently commissions artists both in architecture and the crafts, and Gillgren has carried out much ecclesiastical work. He is technically expert, and also makes silver vessels and cutlery. In 1955 he succeeded Erik Fleming as head of the metalwork department of the School of Arts, Crafts and Design.

Sigurd Persson is a splendid example of how an artist-craftsman can also be an industrial designer. He has his own workshop, where he makes choice and exclusive things of marked individuality, austere but with a certain suppleness. He designs cutlery for hand and industrial production, as well as cooking-pots, dishes, stainless steel cutlery, and plastics. Similar work is done by Åke Strömdahl, who likewise both runs his own workshop and undertakes industrial design. He has a fine sense of form, and like so many silversmiths learnt the craft from his father—a natural way of acquiring professional sureness of touch. He too is typical of modern artists in working both on exclusive gold- and silver-ware and on mass-production goods such as plastics.

All the above-mentioned silversmiths also produce fine jewellery. Wiwen Nilsson's facet-style also appears in his work in this line, which is large and heavy, with the stones carefully selected and cut into table- or cabochon-form. Gillgren works mostly in gold of different shades with precious stones, and has a more delicate style. Sigurd Persson's jewellery is striking in appearance and decorative, with the monumentality of small-scale things. Strömdahl is the most versatile, with both expensive diamond jewellery and effective everyday ornaments such as handsome bangles and necklaces of soft-ground Swedish minerals. Between these two extremes, moreover, he produces a large intermediate range.

There is also a large group of young jewellery-artists, who took part in an interesting exhibition at the Stockholm National Museum in 1959, which showed that something new was on the way to replace the often quite banal jewellery of the international type. Examples of these young pioneers are Inga-Britt Dahlquist and Torun Bülow-Hübe, whose work, though in different ways, shows affinities with modern sculpture. The former has a more sure and succinct style: she combines silver with interesting Gotland fossils, thus stressing the aboriginal urge for personal adornment. Torun Bülow-Hübe uses more gentle and feminine forms and materials. Her ornaments often fit closely to the wearer's skin, and she frequently rounds them off with Graal-glass amulets from Orrefors, old rock-crystals, or stones from the beach.

Cutlery is an important field for the silversmith. For those who could not afford silver, electroplate was formerly the most usual substitute both in cutlery and dishes: but it was never more than a substitute, with false pretences—the silver surface soon wore off to reveal the base metal. It has now been ousted by stainless steel, which is Folke Arström's material. He has worked for many years for Gense, the leading firm in this line, and has there attained a thorough knowledge of processing methods and appropriate form. His cutlery is genuine, well-modelled, and free of extravagances. Pierre Forsell, who also works for Gense, began as a silversmith, but has adapted himself to stainless steel with a sure appreciation

Bruno Mathsson's room at the Interbau exhibition, Hansaviertel, Berlin, 1957. "A synthesis of function, structure, and the expressive value of the form." Swedish mid-Twentieth Century furniture, actually designed in the early Thirties and thereby showing that a well-designed model can hold its own even when fashions change.

of the material. Ainar Axelsson also has designed excellent cutlery and other things in this material for Goldsmiths Ltd., Stockholm.

Recently Gregor Paulsson, Professor of Art-History at Uppsala University, published with his son Nils *Use and Appearance of Objects*, an interesting variation of the phrase 'more beautiful everyday things' of some forty years before. Ulf Hård of Segerstad has attempted to sum up the designer's problems in *The Objects and Ourselves*.

Our environment contains many objects, and their number steadily increases. How much more is desirable or possible with regard to form, material composition, and decoration? Ornament is not nowadays used to excess, though we can hardly say with Le Corbusier: "l'Art décoratif moderne n'a pas de décor". Aesthetic purposes are not obtrusive in well-designed useful wares, but we are concerned that things should be good to look at and pick up and handle. For this reason much care is now taken with the construction even of tools and machines, and the field of work for 'the community's specialists in design' has become notably wider. Many of the artists mentioned above also work at this type of designing, and as typical examples we can name Sigvard Bernadotte and Acton Björn. Their wide sphere of activity includes tools and implements, kitchen utensils, and office machines, as well as decorative patterns for plastic cloths. Carl-Arne Breger has designed excellent plastic articles and sanitary ware, Jan Wilsgaard is responsible for the body of the Volvo Amazon car; and we have already mentioned, to name but a few, Carl-Axel Acking, Folke Arström, Age Faith-Ell, Pierre Forsell, Sven-Arne Gillgren, Stig Lindberg, Sven Palmqvist, Astrid Sampe, and Åke Strömdahl.

The things which surround us at home, outside, and at work, all have significance not only in the functions they fulfil but in their aesthetic qualities: i.e., the impression they make on our senses, especially sight and feeling. Without devoting ourselves to fetishes, we must recognise that the objects about us and our environment exert an influence. They need human, and not merely technical, values: they are, after all, made for us humans. They must be based both on common-sense and on feeling. Some have mainly practical, others more decorative, purposes. The people who have given them form and colour represent a complete spectrum of applied artists, practical artists, designers, or whatever we choose to call them, who, in the words of August Strindberg, are concerned with 'everything separate and movable which makes a house into a home for living beings'.

ILLUSTRATIONS

All units of measure in the captions that follow are given according to the metric system.

1 cm. (centimeter) = 0.3937 inches.
1 litre = 1.7598 pints
                or 1.0567 liquid quarts.

1: Cupboard in golden birchwood, designed by CARL MALMSTEN, Sweden, 1953. Malmsten designed this cupboard for his own home, and has papered its interior in the same manner as the room, thus emphasising the lightness of the glass doors. This piece is typical of Malmsten's conscious roots in tradition.

2: Armchair in mahogany, covered in green plush: designed by CARL MALMSTEN, 1936, and made in his own workshop. Woollen carpet in 'rölakan' technique, designed by INGRID DESSAU, 1958, woven by the Kristianstad domestic crafts association. Vase designed by *Arthur C:son Percy*, 1950, made by *Gullaskruf* glassworks.

Malmsten can also strike a bourgeois note, as in this 'lawyer' armchair, which has obvious affinities with the late Eighteenth Century period so influential in Swedish ideas of style. It is nevertheless individually designed and constructed, and characteristic of one aspect of his output.

2

3: Round table with mahogany top and laminated plywood legs, designed by BRUNO MATHSSON, Sweden, 1950 (chair 1932), made by the *Karl Mathsson* firm, Värnamo.

Mathsson is a modern designer of international repute, since his pieces are suited to modern life and demonstrate new possibilities, and in particular fulfil the three basic principles of good useful articles—functional suitability, appropriateness of material and technique, and attractive and rational outward form. Natural circumstances lie behind his work as a designer of the modern environment. He was, so to speak, born in a furniture workshop in the heart of Småland, a part of Sweden which is poor in agriculture but rich in forests, enterprise, skill, and drive, and which has long supported itself by crafts and industry. Mathsson early tackled the task of analysing the functions of useful things, adapting new methods for use with the classic furniture material—wood—and with these in mind modelling pieces with an unmistakable Twentieth Century stamp. His construction is based on bearing elements made of thin layers glued together in the same line of grain and bent into an appropriate form, which prove adequate in spite of their slender dimensions. The 1932 chair shown here illustrates Mathsson's sure sense of form, at the time when he was still working with conventional media. The table is 25 years later: its legs show the laminated structure and the curves which give support in two directions. The material is hard-wearing beech. As his output is limited, each piece receives individual treatment. His woods always keep their natural colour. This picture was taken in Mathsson's exhibition house in Värnamo, which he designed and built himself. In recent years he has built quite a number of houses, and in these too he adapts the principle of the concordance of functions, material, and design, by means of quite novel solutions.

4

4: High-backed easy chair and working chair, both with plaited leather, designed respectively in 1943 and 1934 by BRUNO MATHSSON, Sweden, and made by the firm of *Karl Mathsson*. A chair can be made comfortable in two different ways: either it can be so large and so fully upholstered that it gives to the weight of the body, or it can be designed with such form and proportions that it requires little or no upholstery. Mathsson definitely works on the latter principle, and avoids upholstery completely. The necessary elasticity is achieved with seats and backs of plaited leather strips or webbing.

5: Armchair in ash with natural-coloured washable leather, designed in 1935 by AXEL LARSSON, Sweden, and made by *Swedish Furniture-works Ltd.* Fitted carpet in green shades made for the councillors' meeting-room at Gothenburg by INGRID DESSAU, *Kasthall Carpet-works*, Sweden.

6: Armchair in maple with separate back- and seat-cushions covered with leather, designed by AXEL LARSSON in 1955 and made by *Swedish Furniture-works*: designed for stacking.

7: Interior with bookshelves of wood supported by frames of plastic-coated metal fixed to the wall: designed by NISSE STRINNING since 1950 and made by *String Design Ltd.*, Sweden. This first item in the now comprehensive range of String furniture was the result of a competition for a practical and inexpensive bookcase. Strinning has subsequently developed the idea in making tables and extending the shelving range to include cupboards, magazine shelves, show-cases, bureaux, etc. Strinning's well-known (and much copied) pieces are a typical element of Swedish furniture around 1960.

8: Upholstered easy chair in elm, with separate footstool, designed in 1959 by ALF SVENSSON, Sweden, and made by *Ljung Industries Ltd.* Standing lamp designed by Svensson in 1956 and made by *Bergbom & Co. Ltd.* Svensson is especially experienced in designing upholstered furniture for mass-production, a speciality of Ljung, who make 'Dux' upholstered pieces. He gives the wood an attractive rounded-off form, and makes the upholstery comfortable without being excessive. His pleasing standard lamp has its shaft made of three laths, held apart lower down by struts to form a base.

9: Armchair in ash and easy chair in oak, both with natural-coloured leather: working-table in ash with linoleum surface and side-table in oak. Designed in 1958 by CARL-AXEL ACKING, Sweden, and made by *Nordiska Co. Ltd.* Acking is one of the most influential of Swedish furniture- and interior-designers active in the Forties and Fifties, partly on account of his work as a teacher and partly because of a series of large and important commissions as an interior decorator. In some cases he has also acted as an architect. He has designed furniture for both manual and industrial production. He has clear modern ideas, a fine appreciation of his material, and a sense for structure, expressed for example in his designing an armchair as an elastic framework in which the leather back and seat are suspended in visible tension. The armchair was originally designed for the newly built Swedish Embassy in Tokyo, which Acking was responsible for furnishing.

7

5

6

8

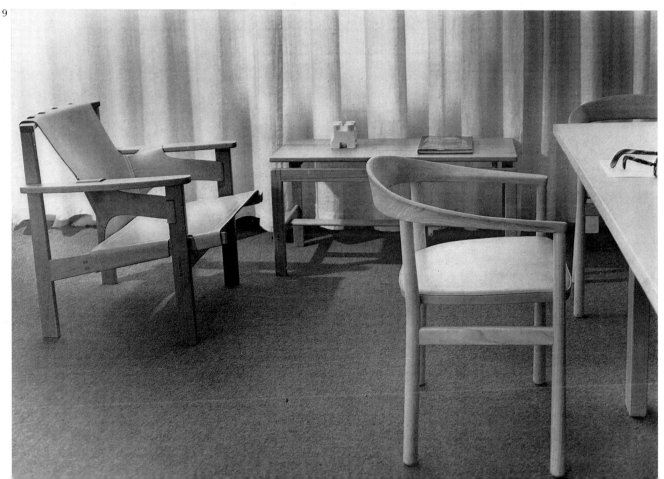

9

10: Cupboard in walnut with roll fronts, 145 cm. high, designed in 1947 by CARL-AXEL ACKING, Sweden, and made on a craftsman basis by *Nordiska Co. Ltd*. Salt-glazed stoneware urn by ARTHUR ANDERSSON, *Wallåkra* stoneware-works, 1948. In his comprehensive work as an architect, interior decorator and furniture-designer, Acking has also managed to design some pieces for handicraft production by cabinetmakers and by a large firm such as Nordiska. In these the means are not allowed to determine the end: they are fully thought-out, and have a character which plainly puts them in the 'mid-Twentieth Century', though at the same time their proportions show a timeless classic restraint.

11: Pinewood cupboard with adjustable shelving, height 160 cm. Designed in 1943 by AXEL LARSSON, Sweden, and made by *Swedish Furniture-works Ltd*. Pile-woven carpet, 150×180 cm., designed by MARIANNE RICHTER in 1950, *Märta Måås-Fjetterström Ltd*. This simple cupboard of common Swedish wood is on display at the National Museum, Stockholm. It is not what one ordinarily understands by a 'museum piece', with its unostentatious and practical form and everyday material, but is nevertheless worthy on its merits of a place among the best products of craftsmanship and industrial art. Larsson was already represented in the Stockholm Exhibition of 1930, and in the Forties and Fifties was prominent as an interior designer, and particularly a designer of furniture. Few have made as thorough a study of the function and construction of furniture, and this has been applied with good taste to handicraft pieces and to the mass-production of the 'Swedish Furniture' firm. He has the ability to think in industrial terms. Before he designed this cupboard he thoroughly studied the functions and dimensions required for storage, and could therefore make a fully considered arrangement of the shelves and trays. This is a typical Larsson piece, both in lay-out and external appearance: pure in style, well-proportioned, and classical.

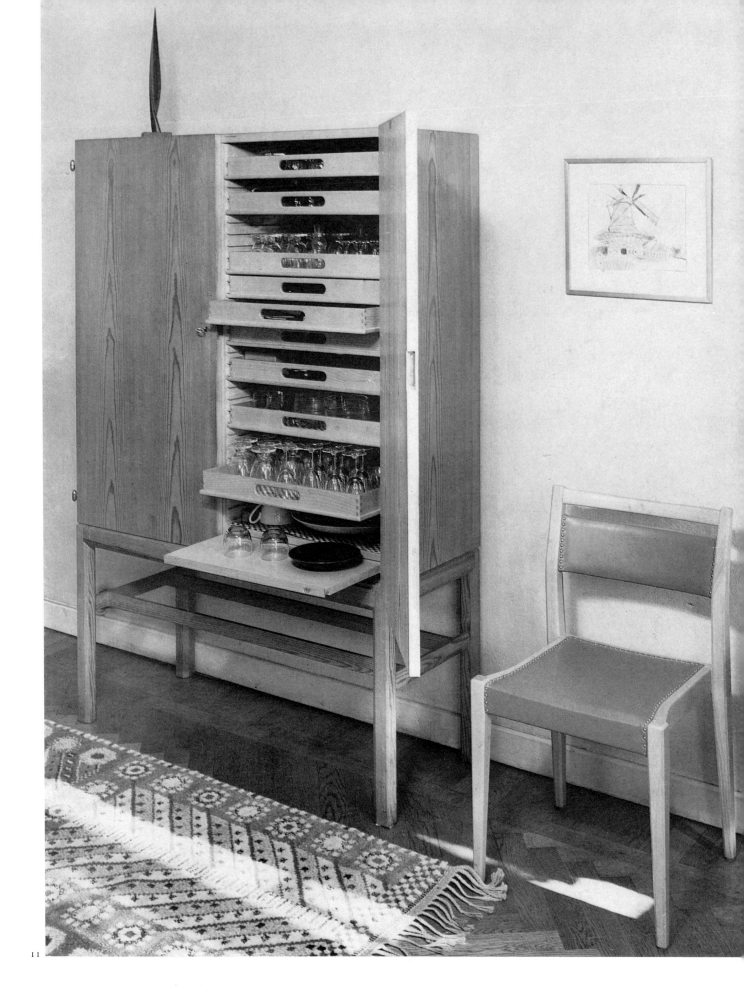

12: Oak dining-room furniture, designed
in 1959 by Björn Hultén, Sweden, and
made by *Bofyra Ltd*. Light-fitting by *Luxus*.
These pieces are notable for practicality
and a form adapted for industrial production, and may therefore be regarded as
typical of Swedish furniture of the present
day. All ornament has been avoided apart
from the skilfully exploited effects of the
material and purely structural details: the
means of expression lies in the proportions.

13: Armchairs in teak with plaited cane
back and upholstered cushion and in oak
with black leather: designed in 1958 by
Karl-Erik Ekselius, Sweden, and made
by *J. O. Carlsson Ltd*. The firm of J. O.
Carlsson is known for its high quality and
craftmanship. Ekselius, who is entirely
responsible for the appearance of its products, works on precisely these lines and
puts restraint and the right choice of material before experimentation. A classical
combination of materials such as mahogany with cane and leather is typical of
his work. The armchair may be regarded
as a demonstration-piece in its distinction
between 'bearing' and 'borne', in its construction, and its sitting-surfaces. The
simply-designed small tables may, with
the addition of thin cushions, be used as
stools.

12

13

14: Living-room in Skogshem Institute
for Supervisory Training of the Swedish
Employers' Confederation furnished by
Sven Kai-Larsen, 1958. Furniture in
Oregon pine, made by *Nordiska Co*. Kai-
Larsen represents a younger generation
of Swedish interior-decorators and furniture-designers, who work in a taut
and matter-of-fact style. Wood is their
material, and like their older colleagues
they are interested in its structural possibilities. But the wood is sawn up into
standard pieces of fixed dimensions, not
treated sculpturally, and these are set at
an angle to each other without rounded
joins. The distinction between the bearing
structure and the upholstered seat and
back surfaces is clearly expressed.

14

15

16

15: Armchair in bent oak or birch, with leather upholstery: designed in 1948 by ALVAR AALTO, Finland, for *Artek Ltd*. Artek pieces are put together on a systematic standardised basis, but their more expensive versions are intended for a very discriminating circle of customers. This chair, with its distinguished austere appearance and its unusually elegant leather-work, takes a place of honour in both spheres.

17

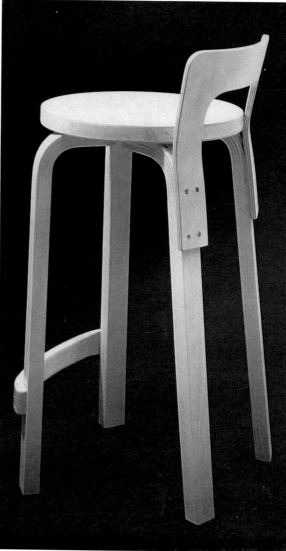

18

16: 'X' stools, designed by ALVAR AALTO in 1954 for *Artek*, Finland. The legs are birch or ash, the top ash or covered with leather: height 44 cm. This stool represents a further step towards more organic solutions of the assembly problem. Here Aalto has rejected separate screwed-in legs (as in fig. 18): these legs 'grow' from the seat, to which they are fastened with three mortice and tenon joints. Each leg is made of five identical laminated pieces. An elegant but not altogether economical construction: much material is wasted in production.

17: Chair of pressure-moulded plywood with metal legs, designed by OLLI BORG, Finland, and made by *Kervo* furniture-makers for the Palace Hotel in Helsinki, 1951. The seat and back are two plywood sheets fastened independently to the metal frame with 16 screws, which also form a decorative feature. This chair is used, for example, in the hotel's restaurant.

18: Stool in moulded birchwood, designed in 1936 by ALVAR AALTO, Finland, for *Artek*. This is a variant of Aalto's proto-type in bent birch. Before the legs are bent their ends are sawn and veneered: they are fastened to the seat with screws. The backrest and the height of the legs are additions to the ordinary stool, which is made three-legged. This construction has been copied in many countries.

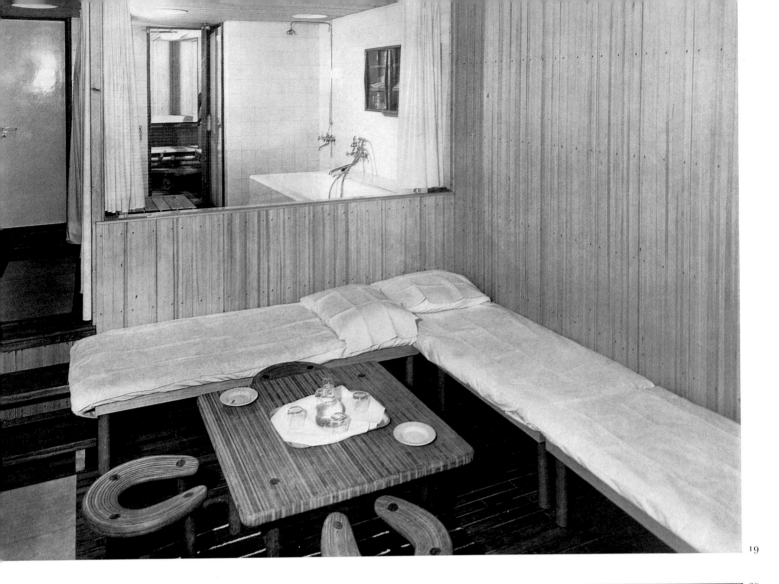

19: Bathroom interior in the Palace Hotel, Helsinki, designed in 1952 by ANTTI NURMESNIEMI. This is not the bathroom proper, but the room where one dries one-self and rests after the bath. Through the glass is seen the washing and shower room, and in the background the wood-lined bathroom itself with a sunlit sauna platform.

20: Bathroom stools in plywood with teak legs, and oak table, designed by ANTTI NURMESNIEMI in 1952 for the Palace Hotel, Helsinki. The rustic horseshoe-form of the stools is functional as well as amusing: they are for use by dripping-wet people drying off after bathing.

21

21: 'Lukki' chair in black-lacquered steel tubing with seat and back of pressure-moulded plastic-coated plywood covered with Teflon: designed 1951 by ILMARI TAPIOVAARA, Finland, for *Lukkiseppo*. Typical examples of Tapiovaara's solidly made, functional small chairs, which are all related in design. The prototype to 'Lukki' may be said to have been 'Domus', which was made in wood, but the metal legs make stacking easier. The quality of this chair is indicated by the fact that after ten years it still sells just as readily, and is used both in private homes and public buildings. It won a gold medal at the 1951 Triennale.

22

22: 'Kiki', fabric-covered metal chair, designed by ILMARI TAPIOVAARA in 1960 for *J. Merivaara Ltd*. Tapiovaara typically makes a virtue of allowing the principles and details of construction to appear plainly, and it is here that the greatest attraction of this chair lies. It won a gold medal at the 1960 Triennale.

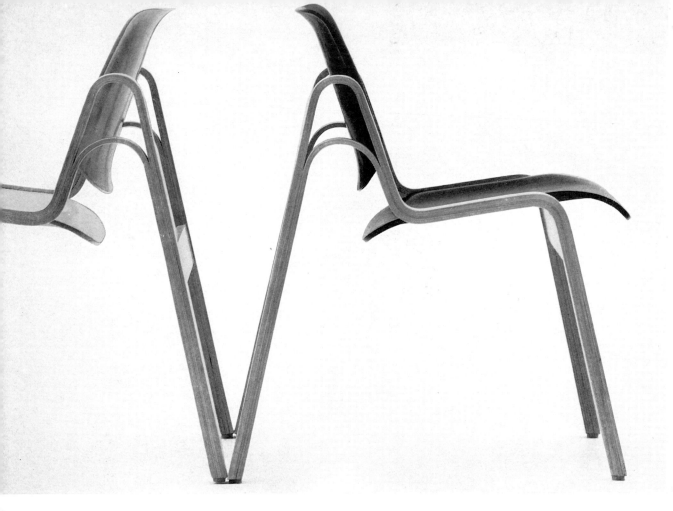

23

23–24: 'Wilhelmina' stacking chair in bent plywood, designed in 1960 by ILMARI TA-PIOVAARA, Finland, for *W. Schauman Ltd.* This is an ideal stacking chair on account of its interesting construction, by the so-called Fontana method. The plywood of the back legs has a supporting element grafted into the curve so that side struts between front and back legs can be eliminated. The seat and back are of pressure-moulded plywood, with or without covering. This chair is made for export: it is packed ready for assembly, and takes remarkably little space in transit – ten chairs in .55 cu.m. Gold medal at 1960 Triennale.

24

25: Blue-painted chair, designed for the *Norwegian Domestic Crafts Association* by AAGE SCHOU. It is based to a certain extent on old Norwegian folk-tradition, but Schou has given it in addition a modern styling, without detracting from its Norwegian character.

26: Table and chair for a lobby, designed by ALF STURE, Norway, and made in pinewood by *Hiorth & Østlyngen*. Panelling in same material. Chair covered with woollen fabric designed and made by ANNELISE KNUDTZON. Sture is one of those Norwegian furniture-designers who have contributed most to modern Scandinavian furniture construction. Several of his models from 1940 and later are of a pioneering nature. Early on he took up anatomical studies, and his construction of a chair's back-line according to medically sound principles appeared at a time when no other Scandinavian furniture-designer had realised the importance of this side of manufacture.

25

26

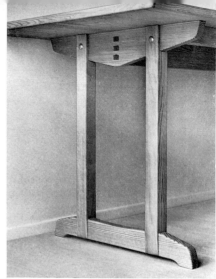

29

27: Chair designed in 1960 by the Norwegian interior-designer ARNE HALVOR-
SEN for *L. Jacobsen Furniture-works Ltd.*,
Egersund. Produced both in oak and teak:
based on a traditional form, and made at
a price which necessitates a simple and
practical construction. It shows complete
mastery in the design of details.

28: Occasional table, designed by the
Norwegian interior-designer ARNE HAL-
VORSEN in 1955 for *Solberg* furniture-
works, Ski. Made in teak, 160×55 cm.,
and can be dismantled and packed in a
carton 8 cm. high. Particular attention
has been given to craftsmanlike manufacture and to the selection of the materials
used.

29-30: Table in acid-stained pinewood,
lacquered turned-chair, and printed linen
fabric, designed by CARL MALMSTEN, Sweden, in 1945, 1940, and 1950 respectively.
It is hard to describe Malmsten's contribution to Swedish interior-decoration and
furniture-design, not to mention cultural
life in general, because it is so comprehensive. As early as 1916 he won first prize in
competition for furniture for Stockholm
Town Hall. He was one of those who
worked most actively for the programme
of the 'more beautiful everyday things'
movement before 1920, and was one of
the bitterest opponents of the Stockholm
Exhibition of 1930, i. e. of internationally-
inspired functionalism. He has always
been a passionate champion of creative
manual work. Malmsten is a poet philo-
sopher, with his roots in peasant culture
and bourgeois comfort. He has made expensive marquetry pieces, but also simple
everyday furniture. He is the most consistent active source of formative ideas for
the furniture, fabrics, and wall decoration
of the ordinary Swedish home. "His object is to achieve functional unity fully
combined with comfort–to give each
room the greatest possible habitability
and atmosphere by means of unconventional groupings and colour combinations." He has had a great influence on
craftwork and on the education of public
taste through his work as a teacher, lectures, exhibitions, and writings. Acid-stained pinewood is a traditional material,
with which he frequently works. The
turned chair he himself calls 'an elegant
spare structure': its painting in colour is
an old tradition in Swedish furniture. The
pottery on the table is by STIG LINDBERG.

28

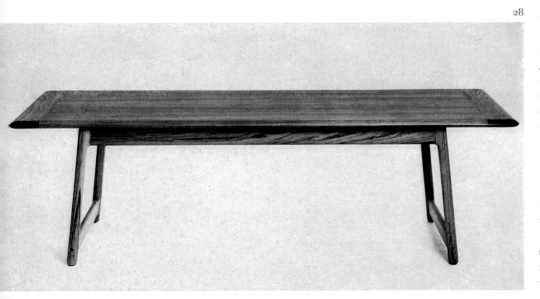

31: Chair in mahogany and Manilla cane with leather seat, and printed linen; designed by JOSEF FRANK, Sweden, in 1948 and 1956 respectively and made by *Svenskt Tenn Ltd*. Frank represents a special line in Swedish furniture, of which his own work is indeed the most typical example but which has decidedly had an important, if rather indefinable, influence. Frank was trained as a designer at the beginning of the century in Vienna, where a typically practical but also likable style was then in the ascendant. Its most prominent representative was Josef Hoffmann, founder of the Wiener Werkstätte. Frank's early work was in this pre-functionalist style. In 1927 he took part in the Stuttgart domestic exhibition which was so important in the development of functionalism. Since 1934 he has worked for the house-furnishing business of Svenskt Tenn in Stockholm, a firm which in a way fulfils in that city the function of the Wiener Werkstätte. Frank designs practically all its output of furniture, fabrics, and light-fittings, besides glass, metal, and objets d'art, as well as whole interiors. His style combines Viennese charm with international matter-of-factness, producing things which are bright and pleasantly gay while always being usable.

31

32

32: Cabinet in mahogany covered with natural-coloured calfskin, designed in 1952 by JOSEF FRANK, Sweden, and made by *Svenskt Tenn Ltd*. The use of choice materials and an austere but attractive form are characteristic of Frank. This cabinet with its many drawers is supported by a wooden frame and covered with such an appropriately exclusive material as natural calf. Narrow gold lines, stamped in the leather as in bookbinding, emphasise the separate drawers, which are further accentuated by the bronze handles.

33: Easy chair of laminated plywood and webbing, modelled by BRUNO MATHSSON, Sweden, 1941, and produced by the firm of *Karl Mathsson*.

Mathsson's chair structures are light and elastic, in a fashion now no longer unusual but which was something new and characteristic of him when this chair was first made.

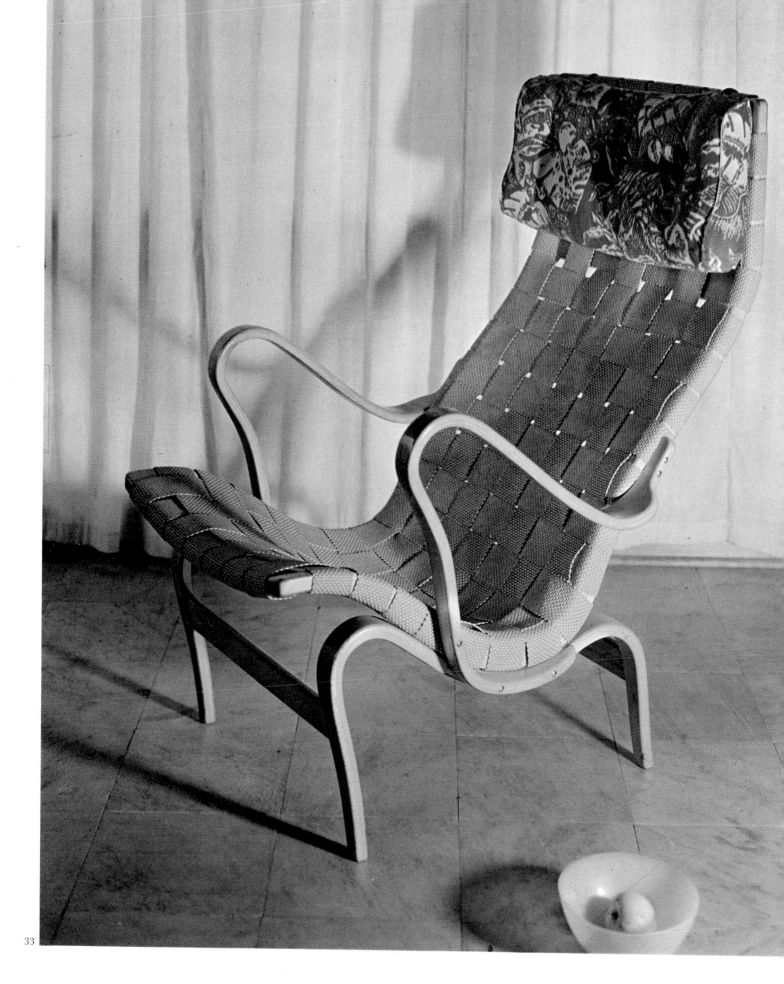

34

was to bring intelligible order into the furnishings of the home. Its working principle was that a careful and patient general study of the functional needs of his work was prerequisite to give the furniture-designer the necessary width of view to produce a generally valid and quite simple solution. Mogens Koch's structural bookcases are the best example of the potentialities of this method of work. With them he solves the problems of book-storage in a manner which has the simplicity of genius. The basic element of this series is a *reversible* box partitioned into small permanent divisions so arranged that inside the rectangle are spaces of three different heights corresponding to the commonest book-formats. Waste space is thus reduced to a minimum. This method of division has the structural advantage that the thickness of the material can be considerably less than in bookcases with separate adjustable shelves. The range includes periodical-cases, under-cupboards for office equipment, record-cases, sets of drawers, etc. The library chair on the right is an improved version of a well-known collapsible outdoor chair; when folded all its parts lie within the width of the front legs.

34: Interior from Villa Mairea, designed by ALVAR AALTO and carried out by *Artek*, Finland, 1939. This house in Norrmark, designed by Aalto for Maire and Harry Gullichsen, was intended for the director of a firm in central Finland, but has also become a Mecca for architects and interior-designers from all over the world. Aalto designed the entire furnishing of the villa, and, together with Maison Carré at Bazoches near Paris, it is the most representative and clear-cut example of the Artek style and Aalto's interior-decoration, in which the slightest details are carefully considered.

35: Structural bookcases and library chair, designed 1928 and 1957 by MoGENS KOCH, Denmark; made in mahogany by *Rud. Rasmussen*'s workshops. In foreground, table and chair designed by KAARE KLINT for the same workshops, and table-lamp designed by Klint for *Le Klint Ltd.* (see text to fig. 70).

Part of the programme of the Klint school

36: Armchair in ipé or palisander, designed in 1951 by OLE WANSCHER, Denmark, and produced by *Rud. Rasmussen*'s workshops. The 'unsupported arm' motif has become popular with Danish designers in the last decade, and nearly all have tried it. Finn Juhl, Børge Mogensen, and Hans J. Wegner, amongst others, have worked on the structural and aesthetic possibilities of the 'broken sternpost'. Wanscher, whose most important output has close affinities with English mahogany furniture of the Eighteenth Century, has also let himself be tempted. In his version the arm-rest shoots boldly forth from the upright in a construction which demands carefully selected wood and first-class craftsmanship. The unsupported arm gives the chair lightness and grace, an impression enhanced by the appearance that back and seat are about to take leave of each other and of the frame. This separateness of the several elements is typical of modern types of chair.

35

37: Chair in oiled beechwood, designed in 1947 by Børge Mogensen, Denmark, for the *Danish C.W.S.* Oak table designed in 1958 by Mogensen for *Karl Andersson & Sons*, Sweden. Lampshade designed in 1958 by Poul Henningsen for *Louis Poulsen & Co.* Curtain (1957) and carpet (1959) designed by Vibeke Klint for *C. Olesen's* Cotil collection.

The basic type which Kaare Klint introduced into Danish furniture with his chair for Grundtvig's church (see fig. 73) was developed further by his pupils. In the dining-chair shown here Mogensen has further simplified the type and made an entirely modern chair, stout enough to withstand daily wear but light and small enough to suit modern living-habits based on the conditions of the small apartment. The table is also a traditional type, of matter-of-fact and practical cut: its prototype was developed in the Nineteenth Century by craftsmen of the North American sect of Shakers.

38–39: Dining furniture in oak and teak, with brass light-fitting, designed by Hans J. Wegner, Denmark, for furniture-maker *Johannes Hansen:* chair 1949.

Hans Wegner is the outstanding Danish chair-designer. His models are stout and bluff, with massive dimensions, and the details are rounded-off so that they stand up to everyday wear and are easy to live with. Their form combines tradition and modernity. In a long series of chairs designed for furniture-makers, Wegner has given special attention to the form of the back-and-arm piece. The frame of this chair, which may be regarded as a classic in Danish furniture, is a familiar, simple, and stable structure, but the uppermost element has received a sculptural treatment which is entirely Wegner's own. The arm- and back-rests, which join each other with a taut curve, completely fulfil

their functional purpose; but in its bluff modelling Wegner has given this chair an additional artistic value which derives less from function than from the material and its potentialities. In such work with the structure and material qualities of wood, Wegner is doing much the same as modern sculptors. Fig. 39 shows the right half of the upper member, and the detail shows with what a sure touch Wegner forms his wood into mobile curves without overtaxing its capabilities. The arms-and-back piece is assembled from three sections of wood, so that the line of the grain is correct both in the arms and back. This method of assembly is not only structurally right but also decoratively beautiful. The joins between the teak upper member and the oak underframe are marked by a slight interruption of line.

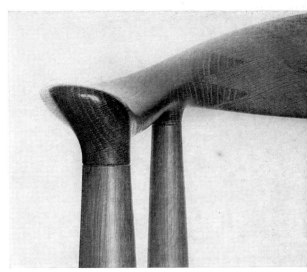

39

40

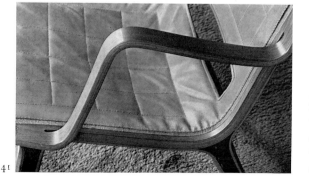

41

40–41: 'Ax' furniture, table and chair in beech and mahogany, chair-seat covered with leather. Designed 1950 by PETER HVIDT and O. MØLGAARD NIELSEN, Denmark, and made by *Fritz Hansen Ltd*.

The major part of the Danish furniture industry may be regarded as rationalised and specialised handwork. Only very recently has there arisen in Denmark an economically sound mass-production industry with sufficient finance to invest in machinery, which makes a complete break with methods of manufacture derived from manual work. Not only has the complete dominance of wood given way to an increasing use of materials such as steel, fibre-glass, and plastic, but wood itself has become a different material with industrial methods of treatment. By cutting into plywood, steam-bending, and various pressure-moulding techniques, wood has become plastic. With their 'Ax' pieces, Hvidt and Nielsen are among the pioneers in this development. The chairs of this series are made with bearing sideframes of beech veneer surrounding a mahogany core. The seat and back may be made of pressure-moulded plywood sheets fixed into a groove in the sidepieces, or, as here, with suspended padded surfaces covered with leather on one side and fabric on the other. Fig. 41 shows the characteristic sidepiece construction: the broad plywood strips are quite simply slit along the middle, and one side drawn upwards to form an armrest while the other is bent downwards to make the frame for seat and back.

42: Armchair in teak with upholstered seat and back, designed in 1945 by FINN JUHL, Denmark, and made by *Niels Vodder*. Flat-weave rug designed and made in 1954 by VIBEKE KLINT. Wood-sculpture by ERIK THOMMESEN.

Finn Juhl's pieces are not as types unusual for the period, but their form shows a clear break from the Danish tradition represented by the work of Klint and his pupils. Juhl consciously rejects artistic influences from the furniture art of earlier times, and aims to give his pieces a value of their own deriving its strength from their affinity in form with modern abstract art.

43: Chair with frame of matt chromium-plated spring-steel, seat-and-back element in cane weave. Designed by POUL KJÆR-HOLM, Denmark, 1957, for *E. Kold Christensen Ltd*. Flat-weave carpet designed and made by VIBEKE KLINT, 1960, for the wedding-room in Tårnby Town Hall, Copenhagen.

Wood is the principal material in modern Danish furniture, but Kjærholm exploits the peculiar potentialities of steel. In his chairs, for example, he has worked with its elastic properties, thereby increasing comfort. In this model the cane-weave is stretched between two elastic side-elements which are not—as in traditional rigid wooden structures—connected at the front edge of the seat and at the top of the back. The weave is merely reinforced at these points with a thicker edge. This untraditional construction means that the person sitting is not bothered by a rigid crossbar behind his shoulders or under his legs. The weave gives naturally to the pressure of the body.

44: Chair designed by ARNE JACOBSEN, Denmark, 1960, and made by *Fritz Hansen Ltd*. Photographed in the Royal Hotel, Copenhagen, which was built in 1960 to Jacobsen's plans.

In upholstered furniture as well, new techniques have inspired hitherto unknown forms. In this chair the broad open bowl is 'baked' with plastic material in a mould; and just as dough rises and hardens in the oven, so this material expands and solidifies when the mould is heated. The plastic bowl is then covered with foam-rubber of varying thickness. This new technique combines great strength with a lightness unusual in upholstered furniture.

44

45

46

45–46: Easy chair in oak, with seat and back in uncoloured stretched hide. Designed 1958 by Børge Mogensen, Denmark, and made by *Fredericia Chair-factory*. Rug in Faroese wool, designed and made in 1944 by Lis Ahlmann.

It is characteristic of modern Danish furniture that designers prefer to use 'natural' materials: untreated and well-worked wood rather than stained or painted, uncoloured leather rather than coloured furnishing-fabric. In this preference lies the wish to make their pieces with first-class materials whose properties gain rather than lose by the effects of daylight and everyday use. Mogensen likes to put together untreated oak and uncoloured ox-hide, as in this chair, in whose straight lines and broad arm-rests one may detect Spanish inspiration. The detail on fig. 46 shows how the sewing and edging of the leather is as thorough as in exclusive saddlery.

47: Group of furniture with table and chair designed 1957 by POUL KJÆRHOLM, Denmark. Table and chair made by *E. Kold Christensen Ltd.*

Kjærholm's desire for austerity in artistic expression, matched with a fastidious choice of materials and an uncompromising demand for technical quality, have parallels in an important element in modern Danish architecture. Their exclusive standard of quality for the most part confines his pieces to public buildings and wealthy homes, but it is precisely in such cases that these uncompromising ideas have produced their best and most clear-cut results in architecture. As in Kjærholm's furniture, what we find here is a combination of influences derived both from Japan and from the Bauhaus, Dessau.

48: Group of furniture in untreated light oak, designed 1958–59 by PETER HJORTH and ARNE KARLSEN, Denmark, for *Interna*. Cover of sleeping-bench designed by LIS AHLMANN and BØRGE MOGENSEN for *C. Olesen's* Cotil collection.

After the Second World War, Danish furniture went through a period of artistic uncertainty. The contemporary demand for novelty, and the cult of artistic individualism, to some extent forced younger artists into a situation where they lost sight of their purpose. In reaction against the aggressive assertion of individuality in international furniture, and to counteract the general tendency to make pieces—especially chairs—into contrived expressionistic sculptures, a group of younger designers looked to some of the ideas of the early Thirties for fresh inspiration. Simplicity of structure has again become the chief consideration, and once more furniture is intended to fit unobtrusively —but not therefore with less aesthetic value—into the room. Straight lines are favoured where there is no functional need for curved forms, and the angles are left sharp where there is no practical necessity to round them off. Hjorth and Karlsen are representative of this young group of modern Danish designers.

48

49: 'Pine-cone' light-shade in copper, designed 1958 by POUL HENNINGSEN, Denmark, for *Louis Poulsen & Co. Ltd.*: diameter 84 cm. This photograph, taken in the Danish Industrial Art Museum in Copenhagen, also shows Henningsen's original drawing for this fitting, as well as a pile-woven carpet designed and made in 1932 by GERDA HENNING: diameter 450 cm. With this shade, originally designed for a Copenhagen restaurant, Henningsen has shown that gaily decorative lighting can be based on technical and scientific principles and on analysis of functional needs. The warm light it gives out is the result of pink coloration on the undersides of the matt copper scales.

49

50

50: 'PH-5' shade in sheet metal, designed 1958 by POUL HENNINGSEN, Denmark, for *Louis Poulsen & Co.*: diameter 50 cm. Henningsen was a protagonist of functionalism, and clearly expressed the movement's principles in his shades where fitness for purpose is central to the design. Ever since he designed his first shade in 1924, he has based his work on scientific analysis of a shade's functions – to intercept, direct, and give tone to the light. Henningsen's shades are all made of separate elements, shaped and assembled in such a way that they cover the bulb and direct the light down upon the table without the rays being reflected more than once. Besides this they give a general light in the room, so that the contrast between the illumination of walls and table is not too marked. Within the shade itself the light is distributed so as to lessen the intensity towards the outer edge of each separate element. In this way Henningsen has avoided the abrupt transition from light to darkness which we find, for example, with an ordinary spherical pendant shade in opal glass. To bring the rather harsh white light from the modern bulb closer to the red end of the spectrum, Henningsen has given the inner side of one element of the shade a red colour.

51

52

51: Toys in painted and unpainted beechwood, designed and first made in 1935 by KAY BOJESEN, Denmark: height of largest dolls 17 cm. The silversmith Bojesen also works in wood: besides his silver vessels and cutlery he has made many kinds of toy – monkeys and bears, horses and cattle, cars and ships, men and women, plain or painted in bright colours. All show his sense of fun and his love for children. Bojesen meets every single requirement for modern toys: his products are strong enough to stand up to the rough-and-tumble of the playroom, sufficiently simple in form and colour to leave room for the child to use his own imagination, and suitable for constructive play.

52: 'Krenit' bowls in pressed and enamelled steel, designed in 1953 by HERBERT KRENCHEL, Denmark, for *Torben Ørskov & Co.*: diameter of larger bowl 25 cm. After a vast amount of experiment, the civil engineer Krenchel has made it possible to produce such bowls from millimetre-thick steel plate. They are machine-pressed cold, and subsequently enamelled in black and colours. They are made in seven sizes, with eight different internal colours, are acid-resisting, and can be put direct on to a fire. These bowls have no rival in mass-produced ware.

53: Trays and containers of styrene plastic: trays (larger 30 × 40 cm.) designed by STIG LINDBERG, 1957; containers (7–16 cm. high) by CARL ARNE BREGER, 1958. Made by *Gustavsberg* works, Sweden. There are many different kinds of plastic: styrene stands comparatively high temperatures and resists shock, and is therefore suitable for articles in household use. Also, as shown, it can be pleasingly coloured. Since plastic is easy to work and colour, it has, at least earlier on, been a happy hunting ground for uncouth forms and glaring hues. But it is not too much to say that the Swedish plastic industry has made a careful search for better solutions, and has employed good artists. In this Gustavsberg has been an example to other firms.

54: Dishes in plywood, designed 1951 by TAPIO WIRKKALA, Finland, for *Stockmann Ltd.*: length 24 and 48 cm. The American magazine *House Beautiful* described one of Wirkkala's dishes in aircraft plywood as the 'world's most beautiful object of 1951'. The same year some of his works in this medium won him several Grands Prix in Milan. Here are shown two examples of forms in the same series which have seldom been published. He has also used the effects of this technique in his tables, where the plywood is inlaid like a kind of marquetry as a decorative element on the table surface.

53

54

55: Suite designed by ALF STURE, Norway, and made by *Hiorth & Østlyngen:* chairs covered with woollen fabric designed by ANNELISE KNUDTZON and produced by *Røros Tweed Ltd.* Sture's furniture has features traceable to Norwegian folk-art, but also an individual element. Tapestry designed by HAAKON STENSTADVOLD especially for this room, the board-room of the Norwegian Meat and Bacon Board, and made by ELSE HALLING at *Norwegian Tapestries Ltd.* The material is wool from 'Old Norwegian' sheep, a variety which is most frequently used in Norwegian tapestry work. It has a quality which results from many years of experiment, and is so soft and glossy that the completed tapestry has a depth of colour beyond the reach of the artist's original scheme. Light-fitting designed by JONAS HIDLE and made at *Høvik* works.

56–57: Dual-purpose table, designed by BENDT WINGE, Norway, and made in teak at *Arna* works. In its higher position this table can be used for dining, with space for eight people. The height in this case is 72 cm., and the extended top 130 × 130 cm. In the lower position it serves as an occasional table, with a height of 52 cm. and a top of 65 × 130 cm. Note the distance between the table-top and the embroidery on the wall in each case.

55

56

57

58

58: Chair in fumed oak, designed 1960 by BENDT WINGE, Norway, for *Aase* turnery-works. The seat and back are fixed to the leg structure with a simple catch, which makes this chair easy to transport. Winge has been for years one of the pioneer Norwegian furniture-designers.

59: Chair in fumed oak with sea-grass seat and back, designed by the Norwegian furniture-designer BENDT WINGE, 1958, made by *Kleppe* furniture-works. This is an ancient type of chair, especially common in Jaeren south of Stavanger. Winge has transposed it into a modern idiom, well-suited for mass-production.

59

60

60: Low armchair of Honduras mahogany, designed by BENDT WINGE, Norway, 1960, for *Møbelindustri Co.*, Egersund. This was designed specially for export: the legs splay out sufficiently for a large number to be stacked on top of each other.

61

61: Oak fireside chair, designed by ROLF RASTAD and ADOLF RELLING, Norway, and made by *Dokka Furniture*. Front and rear legs are at the same angle, and the arm-rests are designed to correspond. This gives the chair an intentional square effect. Rastad and Relling have for years designed all their models in collaboration.

62: Low armchair in teak and leather, designed by the Norwegian interior designers ROLF RASTAD and ADOLF RELLING. This chair was planned for industrial production, and is made by *Bahus* at Os near Bergen. Special care is taken in its manufacture, which maintains craftsmanlike standards throughout.

63: High armchair in teak with cane seat, a variant of no. 62, and designed and made by the same sources.

64: Dining table and chairs in teak, designed by ROLF RASTAD and ADOLF RELLING for *Bahus*, Os, near Bergen. The chairs have seats of light coloured leather. In recent years the Norwegian furniture industry has achieved such high standards of quality that much of its output will stand comparison with the best produced by hand craftsmen.

63

64

65: Chair in teak, with adjustable back and seat, designed by FREDRIK A. KAYSER, Norway, 1960, and made by *Vatne* armchair works. This is a conscious attempt to improve on a common Norwegian type. It is mass-produced, and the quality of its production is highly satisfactory.

66: Armchair in teak and leather, designed by the Norwegian interior-designer TORBJØRN AFDAL and mass-produced by *Nesjestranda* furniture-works.

67: Book case and storage unit, with table, designed by IB JUUL CHRISTIANSEN for *Soltvedt* furniture-works, Florvåg, Norway. The chair, like the shelving, is in teak, and has a cane seat: designed by ROLF RASTAD and ADOLF RELLING for *Bahus*, Os, near Bergen. Light-fitting designed by BIRGER DAHL and put into production by *Sønnico*.

66

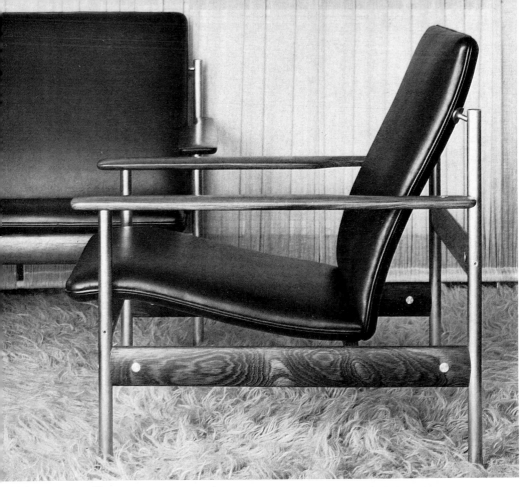

68

69

68: Settee and armchair in palisander, chromium-plated steel, and black leather, designed by SVEN IVAR DYSTHE for *Dokka Furniture*. Dysthe is one of the youngest Norwegian furniture-designers; but, more than promising, he has already shown himself able to introduce new developments. These pieces can be dismantled for transport. Dysthe has also designed a table and armless chair in the same series.

69: Chair of solid steel and leather, designed by the Norwegian interior-designer TORMOD ALNÆS, 1958. The materials were chosen to allow independence of line, and possibilities for industrial production were a secondary consideration.

70: Chair and writing-desk with separate chest-of-drawers, designed in 1930 and 1933 respectively by KAARE KLINT, Denmark, and made in Cuba mahogany by *Rud. Rasmussen*'s workshops. Top of desk and seat and back of chair covered in leather. The top section of the chest-of-drawers holds a typewriter, which with the help of a hinge can be swung out and up to the proper height.

Klint made several of his most important types of furniture in the years around 1930. Starting with a thorough, scientific investigation of requirements, he designed a series of storage units whose internal dimensions were determined by the size of the articles to be kept in them. Their exterior was plain and objective, and fitted closely around the things inside. The artistic quality of this writing-desk derives from mid-Eighteenth Century English furniture, and through this also from Chinese examples. If the chair shown here is compared with one by Chippendale, it will be seen that Klint has transposed the solid and structurally-built lower part almost unaltered, but with the back he has abandoned the open and highly ornate framework of the original. The padded back is taken from another chair-type of that period, with leather-covered seat and back but rococo legs. By thus combining functional details from two chairs he has adopted the structural joinery of the period but has avoided its 'period' styling.

71

72

71–72: Silverware cupboard in palisander, designed 1937 by RIGMOR ANDERSEN, Denmark, and made by *Rud. Rasmussen's* workshops. Stoneware bowl with sculptured relief ornamentation, made in 1935 by AXEL SALTO for the *Royal Copenhagen Porcelain Manufactory.* Flat-weave carpet with blue and green stripes, designed and made by LIS AHLMANN, 1938.

Like Kaare Klint, his pupils also made a careful study of storage units. The artistic effect of this silver-cupboard lies in its quite simple relative proportions and in the exquisite workmanship of its precisely defined unbroken surfaces of wood. Its breadth is exactly twice its depth, so that when the doors are opened they fold back closely to the sides and completely cover them. At the corners the doors and the sides of the cabinet meet at less than 45 deg., so that the thickness of the sides is not apparent from the front. The unit therefore appears as a compact block, into the surface of which the elegant brass fittings are inset. Behind each door are five drawers, with fronts all of equal height but with interiors subdivided horizontally by inserted shelves. The detail on fig. 72 shows the precise bevelling of the edges and the finely made fingerholds in ebony, which lie inset in the surface like the brass fittings.

73: Chair designed 1933 by KAARE KLINT, Denmark, for Grundtvig's Church, and made in beechwood by *Fritz Hansen Ltd.* Klint did not look for inspiration only to Eighteenth Century England. He used serviceable details from any age and culture which suited his constant concern for the functional. When he had to design a chair for use in Copenhagen's Grundtvig Church (built to the designs of his father, P. V. Jensen Klint, (1853–1930) and completed by Klint himself) he made an improved version of the simple folk-type found everywhere in French and Italian churches. It proved an excellent chair for its purpose, so uncommitted and timeless in character that it soon found its way into homes. It was Klint's only mass-production piece.

74: Sideboard and chest-of-drawers in teak with brass fittings, designed 1958 by Børge Mogensen, Denmark, for *P. Lauritsen & Sons* furniture-works. Left, chair designed by Mogensen for the Danish C.W.S. (see text to fig. 37).

Klint designed his furniture as types, not as unique pieces, and many of his models are therefore the natural forerunners of the rationalised mass-production of today. In making storage units for the home, his basic principles of design have been influential and his aesthetic ideals have also been adopted. Like Klint, Mogensen has worked with a simple block. In these austere storage units he has adapted Klint's clear division of pieces into simple box-forms from exclusive hand-work to industrial production of high quality. The sideboard doors are each in two sections, reducing to a minimum the space which must be kept clear in front.

73

74

75: Chair in oiled beechwood, designed 1950 by HANS J. WEGNER, Denmark, for *Carl Hansen & Son*. In Danish furniture, Chinese influences are not confined to storage pieces. In this completely modern industrial chair the traces are slight but the line of descent goes back–through earlier models designed by Wegner–right to the Chinese chair in the Copenhagen Museum of Industrial Art. The steam-bent backpiece, the elegantly curved conclusion of the rear uprights, and the broad backboard (in this case cut into Y-form) are all elements deriving from traditional Chinese chair-types.

76: Folding chair in fumed oak with caneplait seat and back: designed by HANS J. WEGNER, Denmark, and made by the furniture-maker *Johannes Hansen*, 1949.

75

76

Behind, cupboards, bookcase, and radio designed 1960 by PETER HJORTH. Rug designed and made 1958 by VIBEKE KLINT. This easy chair is in principle just as simple as other Danish collapsible furniture shown in this section; but its sculptural massiveness and the organic flow of its side-pieces and struts distinguish it from the conscious lack of period of other models, and it draws its artistic strength from Wegner's highly individual grasp of form. When folded it has a curved surface. On the crossbar between the front legs is a notch by which it can be hung on a peg in the wall.

77–78: Folding stool in ash with seat of natural coloured canvas, designed c. 1933 by KAARE KLINT, Denmark, and made by *Rud. Rasmussen's* workshops. Furniture pieces with a mechanical element–principally collapsible chairs and tables–now form a numerically large part of Danish output. The range is not comprehensive, but several types have been made, and for a mathematically-minded nature such as Klint's the idea of complete collapsibility was a standing challenge. In this little stool the original structural idea, masterly in its simplicity, is an artistic element in itself. Each pair of legs, as shown in fig. 78, is cut out of a single round bar of wood.

79: Deck-chair in teak, with cushion covered with natural coloured canvas, designed 1933 by KAARE KLINT, Denmark, and made by *Rud. Rasmussen's* workshops. Klint made the further improvement of common types of furniture the principal objective of his school. For example, he found in the deck-chair–known to most people from passenger-liners–a model entirely suitable for modern use. He developed it in such a way that its mechanics functioned perfectly, and had it made with first-class materials and craftsmanship. When folded up the chair makes a compact block, with the taut curves completely coinciding. The small folding table in the background, with its screwed-on raised rims which leave the corners clear, is likewise a refinement of a well-known piece of ship-furniture.

77

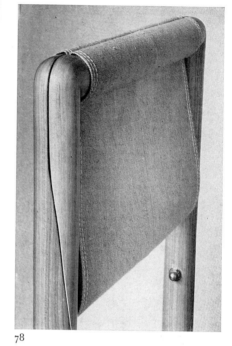

78

79

80

81

80–81: Collapsible chairs and table, designed by MOGENS KOCH, Denmark, in 1938 and 1960 respectively, and made by *Interna*. Chairs in beechwood with seats and backs of unbleached linen; table with beech underframe and teak top. Koch is another furniture-designer who has worked on the improvement of stout traditional types of chairs and open-air furniture, and he has thereby achieved a completely simple structure – the bare bones of a chair. These chairs depend for their aesthetic effect purely on the structural clarity and precise dimensions of their frames. In this case the light folding chair of the film director has been his starting point, and it says something for the universal validity of this type that though designed in 1938 it was first put into mass-production in 1960. Fig. 81 shows some of the special brass fittings, and how the upper part of the cross-legs is bevelled on the inner side to allow the chair to be folded up tightly without catching the material of the seat. The table can also be folded up, and in the closed position the underframe fits in between the cross-bars on which the slats of the top are screwed. The top is not a complete circle, but has a segment missing parallel with the slats on two sides, so that two or more tables may be set in a row with their straight edges touching.

82: Chair in cane and basket work, designed in 1958 by TORSTEN JOHANSSON, Denmark, and made by *R. Wengler*.
The structural properties of cane are so unique that it can hardly be replaced by any other material. It is tough, pliant, and if used properly is easy to shape. It is light, and chairs made of it are comfortably springy. But binding up a bamboo chair frame and then weaving a bowl-form to sit in must always be a manual task: for this reason cane furniture, in spite of its unpretentious material, is nowadays comparatively expensive. Nevertheless it is precisely these special properties which have allowed Danish basket-makers to survive industrialisa-

82

tion, though only with a small and exclusive production.

83: Chair in cane and basket work, designed 1951 by NANNA and JØRGEN DITZEL, Denmark, and made by *R. Wengler*. Basketry is a craft whose forms are to a great extent determined by its material, and it has therefore been only slightly affected by changes in style. Even so, this has not prevented the development of new forms. This chair is something new, but it does not overstep the natural limits of the material. Like traditional basketry it draws its artistic value from the material's unity and handsome fabric-like character.

83

84

84: Easy chair in teak with padded seat, back, and armrests covered in leather. Designed 1949 by FINN JUHL, Denmark, and made by the furniture-maker *Niels Vodder*. Juhl's pieces emphasise the 'bearing' and the 'borne'. The component parts of these chairs thus divide into upholstered 'flakes' which support the sitter where required, and an open wooden frame supporting the upholstered element. Their artistic tension springs from the vital balance between the slender curves of the frame and the solidity of the upholstered parts.

85: Armchair in teak, with padded seat and back covered in natural leather: designed 1960 by EJNER LARSEN and A. BENDER MADSEN, and made by the furniture-maker *Willy Beck*. The two furniture-designers Larsen and Madsen have spent years on the continual improvement of a few types, in which they have constantly repeated the same structural and artistic motifs. This chair is thus the latest of a long series in which they have used an arm-and-back element of moulded plywood. The characteristic crosspieces, designed to allow plenty of vertical space for the legs of the sitter, with their smoothly curved horizontal profile, are also a persistent element in their chair models.

85

86–87: Cedarwood bed, designed and made 1943 by PEDER MOOS, Denmark. Unique pieces of furniture, made in one specimen only, are rare nowadays: and a furniture-maker who designs and makes his models single-handed is a rare individual. In this bed we see the craftsman's delight in his own breadth of skill expressed in a smoothly modelled large piece achieved by gluing together small laths. Influences from the Art Nouveau period survive in Danish furniture in Peder Moos' ideas of form.

87

86

88: Dining-chair in palisander, with padded seat covered in black leather: designed 1956 by OLE WANSCHER, Denmark, and made by furniture-maker *A. J. Iversen*. The new materials available to industry have allowed greater freedom in chair-design than hand-craftsmen have yet caught up with. But with many new types of chair before them, craftsmen have also felt the desire to break away from the purely static structure supported in all directions. An entire series of modern Danish chairs has thus used backrests with prominent projections. In this elegant example Wanscher shows how boldly a craftsman's chair may be made, without its untraditional form seeming unnatural in relation to traditional technique. The slender backrest is made from two pieces glued together in the middle. In this way the form follows the run of the grain as far as possible, and the danger of breakage is minimised.

89: Fireside chair in teak, with padded seat covered in black leather: designed 1940 by TOVE and EDVARD KINDT-LARSEN, Denmark, and made by *Gustav Bertelsen & Co.* Despite its robust form, this is light compared with other easy chairs. With its tightly padded continuous seat-and-back element, it combines the lightness of a wooden with the comfort of a heavily upholstered chair. When it appeared it was a structural innovation, and its method of construction has been repeatedly adapted by other designers with widely differing results. Compare, for example, Finn Juhl's version of 1945, shown in fig. 42.

89

90: Chair in laminated beechwood, designed 1957 by ARNE JACOBSEN, Denmark, and made by *Fritz Hansen Ltd.* Jacobsen's finest work in furniture is found in his pressure-moulded plywood chairs. Starting with the three-legged dining-chair of 1953 shown below, he has designed a long series of excellent models for various purposes. In this example the underframe is also made of laminated wood. Like the rest of Jacobsen's pieces, this is international in cut but Danish in its elegant polish and the care with which it has been made. It is mass-produced, but not ejected from a slot-machine. Its creation is jealously watched from plywood to finished chair. Its elastic body has gone through many tests before it is allowed to leave the factory for the user (in this case a single-family house planned by Jacobsen).

91: Chair in black-treated pressure-moulded beech plywood: designed 1953 by ARNE JACOBSEN, Denmark, for *Fritz Hansen Ltd.* This small chair is a classic example of a perfected industrial product. It is comfortable to sit on, and full use is made of the springy qualities of the steel and the plywood. It can be stacked, takes little space in the small modern dwelling, is cheap to buy, and strong in use. In spite of its highly individual and elegant form, it is perhaps the most popular of modern Danish pieces of furniture. Its popularity arises from its harmony with other modern products such as scooters, small cars, and modern kitchen-ware in enamel and stainless steel.

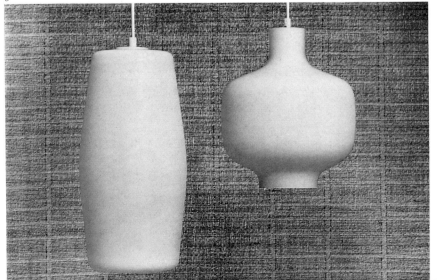

92

93

96

94

95

92: Lampshade of plastic ribbon stretched over wire frame, made 1954 by BENGT JOHAN GULLBERG, Sweden. As a material, plastic has gone its triumphant way with many abortive experiments; but it is plainly now beginning to find a style of its own, at least in Sweden. In that country much care has been taken in working out the appropriate uses and forms for this easily worked and very useful but potentially dangerous substance. Gullberg, who is full of ideas, has constructed his shades on a simple but effective system in which the strips of plastic are so placed that in combination they cover the bulb and at the same time give a decorative effect.

93: 'Fruit lamp' shade in folded paper, designed 1944 by KAARE KLINT, Denmark, for *Le Klint Ltd*. Height 54 cm. The folded lampshade was invented as early as 1901 in the home of the builder of Grundtvig's Church, P. V. Jensen Klint. "My father did various jobs in pottery, including a base for a paraffin lamp," wrote Kaare Klint in 1943, "and then he set out to make a folded shade of character, to match the base. It was one evening, I remember, and father's friend Captain Jeppe Hagedorn, who was on a visit, was also put to work to give the shade a vertical neck. That evening the solution was found, and to the joy of all the family it was the captain who discovered it. Later on we children taught others the art; and I remember how cleverly my friend the architect H. H. Koch handled the technique, producing complete faceted globes." Through friends, and friends' friends, the demand for Klint's shades became so great that in 1943 they were put into mass-production.

94: Lampshade of fabric over wire frame, designed 1947 by THORE AHLSÉN, Sweden, and made by *Pia Ltd*. Thore Ahlsén and his brother Erik have done important work as architects for the Co-operative Association in Sweden. It is interesting when architects take on a limited but

nevertheless important piece of work such as designing lampshades. Ahlsén's Pia shades show a pure modern architectonic construction. Diagonal wire stiffeners extend the fabric covering, which is a simple bag easily put on or taken off. The bulb filaments cause patterns on the underside.

95: Glass lampshade, designed in 1957 by CARL FAGERLUND, Sweden, for *Orrefors* glassworks. One of the functions of a shade is to screen the light-bulb. This is done either by using an opaque material which reflects the light or by using a material which eliminates dazzle. For the latter purpose, glass is particularly suitable. The amount of light which passes through it can be modified as required, and it can be coloured as one chooses. Fagerlund has worked on these problems for Orrefors for twenty years. Here he gives a solution in two kinds of glass: opal and coloured transparent.

96: Two pendant glass shades, the taller 35 cm.: designed by ARNULF BJØRNSHOL, Norway, and made at *Høvik* works. For many years few Norwegian artists were interested in light-fittings, and production was much influenced by foreign models. Recently the industry has woken up to the possibilities in quality wares of this type, and firms now employ a number of artists.

97: Glass chandelier, designed by the Norwegian architect JONAS HIDLE in 1959. Hidle makes a speciality of designing glass light-fittings for churches, assembly-rooms etc. This example, with a diameter of 150 cm., was made in collaboration by *Høvik* and *Hadeland* glassworks for the Oslo Chamber of Commerce. It is of clear crystal and shining nickel-plated brass.

98: Chandelier in matt-surfaced brass, designed by JONAS HIDLE, Norway, 1959: diameter 190 cm. Made at *Høvik* works for the county hall at Baerum, which was designed by the architects Magnus and Anton Poulsson at the end of the Fifties.

97

98

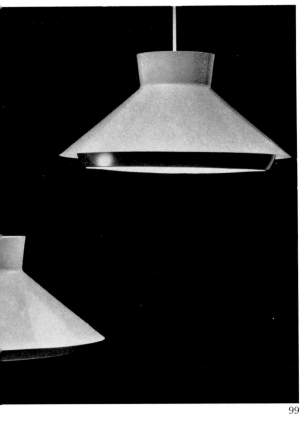

99

101

102

100

99: Shade in painted metal and acrylate, designed 1955 by LISA JOHANSSON-PAPE, Finland, for *Stockmann/Orno*. Diameter 45 cm.

100: Shade in acrylate and brass, designed 1959 by YKI NUMMI, Finland, for *Stockmann/Orno*. Diameter 40 cm. The shade is double, the inner one being of opal acrylate, the outer of grey, light brown, or dark brown, clear acrylate. This results in the shade appearing from any direction to be light coloured with a broad dark edge.

101: Small shade of opal acrylate with lower part in metal; designed 1955 by LISA JOHANSSON-PAPE, Finland, for *Stockmann/Orno*.

102: Light-bulbs in opal glass, designed by TAPIO WIRKKALA, Finland, for *Airam Ltd*. Metal holders designed by the same artist and made by *Idman Ltd*. In production 1960. These decorative bulbs, which are obscure at the sides and throw a clear unshaded light downwards only, won the versatile Wirkkala his second Grand Prix at the Milan Triennale of 1960.

103: HANNA CHRISTIE ABRAHAMSEN, Norway, turns her wooden bowls with a sensitive feeling for form. She chooses her material from the most varied types of wood, and makes things which in every single case follow the structure of the particular piece of wood as far as possible. The bowls shown were made in 1960: smaller 10 cm. high, diameter 26 cm.: larger 10.5 cm. high, diameter 38 cm. They stand on a black and white fabric of wool and linen, designed and made by SIGRUN BERG.

104: Oval wooden bowl, 25 cm. long, and wooden salad-servers: designed by AAGE SCHOU for the Norwegian Domestic Crafts Association. Schou designs furniture, toys, and articles in wood and metal, and in this field he has brought about a renaissance in Norwegian domestic crafts in a simple restrained idiom and with notable understanding for the material.

103

104

105

105: Salad bowl and servers, designed and made in teak by KAY BOJESEN, Denmark, 1949. Diameter 25 cm. When Bojesen designed this salad bowl he started with the most simple and perfect of all mathematical bodies, the sphere. But mathematical strictness has been modified in the curved handles, and with the rich grain of the wood which sets off the form. In nearly all his work in wood Bojesen starts with simple lathe-turned shapes, in which we can clearly observe the process of production at the lathe-bench.

106: Bowl in oiled teak, designed 1949 by FINN JUHL, Denmark, for *Kay Bojesen*. Maximum diameter 37 cm. Juhl and Bojesen produced this bowl, which is at once a practical object and a pure sculpture, with the ancient wood-turning technique. The form was first lathe-turned in the usual way, and then the top edge was cut down with a sure hand. From the side this cut appears as a segment of a circle.

106

107

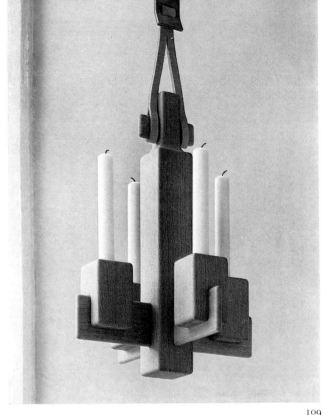

109

108

107: Dish in fir-root from *Kronoberg Dome-stic Crafts*, dish in birch-root from *Väster-botten Domestic Crafts*, and bread-box of fir-chips from *Borås* (Västergötland) *Do-mestic Crafts*. Diameters respectively 51, 26, and 32 cm.: all Swedish. Domestic craft-work in Sweden occupies both male and female members of the family. The wo-men concentrate on fabrics, while the men work in wood and metal. Using a knife as their only tool, they produce a great deal of the most interesting domestic craftwork in material and technique. The large dish was made in Småland, where there is plenty of timber, the smaller one in North Sweden; and the box, in which the rounds of rye-cake are kept, comes from a part of West Sweden where the land is poor and where people therefore rely to a great ex-tent on crafts for a living. All three are traditional in form and technique, but with their natural material and technical quality they are timeless and well-suited to use in modern surroundings.

108: Dishes in teak and birchwood, olive-prong in ebony and horn, butterknife and spoon in walnut and maple, all designed and carved by JOHNNY MATTSSON, Swe-den, 1950–60. Mattsson has refined and developed the domestic craft tradition of wood-working. He has an obvious inher-ited feeling for wood and the other mate-rials he works with. As a designer he is self-taught, but he has achieved masterly re-sults in the direction of refinement and restraint. He has designed models for in-dustrially-made bowls and for glass.

109: Oak chandelier for four candles, 60 cm. high, carved by FORSE GNISTA, Swe-den, 1959. Gnista's interesting works in wood are notable for individuality of style and appreciation of the material. Along-side the modern interest in the design of industrial products, there is a vigorous movement among younger hand-crafts-men for working in natural materials and

giving them functional form. This is Gni-sta's line, and he combines it with an evi-dent enjoyment of structure-values.

110: Four bowls, the large one in ebony, 32 cm. wide, the rest in Coromandel ebony, lignum vitae, and palisander, c. 9 cm. Carved by Co DERR, Sweden, 1959–60. Modern practical articles are increas-ingly made in new materials and with new methods. 'Classical' materials still how-ever hold their own, thanks to the beauty and character in their structure and co-lour. Co Derr has a passionate affection for wood, choosing his materials with care and carving his handsome bowls with feeling.

111: Two cotton weaves by AGE FAITH-ELL, Sweden: checked dress-material,

110

1958, woven by *MAB & MYA*, and ribbed cotton fabric, 1960, woven by *Eriksberg* weaving-mills. The textile tradition of making patterns in the fabric with changes in the binding system and with simple colour changes is maintained by several Swedish women weavers. Age Faith-Ell is one of these: she has wide experience, including practical work abroad, she champions quality, and as an industrial artist she has been able to see some of her designs realised in logically composed machine-woven fabrics.

112: Two printed cotton fabrics, designed by Astrid Sampe for *Nordiska Co. Ltd.*, Sweden, 1960. The textile programme of a large store includes printed fabrics. Besides organising its production, Astrid Sampe has also designed several of the firm's patterns.

113: Double-weave, 160×80 cm., designed and made in 1960 by Kaisa Melanton, Sweden. Kaisa Melanton belongs to the Friends of Handicraft Association, and works for it with ecclesiastical and secular weaving. She also designs industrial textiles, and has her own workshop where she weaves decorative compositions such as this double-weave called 'Africa'. Double-weaving is a peculiar multiple-shaft technique, carried out with two weaves in light and dark elements, 'positive' on one side and 'negative' on the other according to the pattern's change from light to dark.

111

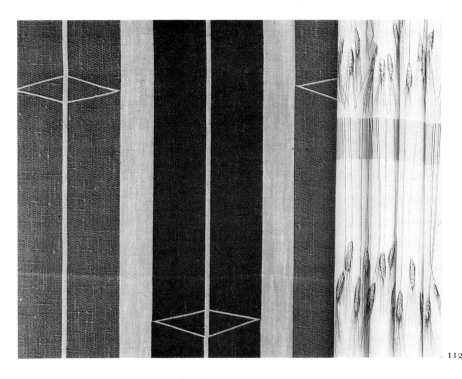

112

113

114: Linen and cotton drapes, designed in 1957 by ALICE LUND, Sweden, and made at *Borås* jacquard-weaving mills. Besides working in her own workshop in a town in Central Sweden, Alice Lund also organises the machine production of various textile factories. The example shown here is a machine-made curtain-fabric, originally made as drapes for the Swedish display of glass and steel at the Milan Triennale of 1957.

115. Linen fabric by ASTRID SAMPE, Sweden, 1960, woven by *Almedahl-Dalsjöfors Ltd.* In this lobby at the Stockholm Royal Institute of Technology Astrid Sampe shows both her fine feeling for textiles and her talent for arrangement. The fabric is in coarse-spun yarn made specially for the purpose. The curtain in the background is also linen, with a white warp and a natural-coloured weft. As director of the Nordiska Company's textile department since 1937, Astrid Sampe has designed a large number of varied products, many of them made by this firm under her personal supervision, others by different firms. These have included both

decorative fabrics and everything normally found in a large firm's house-furnishing department–carpets, printed and woven furnishing and curtain-fabrics, household linen, and much else. In addition she has a great talent for organisation, shown in her choice of product and aesthetic values, her planning and carrying out of commissioned work, her production programmes, and her sales collections.

116: 'Lianas', curtain printed in dark brown on natural ground: designed 1951 by GUDRUN STIG AAGAARD, Denmark, for *L. F. Foght*. Gudrun Stig Aagaard is one of those Danish textile-artists who have consciously designed their curtain patterns in accordance with functional demands. Many of her patterns, like the one shown here, are formed with a single colour on a natural ground, and all make use of the enrichment of the flow of line which results from the natural folds of the material when it is hung. Like all good length patterns they can also be cut anywhere without much waste of material.

117: Two printed cotton fabrics, designed 1959 by ULLA ERICSON, Sweden, and made by *Stobo Ltd*. Ulla Ericson, unlike most Swedish industrial artists, is not tied to one or more firms but is a free-lance in the proper sense of the term. She has designed patterns for both printed and woven fabrics, floor-coverings, and also jewellery. These two patterns won first prize in a competition in 1959. The oak leaves are printed in shades of green upon white: the birds in black, with red beaks, on a white ground.

116

117

131

118–119: Open-weave curtain in natural-coloured wool with inset plastic threads, designed and made 1958 by PAULA TROCK, Denmark, for *Unika Vaev Ltd.* Coat in natural woollen fabric woven by Paula Trock, model designed and made-up by fashion-designer ASTRID FOG, 1960. As a weaver Paula Trock has taken the lead in the work of raising the quality of Danish textile materials, with the help of a small output of yarns produced by 'Spindegaarden'. She is particularly interested in yarn for curtains. She realised that modern houses with large massed window-areas required a new type of curtaining, and that the artistic appearance of living-rooms depended largely on the treatment of incoming daylight. Starting with this appreciation of light as an independent element of house design, she began to produce special curtain-yarns of loosely-spun woollen fibres, and to weave open-work curtains which let light through but also refracted and softened it. The first such types of yarn were produced entirely at 'Spindegaarden', but later they were successfully adapted for industrial production. The beautiful material made from this yarn has also been used by Danish and foreign fashion-houses. Fig. 119 shows an enlarged section of a curtain, with its open weaving and the loose-spun threads whose tangled fibres filter the light.

120: 'Moon': appliqué wall-hanging, designed and made 1959 by ANN-MARI KORNERUP, Denmark. In Denmark embroidery retains a prominent place amongst women's handicrafts. In spite of modern shyness of all work which demands time and patience, embroidery still remains an element in Danish households. It is under the aegis of the Society for the Promotion of Handicrafts, which since 1928 has maintained a craft school, a workshop, and a shop, in all of which embroidery has been the main concern. Many modern textile-artists belong to the Society: Ruth Christensen, Ann-Mari Kornerup, Rolf Middelboe, and Bjørn Wiinblad, amongst others, have provided designs for embroideries. Work has been done in traditional embroidery cross-stitch, white-work, etc., but also in appliqué and free stitchery. The hanging shown is an example of these completely modern works. It consists of up to three layers of material, with gaps showing the lowest layer, thus producing an effect of depth and a play of colour. In the square central panel the composition stands out in embroidered decoration made with free stitching.

121

122

121: Rug designed and made by JULIANA SVEINSDÓTTIR, Denmark, c. 1950. 115 × 220 cm. Danish artists who are painters or sculptors by training work in many branches of handicrafts, and representatives of the fine arts are thus found for example in ceramics, silver, textiles, and industrial design. The painter Juliana Sveinsdóttir is a notable figure in textiles. Here, as a characteristic example of her products, is

shown a knotted-pile rug with an abstract theme based on the study of a bird's wing in flight, a motif which she has repeatedly used in rugs. The background is golden-brown and the figures in grey and black are in natural sheep's wool shades.

122: Decorative fabrics in double-weave: 50 × 25 cm. Made at the State Industrial School for Women under the direction of the Norwegian textile artists RAGNHILD TRETTEBERG and ELI MARIE JOHNSEN. Orange patterns on a ground of shades of blue, in hand-spun wool from 'Old Norwegian' sheep. Double-weaving is an ancient technique, recently revived in Norway.

123: 'Arabesque', wall-hanging of linen in damask technique, designed and woven 1957 by DORA JUNG, Finland, in her own establishment, the Jung Textile Studio: 125 × 32 cm. Woven in close linen on a backing of coarse dyed cotton.

124: 'H 55', wall-hanging linen in damask technique, designed and woven in 1955 by DORA JUNG, Finland, in her own workshop: 280 × 90 cm. Woven in dyed and unbleached linen and dyed cotton: a good example of her restrained and aesthetic patterning and colour-schemes, outstanding precisely because of its restraint.

124

123

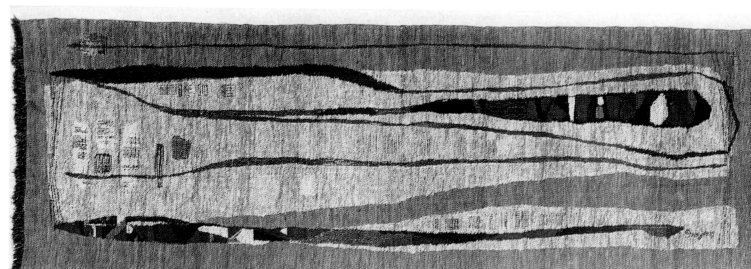

125: 'X-tra', machine-woven damask linen, designed 1956 by DORA JUNG, Finland, for *Tampella*: 160×130 cm. Besides the well-known output of her own workshop, Dora Jung also to a certain extent makes designs for industrially produced damask-weaves. The one shown has a bleached warp and black weft. It is also made completely bleached, and in grey and brown. Grand Prix at 1957 Triennale.

126: Woollen decorative fabric in 'smettevev' (weaving with hand-sitching) made at the State Industrial School for Women, Norway, under the direction of RAGNHILD TRETTEBERG and ELI MARIE JOHNSEN. Earthenware cup and saucer designed by RAGNAR GRIMSRUD and made by *Figgjo Fajance Ltd.*: matt glaze in light golden-brown tones.

127: Detail of coarse damask weave with coloured inlay, designed and made in 1960 by DORA JUNG, Finland, in her own workshop. 34×55 cm.

127

125

126

128: Cotton fabric and woollen furnishing-fabrics, from the Domestic Crafts Associations of Ångermanland, Medelpad, and Östergötland respectively: all Swedish. Home-woven fabrics reflect the folk characteristics of different parts of the country. The northern provinces use intense colours, as in Lapp costume: in Central Sweden colours are lighter, but strong: the south-eastern parts use pink and light blue, and fertile Scania furthest south has deep colours. These fabrics help to illustrate this: the deep-coloured cotton in blue and red is from Medelpad, and the furnishing-fabric in grey, in a technique called 'hålkrus', is from the province to the north. The bright furnishing-fabric in yellow and browns is from Östergötland, a very fertile part of eastern Central Sweden.

129: Bedspread in cattlehair, 120 × 180 cm., from the Norrbotten Domestic Crafts Association, Sweden. Even fabrics for quite practical purposes were generally given a decorative appearance in folk-art. Thus this bed-cover or 'rana' has been given a richly striped pattern, very different from rustic flower-designs and having a studied colour-effect.

129

131: Detail, c. 120×150 cm., of a piece of double-weaving measuring overall 6× 2 m., designed 1958 by ALF MUNTHE, Sweden, and made at *Lekattgården* weaving studio. Munthe is one of the painters who since about 1920 have worked for handicrafts and industrial art. For many years he worked for the Friends of Handicraft Association, and he has made many church and secular fabrics as well as tapestries and pieces for room decoration. Amongst his largest works are an embroidered balcony frieze for the Scandia Cinema in Stockholm, designed by E. G. Asplund in 1922, and a large doubleweave behind the altar of Skövde crematorium (1947). The double-weave illustrated here, with its rich and cheerful colour-scheme and its strictly textile style, is typical of Munthe's later work. It was made for the reading-room of the Stockholm City Record Office.

132: Tapestry-woven curtain, 25×5.5 m., designed 1959 by BARBRO NILSSON, Sweden, and made by *Märta Måås-Fjetterström Ltd.* This may be regarded as an object of use, though it fulfils a strongly decorative function. It shuts off a dreary and traffic-ridden street scene, and creates a pleasant atmosphere in the entrance-hall of the large Folksam insurance building in Stockholm. Barbro Nilsson, who was responsible for its design and manufacture, works with an unusually genuine handicraft quality by modern Swedish standards, without compromising with industry. Since 1942 she has been the artistic director of Märta Måås-Fjetterström Ltd., which carries on the firm founded by the great Swedish textile-artist of that name in Båstad, and which weaves by hand only. Barbro Nilsson shows her strong sense of the decorative and her exceptionally formidable knowledge of textiles. Through her work as a teacher, e. g. as head of the textile department of the School of Arts, Crafts and Design for ten years, and through her management of the Märta Måås-Fjetterström firm, she has had a great influence on the appreciation of quality and design in fabrics for a whole generation of Swedish textile-artists,

130: Woollen drape in 'rölakan' technique, 150×220 cm., designed 1960 by BARBRO NILSSON, Sweden, and made by *Märta Måås-Fjetterström Ltd.* Besides the many large decorative works she has undertaken, Barbro Nilsson has also made many smaller fabrics such as drapes and especially floor-coverings.

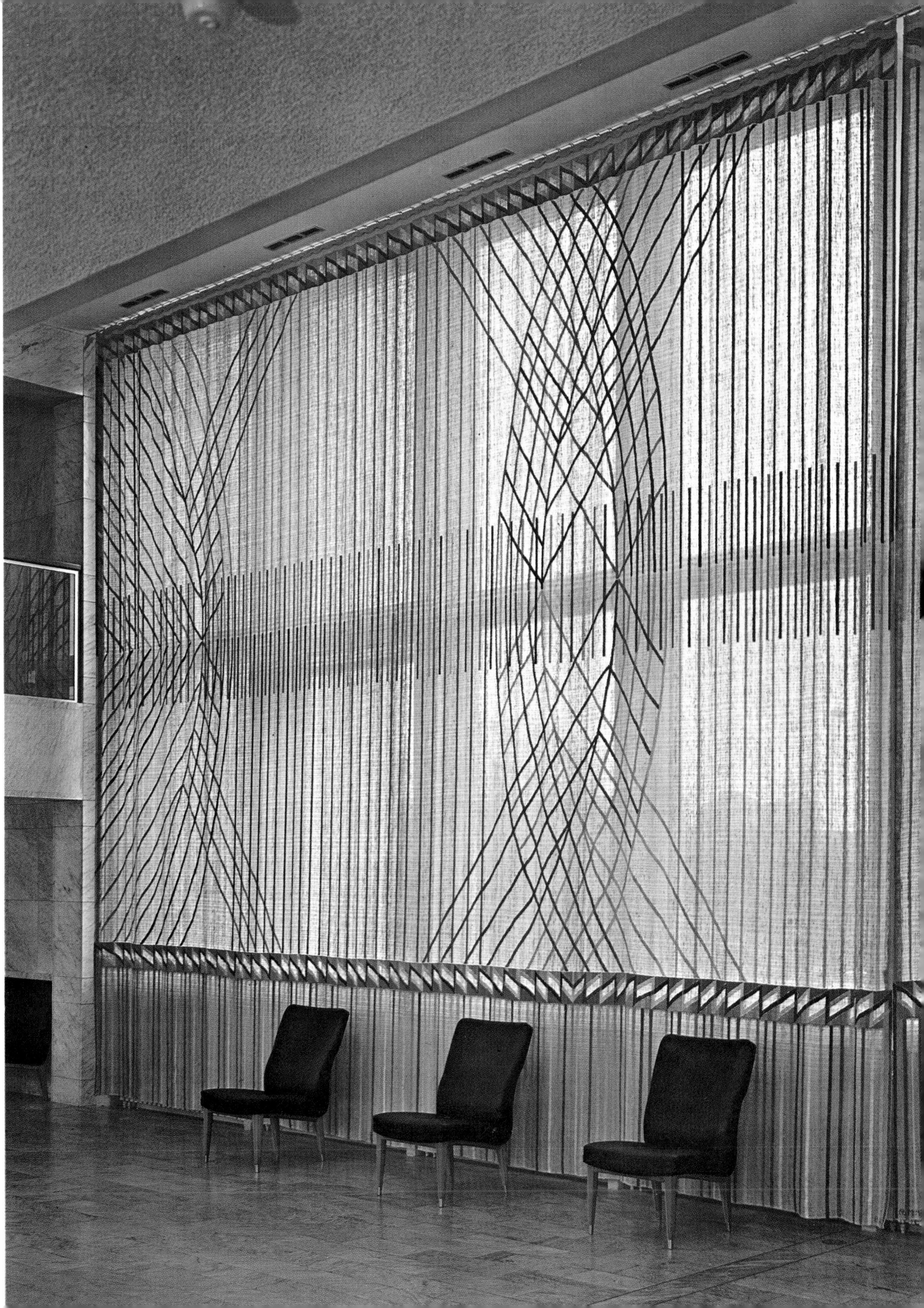

133

134

133: Appliqué panel in linen, 120×150 cm., designed and made 1952 by SOFIA WIDÉN, Sweden. Sofia Widén played an important part amongst the middle generation in Sweden. With her inspiration and technical expertise she made many church and secular fabrics before her unexpected death at the age of 60 in January 1961. It is not surprising that this panel, 'Lapponia', has found a place in the collections of the National Museum in Stockholm. It is typically Swedish in its theme, its restricted colour-scheme, and its choice materials.

134: Balcony frieze in tapestry-weave, 80 cm.×24 m., designed 1956 by ALICE LUND, Sweden, and made in her own workshop. Much of the art-handicraft of recent years has been commissioned by the State Church and independent Churches. Weavers, sculptors, silversmiths, and painters adorn church interiors. Textile craftsmanship has contributed in the form of church vestments and purely ritual fabrics like altar-cloths and wall-hangings. This tapestry weave decorates the front of a gallery in an independent church in Stockholm. Alice Lund belongs to that school in Swedish textile-art which works principally with decorative effects produced by purely technical means, quiet, restrained in its use of colour, and highly skilled.

135: Rug, 180×245 cm., designed 1959 by ULLA SCHUMACHER-PERCY, Sweden, and made in her own workshop. Here she produces amongst other things a range of large knotted rugs. The one shown is from a series of seven which she exhibited at Stockholm in the spring of 1960. It is called 'Variation on a Theme: 6'. She uses the highly expressive technique of rug-making in decorative compositions with refined colour-effects.

136

137

138

136: Woollen rug made in the 'rya' technique, 130 × 180 cm., designed 1959 by INGRID SKERFE-NILSSON, Sweden, and made in her own workshop. Here, in the university town of Uppsala north of Stockholm, she produces all kinds of handmade fabrics. Her rugs are made as complete colour-compositions, either in shades of grey or in a colour-scheme as powerful as this.

137: Tapestry-woven rug, 155 × 180 cm., designed 1950 by MARIANNE RICHTER, Sweden, and made by *Märta Måås-Fjetter-ström Ltd*. The three artists here, Barbro Nilsson, Ann-Mari Forsberg, and Marianne Richter, all work in a rich style, using several freer techniques which are less restricted than those of regular weaving. The rug shown, with its bold hen motif, is made in a technique which approximates to that of tapestry.

138: Carpet in 'rölakan' technique, 150 × 280 cm., designed 1960, and cotton-print designed 1945, by ELSA GULLBERG, Sweden. Painted chair designed by SVEN-ERIK FRYKLUND, 1954, and made by *Hagafors* chair-works. Elsa Gullberg's work in Swedish textiles goes right back to about 1910, when she helped to establish both handicrafts and industrial production on a basis of popular tradition. She has for many years played a part in Swedish domestic crafts and the Crafts Association. Later she founded her own firm for fabric production and furnishing, and in 1955 she handed this over to her children. She still produces new ideas for textiles, as in this carpet, designed so that a domestic weaver can make it in any size she chooses by following a simple pattern and colour-scheme.

139: Rug made in the 'rya' technique, 110 × 140 cm., designed 1958 by BIRGITTA GRAF, Sweden, for *Elsa Gullberg Ltd*. Rugs often perform a quite decorative as well as practical function, and here Birgitta Graf has worked out a most interesting colour theme. She is comparatively young, and since 1955 has been employed by Elsa Gullberg Ltd. She also designs printed fabrics for house-furnishing and clothes.

140: Woollen carpet in 'rölakan' technique, 230 × 330 cm., designed 1958 by EDNA MARTIN, Sweden, and made by the Friends of Handicraft Association. As shown in this example, called 'Piscina' (fish-pond), Edna Martin works in a decorative style which fills the given surface without exaggerated elaboration.

139   140

143

141

141: Handwoven carpet in 'rölakan' technique, 250 × 250 cm., designed 1958 by INGRID DESSAU, Malmöhus domestic crafts, Sweden. Swedish Domestic Crafts Associations are centres which preserve the feeling for quality and the handicraft tradition, give employment to home weavers and textile artists, and serve as nurseries for their development. Ingrid Dessau works for various associations, and also designs products for industrial manufacture. She is likewise represented in the furniture section of this book with machine-woven carpets from Kasthall carpet-factory. She prefers the simple and strong Kelim-like 'rölakan' technique, but occasionally also makes soft long-pile rugs. Her patterns are formal and mostly geometrical, and of unusual clarity. Her colour-schemes vary from white and shades of grey to this intense orange, but are never variegated.

142: Weaving of wool and linen in the so-called 'HV technique', designed and woven in 1960 by INGA BRAND, Sweden. 150 × 220 cm. Inga Brand is still young, and was trained at the Gothenburg school of Art and Design. The weave shown was made with a technique developed experimentally by the Friends of Handicraft Association (HV) in Stockholm. It is a two-shaft technique with a through weft and inlaid threads.

143: Rug made in the 'rya' technique, 130 × 190 cm., designed in 1958 by VIOLA GRÅSTEN, Sweden, and made for the *Nordiska Company's* floor-covering department. Rug-knotting is an ancient technique in Sweden and Finland. The woollen or linen yarn is fixed to a woven base by special knots. The rug can have a deep pile, with the pattern therefore blurred and changing according to the lie of the tufts. This gives it an expressionistic character, suited to the colour-composition, instead of a rigid construction. Viola Gråsten, with her expressive colour-sense, is specially equipped for this technique. She had already made a name with her rugs before she left Finland for Sweden, and here she has continued with them, at first with Elsa Gullberg and later with the Nordiska Company's textile department.

142

144

144: Tapestry weave, 185 × 220 cm., designed 1955 by ANN MARI FORSBERG, *Märta Måås-Fjetterström Ltd.*, Sweden. The textile workshop in which this was made carries on the rich and decorative style of its founder in various techniques. The theme of this piece came from mediaeval Swedish legend: the Danish king Valdemar collected a ransom from the town of Visby in Gotland, but on the way home his ship sank with all its magnificent treasures, which have never been recovered.

145: Appliqué panel in linen, 200 × 240 cm., by STEN KAUPPI, Sweden, 1959. Appliqué work is technically akin to painting, and requires a developed sense of composition and colour. Kauppi has both: he works in the tapestry technique, and to some extent with embroidery, in which he shows fine draftsmanship. He comes from the far north of Sweden, works in fine arts, and has made a considerable number of textile compositions for the Friends of Handicraft Association in Stockholm.

145

146: Knitted cardigan in angora wool, pattern designed by ANNIKA MALMSTRÖM, made by *Bohus Sticking* under the direction of EMMA JACOBSSON, Sweden. An inherited sense of quality, given definite aesthetic direction and organisation, produces first-class products such as the knitted garments which go under the name of Bohus Sticking. During the depression of the Thirties, when there was much unemployment among the quarrymen and fishermen of a district on the Swedish west coast where Emma Jacobsson was the governor's wife, she succeeded in organising home-knitting with the original object of giving relief employment. She took care that yarn of good quality, as well as attractive colour-schemes, were provided. Since then Bohus Sticking has developed into a really fine branch of Swedish domestic crafts.

146

147: Appliqué panel of linen, designed and made by EDNA MARTIN, Sweden, 100 × 100 cm. This work in the free appliqué technique shows Edna Martin's decorative love of colour. She calls it 'Grandiflora', from which it appears that the motif has a botanical inspiration. For decorative purposes this idea has been strongly stylised, but this has been done on the basis of a study of nature. There are various trends in modern Swedish textile art, most plainly distinguishable in floor- and wall-coverings. At one extreme is a completely patternless style, and at the other a vigorous one with almost oriental wealth of detail. In cotton fabrics we find the same contrast. Woven furnishing-fabrics show chiefly stripes, dots, and rectangles. Edna Martin has worked on all types of household fabrics and on dress-material. As director of production for the Friends of Handicraft and head of the textile department of the School of Arts, Crafts and Design in Stockholm, she has a commanding position in textiles generally and an important influence on the growth of textile art.

147

148: Two printed fabrics of linen and cotton, designed by GÖTA TRÄGÅRDH in 1956 and 1958, and a print designed by AL EKLUND 1959, all made by *Stobo Ltd.*, Sweden. Printed fabrics have a prominent place amongst modern furnishing textiles, especially as a decorative element. Consequently the Swedish market has a large selection of printed materials. Göta Trägårdh is a versatile artist in fashion- and pattern-design: she assembles Stobo's collections. Al Eklund is a young and talented artist, full of ideas.

149: Prints designed by VIOLA GRÅSTEN, Sweden: linen for *Nordiska Co.* (1958) and cotton for indoor wear, for *Mölnlycke* weaving-mills (1960). Viola Gråsten is one of Sweden's most outstanding figures in textiles. Besides being an unusually fine rug-weaver, she provides the market with excellently printed industrial fabrics.

150: Material in natural-coloured Faroese wool, designed and made in 1953 by LIS AHLMANN, Denmark. This shows material qualities which can be derived only from hand-weaving, and we can see the artistic strength and calm which an experienced artist can achieve with quite simple means. It is all the work of a single artist: from the sack of wool through sorting, carding, spinning, and weaving, Lis Ahlmann has herself completed the whole process.

151: Detail of upholstered settee covered with woollen furnishing-fabric designed 1954 by LIS AHLMANN and BØRGE MOGENSEN, Denmark, for *C. Olesen*'s Cotil collection. The Danish textile industry has only in very recent years achieved an artistic strength of its own. Many artists have contributed to this, but Lis Ahlmann and Børge Mogensen in their work for C. Olesen were the first to set technical and artistic standards of quality on a sufficiently broad front to raise those of the entire Danish textile output. They have helped to win respect for the work of the artist with their 'anonymous' household fabrics, furnishing-materials, and curtains. With collaboration between weaver and furniture-designer, textiles have achieved a place alongside the best in Danish furniture and furnishings. The furnishing-fabrics shown are part of a series which as well as checked patterns includes single-colour materials and mixtures corresponding to the panels in the checks. As shown here, the different materials of the series may be combined on the same piece of furniture.

151

152: Section of wall-hanging designed and made in 1959 by RUTH HULL, Denmark: size of section 100×134 cm. In fabric-printing also, those concerned with the material quality of their products have sought out ancient and simple techniques which are still used in primitive cultures, for example, fabric patterns made by dyeing with resist areas or with binding the material. In this wall-hanging Ruth Hull first folded the material lengthwise in broad layers and then rolled and tied it tightly about every 20 cm. Then she dipped some of the tied parts of the roll in grey dye, untied it, refolded it differently, and dipped it again. Since the dye only penetrated lightly to the innermost layers, this process produced a groundwork pattern of rectangles in very varied shades. Over this the fabric printer laid a second pattern of different coloured rectangles executed in silk-screen technique, and finally the composition was completed with black lines made with a brush.

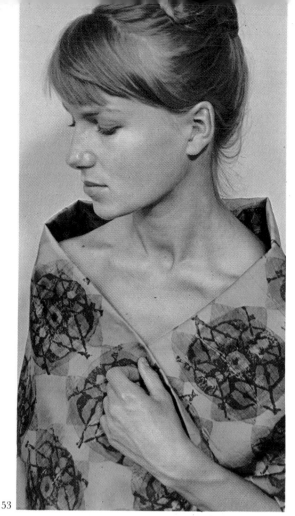

153

152

153: Silk decorated with block-printing, designed and made in 1960 by DORTE RAASCHOU, Denmark. Block-printing is the simplest of all fabric-printing techniques, and this example shows what elaborate patterns can be produced with very little equipment. The pattern is printed with blocks cut in wood or linoleum. In this case two blocks were used: first a surface motif shaped like a butterfly was printed on the fabric, then this same block was turned at right-angles and printed again over the first impression, and finally the pattern was completed with a rose-motif in line. To achieve a surface alive with contrast between the partly and completely covered parts, Dorte Raaschou did not put the dye on the block with a pad or roller but with a brush.

154

155: 'Lightning', flat-weave woollen rug, designed and made in 1952 by VIBEKE KLINT, Denmark. 115×220 cm. In its colours and patterns this was inspired by American Indian textiles. Like primitive folkweaves, its pattern is based on a simple weaving technique – the 'lightning' method which has given it its name. This was the first of a long series of Vibeke Klint's flat-weave rugs, using the same pattern-motif but increasingly independent of the original prototype, and with each rug built up in shades of a cardinal colour. She has worked particularly with close tones of blue-red and yellow-brown.

154: Flat-weave rug in vegetable-dyed wool, designed and made in 1959 by ANNA THOMMESEN, Denmark. Many handcraftsmen in Scandinavia nowadays aim in their work to counteract the technical perfection and intellectual design of industrial products. They often look to primitive examples for inspiration, both for decoration and, often to a greater degree, for material qualities. This applies, for example, to Anna Thommesen's floor-coverings. She is convinced that art-handicraft must be personally carried through every stage of production: design, colour, and construction are for her essentially bound together. She always bases her compositions on colour-impressions derived from Nature, and in building up patterns she always emphasises the lines of the threads. The colour-content in this mat was inspired by the shades of yellow and grey shown by grass in a mild winter, as it stands with a few new fresh green shoots between the half-withered stems.

155

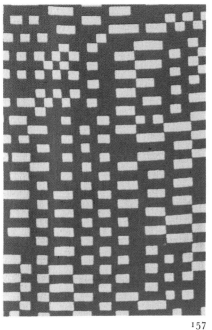

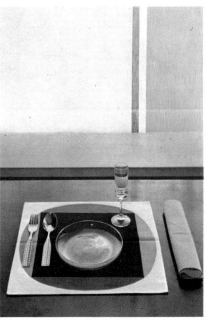

156   157   158

156: 'Beirut', fabric-print designed and made in 1958 by MARIE GUDME LETH, Denmark. Work on the potentialities of colour-effects is playing an ever increasing part in Danish printed household-textiles. The representative designs of the Thirties, and the flower orgies of the Forties, were followed in the Fifties by strict geometrical patterns with rich colour effects achieved by over-printing, giving a great variety of tones in addition to the actual printing colours. Starting with a series of small-figured and narrow-striped fabrics of the early Fifties, a large output of domestic fabrics has appeared in recent years with large restrained patterning but rich colour-compositions. These match in principle the clarified room-shapes and large well-defined areas of window and wall in modern architecture. The fabric-printer Marie Gudme Leth, who introduced screen-printing to Denmark in 1934 and thereby made it possible for hand-printed material to reach a larger public, has also with her great experience taken a major part in this latest development.

157: 'Tasco' fabric-print, designed 1957 by ARNE JACOBSEN, Denmark, for *Grautex Ltd.* Jacobsen's most recent fabric-printing is also dominated by colour-work. From the flower-riots of the war

years, by way of abstract compositions with a naturalistic element, he has now reached completely geometrical designs in which a rhythmic arrangement of rods and circles merely provides the ground-work for an artistic effect in which the interplay of colour is the most important element. In a few recent prints he has worked more freely, for example with completely abstract design.

158: Place-mat designed and made in 1960 by ROLF MIDDELBOE, Denmark. In the background, a section of cotton weave designed by Middelboe for *Unika Vaev Ltd.* As a fabric-printer, Middelboe works chiefly with clear mathematical compositions made by overprinting regular and uniform pattern surfaces in single colours. In this example the design was produced by four superimposed printings of a figure shaped as a square with a segment of a circle attached to one side. At the edges the four colours are pure, and in the square central panel is a vigorous composite colour with a great effect of depth. Middelboe also designs machine-woven fabrics. The cotton cloth in the background is an example of the positive results of the increasing concern of manufacturers to have the services of good artists even for inexpensive everyday goods.

159: Stage curtain in Munkegaard School, Gentofte, Copenhagen, designed 1955 by ARNE JACOBSEN, Denmark, and made by *Kirsten* and *John Becker.* 4.25×15 m. In Denmark large pieces of decorative work for public buildings are usually carried out by painters and sculptors; but in recent years there have also been cases of artist-craftsmen being employed to give a strong artistic element to more practical items. One outstanding example of this is the fabrics at once practical and decorative woven by Kirsten and John Becker for Munkegaard School to the sketches of the architect, Arne Jacobsen. The chief of these was the stage curtain in the school hall shown here. The base is a coarse flax yarn in a pure red dye, and the inlaid panels are of woollen thread in six different shades from pink, yellow, and orange to red and purple. Separately each colour is so intense that in combination with the visible parts of the base the desired tones are produced. The curtain was woven on a carpet loom as broad as the width of the weave. At the other end of the hall a large window area stretching right across is covered with a transparent curtain of natural coarse-spun woollen yarn, with a pattern inserted in black.

162

160  161

163

160: Trial-piece for a window curtain in Skive Teachers' Training College, designed and made in 1960 by TUSTA WEF-RING, Denmark. 127×220 cm. Tusta Wef-ring's work as a fabric-printer shows affinities with some elements of modern abstract art. Her compositions are made with dramatic vigour of line and with strong colour-contrasts. As in the example shown, she normally uses brush-painting alone. Since this curtain was specially made for use on a window wall of a single-storey school building it is, unlike most such fabrics, coloured on both sides. In addition, care has been taken with the translucency of the colours.

161: Rug designed and made in 1960 by LISE PLUM, Denmark: 110×172 cm. As in most other branches of textile art, rug-makers also have abandoned pattern-design proper in favour of work based on colour and material. Artistic expression in floor-coverings has become that of the painter rather than of the draftsman. This rug is an example: a simple division into panels is the sole background for Lise Plum's distinctive colour-composition, the effect of which arises from the contrast between folk-solidity and refined elegance to be found in most of her products. It is not unusual in her work for crude earth-dyes, as here, to be set against distinctive fashionable colours. Notice also that the separate panels of colour are composed of threads in several shades.

162: Woollen fabrics designed and made in 1960 by ELISABETH HAVE, Denmark. As a weaver Elisabeth Have has won a prominent place amongst young Danish textile artists because of, amongst other things, her independent eye for colour. Her soft and light woollen fabrics, used principally for curtains and dresses, take their character from the contrast between her interest in ancient folk-culture and her appreciation of the present-day use of colour in the world of fashion. Her fabrics thus have an element of folk-craft in their material qualities, but are completely modern, refined, and elegant in their remarkable colour compositions. The dark yellow material, here shown as made for curtaining, is for example also made in a version with slender inlaid gold threads which transforms it into an exclusive dress-material.

163: 'Spring', hanging designed and made in 1960 by FRANKA RASMUSSEN, Denmark: 250×85 cm. Tapestry weaving in the traditional manner is virtually extinct in Denmark, but, as in other Scandinavian countries, knotted pile and flat-weave wall-hangings are made. Franka Rasmussen holds a special place amongst the group of artists who use textiles primarily for artistic expression. Unlike most, she employs material effects of various kinds in one design. Like many modern painters and sculptors, she is less concerned with colour and form and more with experiments in material and structure. A common trait in her recent tapestries is therefore the combination of flat-weave patterned surfaces with parts in close and open rug-technique. She also combines materials of different character: in the weave shown she has for example used threads of hemp, various single- and two-ply wools, and flax. She bases her designs on impressions of nature, and aims to evoke natural experiences simply with structure, colours, and geometrical figures such as circles, ellipses, rectangles, and straight lines. By giving her works such titles as 'Twilight', 'Dawn', and 'Dusk', she helps her public to grasp the natural mood she wishes to convey.

164: Wall-hanging designed and made by RUTH CHRISTENSEN, Denmark: 90×230 cm. In fabric-printing the line of demarcation from pure art completely disappears: only the material distinguishes the decorative textile-artist from the painter. Ruth Christensen's compositions for wall-hangings are not planned or sketched in advance, and she never repeats a design. Every single brush-stroke therefore represents the immediate inspiration of the moment. In the example shown the ground was block-printed and the shades of red and the gold lines applied with a brush.

165: Dress-material designed and made in 1960 by ANNETTE JUEL, Denmark. Collaboration between Danish textile-artists working individually and the country's fashion-designers has only very recently become a reality. But now contact has been established, with the result that several young weavers and fabric-printers produce materials especially for dress-making. These are not mass-produced, but are used only for model dresses for which they have been specially made. The material shown is made in diaper pattern, with an alternating warp and weft effect, a weaving technique which both produces a slight effect of depth and allows the separate colours to stand out clearly.

164

165

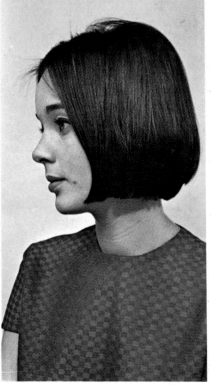

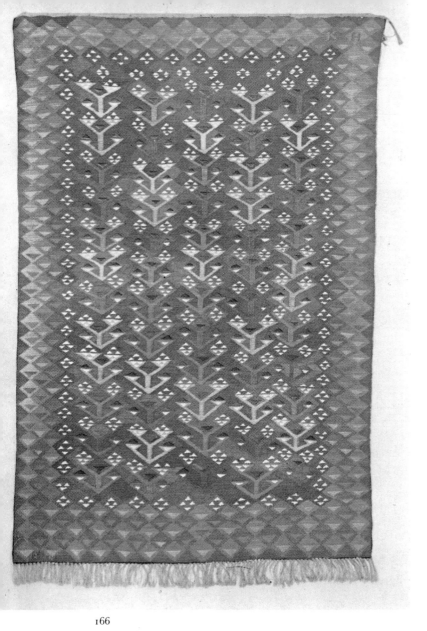

166

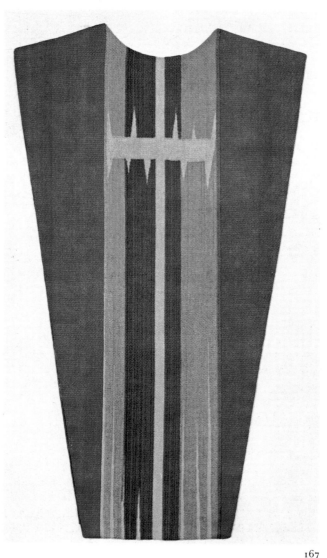

167

166: Tapestry-woven rug, designed and made by KJELLAUG HØLAAS, Norway: 162 × 107 cm. Hølaas is head of the State School of Crafts and Industrial Art.

167: Chasuble, designed by GRETE LEIN, made in the experimental workshop of the State Industrial School for Women, Norway, under the direction of its head, Signe Haugstoga. This workshop, through its experimental work in colour and materials, has made a great contribution to Norwegian church fabrics.

168

168: Woollen furnishing-fabric, designed by SIGRUN BERG, Norway, for *United Woollen Mills.* One of a series which was awarded a gold medal at the Milan Triennale of 1960. Sigrun Berg bases her work on old Norwegian traditions, but has aimed to adapt her furnishing-fabrics to the requirements of machines. In her collaboration with the above firm she has raised industrial products to a high level.

169

169: Pile-woven rug, 120 × 123 cm., designed and made by GRETE LEIN, Norway. The material is the outer wool of 'Old Norwegian' sheep. Grete Lein has shown herself to possess unusual talent as a textile artist. She has won prizes with patterns for factory-made cloths, and she makes rugs and other textiles for the adornment of the home; but she is primarily interested in church fabrics, and in this sphere her achievement has been such as to produce a renaissance in Norway.

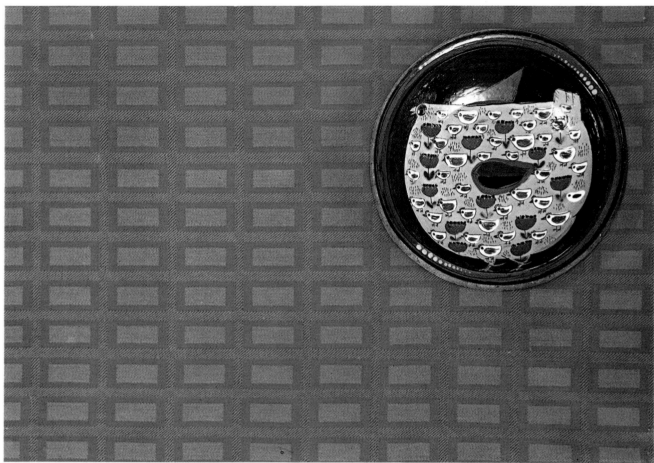

170

171

170: Woollen furnishing-fabric, designed by BIRGIT WESSEL, Norway, and made by *Vakre Hjem* ('House Beautiful'). Birgit Wessel's products show a restrained tone which makes them very suitable for modern interiors. They are marked by cultural values and understanding of quality. Dish of chamotte stoneware, diameter 50 cm., made by ROLF HANSEN, Norway. Hansen's products are generally made in a coarse material, with the clay itself having a large share in the desired effect. His forms are simple and original, but in decorating his pottery he shows little restraint and masters his media in an often striking manner. A burlesque humour gives his work an element of fun which really brightens existence.

171: Woollen fabric, amongst other things used as an altarcloth. Made at the State Industrial School for Women's experimental workshop, under the direction of SIGNE HAUGSTOGA, Norway. Dish in chamotte stoneware made by MARGRETHE VON DER LIPPE, Norway, diameter 46 cm. Margrethe von der Lippe's husband Jens is also a ceramic artist.

172: Hand-knotted rug, designed by ARNE LINDAAS, Norway, for *Sellgren* weaving-mills. This firm some time ago organised a competition for rugs which anyone could make as a hobby, and the one shown here was awarded a prize. Lindaas, who is one of the most versatile Norwegian practical artists, won several prizes in this competition. He works with the greatest variety of materials: he makes designs for fabrics in several weaving techniques, but is equally ready to express himself in glass, wood, metal, ceramics, or ivory.

173: Rug, partly pile-woven, designed by the painter KNUT RUMOHR and made by ANNELISE KNUDTZON, Norway: 190 × 175 cm. Made with 'decorative weaving-yarn', machine-spun wool from 'Old Norwegian' sheep specially suitable for decorative fabrics.

172

173

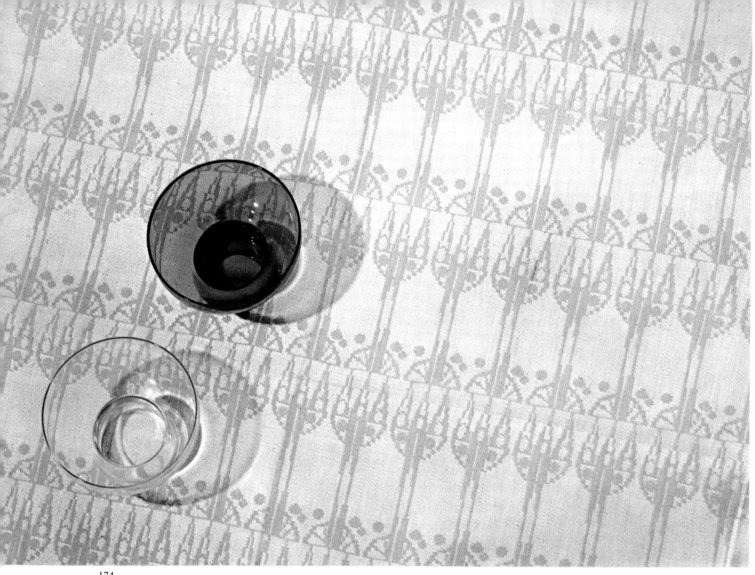

174

175

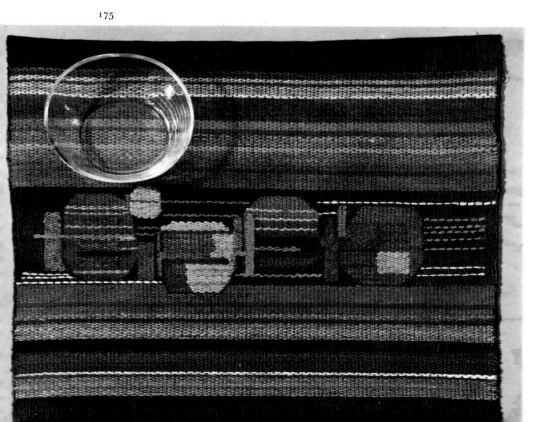

174: Damask cloth in linen, woven on thirty shafts, designed and made under the direction of ELI MARIE JOHNSEN and RAGNHILD TRETTEBERG at the State Industrial School for Women, Norway. Glass bowl designed by ARNE LINDAAS for *Norsk Glassverk*.

175: ELI MARIE JOHNSEN, Norway, has mastered many of the technical potentialities of textiles, and has an outstanding talent for design, both for weaving and for sewing. This decorative fabric in 'smettevev', a weave with hand-stitching, is a good example of her graphic powers and sense of colour. 45×33 cm. Glass bowl designed by ARNE LINDAAS for *Norsk Glassverk*.

176

176: Woollen curtain-fabric, designed and made by ELISE JAKHELLN, Norway. Furnishing-fabric by the same artist, with woollen weft and cotton warp. Elise Jakhelln has a comparatively large workshop by Norwegian standards, working with 8–10 weavers. She frequently collaborates with architects and interior-designers, and takes on special commissions. All fabrics from her workshop are of a high standard of craftsmanship and artistic quality. Chair designed by ALF STURE for *Hiorth & Østlyngen* c. 1940. The floor-carpet is a so-called 'grene', a type made in Norway for ages on quite primitive looms. North American Indians use the same technique and the same type of loom.

177: 'Midsummer Night', embroidery, designed and sewn by ELI MARIE JOHNSEN, Norway: 90×28 cm. The jug, made by KARI and ALF ROGNVED, stands on a hand-printed fabric designed and made by INGER GULBRANDSEN.

177

178: Tablecloth of printed cotton, designed and made by INGER GULBRANDSEN, Norway. The porcelain bowl is an example of KONRAD GALAAEN's work, made at *Porsgrund* porcelain-works: largest diameter 20 cm.

179: Hand-printed cotton fabrics, designed and made by INGER GULBRANDSEN, Norway. From the moment when she displayed her first fabric-prints, Inger Gulbrandsen has been an individual figure amongst Norwegian textile artists. Her patterns generally consist of lines in rhythmic arrangement, with a restrained musically attuned colour-scheme.

180: Hand-printed curtain-material by LIV HASSEL, Norway. Bird-figure designed and made by KÅRE MJØS in chamotte stoneware, 39 cm. long.

179   180

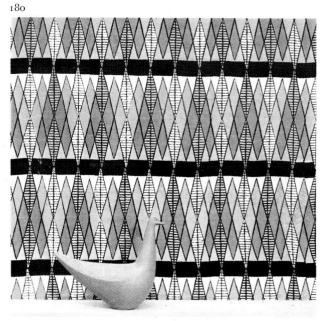

181: 'Doves', wall-hanging in linen damask, designed and woven in 1950 by DORA JUNG in her own workshop, Finland. 92 cm. high. Coloured inlay is used sparingly and with refinement in this fabric, which won a Grand Prix at the 1951 Triennale. The structure in this case, unlike the other hanging shown in fig. 182, is completely even and the technique normal damask-weave. She has repeated the same dove-motif in an uncoloured damask hanging called 'Piazetta', which is mass-produced.

182: Linen wall-hanging in damask-weave, designed and woven in 1957 by DORA JUNG in her own workshop, Finland: 150×150 cm. This is one of the earliest works in which she distinguished the different fields of the pattern by a variation of structure as well as of colour. For example the upper panel, because of its coarser yarn, stands almost in relief in relation to the rest of the surface. It is also emphasised with a slight touch of colour in 'blue net'. Apart from this the material used is principally natural-coloured linen. The technique is a combination of damask weave and 'snärjning', a Swedish technique resembling the oriental soumak-weave.

181

182

183

184

183–184: Machine-woven cotton fabrics, designed in 1960 by KIRSTI ILVESSALO, Finland, for *Barker-Littoinen*.

185: 'Woodpecker', woollen rug, designed in 1954 by KIRSTI ILVESSALO and made in the workshop of the *Friends of Finnish Handicraft*. 120 × 160 cm. The pattern of this glowing red rug recalls links with ancient rustic decorative elements, from which this artist often draws inspiration without ever descending to pastiche. It won a Grand Prix at the 1954 Triennale. Bought by Victoria and Albert Museum, London.

186: Woollen scarves, designed 1960 by
UHRA SIMBERG-EHRSTRÖM, Finland, for
Inhemsk Ull (Native Woollens) *Ltd.*

187: Machine-woven cotton fabric, designed 1960 by ULLA SIMBERG-EHR-
STRÖM, Finland, for *Finlayson-Forssa.*

186

187

188

189: 'Four Colours', woollen rug, designed by UHRA SIMBERG-EHRSTRÖM in 1956 and made in the workshop of the *Friends of Finnish Handicraft:* 120 × 160 cm. The name is descriptive – Uhra Simberg-Ehrström is the most accomplished colorist amongst Finnish rug-artists, and her compositions often consist simply of an arrangement of colour-panels. The dense and heavy, but also sensitive, colours in this rug are also found in several of her industrial products.

188: 'Time', woollen rug, designed 1956 by EVA BRUMMER, Finland, for *Neovius Ltd.*: 120 × 160 cm. The hour-glass motif, also implied in the rug's name, has appeared in many of Eva Brummer's rugs over a long period. It is also found in the work of other artists.

189

190: 'Limetree', woollen rug, designed in 1951 by LOTTA RING, Finland, for the *Friends of Finnish Handicraft*.

191: 'Field', woollen rug, designed in 1954 by TOINI NYSTRÖM, Finland, for the *Friends of Finnish Handicraft*. 120 × 160 cm.

192: 'Ares', woollen rug, designed in 1960 by RITVA PUOTILA, Finland, and made in the workshop of the *Friends of Finnish Handicraft*. 120 × 160 cm. Puotila is a quite new name in rug-making. She made her debut when she competed successfully at the 1960 Triennale. She brings a quite fresh use of colour to this branch of art.

191

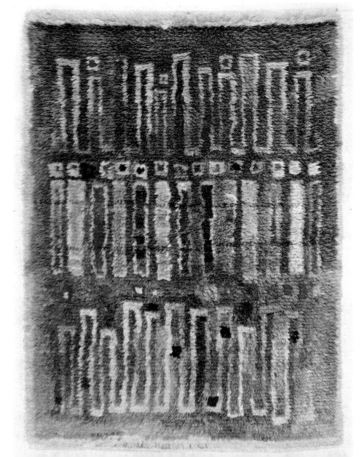

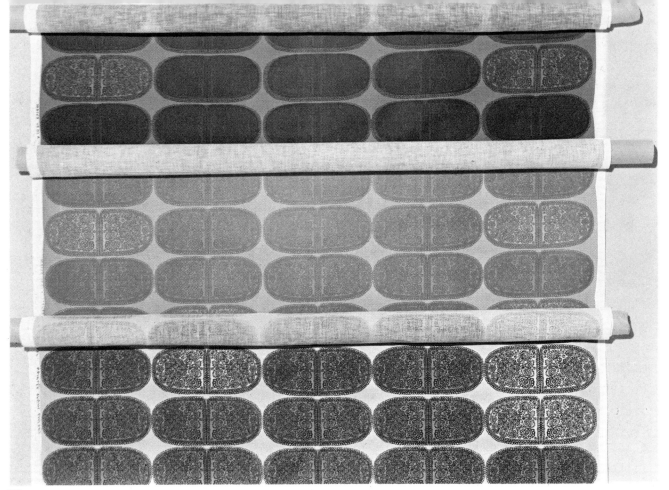

193

193: 'Tantsu', hand-printed cotton fabric, designed 1960 by MAIJA ISOLA, Finland, for *Printex*.

194: 'Rötti', hand-printed cotton fabrics, designed 1956 by VUOKKO ESKOLIN, Finland, for *Printex*.

194

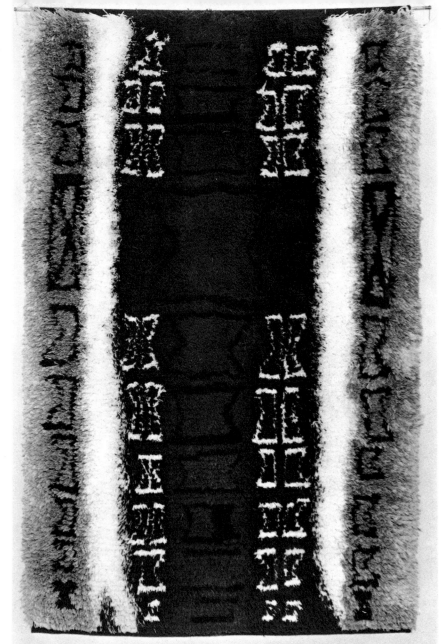

195: 'Sundial', woollen rug, designed 1955 by KIRSTI ILVESSALO, Finland, and woven in the workshop of the *Friends of Finnish Handicraft*. 120×175 cm.

196: Machine-woven cotton fabric, designed 1960 by KIRSTI ILVESSALO, Finland, for *Barker-Littoinen*.

195

196

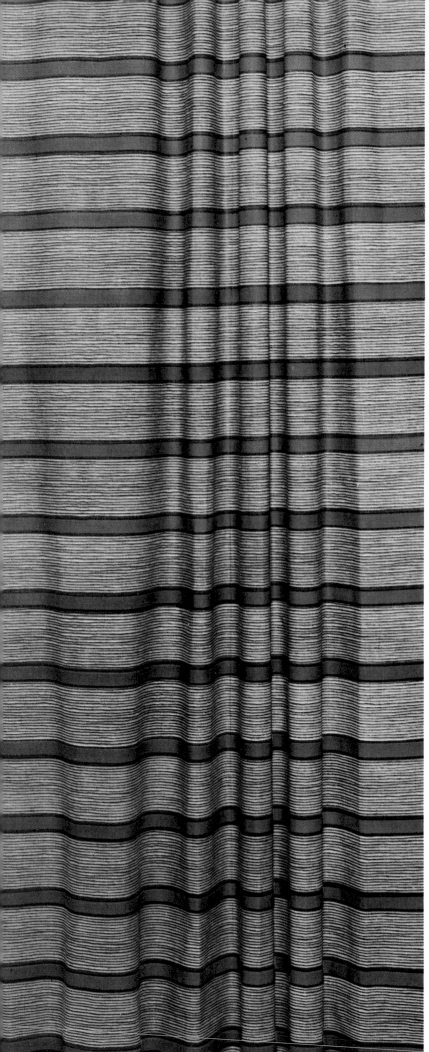

198

197

197: 'Tilda', hand-printed cotton fabric, designed 1959 by MAIJA ISOLA, Finland, for *Printex*.

198: 'Stones', hand-printed cotton fabric, designed 1955 by MAIJA ISOLA, Finland, for *Printex*.

199: 'Kukkapää', hand-printed cotton fabric, designed 1960 by MAIJA ISOLA, Finland, for *Printex*.

200

201

200: Glass vases, designed by ARNE JON JUTREM, Norway, and made by *Hadeland* glassworks: tallest 22 cm. Norwegian glass-production has not in the past been no-table for experiment, but in recent years designers have been given more opportu-nity to carry out their artistic ideas in Norwegian glassworks. Through close col-laboration with the craftsmen in the glass-works, artists have thus been able to achieve very satisfactory results. The vases shown remind one of the glass of ancient times, but nevertheless have a certain individual touch, expressing Jutrem's exceptional joy in creation.

201: Cocktail set, designed by WILLY JO-HANSSON, Norway, and made by *Hadeland* glassworks. Johansson joined Hadeland, where his father was one of the leading craftsmen, at the age of sixteen. Since then he has remained there, except for breaks for training and study. He has learnt all the rich possibilities of glass as a material, and has used his knowledge to put his own stamp on the works' large output. Johans-son's artistic individuality, and his thor-ough knowledge of craft processes, have enabled him to enrich Norwegian glass, from moulded ware to the most expensive crystal, with forms which are simple and natural as well as pre-eminent in quality. The cocktail set stands on a printed cur-tain-material designed and made by LIV HASSEL.

202: Glass vase and bowl by ARNE JON JUTREM, Norway, made by *Hadeland* glass-works. Vase 26 cm. high. Jutrem experi-ments continually, and has a many-sided training behind him. He is a painter and draftsman, designs book-bindings and tex-tiles, and works in metal, with a full understanding of the peculiarities and de-mands of each material. But he is fore-most a glass-artist, and has played a large part in establishing Norway's present po-sition in this field. At Hadeland he has taken on all the various tasks which fall to an artist at a large glassworks.

203   204

203: Glass vase, designed by SEVERIN BRØRBY, Norway, and made by *Hadeland* glassworks. Brørby belongs to the younger generation of artists at this ancient glassworks. Though only 28, he has already made himself an independent niche, and has shown himself to have completely individual ideas and strict standards both of artistic expression and artistic design.

205

204: Glass vases, designed by AXEL MØRCH, Norway, and made by *Norsk Glassverk* (Norwegian Glassworks) *Ltd.*: 12 and 23 cm. high. For many years Hadeland was the only glassworks of importance in Norway; but latterly Norsk Glassverk has shown remarkable determination to concentrate on quality products, and Axel Mørch, who is permanently employed by this firm, has designed a large quantity of practical glassware, with a technical as well as artistic object. His vases and bowls have attracted most attention, and their chief quality lies in the combination of simple forms with fine glass material. The vases stand on a double-weave table-runner of hand-spun outer wool of 'Old Norwegian' sheep, made at the State Industrial School for Women under the direction of ELI MARIE JOHNSEN and RAGNHILD TRETTEBERG.

205: Blue and brown glass vases, 9 and 14 cm. high, both designed by AXEL MØRCH, Norway, and made by *Norsk Glassverk Ltd*.
Examples of the artist's unaffected form and understanding of the value of light refractions in the glass.

206: Glass vases designed by SEVERIN BRØRBY, Norway, and made by *Hadeland* glassworks: tallest 18 cm. These show a thorough knowledge of production possibilities, and Brørby has made intelligent use of the peculiar properties of the material.

206

207: Double decanters in glass, designed
1957 by KAJ FRANCK, Finland, for *Wärt-
silä/Notsjö:* height 35 cm. The opportunities for colour-combinations in these
double-decanters, in which the upper
section can serve as a container or purely
as decoration, are infinite. They are typical of Franck's gay humour, combined
with concern for the practical.

208: Glass cocktail-mixers, designed 1955
by KAJ FRANCK, Finland, for *Wärtsilä/
Notsjö:* height 23 cm. Franck prefers the
natural cylindrical form in his practical
glass as well. These examples take their
individuality from their delicately chosen
colours alone. With a Franck design it
goes without saying that the lip is war-
ranted drip-free. Grand Prix at 1957
Triennale.

209: Decanters and glasses, designed 1958
by KAJ FRANCK, Finland, for *Wärtsilä/
Notsjö:* height 32 cm. Though they are
mass-produced, the individually-coloured
stoppers make each of these inexpensive
decanters a unique work of art. Many of
the 'hens' are claret-coloured, and these
decanters are equally suitable for red wine
or for brandy. The lowest part of each
stopper is covered with cork. These belong to a series for which Franck was
awarded the La Rinascente prize, Gran
Premio Internazionale Compasso d'Oro.

210   211

212

210: Stacking bottles, designed 1959 by TIMO SARPANEVA, Finland, for *Iittala* glassworks: height of each 15 cm.

211: Crystal vases, designed 1955 by TAPIO WIRKKALA, Finland, for *Iittala* glassworks: height 21 and 34 cm.

212: Art-glassware, designed 1960 by TIMO SARPANEVA, Finland, for *Iittala* glassworks: height 15 cm.

213: Crystal bowl, designed 1957 by TIMO SARPANEVA, Finland, for *Iittala* glassworks: height 12 cm. Pure clear crystal is Sarpaneva's chief medium of expression as an artist in glass. In his work for Iittala he most often uses abstract sculptural forms with a skilful use of the

213

effect of enclosed air-spaces in the glass-metal. Equally fine refractive effects are also achieved in pieces of completely simple and select form such as this bowl with its thick base and sensitively tapered rim.

214: Bowl and jars in transparent coloured glass with dark violet bands and spot in the base, designed 1960 by PER LÜTKEN, Denmark, for *Holmegaard* glassworks. Height of tallest jar 26 cm. No other material is as suitable as glass for giving the imagination free play. A skilled glass-blower can blow any–even the most remarkable–form, and a skilled glass-cutter can decorate it with the most ingenious ornamentation: but in all too many methods of treatment glass can be deprived of its most distinguished characteristics–its airy transparency, and the smooth roundness of form in which we can still make out the glowing viscous

lump of metal. Restraint is needed to avoid excess, and this Per Lütken has learnt in nearly twenty years of work with glass. The hall-mark of his later work is natural form derived from a simple process. The products shown here are the result of an ancient glass-maker's tech-

nique: before the mass of clear glass is blown to its final shape, the craftsman adds filaments of violet glass to the outside and the spot at the base. The two shades of glass are then worked into each other, and finally the vessel is blown inside a mould of wet wood.

214

215: Two vases of crystal glass with coloured layering, 16 and 22 cm. high. Designed 1957 by MONICA MORALES-SCHILDT, Sweden, at *Kosta* glassworks. Glass vessels may be made with different coloured layers. Subsequently a few large facets may be cut down through the layers of colour, revealing how these lie in relation to each other and achieving an interesting refractive effect. Monica Morales-Schildt, who is much-travelled and knows a great deal about foreign applied art, represents the most continental element in Swedish glass. She works almost exclusively in coloured glass.

216: Bowl, 18 cm. broad, and vase, 20 cm. high, of crystal glass with coloured layer on the inner surface. Made 1959 by VICKE LINDSTRAND, Sweden, at *Kosta* glassworks. Lindstrand, who has worked so much in colours, naturally likes to introduce them into his glassware, which takes the form of heavy abstract shapes with a strong colour content. Glass can be coloured either by colouring the body of the glass itself or else by the use of a coloured layer and the latter may be on either the outer or the inner surface.

215

216

217: Large 'Fuga' bowl, 31 cm. high and 57 broad, designed by SVEN PALMQVIST, Sweden, for *Orrefors* glassworks. Pile-woven rug designed by BARBRO NILSSON 1955, made by *Märta Måås-Fjetterström Ltd.*

218: Oval bowl in crystal glass, 30 cm. broad, with inset coloured filaments and air-bubbles: designed 1958 by EDWARD HALD, Sweden, at *Orrefors* glassworks. The technique used here was worked out experimentally at Orrefors in the years 1915–20, and is called Graal. It uses Emile Gallé's layering technique in a new way, with the etched, cut, or engraved patterns melted into the glass. This gives the artist great opportunities for colour-effects. Hald, who was originally a studio painter, has produced many remarkably interesting works in this technique. He began work at Orrefors as early as 1917. The bowl shown here is an elaborate version of the Graal technique which the artist calls Aqua-Graal, since the regular lines of small bubbles give the impression of water.

219: Bowl with colour ornamentation in the glass, 20 cm. high, 32 cm. broad, designed by SVEN PALMQVIST, Sweden, at *Orrefors* glassworks. Palmqvist has worked in glass, exclusively at Orrefors, since 1927. He has been through the factory's engraving school, and has subsequently obtained further training. He is an experimentalist, and works out with quiet concentration the processes for making practical ware in the Fuga series and this version of the Orrefors Graal technique which he calls 'Ravenna'. The variety and depth of colour of the decoration makes one think, though without comparison, of the more exclusive ceramic materials.

217

218

219

220: Wineglasses of crystal glass, 28–53 cm. high. Designed 1956 by NILS LANDBERG, Sweden, and made at *Orrefors* glassworks. This 'tulip' glass is made with a coloured layer on the inner surface, and in the stems this layer stands out beautifully beneath the clear glass. The thin bowl is blown, and the elegant stem and foot drawn out of the same two-toned piece of glass instead of being assembled from separate pieces. The edge of the foot is turned up to form a beaded rim. This work demands much concentration from the artist, and the highest degree of collaboration between him and the skilled glass-blower. In the brief moment of creation the material must stand up to a severe strain.

221: Three bottles of coloured glass, 15–20 cm. high; designed 1959 by ERIK HÖGLUND, Sweden, and made by *Boda* works. Höglund is a young man, and began as a sculptor. He takes great delight in trying out the possibilities of different materials. His glassware also shows a spontaneous joy in modelling. In colours, structure, and technique his glass reminds one of the eras before the Eighteenth Century, which has had such an influence on general Swedish ideas of taste. It gives a gay and confident impression, breaks away from what is commonly prized and accepted, and takes a new and primitive line valid both in Scandinavia and elsewhere.

221

222: Spherical vase of crystal glass, 37 cm. high, designed 1955 by INGEBORG LUNDIN, Sweden, and made at *Orrefors* glassworks. This vase incarnates all the lightness in the concept of glass, a great bubble, made entirely in the glass-house in a form which has the surprise-effect of the really natural. Ingeborg Lundin can occasionally be over-elaborate; but in this vase, called 'Apple', she shows that she can also be spontaneous.

223: Prism-shaped crystal vase with engraving: designed 1959 by INGEBORG LUNDIN, Sweden, and made at *Orrefors* glassworks. Spheres and cylinders are the most natural shapes for blown glass, and therefore it is encouraging to try a completely different form. Ingeborg Lundin is represented here both by a sphere, a glass bubble, and this prism, whose character she has accentuated with abstract cutting, unpolished and left matt. This is a technique she often uses: it gives a graphic effect, as distinct from polished cutting, which produces light-refractions. She has achieved the latter in the form itself, which collects and refracts the light.

223

224: Three asymmetrical vases, 11–28 cm. high, of crystal glass with cutting. Designed 1955 by VICKE LINDSTRAND, Sweden, and made by *Kosta* glassworks. When glass is blown, in accordance with a physical law it is of equal thickness at every point: but there are tricks for preventing this. Lindstrand has made use of these to get the air-bubbles in his vases placed asymmetrically. This sort of thing is typical of him: his active talent is always searching for 'different' effects. He is the expressionist in Swedish art-glass; and he looks outside the balanced classicist world for his media and expression, with a lively perception of modern trends. He has worked in other fields, in poster-design, studio painting, and ceramics. The glass-artist's medium seems most naturally suited to him, because this material has to be shaped with the inspiration of the moment in a few glowing minutes–in a form which, once set, cannot be added to but only cut away, worked down into, and further decorated.

225: Vase and bowl of crystal glass with inset air-cavity decoration: vase 22 cm. high, bowl 20 cm. broad. Designed 1955 and 1956 by BENGT EDENFALK, Sweden, and made by *Skruf* glassworks. As a material glass has many aesthetic assets, of which transparency and light-refraction are the most prominent. It can be made into light bubbles or heavy masses. Edenfalk's glass is massive, but still gives an effect of lightness because of the air-bubbles inset into its thick walls in interesting groupings.

226: Engraved crystal vase, 25 cm. high, designed 1960 by GUNNAR CYRÉN, Sweden, and made at *Orrefors* glassworks. The methods used in decorating glass may be divided into those carried out in the glass-house while the material is still hot and those which must wait till it has cooled. Among the latter is engraving, whereby with cutting equipment and copper wheels one can trace ornaments and figures, matt or shining, on the surface of the glass. Cyrén was trained as a silversmith, and his ideas of form are based on that craft. His particular interest is engraving, which won Orrefors international renown in 1925. This firm, with its staff of first-class glass-engravers, is especially well placed to follow out his intentions.

227: Oval bowl of crystal glass with engraving, 20 cm. broad, designed 1955 by EDWARD HALD, Sweden, and made at *Orrefors* glassworks. Hald is one of the most prominent of the generation of Swedish artists who before 1920 followed the call for improved industrial products. He has worked at Orrefors since 1917, and was its chief for many years. He has a great output behind him, and has had much influence on the glass of his contemporaries. This bowl with its light engraving shows his characteristic traits—no heaviness, but 'esprit' and a masterly appreciation of what is appropriate to glass.

227

228

229

228: Two sets of table-glasses in semi-crystal, designed 1957 by NILS LANDBERG, Sweden, and made at *Orrefors* glassworks. Table-glasses each have a particular purpose, and therefore particular dimensions and capacity. It is an example of human ingenuity that they can be made as different as those shown, when the difference lies not in decoration but solely in form. The set on the left is uncoloured. The stems were not attached but were drawn out from the same piece of glass as the bowl, which can be seen in the way in which the inside of the bowl follows the transition to the stem. The same applies to the transition from stem to foot, and this is beautifully finished with a raised edge. The other set is in grey glass, less upright than the first, but with a handsome upward-reaching profile. Landberg belongs to the middle generation at Orre-fors, learnt the craft in the firm's engraving school, and has been one of its artists since the beginning of the Thirties. He has an elegant sense of form, a brilliant mastery of technique, and a perfect knowledge of the material's possibilities.

229: Set of table-glasses in semi-crystal, designed 1956 by VICKE LINDSTRAND, Sweden, and made at *Kosta* glassworks. Kosta glassworks, founded in 1742, has a strong tradition in table-glass. Even an artist as independent as Lindstrand is bound by tradition, in this case by the artistically limited possibilities of table-glass. With his very varied talents, he can at one moment make surely formed and (in the best sense of the word) traditional table-glass, and at the next completely abstract sculptures in the same material.

230: Glasses, and jug 21 cm. high, designed 1958 by KJELL BLOMBERG, Sweden, and made at *Gullaskruf* glassworks. The products of glassworks have a character of their own, stamped by traditional techniques, appropriate methods of production, and the particular talents and training of their staff of craftsmen. At the same time, they are influenced by the aesthetic and business chiefs of the firm and by the needs of the market. Blomberg is able to make a happy use of Gullaskruf's facilities, and to add new and individual traits. His predecessor at the works, Hugo Gehlin (d. 1953), Arthur Percy, and the firm's late chief William Stenberg, developed the works' glass compositions and its excellent craftsmanship by having form and decoration mostly completed in the glass-house and only to a minor extent 'improved' with cutting and engraving. Blomberg, who is still young, has continued to work on the same lines, both with objective practical glassware and more decorative glass.

231: Glass bowls of various sizes, centrifugally formed: produced by *Orrefors* glassworks according to the technique and form of SVEN PALMQVIST, 1950, Sweden. The idea of 'design' goes back to the beginnings of craft-work, but today the expression is more topical than ever. It now applies not only to the outer form alone but also to its relationship with function and with the process of manufacture. It would be hard to find a better example of a natural and simple design than Palmqvist's Fuga series. For these functional forms he himself invented an unconventional process in which the rapidly rotating molten metal is flung outwards by centrifugal force. This gives smooth natural forms such as can hardly be achieved by any other method.

232

232: Soft-drink glasses, in clear violet or smoky glass: designed 1960 by KAJ FRANCK, Finland, for *Wärtsilä/Notsjö*.

233: Wineglasses in various sizes and colours, designed 1959 by KAJ FRANCK, Finland, for *Wärtsilä/Notsjö*. The artist's object here was to make glasses for claret and other wines in as simple a form as possible, but at the same time to keep something of the appropriate festive atmosphere. The result was these modernised tumblers. They also have the practical advantage of being stackable.

233

234

234: 'Soap Bubbles', glass vases designed 1950 by KAJ FRANCK, Finland, for *Wärt-silä/Notsjö*. Smoky or clear-smoky: in two sizes, 32 and 22 cm. high. Another example of Franck's sense of the value of simple forms. The glass is very thin, and is equally suitable as a vase for slender flowers or twigs or as a purely decorative object in itself.

235: 'Woodcock', glass figure by KAJ FRANCK, Finland, 1953: made at *Wärt-silä/Notsjö*. Height 6–8 cm. The bubbles and sooty spots in the glass are produced by mixing iron with the glass material.

235

236: 'Ice-block', crystal vase designed 1960 by Tapio Wirkkala, Finland, for *Iittala* glassworks: height 20 cm. Amongst Wirkkala's best works of the early Fifties was the crystal bowl 'Iceberg', which had sharp edges and a form so dynamic that it seemed as if petrified in the middle of an explosion. With 'Ice-block' the artist, after a long series of strictly geometrical works in clear or clear-and-coloured crystal, has returned to this nature-inspired form. The fluted surfaces give a peculiar illusion of melting ice. Gold medal at 1960 Triennale.

237: Bowl in cut crystal, designed 1951 by Tapio Wirkkala, Finland, for *Iittala* glassworks. 30 cm. long, 8 high. A very simple piece, but with tensions between the curves and angles and with refractions in the mass. Bought by Museum of Modern Art, New York: Grand Prix at 1954 Triennale.

237

238

238: Stacking glasses in three sizes, designed 1951 by SAARA HOPEA, Finland, for *Wärtsilä/Notsjö*, Made in three colours: violet-blue, smoky olive, and clear ruby.

239

239: 'Neptune' tumblers, with cut base, designed 1946 by GUNNEL NYMAN, Finland, for *Wärtsilä/Notsjö*. Made in five sizes, in clear coloured glass only. Gunnel Nyman's name is chiefly associated with the elegant art-glass which she produced for several of Finland's leading glassworks before her premature death; but she also made good practical glass such as this. Glasses with heavy solid bases are, as the name implies, intended for use on shipboard.

240

240: Large soft-drink glasses and small wine glasses, designed 1960 by HARRY MOILANEN, Finland, for *Wärtsilä/Notsjö:* in smoky or clear glass.

241

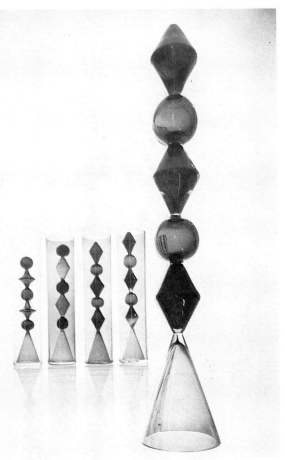

241: Crystal vases in the 'Polar' series, designed 1959 by HELENA TYNELL, Finland, for *Riihimäki* glassworks. From the left, 'Northern Lights', in three sizes, 22, 28, and 16 cm. high, in blue-green and red-clear green: 'North Star', blue and clear, 9 cm. high: 'Midnight Sun', red and clear, 9 cm. high: 'Lapp Hat', dark blue and clear, 12 cm. high. This is a representative collection of the artist's latest art-glass. The colours of 'Northern Lights' are achieved with an ordinary layering technique with three blowings and the coloured layer inmost, but cutting in a great number of crystalline forms gives an amazingly rich play of colour. In 'Lapp Hat' too, complex cutting produces rich effects from the blue innermost layer.

243

242

242: 'Midsummer Pole', figure in dark blue, violet, and orange glass. Designed 1957 by NANNY STILL, Finland, for *Riihimäki* glassworks: 30 cm. high. The bold colour combination is very typical of Nanny Still's art-glass. On the other hand she has also made matter-of-fact practical glassware, such as the very simple and inexpensive Viiru series, and the taut 'Black & White' range in opal-white and black. She has another version in which the pieces illustrated are set in cylindrical vases with different colour-tones.

243: 'Saturn', glass vase in three sizes, designed 1960 by NANNY STILL, Finland, for *Riihimäki* glassworks. Made in two colours, violet and golden. Height 4, 5, and 12 cm. The vases can also be used as candlesticks.

244: Bottle in clear glass, with metal fitting to stopper: height 13.5 cm. Designed by ARNE JON JUTREM, Norway, for *Hadeland* glassworks. The foursquare but rounded form gives this bottle a changing play of line which makes for life and interest in its surfaces.

245: Glass vases, 14 and 11.5 cm. high: designed by ARNE JON JUTREM, Norway, for *Hadeland* glassworks. These vases derive their character from the interrelation of the form and the clear glass with its irregular white dots. It makes us think automatically of sculpture carved in ice.

244

245

246: Drinking glasses, designed by ARNE JON JUTREM, Norway, for *Hadeland* glassworks, 1958. A form as austere as this makes great demands on the quality of the glass. There is no decoration or break of line to conceal any technical flaws. Jutrem works very closely with the craftsmen in the glasshouse: he knows the glass material they are using, and fully understands their sensitive precision. This makes it safe for him to design such simple glasses.

247: Pressed glassware, designed by WILLY JOHANSSON, Norway, for *Hadeland* glassworks. Diameter of dish 33 cm. The simplicity and naturalness of Johansson's many-sided work in glass is plainly seen in the sets of pressed glass he has designed. This is his latest, designed in 1960.

247

248: Steel-grey drinking-glasses, designed by WILLY JOHANSSON, Norway, for *Hadeland* glassworks, 1958. These have the simple and almost inevitable shape which appears in so many of this artist's products. The grey tone accentuates the lines of their natural form.

249: Brown glass vase, rim in clear glass: 8.5 cm. high, 11 cm. diameter. Designed by WILLY JOHANSSON, Norway, for *Hadeland* glassworks, 1960.

249

250: Bowl, diameter 14 cm., and vase, height 25 cm. Designed by WILLY JOHANSSON, Norway, for *Hadeland* glassworks, 1960. Johansson has consciously achieved a surface effect with the visibly grained structure of the material.

251: Caraffe, tumbler, and vase in clear glass, designed by ARNE LINDAAS, Norway, for *Norsk Glassverk*. Caraffe 17 cm. high. Lindaas is an artist who has made a contribution in several different fields. He designs fabrics, glassware, ceramics, work in wood, etc., with the same apparent ease. But he has a thorough knowledge of the materials he works with, and a long period of study at the glassworks lies behind his glassware.

252: Table-glasses designed by AXEL MØRCH, Norway, for *Norsk Glassverk Ltd*. Mørch was awarded a silver medal for his exhibits at the 1960 Triennale. He is 35 years old, and in Norway great things are confidently expected of him.

251

252

253

253: Wine decanter and glasses, designed 1957 by JACOB E. BANG, Denmark, for *Kastrup* glassworks. Height of decanter 23 cm. Bang discovered a decanter which pleased him in a 19th century oil painting of a scene in an Italian inn. It was made as one continuous body, having thereby greater unity of form than ordinary decanters divided into neck and flask. He worked on this type for some time, and eventually reached the model shown here. As compared with the original, it is more taut and rather more square in form. The neck is also broader, so that it fills the hand when grasped. In a little book of impressions from travel in Italy (*Italienske Bagateller*, 1959) Bang writes: "The things we live with should be sound, pleasant, and practical, real friends who say what needs saying and do what needs doing, quiet, and without superfluous elements and assertive personality." His own practical glassware is in accordance with this manifesto.

254

254: 'Stump' drinking-glasses, designed 1959 by GRETE MEYER and IBI TRIER MØRCH, Denmark, for *Kastrup* glassworks. In recent years Danish industrial designers have done much work on the problems of storage in the home. Not only have cupboards and drawers been analysed and worked upon, but also the space requirements of separate articles have been taken into account. In this table-glass the two women designers have produced stackable glasses, to save space in the kitchen cupboard and on the kitchen table. Stacking can, as shown, be done in two ways, but in each case the glasses rest on each other in such a way that the thin glass wall is not subjected to the outward strain which arises in stacking tumblers of the usual shape. This is particularly important in washing up, since temperature changes set up further strains in the glass, which combined with outward pressure can cause breakage.

255

256

257

255: Teapot, beakers, and jug in earthenware, made in slip technique by JENS VON DER LIPPE, Norway. Height of jug 17 cm. Jens von der Lippe's pottery is based on earlier Norwegian tradition, but is nevertheless strongly marked with his own personal ideas. His products have their intrinsic value, but besides this they have a special importance in that they are made by an artist who is also in charge of the ceramics department at the State School of Crafts and Industrial Art. Jens von der Lippe has been an inspiring influence on his pupils, because of the intense creative joy which fills him and is apparent in his work as a potter.

256: Porcelain dishes, designed by EYSTEIN SANDNES, Norway: 35×25 and 25×23 cm. Parts of a service made by *Porsgrund* porcelain-works, in which effects depend chiefly on the contrast between the dark-brown and white parts. Sandnes shows calm and balanced design in his products. He has an objective artistic judgement, and takes full account of the needs of industry. Besides designing porcelain he has a large output of earthenware and glass behind him. Linen cloth designed by BIRGIT WESSEL and made by *Joh. Petersen's* linen-mills.

257: Stoneware vases by ERIK PLØEN, Norway: tallest 46 cm. When we see an assortment of work in ceramics, it is often hard to tell which artist made any particular object: the means of expression are, after all, limited. But there can be no possible doubt about Pløen's work: it is quite in a class by itself, and has an individuality peculiar to this hard-working artist.

258: Stoneware vases and bowl by DAGNY and FINN HALD, Norway; bowl 26 cm. high, 34 cm. diameter. These artists work without assistants, and the things they create have so much of the personality of both that it is impossible to regard this married couple as two separate artists. They express themselves in an easy and natural form-idiom, and take great care to make their glazes and decoration harmonise with the characteristic simplicity of stoneware.

259: Stoneware vases by DAGNY and FINN HALD, Norway: the nearer 20 cm. in diameter, the further 20 cm. high. The vases are characteristic of these artists' products, which are a valuable addition to Norwegian stoneware. This has no earlier tradition to draw upon, since stoneware production began only in recent years in Norway.

260: Assortment of recent works in stoneware by ERIK PLØEN: tallest 21.5 cm. Pløen is one of the outstanding figures among Norwegian ceramic artists. He normally expresses himself in austere forms often based on the architectonic lines of earlier cultures, but the glazes and decoration he puts on them are entirely his own. In technique he is an exceptionally skilful potter, with complete mastery of his media. He works quite alone, in his own studio.

260

261: Stoneware jars with dense, partly matt, iron glazes, made in 1957 by CHRISTIAN POULSEN, Denmark: height 24 cm. Most modern Danish stoneware is made by the large factories through the collaboration of potter, chemist, and artist. Poulsen is one of the few who make it single-handed. His latest works are simple tautly modelled vessels with a massive body and a very thick glaze which often droops towards the base. He does not regard every separate piece as a thing complete in itself, but sees all his work as a coherent artistic manifestation. His glazes are therefore closely attuned to each other, and for that reason make their strongest impression when they are put together in contrast and harmony.

262: Stoneware tureen with brush decoration in blue on a grey ground, covered with transparent white glaze. Made in 1952 by GERTRUD VASEGAARD, Denmark, at *Bing & Grøndahl* porcelain-works. Diameter 19 cm. At Bing & Grøndahl several younger artists have worked for years with 'blue painting', a special technique deriving from the work of the architect Carl Petersen at this factory round about 1910. They have all used it mainly in connection with porcelain; but Gertrud Vasegaard has employed it particularly in her stoneware, with its forms based on the honest household stoneware vessels of earlier times. This tureen is typical of her blue-painting. The colour does not, as in the world-famous Danish under-glaze painting, lie under the glaze as beneath glass. In firing it is absorbed into the glaze, and combines with it to form the outer surface. Aksel Rode collaborates in making the glaze and the dark greenish-blue colouring which Gertrud Vasegaard uses.

261

262

263: Stoneware bowl in 'fluted' style, made in 1939 by AXEL SALTO, Denmark, for the *Royal Copenhagen Porcelain Manufactory* and the *Faience Manufactory Aluminia*. Height 11 cm. In Salto's stoneware the material and the decoration harmonise in an unusual fashion. By means of modelled or deeply incised ornamentation the body projects through the glaze and reveals its own material effects. In this bowl the glaze softens the cut relief, but at the same time accentuates it by settling in different thicknesses, thinnest on the projecting edges and thickest in the depressions. Even after firing the bowl keeps the character of the wet clay from which it was made. One realises why the potter when working on the decoration put little pressure on the circular form.

264: Jars in, respectively, the 'budding' and the 'sprouting' style, made in 1937, 1930, and 1948 by AXEL SALTO, Denmark, for the *Royal Copenhagen Porcelain Manufactory* and the *Faience Manufactory Aluminia*. Foremost jar 18 cm. high. Salto used the 'budding' style to carry out his experiments with the interplay of material and glaze. He is still concerned with 'ceramic ornament', but in the later style it is as though the inner tension had grown greater, as if the 'innate force of the thing' – as Salto call its – had begun to move under the enclosing surface. Finally, in the 'sprouting' style, the emergent life-force breaks out through the unity of the form, forcing outwards in long spines over which the glaze divides and runs like lava.

263
264

265

265: Stoneware bowl with green glaze on the inner side, made in 1960 by KIRSTEN WEEKE, Denmark, for 'Saxbo'. Diameter 28 cm. Kirsten Weeke has been one of the staff at Saxbo who have helped to bring out the new Saxbo style. The bowl shown here is typical of some of her work. Its form is heavy, its outer surface rustic, and its decoration bold and painter-like. The material is a combination of stoneware and chamotte, covered externally with a dark slip through which the decoration has been cut.

266

266: Bowl and jar in stoneware, made in 1959 by PEDER RASMUSSEN, Denmark. Height of jar 26 cm. Rasmussen finds many of his materials literally just outside his door—in cinders from a fire or in kilns at a works where seed-pods are used for firing, etc. These chemicals are the same as those which can be bought, but are full of impurities and thus give the vigorous effect in structure and colours which many younger Danish ceramic artists cultivate in protest against the perfection of products from the large factories. In these two pieces a yellowish-grey stoneware clay has been used. The bowl has an iron and ash glaze, which droops heavily towards the base without completely covering it. The jar, which has a triangular section, was first treated with an ash glaze and then with an alkali glaze. In firing the two chemicals have interacted and made odd runs and figures on the smooth surface.

267

267: Bowl and jar in high-fired earthenware, made in 1960 by GUDRUN MEEDOM BÆCH, Denmark. Height of jar 20 cm. After leaving Bing & Grøndahl in 1953, Gudrun Bæch has worked entirely in her own studio, single-handed. She collects her materials from the vicinity. She washes her own clay, thins it with sand from a bank by the Limfjord, and herself burns

the apple- and alder-wood ash to make her glazes. Her forms are simple, and her decorations move sensitively around them in a lively rhythm. The decoration on the large jar was cut into the red clay and the depressions filled with white slip. The bowl decoration was painted with cobalt. The smooth vital character of the surface is achieved by the ash glaze boiling up at a late stage of firing into bubbles, which break and melt out again.

268: Stoneware jar, made in 1960 by EDITH SONNE BRUUN, Denmark, for *Saxbo*: glaze by NATHALIE KREBS. Height 21 cm. When Saxbo's artists began in the late Fifties to cultivate rustic and vigorous effects, the 'classic Saxbo style' was replaced by something new. Smooth polished forms gave way to powerful, often massive, large-girthed shapes, and the glaze was allowed to run over the rough material and make its own bluff patterns. This jar is typical of the new type of Saxbo product. Chamotte (crushed burnt clay) is mixed into the dark stoneware clay, giving a surface with hollows and grooves in which the dark-brown glaze can collect. Where the glaze lies thicker it appears a darker colour.

269: Stoneware jar with lid, made in 1960 by EVA STÆHR-NIELSEN, Denmark, for *Saxbo*: glaze by NATHALIE KREBS. Height 90 cm. Eva Stæhr-Nielsen does not personally throw her vessels and jars. She draws them on large sheets of paper and leaves it to others to form them in clay. But she herself supervises the process, modifies the forms, perhaps models them, touches up lines and curves, and finally cuts the surface ornament. The jar shown, which is in red chamotte clay, was modelled after throwing, so that the section is oval. The low relief was then cut in the broader sides, and the panels painted, before it was glazed.

268

269

270

271

272

270: Earthenware jug, made in 1960 by LISA ENGQVIST, Denmark: height 18 cm. Lisa Engqvist carries on the folk-pottery tradition with its delight in colour. This jug was first thrown in open vase form; then the spout was made by pressing the sides together, so that a large and a small opening were formed. The 'web' between these two was then cut away, separating the spout from the body. The handle was made with the fingers, and is decorated with stamping on its smoothed-off joins with the body. Other stamped ornament runs in a belt round the jug and accentuates its form. The glaze was put on by dipping. This jug is the best possible example of a form which arises directly from the work of the hands with clay. It was not based on previous sketches on paper, but took shape on the wheel.

271: Stoneware made in 1960 by CONNY WALTHER, Denmark: diameter of bowl 28 cm. Beginning with simple folk-pottery forms, Conny Walther in her small studio has produced bowls, jars, and oval phials with smooth heavy forms. As in the examples shown, she often uses small stamped or incised motifs to accentuate the form; but for her the essential point is the material effects of the rustic cha-motte-clay and the thick smooth glazes.

272: Two earthenware jars, made in 1960 by BIRTE WEGGERBY, Denmark: height of larger 60 cm. In her ceramics Birte Weggerby aims at a harmony of material, form, and decoration. "The form should determine the decoration and the material effects," she says, "and the decoration conditions the form." The pot-men shown were modelled in yellowish chamotte clay, and then decorated with black and white slip. After the first firing they were given a blue alkali glaze, which appears olive-green on the clay, pure blue on the white slip, and dense blue-black on the black.

273: Unglazed and salt-glazed stoneware, made in 1960 by NILS KÄHLER, Denmark, at *Herman A. Kähler*. Height of teapot 11 cm. Common earthenware has been used for practical pottery for centuries, but it seldom satisfies modern demands for cleanliness and durability. Stoneware, on the other hand, can hold its own very well indeed beside faience and porcelain, and with rationalised production it can also compete in price. Nils Kähler has produced, for Herman A. Kähler in Næstved, just such a competitive output of practical ware in unglazed and salt-glazed stoneware. The tea-pot in the foreground is a variant of a traditional and quite simple thrown form. The material is fine-grained clay with a lively surface.

274: Earthenware dish, made in 1959 by GRETE LINDBLAD, Denmark: diameter 37 cm. Grete Lindblad uses her ceramic media as a painter uses his, only replacing the canvas with a pottery surface and the brush with a cowhorn filled with coloured glaze. This dish was thrown in red clay and completely covered in protective glaze. Before firing this glaze looks grey: only in the heat of the kiln do its strong and sparkling colours appear.

275: 'Patella' oven-proof ware, designed in 1957 by MAGNUS STEPHENSEN, Denmark, for the *Royal Copenhagen Porcelain Manufactory* and *the Faience Manufactory Aluminia*. Maximum diameter of large casserole 24.5 cm. In recent decades there has been in Scandinavia a move away from the dining service. Changed eating habits, and different kinds of food, have given rise to a demand for practically-designed serving units which can be bought separately, and which can take their place on the table alongside other articles. Stephensen's 'Patella' ware was designed to meet this need. As colour-pattern he supplied a withered and spotted oak-leaf, and the brown glaze was specially made for this series. The desired colour-effect was completely achieved, and incidentally the glaze proved to be most efficient in covering any iron-spots in the material. A poetic fancy thus had the effect of reducing the factory's proportion of rejects.

273

275

276: Stoneware bowl, 23 cm. broad, and vase, 17 cm. high, by WILHELM KÅGE, Sweden, made in 1959 at *Gustavsberg* works. It has often been pointed out that there is close contact between Swedish industrial art and art-handicrafts, and that the same artists work both in an exclusive studio and in the design department of a factory. Kåge, for example, during all his time as artistic director at Gustavsberg has worked both on rational practical ware for mass-production and on exclusive products of a sometimes burlesque and sometimes wholly serious nature. In his work one can also see a painter's marked love of colour. One kind of stoneware which he has worked with since 1940 he calls Farsta, after the island Gustavsberg stands on. This has been described as lightly-fired stoneware or high-fired earthenware. In any case, it is the material which suits Kåge: it has a heavy clay and a powerful ever-changing colour-scheme.

277: Earthenware bowl, made in 1960 by LISBET MUNCH-PETERSEN, Denmark: diameter 15 cm. Like Axel Salto, Lisbet Munch-Petersen draws her inspiration from impressions of Nature—fruits, seed-pods, and pinecones may be recognised in her ceramic forms, and in the composition of her glazes one can sense the moss-covered boulders under the cliffs of Bornholm where she has her studio. In the thin sides of this bowl she has carved a simple leaf-decoration, which attaches itself naturally to the form. The bowl has a light glaze, which droops downwards but leaves the base uncovered.

278: Stoneware urn, 32 cm. high, thrown by BERNDT FRIBERG, Sweden, at *Gustavsberg* works. Friberg was trained as a thrower, and everything he signs was thrown by himself personally. He works exclusively with form and glaze, and handles both in a masterly manner. The form is always distinguished and simple, never decorated, and the glazes are tranquil and never of the 'eruptive' variety favoured by some artists.

276

277

279

279: Two vases and a jar in stoneware, made in 1960 by STIG LINDBERG, Sweden, at *Gustavsberg* works. Besides his comprehensive work in design for mass-production, Lindberg also makes interesting and brilliantly designed stoneware with skilfully employed glaze effects.

280

280: Bowl and two vases in stoneware, made by ERICH and INGRID TRILLER, *Tobo* stoneware-studio, Sweden. If one talks of 'pure' stoneware, the Trillers' may be taken as an example. The forms are simplified to the utmost, and any decoration, even a simple incised or painted line, is unthinkable. Material, form, and glaze are everything, according to the principles which this pair have upheld through the years. There is nothing here for the sensation-seeker, but sound 'right' articles of high quality and with a charm which lies precisely in their rejection of effects. Since 1935 the Trillers have carried on their stoneware workshop north of Uppsala in a collaboration which is outstanding, with Ingrid specially concerned with aesthetics and Erich with technique –in so far as these two elements can, in the long run, be distinguished.

281

281: Earthenware dishes, c. 40 cm. in diameter, with slip as well as painted and incised decoration. Made by HERTHA HILLFON, Sweden, 1960. Hertha Hillfon is a notable figure in Swedish ceramics. She began her training as a potter quite late in life, impelled by strong artistic ambitions. In the course of the few years in which she has so far worked in her own studio, she has aroused well-merited attention and created an independent place for herself. She has also had an influence on others, especially the young, but this has so far only produced reflections of her own strong personality as an artist. She often works sculpturally, and uses clay, glazes, and colours as media for expressing her free artistic ideas. But she also uses ordinary practical forms like bowls, mugs, and jars, as simple bases for a decorative scheme.

282

282: Three stoneware jars, 24–36 cm. high: made by CARL-HARRY STÅLHANE, Sweden, at *Rörstrand* porcelain-works. Stålhane is one of those artists who exploit the possibilities of stoneware to the uppermost. These extreme potentialities are massiveness and aptitude for primitive expression. But it is a very refined primitivism, which sounds like a paradox. His forms are large and simple, and glazed with materials from neighbouring geological deposits. Stålhane has been through several stages of development since he assisted Isaac Grünewald in painting faience at Rörstrand round about 1940. By way of an elegant Sung period in his art, and surface glaze decoration on asymmetrical forms, he has now reached his present massive style. He has also designed table-services and other practical ware, and in this double output of industrially-made useful products and exclusive experimental ware he is in line with other Swedish artists.

213

283

284   285

283: Chamotte stoneware, 5–13 cm. in diameter, by KARIN BJÖRQUIST, 1960. Sculpture in the same material, 35 cm. long, by LISA LARSON, 1958. Made at *Gustavsberg* works, Sweden. Linen fabric from Swedish Domestic Crafts Association. Most porcelain works in Scandinavia have studios where artists can experiment and express their decorative ideas. Karin Björquist and Lisa Larson belong to the youngest generation at Gustavsberg. They work in, amongst other things, chamotte stoneware, on which they sketch, paint, and glaze–each expressing her own quite different temperament. Karin Björquist has a quite massive geometrical idiom, quiet and introspective, while Lisa Larson, with high spirits and a freer style, makes the clay into amusing people and animals.

284: Egg-shaped earthenware containers, 25 cm. high, made by HANS HEDBERG, Sweden, 1959. Hedberg had his training as a potter in Italy, and now lives in the South of France. Nevertheless his work represents an extrovert element in Swedish art-craftmanship. He works with large simple forms, predominantly decorative in function. The egg-shaped containers shown can certainly be used to keep something in, but they must be primarily regarded as 'for enjoyment', not least for their colouring. They rest on metal stands.

285: Dish in black-stained chamotte earthenware, with glaze decoration, diameter 40 cm. Made in 1957 by INGRID ATTERBERG, Sweden, at *Upsala-Ekeby Ltd.* Besides her models for mass-produced practical wares, Ingrid Atterberg makes decorative things which express her artistic temperament. She uses practical forms–bowls, dishes, and jars–but gives them a decorative significance in addition to their purely functional purpose. She likes to give her earthenware additional effects by firing it to the limit of heat which it can stand, or by staining the clay or mixing in grains of previously-fired clay (chamotte). She generally uses the colder section of the colour-scale, and her designs are geometrical.

286: Three jars of chamotte stoneware, externally unglazed. Made by SIGNE PERSSON-MELIN, Sweden, 1960. This artist

286   287

takes the material as her starting-point, and to achieve the greatest possible effect from it she gives her pots large enclosed forms, sometimes with simple decoration in relief. She contrasts glazed with unglazed surfaces, and works in a limited colour-scale dominated by the hue of the clay itself. She also shows her sense of the monumental in decorative works. In the new People's House in Stockholm, opened in 1960, she has carried out a very large scheme of ceramic wall-decoration in collaboration with the sculptor and ceramic artist Anders Liljefors. Her workshop produces an attractive array of bowls, jars, and jugs, equally stamped with her fine sense of form and material.

287: Wine-jars, 32 cm. high, of salt-glazed stoneware, and earthenware bowl, 26 cm. diameter. Made by TOM MÖLLER, Sweden. Möller and his Danish-born wife

Grete have shared a studio in Stockholm since 1943. There they produce attractive practical ware and decorative articles in earthenware and stoneware. Möller also works with glass, which he has made for Alsterbro and since 1960 for Reijmyre, both in Sweden. He and his wife are typical artist-craftsmen, and have meant something in their circle. Möller is, for example, chairman of the artist-craftsmen's sales organisation in Stockholm.

288: Bowl and teapot in earthenware, made in 1959 by GRETE MÖLLER, Sweden. Grete Möller is Danish by birth, and was trained at the Copenhagen School of Arts and Crafts. She and her husband Tom are both potters and artist-craftsmen in the best sense of the term. They complement each other splendidly, since Grete, as one would expect, has a feminine and Danish gentleness.

288

289

289: Parts of a service of heat-resisting felspar-porcelain, designed in 1954 by SVEN ERIK SKAWONIUS, Sweden, for *Upsala-Ekeby Ltd.*, Karlskrona. Cotton cloth from *Almedahl-Dalsjöfors Ltd.* The separate parts of this well-thought-out series can be used in combination and stacked upon each other. They are dimensioned to suit Swedish practice, and also to fit the average oven. The measurements and functional forms were worked out in consultation with the State Consumer Research Institute.

290

290: Parts of an earthenware service with opaque glaze, designed in 1955 by ARTHUR C:SON PERCY, Sweden, and made at *Upsala-Ekeby Ltd.*, Gävle. Arthur C:son Percy was originally a 'pure' artist, trained by Matisse. He belongs to the generation which made Swedish industrial art famous, especially through the Paris Exhibition of 1925. In 1923 he joined Gävle porcelain-works. He is still a painter, and besides ceramics has designed patterns for fabric-printing and in recent years also glass for Gullaskruf.

291

291: Earthenware teacups with copper-printed decoration, designed in 1951 by ARTHUR C:SON PERCY, Sweden, and made at *Upsala-Ekeby Ltd.*, Gävle. Tray in pinewood from South Kalmar Domestic Crafts Association. This is typical of Percy's later products: a simple but individually proportioned form, and a rich and well-composed decoration.

292

292: Cooking- and serving-ware in oven-proof earthenware designed in 1954 by MARIANNE WESTMAN, Sweden, and made at *Rörstrand* porcelain-works. Marianne Westman has been attached to Rörstrand since 1950, and devotes herself to modern beautiful everyday things. The decoration is done by copper-printed outlines and under-glaze painting.

293

293: Jar in red chamotte earthenware, with black glaze: 56 cm. high. Designed and made by EDGAR BÖCKMAN, Sweden, 1950. Böckman belongs to the pioneer generation of the period between 1910 and 1920. Then he worked for Höganäs-Billesholm, but has since had his own workshop and was for a decade head of the ceramics department at the State School for Arts, Crafts and Design. Formerly he decorated his work to some extent, but gradually he has gone over to working almost exclusively with effects of form and material.

294: Unglazed coarse stoneware sculpture in brown and blue, 40 cm. high, made in 1960 by TYRA LUNDGREN, Sweden. Tyra Lundgren has a unique place in Swedish industrial art. She was originally trained as a sculptor, and began early to treat ceramics sculpturally. By this route she came to applied art at various ceramic works including 'Arabia' and Sèvres, and then also in glass, as with Venini at Murano. She now works chiefly with purely sculptural treatment, reliefs, and ceramic figures. She has a vigorous decorative style, and is excellent at playing off against each other the ceramic materials and the structures and colours of the glazes.

294

217

295

295: Stoneware pots and jugs, 6–27 cm. high, with grey-green glaze. Made in 1960 by JOHN ANDERSSON, Sweden, for *Andersson & Johansson*, Höganäs. John Andersson learnt throwing and the craft of ceramics from one of the firm's two founders, Karl Andersson, and he has always worked there. He is an example of the not altogether common combination of designer and craftsman in one individual. He has achieved and developed his sense of form and material effects in the course of his daily work. He makes practical earthenware in accordance with earlier pottery traditions, and his products have become very popular.

296

296: Spice jars, flasks, bowl, and jug (height of jug 17 cm.) in brownish part-glazed stoneware. Designed and made from 1955 by SIGNE PERSSON-MELIN, Sweden. This artist has aroused great interest among the younger independent Swedish ceramic artists with her individually designed practical wares. She also makes large monumental forms, and displays this side of her talents equally in decorative work (see caption number 286).

297

297: Soup-bowl in grey-brown-red stoneware, with plates of felspar-porcelain. Designed and modelled by CARL-HARRY STÅLHANE, Sweden, and produced by *Rörstrand* porcelain-works. Linen fabric from Swedish Domestic Crafts Association. In this thin-walled soup-bowl and the graceful white saucers Stålhane strikes a note in which he is a master—lightness and elegance.

298: Set of oven-proof porcelain with green glaze and unglazed rims: modelled in 1958 by KARIN BJÖRQUIST, Sweden, and produced by *Gustavsberg* works. Linen cloth from Swedish Domestic Crafts Association. During the Forties and Fifties the old idea of a dining service was partly abandoned. Complete services are retained for special occasions, but for everyday use only plates, bowls, and dishes are required, which must be solidly made and capable of use in combination with other articles. The set shown is therefore appropriately called 'Everyday'. Karin Björquist is a young artist who works calmly and consciously in a style which has parallels in Höglund's glass and Gnista's products in wood.

298

299: Bowl, pots, and dish in black earthenware, with varying dark-green glazes on the inner sides. Dish 38 cm. long. Designed in 1956 by INGRID ATTERBERG, Sweden, for *Upsala-Ekeby Ltd.* This type of earthenware is fired at a comparatively low temperature. The material is porous, and therefore cannot be thrown too thin but must have solidity. Combined with intense colours and glazes, it is seen at its best in more countrified objects. Ingrid Atterberg has worked on earthenware at Upsala-Ekeby since 1944. She understands her material, its many decorative possibilities, and its technical limitations. She intended the pieces shown for serving fish, hence the name 'Smögen', which is that of a well-known Swedish fishing-port.

299

300

300: Jars in dark earthenware with white glaze and decoration in several colours: 11–17 cm. high. Modelled in 1960 by MARI SIMMULSON, Sweden, and produced at *Upsala-Ekeby Ltd.* Mari Simmulson uses more vigorous decorative effects and more varied motifs, which derive from the Baltic environment in which she had her training. Earthenware therefore suits her well, being easy to shape and giving great opportunities for effects of colour and material.

301

302

301: Parts from a service in a series of oven- and fire-proof felspar-porcelain with relief decoration and cobalt painting beneath the glaze. Tallest piece 21 cm. Designed in 1954 by HERTHA BENGTSON, Sweden, for *Rörstrand* porcelain-works. Plastic tablecloth with pattern designed by LOUISE FOUGSTEDT in 1958, made by *Jönköping-Vulcan Ltd*. Meals are the regular time for the modern family to get together, and this gives a special interest to the things on the table. Hertha Bengtson has a happy touch in this field, and endows her products with a natural and practical form. The 'Koka' service is a good example of this: the forms are impersonal, the knobs and handle ceramically correct. The broad band in that ancient ceramic colour cobalt-blue stands out against the white porcelain.

302: Service-ware in greyish earthenware, decorated with cobalt and spots of glaze. Designed and painted in 1959 by MARIANNE WESTMAN, Sweden, and produced by *Rörstrand* porcelain-works. Cotton cloth designed by VIOLA GRÅSTEN, 1960, and made at *Mölnlycke Textiles Ltd*. Marianne Westman has a definite place among Rörstrand's artists as the one who produces the 'enjoyable' and uncomplicated satisfying things, genuine practical ware, which she always decorates, generally in bright and light colours.

303: Coffee service in bone-china, designed in 1948 by STIG LINDBERG, Sweden, and made at *Gustavsberg* works. Lindberg has unusually versatile talents in industrial art. He has successfully designed fabric-prints, posters, wrapping paper, playing cards, enamel, glassware, and plastics, and tries his hand at other forms of industrial design. But he is primarily a ceramic artist, and as such he has worked for Gustavsberg since 1937. He has behind him a large output of service-ware and similar things, chiefly made in the materials Gustavberg now specialises in – earthenware, bone-china, (which in Sweden is made only here) and stoneware. He is a rationally minded artist, and at the same time gifted with an unusual flair for flowing decoration. His work covers a great range of types from the simple industrially-made to the complex and romantic. This coffee-service in white bone-china is typical of his elegant practical forms. He also designed the plastic tray, which is made in blue, red, black, and white by the same works.

304: Pieces of a partly fire-proof service, designed in 1955 by STIG LINDBERG for *Gustavsberg* works. The combination in this service of parts made with materials differing according to suitability for various purposes is a definite step forward from the uniform dining-service. The vessels intended for cooking over a flame, and the pot and teapot, are in fire-proof brown ware; the coffee-cups are in bone-china, the plates in earthenware, and the baking-dishes are heat-proof. The dishes are also intended to be taken direct from the hot-plate or oven to the dining-table. All the latter pieces have a line decoration in the same brown as the first two. The forms are simple and rational, allowing many different combinations, and are thus typical of both designer and manufacturer.

305: Teapot and bowl in red unglazed earthenware, designed and made by ALF and KARI ROGNVED, Norway. Diameter of bowl 16 cm., height 5.5 cm. The decoration is incised into the clay, and the depressions filled with white glaze.

304

305

306

306: Jar and bowl in chamotte stoneware, made by ROLF HANSEN, Norway. Height of jar 22 cm. Hansen has scratched his linear patterns in the white glaze, a technique he often uses in decorating his simple earthenware forms.

307: Stoneware vase with grey-brown glaze, made by MAGNE KVILSTAD, Nor-

way, 1959. Height 27 cm. Kvilstad's works often have a monumental character, even when they are comparatively small, and they all show his strict demands on himself and his craft. Small stoneware bowl in brownish tints, by KÅRE B. FJELD-SAA, made by *Stavangerflint Ltd*. Diameter 14 cm.

308: Flame-proof earthenware, called 'flint' in Norway, with polychrome decoration, designed by HERMANN BONGARD and made at *Figgjo* faience-works. Bongard expresses himself in several different media. He is a glass-artist, a book-binder, a draftsman, and also much concerned with wood and metal. The fabric is linen with grey and black stripes, designed by BIRGIT WESSEL for *'Vakre Hjem'*.

307

308

309: Jugs for hotel use, in black and white porcelain, designed by TIAS ECK-HOFF, Norway, for *Porsgrund* porcelain-works, 1960. The jugs as well as their lids can be stacked, and they are specially designed to withstand rough handling. Made in four sizes, capacity 112, 84, 56, and 28 cl.

310: Household jars with lids, specially made for refrigerators. Designed by EY-STEIN SANDNES, Norway, for *Porsgrund* porcelain-works, 1959. White and dark-brown glaze. Height of tallest 11.5 cm. The flat lids make stacking possible, and the lids can also be used as saucers beneath the jars.

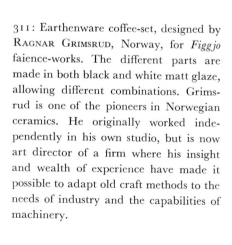

311: Earthenware coffee-set, designed by RAGNAR GRIMSRUD, Norway, for *Figgjo* faience-works. The different parts are made in both black and white matt glaze, allowing different combinations. Grims-rud is one of the pioneers in Norwegian ceramics. He originally worked inde-pendently in his own studio, but is now art director of a firm where his insight and wealth of experience have made it possible to adapt old craft methods to the needs of industry and the capabilities of machinery.

312: Coffee-set in white porcelain with grey pattern: height of jug 21 cm. Designed in 1959 by EYSTEIN SANDNES, Norway, for *Porsgrund* porcelain-works. Coloured cotton fabric made at the State Industrial School for Women.

313: Plate and dish in white porcelain, designed by EYSTEIN SANDNES, Norway, 1960, and made at *Porsgrund* porcelain-works. Stainless steel cutlery designed by TIAS ECKHOFF, Norway, for *Danish Cutlery-works*.

314: Earthenware bowls, designed and made by ANNE-MARIE BACKER MOHR, Norway, 1959. Diameter of largest 20 cm. Glossy brown glaze: unglazed surfaces reddish-brown. Anne-Marie Backer Mohr was a pupil of the English ceramic artist Bernard Leach, and thereby acquired an understanding of the inherent values of simple forms and of the relation between glazed and unglazed surfaces. But primarily she expresses delight in good craftsmanship.

315

316

317

315–316: 'The Round of Love', punch-bowl in high-fired earthenware, made in 1957 by Lars Thirslund, Denmark. Outside unglazed, interior decorated with stamped ornament and covered with semi-transparent blue-green glaze. Diameter 45 cm. Thirslund calls this 'a punchbowl for spontaneous devotees of beauty'. On the sides he has pictured eight love-scenes from all over the world. These reliefs were first carved in clay panels, which were fired and then used as stamps. Fig. 315 shows the mediaeval Danish couple Hagbart and Signelil, Adam and Eve, and David and Bathsheba. Fig. 316 shows the David and Bathsheba panel. When the punch is drunk a ninth relief appears on the bottom of the bowl, representing 'You and me'.

317: Dish in high-fired earthenware, made in 1960 by Marianne Herlufs-datter, Denmark. The glaze decoration on the interior is in clear bright colours: green, blue, and manganese violet. Diameter 43 cm. This dish, with its simple form and glaze decoration and the naive lion on the base, is typical of Marianne Herlufsdatter. Like her husband Lars Thirslund, she carves her ornament in clay panels which are fired and used as stamps. Her ceramics are straightforward and artless like those of rustic potters of earlier days. The glaze ornamentation, in keeping with the character of the pieces, is diagrammatic or geometrical, and fits naturally and organically into the form of pots and dishes. The stamped decorations are large and clear, and can be seen from a distance.

319   320

318: Stoneware bowl made in 1959 by GEORG HETTING for *Bing & Grøndahl* porcelain-works: diameter 31 cm. In this bowl Hetting uses carved relief, as in so many of his other works. The ornament is a vigorous effective figure rhythmically and precisely repeated all round the vertical sides of the bowl. At the foot the glaze was wiped off before firing, so that the light ferrous chamotte clay stands out in contrast with the green celadon glaze.

319: Stoneware jar made in 1960 by FINN LYNGGAARD, Denmark: height 22 cm.

With its stiff angular form and the sharp precise profile of the neck, this jar is typical of one side of Lynggaard's work. It was thrown in chamotte stoneware clay, and then beaten into a rectangular section. The glaze is a white-streaked felsparglaze, put on in such varying thickness that bulges have resulted.

320: Stoneware jar with olive-brown glaze over greyish-brown surface, made in 1960 by ERIK REIFF, Denmark: height 27 cm. Reiff found his inspiration for this jar in a fruit, and in the first examples

he made he attempted to keep as close to the original as possible. When after a few months' break he examined what he had done, he discovered that he had unconsciously moved away from the form of the fruit towards a more upward-reaching form. This is the final version, which may be regarded as an experiment in putting together different thrown shapes with convex, concave, and straight outlines. On the sides the impressions made by the artist's fingers as the wheel turned may be faintly traced. When the brown glaze collects in runnels, it appears darker because of its greater thickness.

321: Porcelain tea-set, designed in 1957 by GERTRUD VASEGAARD, Denmark, for *Bing & Grøndahl* porcelain-works.

Ancient oriental ceramics have had much influence in Denmark, as in all western countries. Chinese, Japanese, and Korean forms and glazes have been adopted and revived in a new Danish version. In this tea-set this influence is obvious. Its porcelain is covered with a transparent lead-glaze, scraped off at the rims and replaced with a red iron-glaze. The teapot handle is, in Chinese fashion, made of a bent piece of bamboo, the cut-down ends of which pass through two eyeholes in the body of the vessel. The cups have no handles, but the rim is slightly out-turned, so that they may be easily grasped with the fingers. The cups are large, and therefore not completely filled, so that there is no risk of burning the fingers. Both hands are used to raise the cup to the mouth. This set is machine-made in a modern factory, but has still kept much of the quality of a unique piece of work. One realises that it was created by an artist with a sound and original appreciation of clay, and one who forms things more with hand and heart than with pencil and brain.

322–323: 'Thermodan' pieces of a coffee-set in porcelain with double insulating walls, designed in 1957 by AXEL BRÜEL, Denmark, for *Danmark* porcelain-works.

Printed cloth designed in 1960 by ARNE JACOBSEN for *Grautex Ltd.*

Handles on cups and jugs have always been a problem in making porcelain. They tend to fly off during firing, they are easily knocked off in packing and transport, and they break during washing-up. Moreover, they take up too much of the limited space in the kitchen cupboard. With these drawbacks in mind. Brüel and Danmark's technicians set out to make a handleless set on quite new principles, and after many attempts succeeded. By making the separate pieces slender enough to grasp in the hand, the handle could be dispensed with: and by giving them double walls – as in ordinary thermos-flasks – they could be sufficiently insulating to be held even if the contents were at boiling point. The fluted decoration on the outside of the jug and cups assists a firm grasp. The outlines are not straight, but bulge slightly in the middle, like classical pillars. In this way Brüel has given the form life, and changed it from a dead mathematical shape to a humanised form.

324: Sauceboat from a porcelain dinner-service, designed in 1960 by EBBE SADO-LIN, Denmark, for *Bing & Grøndahl*.

In this service, as well as in the other he designed in 1932, Sadolin has used a natural and unaffected form-idiom and has avoided any mark of datable fashion. Each article has a simple, finished shape, based on practical needs and a disciplined restraint.

322

323

321

324

325

326

325: 'Kilta' cream-jugs designed in 1948 by KAJ FRANCK, Finland, for *Wärtsilä/ Arabia:* on the market since 1953. Capacity 20 cl. These are made in the same material and colours as the rest of the ware in the 'Kilta' series which was awarded a Grand Prix at the 1957 Triennale.

326: Bowls in vitreous enamel made to pack into each other. Designed by KAJ FRANCK, Finland for *Wärtsilä/Maskin & Bro.* Produced in 1957. Largest diameter 24 cm., smallest 10 cm. These thin smooth bowls are made in six colours: red, white, light-blue, blue-green, yellow, and cobaltblue. Grand Prix at 1957 Triennale.

327

327: 'Kilta' heat-proof plate and dish in high-fired earthenware: modelled in 1948 by KAJ FRANCK, Finland, for *Wärtsilä/Arabia*. On the market since 1953. Glass by Kaj Franck, 1959, for the same combine's Notsjö glassworks. 'Triennale' cutlery in stainless steel by BERTEL GARD-BERG, 1957, for *Fiskars Ltd*. The plate is easy to make because of its straight-profiled rim. Made in five colours: white, black, yellow, blue and green; dish in white only. This inexpensive series is very comprehensive (cf. figs. 325 and 328) and the several well-chosen colours allow a large number of individual combinations.

328: Coffeepot with lid in heat-proof earthenware, with sugar-bowl and cream-jug. Designed in 1948 by KAJ FRANCK, Finland, for *Wärtsilä/Arabia*. On the market since 1953. Parts of the 'Kilta' series, which comes in white, black, yellow, blue, and green.

328

329

329: Stoneware vases, designed and model-led by OKKI LAINE, Finland, for *Kupittaan Savi*; height 20–23 cm.

330: Stoneware vases, designed and mo-delled by OKKI LAINE, Finland, for *Kupittaan Savi:* height c. 25 cm.

330

331: 'Liekki' heat-proof ware, designed and modelled by ULLA PROCOPÉ, Finland, 1957, for *Wärtsilä/Arabia*. Diameter of largest skillet 24.5 cm. This earth-brown ware is so made that the pieces may be stacked, and the lids may be used as serving dishes.

332: Filter coffeepots in vitreous enamel with plastic handles. Designed by ANTTI NURMESNIEMI, Finland, for *Wärtsilä/Maskin & Bro*. Produced in 1958: capacity 1.5 and .7 litre. Made in red, yellow, and light-blue.

333: 'Rustak' stoneware designed by ULLA PROCOPÉ, Finland, 1960, for *Wärtsilä/Arabia*. Diameter of pie-dish 33 cm., of casserole 19 cm. Colour autumn-leaf brown.

334

335

334: Stackable coffee-cups in ivory-coloured porcelain, designed by KAARINA AHO, Finland, 1957, for *Wärtsilä/Arabia*. Silver medal at 1957 Triennale.

335: Egg dish with lid: earthenware with mustard-yellow ground and black domino. Designed by KAARINA AHO, Finland, 1953, for *Wärtsilä/Arabia*. Height 15 cm., length 20 cm. A modern version of the classic egg-hen for the breakfast table.

336: Bowl in eggshell porcelain, designed and made by AUNE SIIMES, Finland, 1951, at *Wärtsilä/Arabia*. Height c. 10 cm. Siimes fashions these exquisite bowls with separate layers decreasing in number towards the rim, giving an elegant effect of increasing transparency. This bowl is white, but pink material is also used.

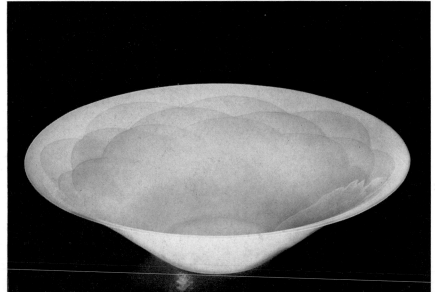

336

337

337: Stoneware pots, designed and produced in 1960 by KYLLIKKI SALMENHAARA, Finland, for *Wärtsilä/Arabia*. Height 41.5 and 39.5 cm. The more dynamic forms of this artist's recent output appear to be the result of a travelling scholarship in America in 1956. This encouraged her to break away from a genre in which she had previously won many laurels but in which she was afraid of getting into a rut.

338: Stoneware pot designed and produced in 1960 by KYLLIKKI SALMENHAARA, Finland, for *Wärtsilä/Arabia*. Height 43 cm. Kyllikki Salmenhaara fires her pottery at high temperatures–1320–1380° C.–and generally uses an off-white clay mixture with a varying content of chamotte of different fineness. She makes her own glazes. The powerful lines of this jar are typical of her most recent products, which are moving towards increased simplicity of form. The glazes also contrast strongly with the birchbark-like surface which she gave her more slender vases of the early Fifties.

338

339: Dish and vase in porcelain, thrown and glazed in 1951 by TOINI MUONA, Finland, for *Wärtsilä/Arabia*. Diameter of dish 44 cm., height of vase 38 cm. The dish was fired at 1300° C., and covered with copper glaze. The chalk-white vase was fired at 1250° C. Toini Muona generally employs simple forms such as these as the basis for her instinctive use of glaze effects. The large dimensions are typical of her work.

340: 'Mother and Child', wall-plaque in chamotte earthenware, made in 1948 by BIRGER KAIPIAINEN, Finland, for *Wärtsilä/ Arabia*. Height 45 cm. This was fired at 1050° C., and is typical of the Byzantin-esque style which Kaipiainen cultivated in his studied figures round about 1950. Later on, during his brief period with Rörstrand, he devoted himself increasingly to surrealistic motifs. A characteristic element in all his output is the nostalgic atmosphere he creates around his human figures.

340

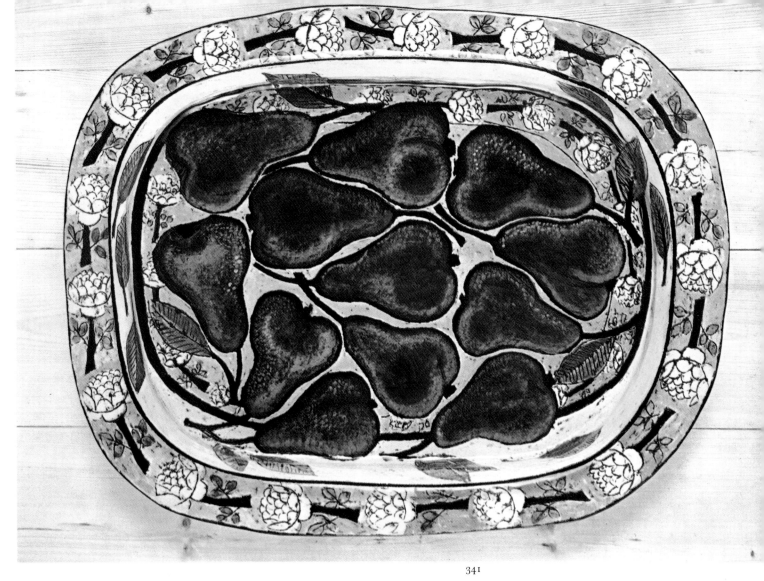

341: Earthenware dish; designed, produced and decorated by BIRGER KAIPIAI-
NEN, Finland, for *Wärtsilä/Arabia* in 1960.
40×55 cm. This is one of Kaipiainen's
recent pieces, but has affinities with the
pottery which won him his first recognition in the Fifties. The incised technique
which he then employed appears here
only as a secondary detail beneath the
under-glaze painting. Some chamotte is
mixed into this lightly-fired material.

342: 'Curlew', figure made with strings
of earthenware beads stretched over a
steel frame. Made in 1959 by BIRGER
KAIPIAINEN, Finland, for *Wärtsilä/Arabia*.
Height and length 110 cm. With this and
similar figures Kaipiainen won a Grand
Prix at the 1960 Triennale. In this
example, composed partly of beads and
partly of flat round medallions, the material is almost free from glaze: the colour
comes from inserted iron-oxide. This artist
has previously been interested in the
bird-motif. In the early Fifties he made a
series of wall-figures in solid earthenware
which foreshadowed this oviparous wonder.

342

343

344

345

346

343: Cutlery in sterling silver, designed in 1956 by BERTEL GARDBERG, Finland, for *Hopeatehdas*. Soup-plate, dinner-plate, and salt- and pepper-containers in high-fired earthenware, designed in 1947 by KAJ FRANCK for *Wärtsilä/Arabia*. Glass by Franck, 1959, for *Wärtsilä/Notsjö*. Linen tablecloth from *Friends of Finnish Handicraft*.

344: Stainless steel spoon with plastic handle, designed in 1959 by BERTEL GARDBERG, Finland, for *Hackman & Co*. Serving-dish in high-fired earthenware by KAJ FRANCK, 1947, for *Wärtsilä/Arabia*. Linen place-mat woven in 1960 by DORA JUNG in her own workshop.

345: Porcelain coffee-cups, designed by KAJ FRANCK, Finland, 1953, and decorated by RAIJA UOSIKKINEN. Made by *Wärtsilä/Arabia*.

346: Preserve jars in high-fired earthenware, modelled in 1953 by KAJ FRANCK, Finland, for *Wärtsilä/Arabia:* capacity .36, .75, and .80 litre. These practical jars, designed to stack, with their pure cylindrical form and bright glaze in concordant colours, are typical of Franck's simple, unpretentious and inexpensive utility ware. These colours are repeated in his plain round or square plates and serving-dishes.

347: Pottery tray with glazed fish-figures, made in 1959 by RUT BRYK, Finland, for *Wärtsilä/Arabia:* 55×42 cm. Rut Bryk's naive-romantic bright paintings on earthenware trays were followed in the Fifties by wall-plaques in thick glaze and deep colours in which naiveté increasingly gave way to studied artistry. In a number of wall-decoration works, e. g. for the Rosenthal factories, this artist later combined unglazed pottery surfaces with glazed panels and figures in high relief. In this tray the glazed surfaces of the fish are separated by thin incised strokes.

348: 'Hen', wall-tile in chamotte, made in 1950 by MICHAEL SCHILKIN, Finland, for *Wärtsilä/Arabia*. Height 40 cm. Schilkin, who was really for the most part a ceramic sculptor, and won recognition with his monumental wall-reliefs, showed in a series of chamotte wall-tiles that he also had a strong feeling for the paint-like effects of glaze. Probably the finest example of this, 'Burbot' (1944), is in the National Museum in Stockholm. 'Hen', which came six years later, clearly shows his development towards greater stylisation of the animal motifs he liked to work with.

348

349: Iron cooking pots, two with enamel, with teak handles. Designed by TIMO SARPANEVA, Finland, 1960, for *W. Rosenlew & Co/Björneborg Machine Shops*. Height 14 cm. Cotton curtain fabric, designed by Sarpaneva, 1960, for *Björneborg Cotton Ltd*. Sarpaneva's most important work was previously in studied craftsmanship and exclusive glassware, but recently he has tried his hand at such practical everyday things as cast-iron ware and cotton-prints. With the help of a special alloy these pots have been made unusually thin. The wooden handle serves also to remove the lids.

350: Stainless steel enamelled bowls, designed by GRETE KORSMO, Norway, for *Cathrineholm*. Place-mat designed by KARI FRONTH for the *Plus* organisation.

351: 'Maya' stainless steel cutlery, designed by TIAS ECKHOFF, Norway, for *Norwegian Pressed Steel*. Eckhoff has designed cutlery for many years, and amongst other things won a Danish competition for silver table-ware. He formerly designed in stainless steel for Danish firms, and the example shown is the first for manufacture in Norway. Soup-bowl and plate designed by EYSTEIN SANDNES for *Porsgrund* porcelain-works. The place-mat is in 'smettevev', a free weaving technique, by ELI MARIE JOHNSEN and RAGNHILD TRETTEBERG.

352: Anodised aluminium bowls designed by BJØRN ENGØ, Norway, and made at *Emalox*. Bowl on porcelain plate 15 cm. diameter. Engø is a typical industrial designer, and has amongst other things worked on furniture, light-fittings, and fabrics. He pays attention to current tendencies, but still gives his products an individual stamp. Place-mat composed by KARI FRONTH for the *Plus* organisation. Stainless steel cutlery designed by ERIK HERLØW, Denmark, for *Norwegian Pressed Steel*.

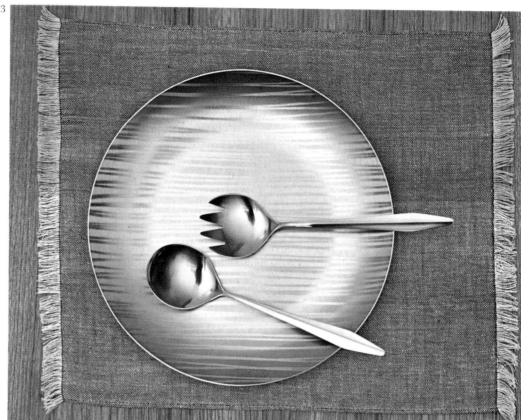

353: Engraved stainless steel dish, designed by GRETE KORSMO, Norway, and made by *Cathrineholm*. Salad-servers in the same material, designed by ERIK HERLØW, Denmark, and made by *Norwegian Pressed Steel*. Place-mat in linen, woven at *Pettersen's* workshop.

354: Enamelled copper bowls, by GRETE KORSMO, Norway, made by *J. Tostrup*. Diameters 23, 15, 11.5, and 9 cm. Grete Korsmo's usual original work in silver and gold must necessarily always be exclusive. She has therefore begun enamelling copper, and in this material her products are much less expensive. The enamel is not transparent, and the appearance depends on line and colour. Fabric composed by BIRGIT WESSEL for *'Vakre Hjem'*.

354

355: Vases in silver and enamel, designed and made by GRETE KORSMO, Norway, at *J. Tostrup.* Tallest 45 cm. The art of enamelling has become a Norwegian speciality, and Grete Korsmo has been, and is still, the pioneer in this field. Through many years of independent experiment she has achieved a technical mastery which has made her name known far outside Norway. She achieves intense colour-effects, with the special qualities of the silver brought out by the translucent enamel. She is a remarkably sensitive artist, and her delight in beautiful lines combined with enamel surfaces has also led her to make outstanding jewellery of individual character. Rug in background designed and made by GRETE LEIN.

356

357

356: Fish-serving dish in sterling silver, designed in 1954 by HENNING KOPPEL, Denmark, for *Georg Jensen Ltd.*: 68 cm. long. With this dish Koppel has reacted against the plain austerity of functionalist silverware. At the same time he has not returned to the over-elaboration of pre-Bojesen times, when love of ornament overshadowed love of the objects themselves. On the contrary, he has continued to develop his work on the basis of a functionalist view of material, and, instead of covering the article with ornament, gives the basic form a sculptural force which is indeed derived from function but incidentally has a conscious artistic aim which connects the object with modern pure art. The parted 'lips' at each end, which suggest a fish's mouth, form a handhold.

357: Gold bracelet with amethysts, designed in 1960 by ERIK HERLØW, Denmark, for *Georg Jensen Ltd*. In this bracelet the gems alone attract attention. They are not set in the normal fashion, but are held out in a slender structure of 'gold claws'. This free method of support allows the light to enter the stones from every angle, and thus makes them sparkle from any viewpoint.

358: Necklace of Swedish stones, designed by ÅKE STRÖMDAHL, Sweden, 1955, and made in his own workshop, *Hugo Strömdahl*, Court jeweller. In a period when personal ornaments are within the reach of all, they are also worn with simple everyday clothes. For this purpose 'precious' materials may be too exclusive, and it is typical that in modern jewellery new decorative materials are looked for. Åke Strömdahl has found one such in Swedish natural stones, which he cuts and polishes to achieve interesting effects.

358

360

359: Pendant, bracelet, and ring in white gold (alloy of gold and platinum) with green Ceylon moonstones. Designed by WIWEN-NILSSON, Sweden, 1956, and made in his own workshop. His jewellery shows the same individual feeling for material as his silverware. Its decorative effect lies in its size, in the simple well-proportioned forms, and the unusually beautiful stones.

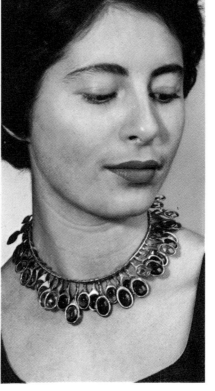

359

360: Neck-ornament with 52 different coloured stones, designed and made in 1960 by ARJE GRIEGST, Denmark, for *Just Andersen Ltd.* With pieces such as this, and Herløw's bracelet in fig. 357, a new era in Danish jewellery has opened. While Danish artists since the war have primarily cultivated the material effects of the metal, the freeing of imports of loose stones and the lowered tariffs have stimulated interest in stone jewellery. Griegst makes precious stones sparkle with unusual brilliance: they are set in rings and held on outstretched brackets so that the light reflected from the skin beneath can shine through and make them light up. The 52 stones are arranged in groups according to colour.

361: Pendant of silver with Mediterranean stones polished by the action of water: designed and made by TORUN BÜLOW-HÜBE, Sweden, c. 1950. She works entirely in pure silver, with semi-precious stones, stones from beaches, quartz, and other smooth materials. Since 1956 she has had her own workshop in France, and in spite of her youth may be regarded as exercising a considerable influence on modern continental style in jewellery. Woollen shawl designed and woven by INGRID SKERFE-NILSSON.

362: Neck-ornament of silver with fossils, designed and wrought by INGA-BRITT DAHLQUIST, Sweden, 1959. It is typical of the whole school of younger Swedish silversmiths, of whom she is one, that they work principally in silver and use non-precious stones. Here the artist has used fossils from Gotland, interesting in structure and form, and in this material she has made quality ornaments for everyday wear.

362

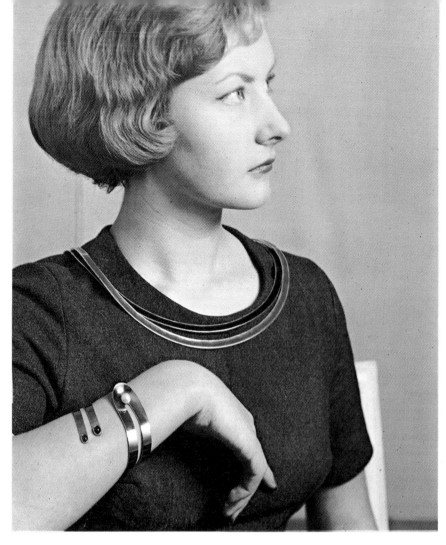

363: Enamel necklet and bracelet in silver with pearls; designed by GRETE KORSMO, Norway, and made by *J. Tostrup*. Grete Korsmo has followed a line of her own, and has understood how to give her ornaments a completely individual form. Though they are often inexpensive to produce, they have both technical and artistic quality. It is worth mentioning that for several years she collaborated productively with the well-known Italian glass-artist Paolo Venini. She designed ornaments, and Venini made the coloured glass for them. Venini's death brought this interesting international cooperation to an end.

364: Silver bracelet designed and made by ELSE and PAUL HUGHES, Norway. In recent years Norwegian work in silver has had a revival. Several young people have produced things which promise well for future developments in this field, Else and Paul Hughes among them. This married couple work so closely together that they may be regarded as one. They have tried their hands especially at jewellery, and everything they make has an individual stamp. They say themselves that their style is a conscious 'reaction against the modernism and streamlining which affect so much at the present day'. Modernism or not, they have given a reviving injection with their jewellery to a craft which has strong and ancient traditions in Norway.

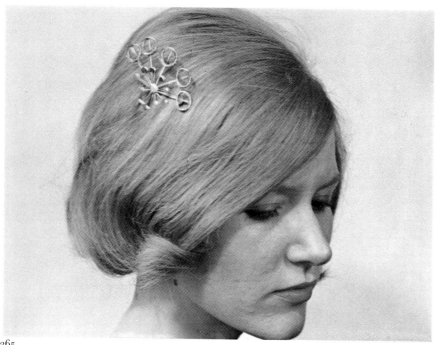

365

365: Hair-clip in silver and enamel, designed and made by TONE VIGELAND, Norway. This artist is also one of the younger generation of Norwegian silversmiths. Many of her works shine with a fresh, youthful, and unconventional delight in creation.

366: Silver necklet, designed and made by TONE VIGELAND, Norway. Her silver jewellery is simple, and in part somewhat primitively made, but has an individual character to which one cannot be indifferent.

366

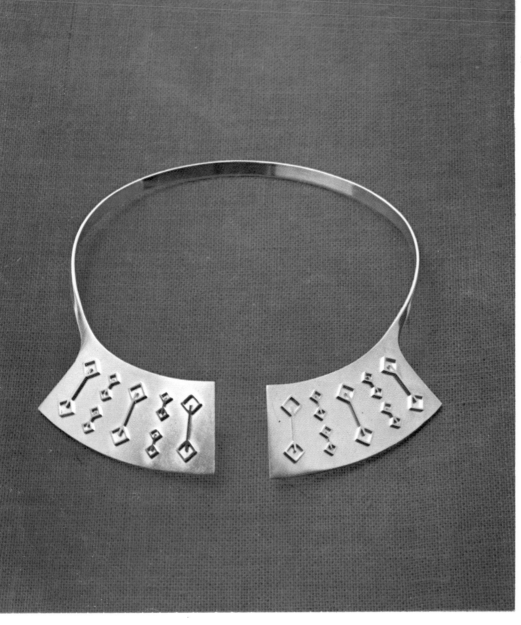

367: Wrought necklet in sterling silver, with soldered relief in red and green Finnish gold. Designed and made by BJÖRN WECKSTRÖM, Finland, 1959, in his own workshop.

368: Two gold rings with clouded topazes and silver ring in niello technique, designed and made by BERTEL GARDBERG, Finland, in his own workshop, 1959. Gardberg holds a unique position in Finland with his silver vessels, but he is also interested in jewellery and in that field has founded a school. These rings are completely typical of him, genuine and restrained in form and faultlessly made. The topazes, gold, and silver are all Finnish.

368

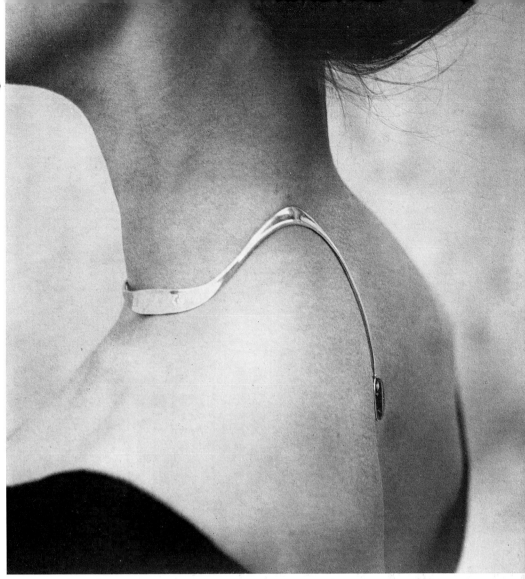

369

369: Neck-ornament in silver, with two Graal-glass 'jewels' by EDWARD HALD, designed and wrought by TORUN BÜLOW-HÜBE, Sweden, 1959. This does not hang round the neck in the conventional way, and in fact only goes half round it. It is hammered out in a single piece, and goes from the back over the left shoulder and across to the right side of the neck. It is sufficiently springy to keep its place and follow the movements of the neck easily.

370: 18 carat gold bracelet, with Finnish clouded topaz, designed in 1958 by EERO RISLAKKI, Finland, for *Westerback Ltd.* The 'spur' round the stone has no structural significance, the piece being opened with a catch and hinge at the sides.

371: Sterling silver necklet, designed and made in 1959 by BÖRJE RAJALIN, Finland.

371

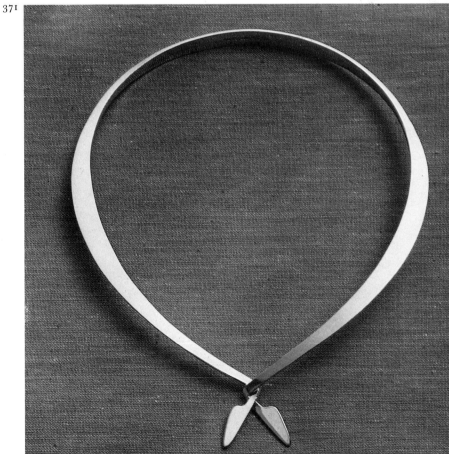

370

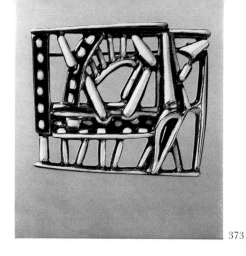

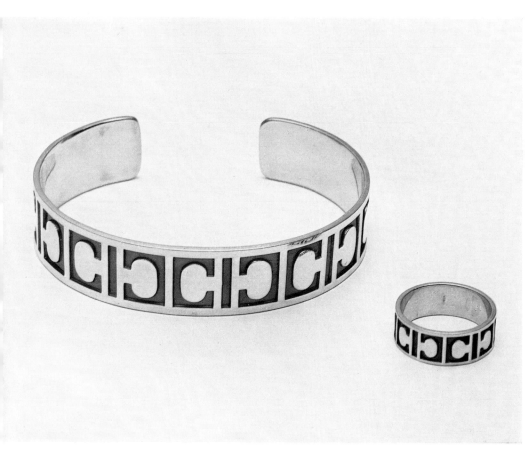

372: Ring and bracelet in sterling silver, with oxidised ornament: designed and made in 1956 by Börje Rajalin, Finland, for *Kalevala Koru.*

373: Ornament in black and white enamel on gold: 5 cm. across. Designed and made by Sigurd Alf Eriksen, Norway, 1960. Eriksen originally based his enamel-work on mediaeval examples. Later he found an individual form of his own, abstract in motif and with complete mastery of craft techniques.

372

374: Silver bracelet by Bertel Gardberg, Finland, 1958. The massive catch and the solid construction give tone to the whole piece.

375: Bracelet in gold, ivory, and ebony, designed in 1947 by ERIK HERLØW, Denmark, for *I. G. Schwartz & Sons.* Aesthetic expression is the all-important thing in jewellery. It represents something extra, which adds interest and distinction to life. Here imagination and spirit are the only realities, and beauty the only function. At the same time, the maker of jewellery must take his material into account just as much as any other practical artist: here too the form must suit its peculiar properties. In this piece Herløw makes use of colour and structure contrasts in three precious materials: gold, ivory, and ebony.

376: Silver necklace designed in 1957 by BENT GABRIELSEN PEDERSEN, Denmark, for *Hans Hansen Ltd.* This piece is typical of Pedersen's work in the linking together of identical elements, which grip each other like linked hands. As in most of his work, both sides are carefully finished: but in this case the outer sides are marked by yellow enamel on some of the links. The catch is indicated by black.

375

377: Bracelet, designed in 1956 by NANNA and JØRGEN DITZEL, Denmark, for *Georg Jensen Ltd.* In this piece we find the same form-idiom as in those from early Danish history, but at the same time it is entirely suitable as a means of expression for the woman of today. It is as simple as her uncumbrous clothing, and made with the same sureness and precision as the good practical wares in her home.

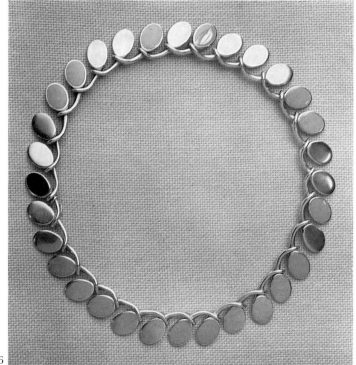

377   376

being decorated. They were made in protest against the earlier style of over-decorated and hammered silver, and appear in pure austere forms. Cubic shapes are dominant, but in a different fashion from so many 'modern' articles of the Thirties. We do not find the abstract mathematical forms of early functionalism here, but a liking for simple plain shapes with a natural vigour of their own and taut lively curves and lines. His products are functional and matter-of-fact, but in no way commonplace. Every single piece has a vigorous form endowed with both imagination and feeling. Bojesen himself has expressed it thus: "Lines must be pleasing. There must be life, blood, and heart in the things we make. They must be human, warm, and alive."

378

379

378: Silver coffee-set with ebony knobs and handles, designed and first made in 1954 by KAY BOJESEN, Denmark. Height of coffee-pot 15 cm. Bojesen was one of the first Danish functionalists in applied art. He had no use for ornamental show-pieces, and he attacked under-proportioned tinny silver. His products were primarily for use, and made to function as appropriately as possible. The spout of a coffee-pot must not drip, handles and knobs on lids must be sufficiently insulated not to burn the fingers, each piece must 'fall' comfortably into the hand, and everything must be made solid enough to stand up to years of daily wear. The coffee-set shown here is typical of Bojesen's container-pieces: each element is strongly made and works properly, and the plain shining silver surfaces are ornamented only by strengthening and curving the rim, which enlivens the form and causes light-reflections over the surface.

379: Silver teapot with ebony lid-knob and handle bound in cane, designed and first made 1938 by KAY BOJESEN, Denmark. Bojesen's vessels are striking without being showy, and decorative without

380: 'Grand Prix' silver cutlery, designed in 1938 and made by KAY BOJESEN, Denmark. Though this set of cutlery is over twenty years old, it is still up-to-date. The fashions of surface treatment so often found in the cutlery industry are completely absent. This was not made to satisfy the unfortunate urge for collecting 'pieces'. It consists of simple utensils, whose form and structure have been carefully thought-out to meet every functional demand. The balance is right, the details and surface treatment allow quick and thorough cleaning, and the form is functionally perfect. Where the traditional shape of a detail has a functional basis—as in the pointed form of the bowl of the spoon—it has been retained: but otherwise tradition has been ignored. This applies, for example, to the length of the handles, which are slightly shorter than the earlier norm. Likewise the knife blade is shorter, and its edge more curved so that more of it can be used in cutting. Finally, the prongs of the fork have been made considerably shorter and stronger than in earlier examples, so that they will not bend in use. This set is still made in silver, and with a few changes of detail has also been adapted to stainless steel.

380

381   382

381: Sterling silver coffee-set, designed
and made in 1957 by INGER MØLLER,
Denmark. The coffeepot lid has an ebony
knob, and the handle is bound with slips
of cane. Height 19 cm. Inger Møller has
made various coffee-sets in silver and
copper, and very few of them are completely uniform. Every time she makes a
vessel she looks for a new shape–not just
to make things different, but to make
them better. This coffee-set can thus be
seen as the result of many years' work and
many determined efforts to make the
form purer, tauter, and more functional,
and to produce the most beautiful effects
of reflection in the convex and concave
surfaces. In this coffeepot the spout has
been given a minute curve at the mouth
to make it drip-free: the drop is, so to
speak, drawn back into the pot. This
curve is repeated on the rear side of the
spout as an artistic refinement.

382: Silver casserole, designed and made
in 1937 by INGER MØLLER, Denmark.
Height 13 cm. Cotton cloth woven in

1936 by LIS AHLMANN. At the time when
Inger Møller made this casserole, she
found her inspiration in the fine old
cooking-pots in copper and aluminium;
and, as in these, the thin almost tinny
structure is strengthened by a folded
rim and a gently curved form at the base.
The handles are bound with silver wire,
which gives some degree of insulation.
Where they are fixed to the body, they
are hammered into a curved surface
which follows the shape of the vessel
closely and gives a firm join.

383: Tobacco canister in sterling silver,
designed and made in 1953 by HANS
BUNDE, Denmark, for *Carl M. Cohr Ltd.*
Height 15 cm. In this stout and vigorous
little canister, Bunde has made a masculine article which does not need to be
treated gently. The handle is elegantly
joined to the lid in an organic union,
which, like the sweeping curves in Peder
Moos' table on which it stands, makes one
think of the form-principles of the beginning of the century.

383

384

385

384: 'Obelisk' cutlery, in stainless steel, designed in 1954 by ERIK HERLØW, Denmark, for *Universal Steel Co. Ltd*. In this set steel may be seen in its own right: it does not imitate silver either in form, hue, or surface treatment. On the contrary, it exploits the advantages it has in comparison with silver—its hard resistant surface and its high breaking-strain, which allow slender dimensions. Technically, 'Obelisk' is something new. Spoons and forks in steel are generally stamped out of steel plate, but all 'Obelisk' pieces are wrought from a single length of rod with the help of a large drop-hammer. Since all three parts are thus of the same material, they are not distinguished by any difference of hue in the steel, such as one finds in many steel cutlery sets in which spoon and fork are stamped out of plate and the knife-blade forged.

385: 'Tulip' cutlery in silver, designed in 1953 by OLE HAGEN, Denmark, for *A. Michelsen*. In this set the shape suggests natural forms—the beautiful relationship between a leaf and its stem. The artist has nevertheless avoided the blurred and imprecise shapes which often result from work with organic forms. Here every element is strictly defined, and beneath the taut surfaces of the handles one perceives that planes and lines are logically carried through. The surfaces of the heads of spoon and fork are carried some way up into the handle, which at this point is shaped like a tube, thereby achieving great strength with a minimum of material.

386: Coffeepot in sterling silver with cane-bound handle and ivory knob on lid: designed in 1950 by ERIK HERLØW, Denmark, for *A. Michelsen*. In his silver vessels Herløw employs entirely modern media and ideas: plain simple forms, a matt undecorated surface, and a thorough consideration of function. At the same time he maintains links with earlier silversmith's work. In some of his products he emphasises the reflecting power of silver by using the rococo period's combination of sharp angles and smooth curves: in others he makes a new version of a traditional form. In this coffeepot he has thus started with a form well-known for hundreds of years and in many cultures, but the result is an individual and quite contemporary work.

386

387

388

387: 'Tuja' cutlery-set in stainless steel, designed in 1955 by MAGNUS STEPHENSEN, Denmark, for *Georg Jensen Ltd*. In designing this cutlery, Stephensen has paid attention both to function and to rationalised mass-production. The knife is forged, while spoon and fork are stamped out of steel plate and pressed into shape with handles which are slightly arched in section. This makes them stronger, since a fluted form is harder to bend than a flat one of the same dimensions. The prongs of the fork are strong, will not bend in use, are well separated, and the intervals are easy to clean. The depression below the prongs is deep enough to pick up gravy. The blade of the knife is short, and because of the angle of the cutting edge to the handle the whole of it can be used for cutting instead of only the end as in earlier knives.

388: 'Caravel' cutlery in silver, designed in 1957 by HENNING KOPPEL, Denmark, for *Georg Jensen Ltd*. For cutlery to be pleasant both to look at and to handle, it is now considered that the flow of surface and line in the separate pieces must be logically and consistently carried through. A spoon or a fork consists – roughly speaking – of an upper and a lower side and edges in between: and where each of these is clearly defined one has a feeling of sureness and satisfaction. Conversely, one has a feeling of uncertainty if one cannot clearly see or grasp where each surface begins and ends. Koppel's 'Caravel' cutlery takes account of this. Upper side, lower side, and edges are carried through consistently, and the bowls of spoon and fork are clearly defined with a clean break in the almost flat upper side. Into this cutlery has gone the ex-

perience Koppel has gained in his work with silver vessels: the parts have sculptural strength, but are all designed to meet functional needs. To this series belong, amongst other things, the salad-servers shown in fig. 388a. The bowls here are made in melamine which, unlike silver, is not discoloured by contact with salad-dressing.

389: Teapot in sterling silver, designed in 1956 by HENNING KOPPEL, Denmark, for *Georg Jensen Ltd*. Like all good silversmiths, Koppel understands how to use the malleability of the metal. His water-jugs and coffee- and tea-pots show skilful treatment, modelling with smooth joins, and beautifully curved surfaces which allow reflections to distribute themselves evenly and show the metal's range of imperceptibly changing hues.

389

388 a

390

390: Coffee-set and tray; designed in 1959 by ÅKE STRÖMDAHL, Sweden, and made at his own workshop, *Hugo Strömdahl*, Court jeweller. Strömdahl is one of those artists who, so to speak, grew up in a silversmith's workshop; he learnt the craft from his father, and follows a traditional line. But he also has a talent for dealing with modern problems of design in other materials. He has, for example, designed excellent plastic ware. As a silversmith he gives his work character with pure undecorated forms and a mass of reflections in its often rounded surfaces.

391

391: Altar-candlestick and communion plate in silver, designed by WIWEN-NILSSON, Sweden, 1959, and made in his own workshop. Height of flagon 34 cm. Wiwen-Nilsson shows marked individuality, not only in his silverware but in art-handicrafts in general. His sound craftsmanship and his thorough knowledge of silver as a material were acquired when he was quite a youngster in his father's workshop. Besides this he has learnt much of historic styles by travel, and in the environment of the university town of Lund has developed an intellectual clarity closely akin to the artistic trends of the Twenties and Thirties. He does not regard silver as a smooth reflecting material: he works with well-defined stereometrical forms, limited to large planes at sharp angles or hemispheres. All trace of the process of manufacture under the hammer is carefully removed, and his products are pure, austere, and massive, clearly defined by light-reflecting surfaces.

392

392: Hexagonal bowl, 13 cm. broad, and pentagonal box, 7.5 cm. tall, in silver. Designed by WIWEN-NILSSON, Sweden, 1945, and made in his own workshop. These objects are typical of Wiwen-Nilsson: clear in form, completely undecorated and technically perfect. The lid fits exactly on the box, whichever way it is put on.

393: Silver teapot and hot-water jug, designed in 1951 by SØREN GEORG JENSEN, Denmark, for *Georg Jensen Ltd.* Joint height, without handle, 19 cm. Søren Jensen's vessels are stoutly made and clear-cut; they have simple cylindrical bodies with precisely defined surfaces and no unnecessary details. The water-jug has a flat lid, to prevent steam from the hot water condensing under the bottom of the teapot.

394: Hand-made silver coffeepot, designed by SIGURD PERSSON, Sweden, 1950, and made in his own workshop. Persson also grew up in the workshop of a gold- and silver-smith, learnt the craft from his father, and had in addition a thorough craft-school training. Starting with a genuine handcraftsman approach, he has experimented with form and structure. Since 1942 he has had his own workshop in Stockholm, where he makes ecclesiastical and secular vessels, cutlery, and unusually individual jewellery. Partly on account of his breadth of outlook and partly because of his fine sense of form, he has also been employed by industry to design pots in enamelled iron, cutlery and dishes in stainless steel, plastic ware, etc. Fig. 418, for example, shows a serving tray designed for Scandinavian Airways, with a set of steel cutlery which it is interesting to compare with his corresponding work in silver. In him one sees an excellent example of a designer who faithfully follows an experimental and exclusive line in handicraft, while at the same time understanding the requirements of machine production and providing good designs for everyday wares.

393

394

395   396

395: Cocktail-shaker and beakers in silver, designed by SVEN ARNE GILLGREN, Sweden, 1958, for *Guldsmedsbolaget, Stockholm*. Modern art-silver has a puritanical character which is far removed from the florid chased surface-treatment of earlier styles. The material is allowed its placid reflection effects, but the form is taut and undecorated–which does not mean any less demand on the craftsman. Gillgren is art-director of one of Sweden's largest silverware firms, and a teacher at the School of Arts, Crafts and Design. Thus

he holds a prominent place amongst the middle generation. In his products he shows great restraint, strong feeling for his material, and a fine sense of form, which he applies as much in cutlery and vessels as in jewellery. He has made much church plate, and amongst his cutlery is a set made for Swedish embassies abroad. Like so many other Swedish designers, Gillgren covers the whole range from exclusive hand-made articles to models designed for industrial mass-production.

396: Silver coffee-set with oxidised engraving; designed in 1959 by SVEN ARNE GILLGREN, Sweden, and made by *Guldsmedsbolaget, Stockholm*. Coffeepot 25 cm. high. Here Gillgren has used pure stereometrical forms, the cone and cylinder, decorated with oxidised engraving at the points grasped by the fingers. The slim coffeepot is undecorated apart from the engraving on the lid and the accent provided by the black ebony handle.

397   398

397: Silver cutlery, designed by SIGURD PERSSON, Sweden, 1945. Linen fabric from *Västerbotten Domestic Crafts*. Cutlery has gradually gone through certain changes. Firstly the prongs of the fork have become shorter, like the blade of the knife, while the handles have noticeably lengthened. This is largely due to changed eating habits and different methods of preparing food. Persson's silver cutlery-set from 1945 has a traditional basis, but nevertheless a quite modern and undecorated form. The noble metal expresses itself only in its tautly rounded forms and clean outlines. This set was originally hand-wrought, but has later come into mass-production.

399

400

398: Silver cutlery designed by SVEN ARNE GILLGREN, Sweden, 1959, and made by *Guldsmedsbolaget, Stockholm.* Linen cloth from *Mora Domestic Crafts.* Nowadays the everyday functions of cutlery have been largely taken over by stainless steel. This has allowed silver to recover its old position as a genuine precious metal without competition from cheap substitutes. Gillgren has finely expressed its characteristic properties, its lustre and smoothness.

399: Coffee-set in silver, designed and made in 1959 by STEINAR FLATHEIM, Norway. The interiors are gilt, and the handle and lid-fitting are in palisander. Flatheim is still only 27, but has already produced a number of works of great interest. They promise a revival in Norwegian art-silver.

400: Tea-caddy in teak with sterling silver lid; designed and made by BERTEL GARDBERG, Finland, for *Hopeatehdas,* 1954.

Height 12 cm. Notice how the hall-marks are used as a decorative feature. They have a practical purpose, and thus dot the i where decoration in the ordinary sense would have been a superfluous intrusion.

401: Hors d'oeuvre fork (1950) and tea-strainer (1952) in sterling silver and palisander, designed and made by BERTEL GARDBERG, Finland. Length of fork 20 cm.

401

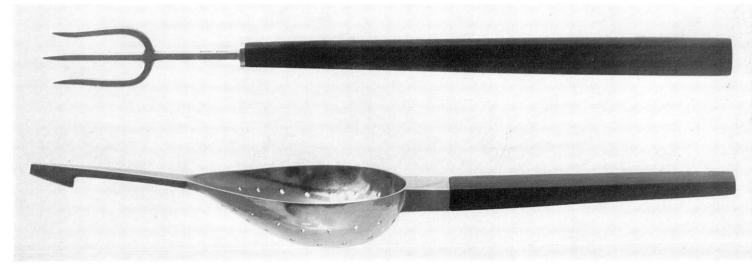

402: Tableware designed by THORBJØRN LIE-JØRGENSEN, Norway, and made by *David-Andersen*. These show what this artist aims to give expression to in his work: the character of the material and a conscious interplay between line and form.

403: Silver jug, designed by THORBJØRN LIE-JØRGENSEN, Norway, and made by *David-Andersen*. Height 14.5 cm. Lie-Jørgensen's works show a sensitive understanding of the potentialities of silver. They are simple and natural, and the character of the metal is given full expression in his vessels.

404: Silver coffeepot, designed by THORBJØRN LIE-JØRGENSEN, Norway, and made by *David-Andersen*. Height 20 cm. Lie-Jørgensen was one man but two artists. As a painter he was one of Norway's finest colorists, with a quite personal depth and weight in his choice of colours. As a silversmith he also achieved excellent results. He worked with the greatest possible simplification of forms and appropriate and balanced line.

403

404

402

405

407

405: Tobacco-canisters in Britannia metal, designed by BERTEL GARDBERG, Finland, for *Hopeatehdas*. On the market since 1958. Anonymous and robust, and highly elegant practical articles in their unpretentious forms.

406: Candle-bracket and reflector in brass, designed by ALF STURE, Norway, and made by *Pusch & Windelstad*. Height 30 cm. Sture is one of those Norwegian practical artists who consciously base their work on old traditions, without thereby limiting their individual artistic achievement.

407: Lidded jugs in stainless steel with plastic knobs, designed in 1959 by FOLKE ARSTRÖM, Sweden, for Scandinavian Airways, and made by *Gense Ltd*.

408: 'Finnline' salad-servers in stainless steel with plastic handles; designed in 1956 by BERTEL GARDBERG, Finland, for *Hackman & Co*. Place-mat in grey-black linen by DORA JUNG. Gardberg has a marked respect for the material he is working with or for, and in his modelling the steel here is given a character fully comparable with that of other metals.

406

408

409   412

410

411

409: Parts of a range of cooking and serving ware in stainless steel, designed in 1960 by ERIK HERLØW and TORMOD OLESEN, Denmark, for *Carl M. Cohr Ltd.* This range of articles for kitchen and table includes a long series of vessels, common to all of which is a basic shape consisting of a cylinder finished at the top with a sloping collar. The advantages of using the same basic form are, firstly, that production equipment can be greatly simplified, and secondly, that there is a general affinity of shape between the different units. The advantage of the collar is, amongst other things, that each unit can be used as a lid for the one of next larger size.

410: Brass tobacco-canister covered with natural leather and with palisander lid. Designed and made by BERTEL GARDBERG, Finland, 1952. A choice example of Gardberg's talent for combining different materials into a—here masculine— happy unity. Pipe-smokers confirm that the shape is ideal when filling a pipe, and the construction is careful in every way. The lid slides on to its brass grip as if greased, and closes the box tightly.

411: 'Canton' serving-dish and casserole in stainless steel, with detachable handles.

Designed in 1957 by BERTEL GARDBERG, Finland, for *Hackman & Co.*: made in three sizes. Largest casserole 21 cm. diameter. In Finland, which has long lacked good practical ware in stainless steel, the Canton series soon became a best-seller. The simple device of the wooden handles functions irreproachably: the slightly down-turned rim of the casserole glides into a groove in the upper side of the handle and is gripped there, and the casserole lid can easily be detached and lifted off by means of a groove in the underside of the handle.

412: Coffee-set in stainless steel, designed in 1954 by MAGNUS STEPHENSEN, Denmark, for *Georg Jensen Ltd.* With this coffee-set, and with a range of pans and casseroles, Stephensen and Georg Jensen Ltd. have spoken out against cheap—often tinny—household ware in stainless steel. The pieces are drawn up over rotating steel cores and then finished and polished by hand, and the final product can compete in quality with the best corresponding work in silver. Since the steel plate is relatively thick, it is not necessary to strengthen the rims with folds or sectional reinforcement and there is similarly no need to curve the plane surfaces.

413: Calculating machine by SIGVARD BERNADOTTE and ACTON BJØRN, Sweden, 1958, produced by *Åtvidaberg Industries Ltd.* As early as the turn of the century a movement arose for giving factory-made tools and machines a form which was functionally and materially correct, and therefore, as many would say, beautiful. An attractive outer form, which harmonises with structure and function, is particularly in demand for everything in the way of office and household tools and machines, and in means of transport. Surface treatment and colour play a prominent part. The firm of Bernadotte & Bjørn, with offices in Copenhagen and Stockholm, has had much success in this field. Amongst other things, they model all Åtvidaberg's output of office machines.

414: Doorhandle, designed in 1960 by BJØRN A. LARSEN, Norway, for *Trio Ltd.* Length 12.3 cm. Bjørn Larsen is an industrial designer who has made a contribution in many fields. It may be only coincidence, but it seems as if Norwegian practical artists are particularly keen on modelling doorhandles. Larsen generally makes his with smooth lines, without losing the decided tautness he likes to give his products.

415: Stainless steel cutlery with black nylon handles, designed in 1956 by FOLKE ARSTRÖM, Sweden, and made by *Gense Ltd.* 'Cottonin' cloth from *Leksand Domestic Crafts.* Arström has been connected with Gense since 1940. This firm is a large producer of stainless steel goods in Sweden, and he has therefore come to take a prominent place in this field and has thoroughly studied the technical problems of steel. The cutlery shown is called 'Focus de luxe'. It is interesting to compare it with Axelsson's set in fig. 417, and see how an object may be achieved in quite different ways. In this case the form of the bowl of the spoon follows the classical egg-shape; the fork has three prongs and is only slightly broader than the broadest part of its handle, and the blade of the knife flows smoothly into the shape of the handle. The black colour of the handles is traditional, but they are made in a new material and form.

416: Fork in stainless steel, for multipurpose use. Designed by PIERRE FORSSELL, Sweden, 1956, and made by *Gense Ltd.* The modern designer tackles the problems of function and form in a fresh and unconventional manner. This object is primarily a fork, but it has a long straight cutting edge and a bowl which can pick up small pieces of food. For buffet suppers, where it is difficult to manage three implements, this combination makes an excellent 'party fork'.

414

415

413

416

417

417: Cutlery in stainless steel and black nylon, designed by AINAR AXELSSON, Sweden, 1956, and produced by *Guldsmedsbolaget, Stockholm*. Linen-cotton cloth from *Östergötland Domestic Crafts*. Stainless steel has broken through as a material for cutlery. Its properties and processing methods, together with modern ideas of form and changed eating habits, have compelled fresh designs. The blade of the knife has been shortened, but its handle lengthened: the bowl of the spoon is often round. The fork in this case has four prongs, which are short and given a bowl-like form so that one can take up small pieces of food. Axelsson has since 1946 been attached to *Guldsmedsbolaget, Stockholm* (GAB), where he works both in silver and stainless steel.

418

418: Place-setting with black plastic tray, grey plastic ware, glasses, and stainless steel cutlery. Designed for Scandinavian Airways by SIGURD PERSSON, Sweden, 1958. Patterned linen cloth and napkin designed by KAISA MELANTON, Sweden. In an aeroplane the purpose and weight of equipment must be reduced to a minimum consistent with pleasantness and comfort. The artist has solved this problem by his choice and co-ordination of materials, form, and colour. The cutlery was designed first, and was the result of an inter-Scandinavian competition organised by SAS in collaboration with the Industrial Art Associations of Denmark, Norway, and Sweden. Persson, who was originally a silversmith and continues to work as such with success, won the first prize, and has since also had the opportunity of modelling the other parts of the ensemble.

BIOGRAPHIES

Apart from the initial letters the following names are listed in the Scandinavian order, whereby the modified vowels are placed at the end of the alphabet.

The figures in brackets at the end of each entry refer to plates in the Illustration Section.

The following abbreviations are used:

Training Institutions:
Stockholm A.C.S.: Stockholm School of Arts, Crafts and Design (Konstfackskolan). Helsinki C.I.A.: College of Industrial Art, Helsinki (Konstindustriella Läroverket, formerly Centralskolan för Konstflit). State I.S.W.: State Industrial School for Women, Norway (Statens Kvinnelige Industriskole). State S.C.I.A.: State School of Crafts and Industrial Art, Norway (Statens Håndverks- og Kunstindustriskole). Copenhagen A.C.S.: Art-Craftsmen's School (Kunsthaandvaerkerskolen).

Exhibitions:
DS: Design in Scandinavia, U.S.A. 1954–57. H 55: Hälsingborg 1955. WG: Finnish Exhibition in West Germany, 1956–57. NF: Neue Form aus Dänemark, Germany, 1956–59. FS: Formes Scandinaves, the Louvre, Paris, 1958. AD: The Arts of Denmark, U.S.A. 1960–61. FZ: 'Finlandia', Zürich, Amsterdam, London, 1961. MT: Milan Triennale.

Museums:
I.A.M.: Industrial Art Museum: Oslo, Copenhagen, Bergen (Westland), or Trondheim (Nordenfjeld). Faenza, M.I.C.: Museo Internazionale delle Ceramiche, Faenza. N.M.: National Museum, Stockholm. R.A.C.M.: Röhsska Arts and Crafts

Museum, Gothenburg. V. & A.: Victoria and Albert Museum, London. F.F.H.: Friends of Finnish Handicraft, Helsinki (Finska Handarbetets Vänner).

AAGAARD, GUDRUN STIG. Danish fabric-printer, b. 1895. Trained at Copenhagen School of Design and Industrial Art for Women, Académie des Beaux Arts des Tissus, Lyons, and with I. G. Farben, Frankfurt-on-Main. Own workshop since 1928. Designs fabrics for L. F. Foght. Has exhibited at home and abroad, inc. AD, and independently in Society for Promotion of Handicrafts. Works bought by Copenhagen I.A.M. (116).

AALTO, ALVAR. Member of Finnish Academy (1955), professor, architect, b. 1898. Trained as architect Helsinki College of Technology, own drawing-office since 1923. Founded Artek firm 1933, operating in Finland, England, U.S.A., Sweden, etc. with house-furnishings and mass-produced furniture. Professor at Massachusetts Institute of Technology 1940–49. Represented in many Finnish and foreign architectural competitions. Honorary doctorate Princeton University. Royal Gold Medal of Architecture (Great Britain), Medal of Honour of Association of Academic Architects, Denmark. Has frequently exhibited furniture, glass, and light-fittings, inc. MT 1936, Paris 1937, New York 1939, H 55, DS, Hansa Viertel Berlin 1956, FS, FZ.

Besides his work as town-planner and architect, which has made him world-famous, Aalto has designed furniture, fabrics, and light-fittings, which he calls 'architectural accessories': in fact, he recognises no frontier between architecture and industrial art. In his furniture he has developed the possibilities of bent wood for three decades, and his products with their combination of rational standardisation and pure and simple beauty have become models of style and have found a large international market. They are closely bound up with the name and principles of Artek, the firm which launched them. The significance of Aalto and Artek as an impetus to Finnish industrial art since the early Thirties is obvious. (15, 16, 18, 34).

ABRAHAMSEN, HANNA JOSEPHINE BRODT-KORB CHRISTIE. Norwegian, b. 1907. Trained Bergen A.C.S. and École Nationale Supérieure des Beaux-Arts, Paris. Pupil of the sculptor Despiau, Oslo Academy of Art. Has worked as teacher of design, architect's assistant, furniture-designer, and interior-designer specialising in house-furnishing and display. Own workshop for turning and carving in wood. Exhibited in all Norwegian exhibitions abroad since 1945. Silver Medal MT 1954. She takes immense care over the modelling of her works, and has a sensitive understanding of the possibilities of different kinds of wood. (103).

ACKING, CARL-AXEL. Swedish architect, b. 1910. Trained Stockholm A.C.S. and Royal Institute of Technology. Own drawing-office since 1939. Has taught furniture-

Carl-Axel Acking

Lis Ahlmann

and interior-design at A.C.S. and form and materials at C. of T. Lunning Prize 1952. Represented in Stockholm N.M. Acking is one of the few Swedish architects who design interiors and furniture as well as building houses. He designed for H 55 the accommodation for the display of fittings and furniture for public buildings. Hässelby family hotel was built to his designs 1954–56. Interior-designer for Hotel Malmen Stockholm, Swedish embassy in Tokio, and ships of North Star Line. His furniture includes both expensive hand-made articles and mass-produced factory pieces. Over the years has designed many pieces for Stockholm craftsmen, sold through the sales-organisation of the city's handicrafts association, 'Hantverket'. Has also designed showpieces for Nordiska Co's. hand-made furniture department, and mass-production pieces for that company's Nyköping works and for Svenska Möbelfabrikerna in Bodafors. (9, 10).

AFDAL, TORBJØRN. Norwegian interior-designer, b. 1917. Trained State S.C.I.A. Employed by Bruksbo Ltd. since 1946. Several prizes in Norwegian furniture-competitions: gold medal at German Craft Fair, Munich 1959. Afdal does not only design models for good individual pieces: he aims to make them go well with each other, to produce a harmonious ensemble. (66).

AHLMANN, LIS. Danish weaver, b. 1894. Trained by Gerda Henning. Own work-

shop since 1933. Since 1953 art-consultant for the C. Olesen textile firm, Copenhagen. Represented at all larger Danish applied art exhibitions at home and abroad, inc. MT, DS, NF, FS, AD. Copenhagen I.A.M. has bought several of her works. (45, 48, 71, 150, 151, 382).

AHLSÉN, TORE. Swedish architect, b. 1906. Trained Stockholm Technical College and Royal Institute of Technology. In Swedish C.W.S. drawing-office 1929-32. Since 1936 has worked independently as architect with brother Erik, and on light-fittings and furniture. (94).

AHO, KAARINA. Finnish ceramic artist, b. 1925. Trained at Helsinki C.I.A. etc. Designer of useful wares at Arabia works since 1946. Silver medal MT 1954, 1957. Represented in Trondheim I.A.M. Exhibited abroad inc. MT's 1954–60, H 55, DS, FS, WG, FZ. (334, 335).

ALNÆS, STEPHAN TORMOD. Norwegian interior-designer, b. 1921. Trained State S.C.I.A. Diplôme d'honneur MT 1954. Exhibited Brussels 1958, MT 1960. Teacher at State S.C.I.A. since 1950. Secretary Applied Art Association, Oslo, since 1956, planned its autumn exhibitions 1956, 1958–60.
Designed official Norwegian applied-art exhibition Kiel 1960. Prefers to experiment with fresh combinations of materials and forms. As exhibition-planner has shown flair for lay-out and simple arrangement, showing each exhibit to the best advantage. (69).

ANDERSEN, RIGMOR. Danish architect, b. 1902. Trained at Academy of Art Copenhagen, where lecturer in furniture and interior design 1959. Represented in Copenhagen I.A.M. (71, 72).

ANDERSSON, ARTHUR, b. 1912 and ANDERSSON, STIG, b. 1919. Swedish ceramic artists, trained by their father in his workshop, Wallåkra stoneware-works, founded 1864, which they have now taken over. Gold medal MT 1954. Represented in Stockholm N.M., Gothenburg R.A.C.M., and museums in Malmö and Hälsingborg. Exhibited at Domestic Crafts Exhibition Stockholm 1948, several times at Gothen-

burg R.A.C.M., H 55, and Lund Art Gallery 1957. (10).

ANDERSSON, JOHN. Swedish ceramic-artist, b. 1900. Works with Andersson & Johansson Ltd., Höganäs, where trained. Prepared Old Höganäs series for H 55, and brought out new Sung series 1960. (295).

ANTTILA, EVA. Finnish tapestry-weaver, b. 1894. Trained Helsinki C.I.A. and University etc. Own workshop in Helsinki, producing tapestries. Gold medal Barcelona 1929, diplôme d'honneur MT 1954. Represented in Helsinki I.A.M., art galleries in Malmö and Fort Wayne Indiana, and V & A. Separate shows in Helsinki 1943, 1949, 1956: Tammerfors 1948, London 1949, Gothenburg 1949, Åbo 1957. MT 1951, 1954, DS. She has a distinct painter-like talent, her tapestries being as rich in tones and as sensitive as oil-painting without renouncing their textile qualities. Her typical works are small coloristic sketches, c. 30 × 30 cm., but her monumental works also deserve mention, e.g. the massive hanging in the Bank of Finland, Vasa, 'Work and Life'.

ARSTRÖM, FOLKE. Swedish designer, b. 1907. Trained at Linköping Craft School, Stockholm A.C.S. and Royal Academy of Fine Art, Stockholm. Own business as designer since 1934. Designed silver and pewter for Goldsmiths Ltd. 1936–40, since then chief designer for Gense Ltd., Eskilstuna, and assistant at BAHCO, Stockholm. Gold medal MT 1951 and distinctions in U.S.A. Gregor Paulsson trophy 1961. Represented in Stockholm N.M. Gothenburg R.A.C.M., etc. Exhibited in Sweden and abroad since 1933. (407, 415).

ASPLUND, ERIK GUNNAR. Swedish architect, 1885–1940. Pioneer of functionalism in Sweden. Leading architect in Stockholm Exhibition 1930. Built Scandia Cinema Stockholm (1923) and City Library (1928) in classicist style. Later responsible for extension of Gothenburg Town Hall and Skogskyrkogården, Stockholm.

ATTERBERG-GÖRANSSON, INGRID. Swedish ceramic-artist, b. 1920. Trained Gothenburg School of Arts and Design. Employed at Upsala-Ekeby Ltd. since 1944, and occasional work for Manicioli Natale C., Montelupo, Italy. Represented in Stockholm N.M., Faenza M.I.C., V & A, Trondheim I.A.M., etc. (285, 299).

AXELSSON, AINAR. Swedish silversmith, b. 1920. Trained Stockholm A.C.S. Employed by Goldsmiths Ltd., Stockholm. First prize in International Design Competition for Sterling Silver Flatware, organised by American Craftsmen's Council, 1960. Exhibited in Sweden and abroad. (417).

BANG, JACOB E. Danish architect, b. 1899. Trained as sculptor, then at Copenhagen Academy of Arts architecture department. Assistant to various architects, then industrial designer for Holmegaard glass-works 1925–42, after which free-lance for e.g. Kastrup glassworks, Nymølle potteries, Pan Aluminium, F. Hingelberg silversmith. Exhibited frequently, inc. MT, DS, NF, FS, AD. Represented e.g. at Copenhagen I.A.M. (253).

BECKMAN, ANDERS. Swedish publicity artist, b. 1907. Fertile in ideas and a prominent designer of posters and print, exhibition-organiser (Swedish Society for Industrial Design Centenary, 1945; Swedish pavilion, New York 1939) and teacher. Since 1939 head of Anders Beckman School in Stockholm, where he trains publicity and fashion artists and illustrators with excellent results.

BENGTSON, HERTHA. Swedish ceramic-artist, b. 1917. Trained at Hackefors porcelain-works, since 1941 employed at Rörstrand porcelain-works. Exhibited at home and abroad since 1948. Represented in Stockholm N.M., Oslo I.A.M., Copenhagen I.A.M., Faenza M.I.C. (301).

BERG, SIGRUN. Norwegian textile-artist, b. 1901. Trained State S.C.I.A. and State Academy of Art. Employed by Teletweed Weaving Co. 1936, own workshop since 1947. Also launched weaving at Trysil on a contract basis. Since 1956 teacher of dyeing at State S.C.I.A. Has undertaken large commissions, e.g. for Bodø Cathedral. Has woven fabrics for royal yacht 'Norge', hotels, and ships. Diplôme d'honneur MT 1954; gold medal

Munich Craft Fair 1958 and MT 1960. Several separate exhibitions. One of Norway's most distinctive textile artists: works principally with a colour-scheme based on old Norwegian traditions but completely adapted to modern ideas. (103, 168).

BERGLUND, ERIK. Swedish furniture-designer, b. 1921. Trained as cabinetmaker, then pupil of Carl Malmsten. Various work for Society for Industrial Design since 1943, e.g. courses, exhibition work; since 1948 particularly with the Society's researches into furniture function, resulting in the publications *Beds* (1950), *Tables* (1957), and *Cupboards* (1960).

BERNADOTTE, SIGVARD. Swedish industrial designer, b. 1907. Count of Wisborg, son of King Gustav VI. Graduate in philosophy, and studied at Royal Academy of Fine Art, Stockholm. Designed silverware for Georg Jensen, Copenhagen, and theatre decoration inc. Theatre Royal, Copenhagen. Also fabrics, posters and furniture. With Acton Bjørn carries on the design business Bernadotte & Bjørn, Copenhagen and Stockholm. Represented in Copenhagen I.A.M. and museums in U.S.A. (413).

BJØRN, ACTON. Danish architect and industrial designer, b. 1910. Trained at the Technical Society's schools and the Academy architecture department. Has designed houses and schools. Began as industrial designer in the Forties, and supervised construction of Boeing and Douglas aircraft for Scandinavian Airways. Partner-founder with Bernadotte of industrial design firm 1948 (see above). (413).

BJÖRQUIST, KARIN. Swedish ceramic-artist, b. 1927. Trained at Stockholm A.C.S. Employed since 1950 at Gustavsberg Studio. Gold medal MT 1954. Represented in Stockholm N.M., Gothenburg R.A.C.M., Trondheim and Copenhagen I.A.M.s, etc. Has exhibited at home and abroad since 1954. (283, 298).

BJØRSHOL, ARNULF. Norwegian designer, b. 1921. Trained at State S.C.I.A. Practised in drawing-office. Editorial secretary of periodical Bonytt 1945–46. Employed by J. Tostrup silversmiths 1944–48, since

Sigrun Berg

then with Christiania Glasmagasin, Høvik works, specialising in light-fittings for ships and hotels. As free-lance has designed refrigerators and mechanical and electrical household apparatus. Has exhibited at home and abroad. Chiefly interested in design of light-fittings, which show his sure sense of line and proportion.

BLOMBERG, KJELL. Swedish ceramic-artist and glass-designer, b. 1931. Trained at Stockholm A.C.S. Designs glass for Gullaskruf glass-works, with which he has been connected since 1955, and pottery for Gabrielverken Ltd., Timmernabben. Has exhibited at home and abroad since 1955. (230).

BOJESEN, KAY. Danish silversmith, 1881–1958. Trained with Georg Jensen Ltd. and at Royal Craft School for Precious Metals, Württemberg. Later worked as craftsman in Paris and Copenhagen: own workshop in Copenhagen 1913. Art-consultant for Bing & Grøndahl porcelain works 1930–31. Held many one-man shows of silver and wood; exhibited frequently at home and abroad inc. MT's (Grand Prix 1951, gold medal 1954), DS, NF, FS, AD. Works bought by many museums, inc. V & A, Kunstgewerbe M. Munich, Stedelijke M. Amsterdam, Oslo, Bergen, Copenhagen, and Trondheim I.A.M.'s., Stockholm N.M. (51, 105, 378–380).

BONGARD, HERMANN. Norwegian artist, b. 1921. Trained at State S.C.I.A. Employed at Hadeland glassworks 1948–55, Figgjo faience-works since 1957, and Oslo Silverware-works since 1958. Also works as free-lance for publishers, and in glass, pottery, silver, wood, and textiles for manual and industrial production. Has carried out monumental decorative works and ship decoration. Holds various responsible offices in Norwegian applied-art organisation. Represented in Oslo and Trondheim I.A.M.s, Växjö glass museum, Whyte Gallery and Smithsonian Institution, in Washington D.C. Has exhibited in Belgium, Denmark, France, Italy, Holland, Sweden, and U.S.A. Gold and silver medals MT 1954: Lunning Prize 1957. A versatile practical artist who insists on austere and objective forms, but takes a freer line with purely decorative work. (308).

BORG, OLLI. Finnish interior-designer, b. 1921. Trained at Helsinki C.I.A. and by travel in Scandinavia, Spain, and Italy, interior-designer for Te-Ma Ltd. 1947–50, in Viljo Rewell's drawing-office 1950–54, with Asko Industries 1954–56. Head of industrial design department at C.I.A., and own drawing-office, 1956. Exhibited at MT 1954, DS, FS. (17)

BRAND, INGA. Swedish textile-artist, b. 1929. Trained at Gothenburg, School of Arts and Design. Has own workshop at Kungälv, where teaches at local Craft School. (142).

BREGER, CARL ARNE. Swedish industrial designer, b. 1923. Trained at Stockholm A.C.S. Studied plastic techniques in England and Italy. Employed by Gustavsberg works to 1960, then founded own firm, Breger Design. 1960 design prize from Swedish Plastic Association.

BRUMMER, EVA. Finnish rug-artist, b. 1901. Trained at Helsinki C.I.A. Has worked independently since 1929. Collaborated with Friends of Finnish Handicraft by exhibiting in competitions and with commissioned rug-designs. First prize in F.F.H. competitions 1953, 1956, 1958: diplôme d'honneur MT 1933, silver medal Paris 1937, Grand Prix MT 1951, diplôme d'honneur MT 1954, gold medal MT 1957. Rugs in Helsinki and Oslo I.A.M.s and Moltzau collections, Oslo. Has exhibited e.g. in Europe, U.S.A.,

Kay Bojesen

Hermann Bongard

Canada, Brazil, MTs 1951–60, DS, FS. Belongs to the older generation of still-active rug-artists. Originally inspired, with others, by the eminent teacher Arttu Brummer, to revive the ancient folk-weave technique in high-quality rugs: still one of the leading rug-artists, and also an eminent painter. (188).

BRÜEL, AXEL. Danish ceramics artist, b. 1900. Trained as painter with Harald Giersing and later with Professor Axel Jørgensen at Copenhagen Academy of Art. Became interested in ceramics and worked at several potteries before starting his own in 1928. Study tour in France 1939. Since 1956 art-consultant for Danmark porcelain-works, as well as working independently. Has exhibited frequently at home and abroad, inc. MTs, DS, NF, FS, AD. Represented in Metropolitan Museum of Art, New York. (322, 323).

BRYK, RUT. Finnish ceramics artist, b. 1916. Trained at Helsinki C.I.A. Employed by Arabia works since 1942. Grand Prix MT 1951, diplôme d'honneur MT 1954. Represented in Stockholm N.M., Copenhagen and Trondheim I.A.M.s, Faenza M.I.C., Zürich Kunstgewerbemuseum. Has exhibited frequently in Europe and America, inc. MTs 1951–60, DS, FS, H 55, WG. In her ceramics the decorative element is the most vital. Work on the wheel means less to her, and she is more interested in two-dimensional painting with unusually strong and brilliant glazes on faience and

chamotte-surfaces. Her former shallow incised technique has now been replaced with deep glazing, which in fact suggests a third dimension even in surface decoration. But the sensitive romantic spirit of her earlier work largely survives in her later and more mature products. These are normally trays, wall-tiles, and plaques of modest size, but she has also built them up into larger wholes of a monumental nature, e.g. open-work screens made of hexagons in faience, and the ceramic wall-surface made for the Rosenthal works in 1960. (347).

BRØRBY, SEVERIN. Norwegian glass-artist, b. 1932. Trained at State S.C.I.A. Qualified engraver. Employed at Hadeland glassworks since 1956. Has exhibited in various European countries. Represented in Trondheim I.A.M. He demonstrated his abilities as an independent glass-artist last year, and has achieved excellent results, especially with experiments in coloured glass. (203, 206).

BUNDE, HANS. Danish silversmith, b. 1919. Trained at Carl M. Cohr silverware works. With A. Michelsen silverworks 1943–50, since 1951 designer for Carl M. Cohr Ltd. Has exhibited at home and abroad, inc. MTs (diplôme d'honneur 1954), DS, NF, FS, AD. Two of his works bought by Landesgewerbe-Museum, Stuttgart. (383).

BÜLOW-HÜBE, TORUN. Swedish silversmith, b. 1927. Trained at Stockholm

A.C.S. Own workshop in Stockholm 1951–60. In Paris since 1960. Has lived at Biot in France since 1958. Gold medal MT 1960, and Lunning Prize 1960. (361, 369).

BÄCKSTRÖM, OLOF. Finnish woodcarver and designer, b. 1922. Self-taught: study tour in Denmark 1959. Since then employed by Fiskars Ltd. as cutlery designer. Silver medal MTs 1957 and 1960. FS, FZ.

BÖCKMAN, EDGAR. Swedish ceramics artist, b. 1890. Trained at Stockholm A.C.S. and at ceramics craft-school in Prague. Employed 1915–27 at Höganäs-Billesholm and 1927–29 at Rörstrand porcelain-works. Principal teacher in ceramics at A.C.S. 1947–57. (293).

CHRISTENSEN, RUTH. Danish fabric-printer, b. 1918. Trained at Copenhagen A.C.S.: own workshop since 1950. Has made industrial prints for C. Olesen's Cotil collection. Represented e.g. at AD. Compasso d'Oro 1957. Works bought by Trondheim and Copenhagen I.A.M.s (164).

CYRÉN, GUNNAR. Swedish silversmith and glass-designer, b. 1931. Trained as goldsmith in Gävle and at Stockholm A.C.S. Society for Industrial Design's medal for proficiency and industry 1956. Employed at Orrefors glassworks since 1958. (226).

DAHL, BIRGER. Norwegian designer, b. 1916. Trained at State S.C.I.A. Light-fitting designer for Sønnico 1944–59. Senior teacher at S.C.I.A. since 1947. Consultant for Vallø carpet factory. Several responsible functions in Norwegian applied-art organisation. A most fastidious designer, as is plainly shown in his wide and valuable work in the field of light-fittings. Also a pioneer in Norwegian wall decorations for many years. (67).

DAHLQUIST, INGA-BRITT. Swedish silversmith, b. 1924. Trained at Stockholm A.C.S. Since 1955 co-owner of a jewellery firm in Malmö with Olof Barve. Represented in Stockholm N.M. (362).

DERR, CO. Swedish woodcarver, b. 1921. Trained at crafts chool in Amsterdam. Dutch-born, but since 1955 has worked in Stockholm and has frequently exhibited his fine woodcarvings. (110).

DESSAU, INGRID. Swedish textile-artist, b. 1923. Trained at Stockholm A.C.S. Has worked for Malmöhus and Kristianstad Domestic Crafts, and for Kasthall carpet-works at Kinna. First prize in carpet competitions organised by Hantverket in Stockholm 1959 and 1960. Lunning Prize 1955. Represented in Stockholm N.M., Gothenburg R.A.C.M., Malmö Museum, etc. Has exhibited since 1953. (2, 5, 141).

DITZEL, NANNA and JØRGEN. Danish furniture-designers, b. 1923 and 1921: Jørgen d. 1961. Trained at Copenhagen A.C.S. and Academy of Art furniture school. Have worked as designers e.g. for Herning weaving-mills, Georg Jensen Ltd., Kold sawmills furniture-works, Ravnholm enamel-works, and Unika Vaev-Ltd. Exhibited frequently at home and abroad, inc. MTs, NF, FS, AD. Several prizes at MTs (gold medal 1960): Lunning Prize 1956. Works bought by Trondheim and Copenhagen I.A.M.s. Published book 'Danish Chairs', 1954. (83, 377).

DYSTHE, SVEN IVAR. Norwegian interior-designer, b. 1931. Trained at Royal College of Arts, London. International Design Citation of American Institute of Decorators. Has won several competitions. One of the younger generation of Norwegian furniture-designers, who has

Ingrid Dessau

already made his mark with his sense of construction and his sound craftsman's training. (68).

ECKHOFF, TIAS. Norwegian ceramics artist and metal designer, b. 1926. Trained at State S.C.I.A. Practised as potter in Denmark, inc. at Saxbo. Designer at Porsgrund porcelain works 1949 and artistic director since 1953. Permanent links with Danish and Norwegian firms as design consultant. Won competition for ceramic decorations for Students' Union at Norwegian Agricultural College 1948. Two prizes for decorative and practical glass in Hadeland competition 1951. First prize for silver cutlery in Georg Jensen's inter-Scandinavian competition 1953. Lunning Prize 1953. Gold medals for porcelain and silver cutlery MT 1954, for porcelain and door furniture MT 1957, for porcelain MT 1960. As designer covers a very wide field, and all his products have a simple and natural objectivity. (309, 313, 351).

EDENFALK, BENGT. Swedish painter and glass designer, b. 1924. Trained as painter at Stockholm A.C.S. First prize in competition for decoration of Stockholm Central Underground station, 1956. Own display in Special Exhibition of International Contemporary Glass, Corning Museum of Glass, 1959. Represented in Stockholm N.M. and Malmö Museum. Since 1954 has exhibited in Sweden and abroad. Employed at Skruf glassworks since 1953. (225).

EKLUND, AL. Swedish pattern-designer and printer, b. 1936. Trained at Anders Beckman School, Stockholm. Designs fabric-prints for e.g. Stobo, Stockholm. Has exhibited in Stockholm, England, and U.S.A., and at MT 1960 (silver medal). (148).

EKSELIUS, KARL-ERIK. Swedish furniture designer and furniture-maker, b. 1914. Trained as furniture-craftsman with J. O. Carlsson in Vetlanda, then with Carl Malmsten in Stockholm and Fritz August Breuhaus in Berlin. Administrative director and furniture-designer with J. O. Carlsson Ltd. since 1950. Represented in Stockholm N.M., Gothenburg R.A.C.M. Has exhibited in, and arranged,

Tias Eckhoff

exhibitions in Sweden and elsewhere since 1954. (13).

ENGQVIST, LISA. Danish ceramics artist, b. 1914. Trained at Copenhagen A.C.S. Worked with Nathalie Krebs at Saxbo 1935–38 and 1952–54. Individual exhibition 1959, and has exhibited frequently at home and abroad, inc. MTs, NF, FS, AD. Represented at Metropolitan Museum of Art, New York, Copenhagen I.A.M. and Louisiana Museum. (270).

ENGØ, BJØRN. Norwegian interior-designer, b. 1920. Trained at State S.C.I.A. Has worked independently since 1948. Designs for several firms. Started his career as furniture-designer in blithe opposition to traditional materials and forms: in recent years has designed light-fittings and bowls in anodised aluminium, and has designed textile patterns. (352).

ERICSON-ÅSTRÖM, ULLA. Swedish fabric- and fashion-designer, b. 1922. Trained at Stockholm A.C.S. and Anders Beckman School. Works as free-lance. First prize in several Swedish textile competitions. Has exhibited since 1955 in Sweden and abroad. (117).

ERIKSEN, SIGURD ALF. Norwegian silversmith and painter, b. 1899. Trained at State S.C.I.A. and Staatliche Zeichenakademie, Hanau. Has worked for J. Tostrup, Oslo, Otto Ulbrich, Hanau, Siemet & Co., Vienna, Schneider, Paris, and Janausch, Pforzheim. Has taught at three

schools in U.S.A. and Goldsmiths' College Copenhagen. Senior teacher at State S.C.I.A. Has exhibited independently and in general exhibitions in various countries. Represented as practical artist at Trondheim I.A.M., V. & A., and Cooper Union Museum New York. (373).

ESKOLIN-NURMESNIEMI, VUOKKO. Finnish textile-artist, b. 1930. Trained in ceramics Helsinki C.I.A. Free-lance, working chiefly with fabric-prints for Marimekko firm. Prizes in Finnish tapestry competition and Kastrup glassworks competition. Gold medal MT 1957; also exhibited in Europe and U.S.A. inc. DS, WG. Fabrics in V. & A. Designed Finnish industrial art exhibition in Boston 1959. (194).

FAGERLUND, CARL. Swedish designer of light-fittings, b. 1915. Trained at Stockholm A.C.S., qualified teacher of design. Since 1946 employed at Orrefors glassworks as designer and maker of light-fittings. Has exhibited at home and abroad since 1955. (95).

FAITH-ELL, AGE. Swedish textile-artist, b. 1912. Trained at Johanna Brunsson weaving-school Stockholm, Akademie für Angewandte Kunst, and Staatslehr- und Versuchsanstalt, Vienna. Silver medal of Stockholm Craftsmen's Union and prizes in fabric competitions. Gold medal MT 1960: has exhibited at home and abroad. Represented Stockholm N.M. and Die Neue Sammlung, Munich. Worked with Swedish Domestic Crafts Association to 1945, Bo Ltd. Copenhagen 1938, Irish Poplin House, Belfast, 1937–45. In Sweden has worked for Claes Håkansson Kinna, Stobo Stockholm, Tidstrand woollen-mills Sågmyra, Mab & Mya Malmö, Eriksberg weaving-mills Kinna. (111).

FJELDSAA, KÅRE B. Norwegian ceramic artist, b. 1918. Trained in Jens von der Lippe's workshop: had his own 1947–58. Since 1958 artistic director of Stavangerflint. Gold medals MT 1956, Cannes 1957. Has exhibited in various countries. (307).

FLATHEIM, STEINAR FRODE. Norwegian silversmith, b. 1935. Trained as goldsmith's apprentice, at craft-school, and at Crafts Association School in Gothen-

burg. Pupil of silversmith Thore Eldh. Distinctions at Higher Industrial Art Day School, where now teaches in metal department. Has done work for Stavanger Cathedral, Stavanger municipality, Bergen and Trondheim I.A.M.s. Own workshop 1960. MT 1960. The youngest Norwegian artist in this book, but has already shown sure talent. His works are of such exceptionally good craftsmanship that he fully merits a place here. (399).

FORSBERG, ANN-MARI. Swedish textile-artist, b. 1916. Trained Stockholm A.C.S. Since 1941 worked at Märta Måås-Fjetterström Ltd. Båstad and for Friends of Handicraft in Stockholm. Teacher of art-needlework since 1953. Has exhibited at home and abroad since 1945. Represented in Stockholm N.M. (144).

FORSSELL, PIERRE. Swedish silversmith, b. 1925. Craft training at Court-silversmith Erik Fleming's Atelier Borgila, Stockholm and at A.C.S., where taught 1952–60. Since 1960 teacher at Craft Teachers' College Linköping. Has worked with Gense Ltd Eskilstuna since 1953, Swedish Metalworks Skultuna since 1955. (416).

FOUGSTEDT, LOUISE. Swedish textile-artist and pattern-designer, b. 1938. Trained at Stockholm A.C.S. Works in Nordiska Co.'s textile department: also designs patterns for oil-cloth and plastic cloths for Jönköping-Vulcan, Anneberg, Småland. (301).

Kaj Franck

FRANCK, KAJ. Finnish artist in glass, ceramics, and textiles, b. 1911. Trained at Helsinki C.I.A. Textile-designer for Te-Ma 1933–37, United Woollens 1937–39, etc. Since 1945 teacher at C.I.A. and art-director since 1960. Has modelled practical pottery for Arabia porcelain-works and glass for Notsjö glassworks. Lunning Prize 1955. Has exhibited frequently, inc. MTs 1951–60 (diplôme d'honneur 1954, Grand Prix 1957), DS, H 55, FS, WG, FZ: with Dora Jung and Gardberg in Gothenburg 1955 and Copenhagen 1956. Compasso d'Oro 1957. Exhibited in N. and S. America. Represented in Gothenburg R.A.C.M., Trondheim and Copenhagen I.A.M.s, V. & A., New York Museum of Modern Art. His great contribution in raising the artistic standard of everyday wares, in ceramics as well as glass, puts him amongst the leading Finnish designers He combines a bold and unusually decorative imagination with practical ability to meet the rationalised needs of industrial production. As production-planner for Arabia's modern practical ware he has a key position allowing full scope to his talents in wide varieties of product. The things he has put his stamp on are produced in such great quantities that his influence is felt in a large percentage of Finnish homes. Happily, the holder of this dominant position has an incorruptible sense of responsibility. This trait, moreover, is combined with humour and a love of playful experiment, never overdone, but producing results which stand above fashion changes and are therefore never wearisome. This frolicsome fantasy is naturally best expressed in glass articles which can ignore any social or rational considerations. (207–209, 232–235, 325–328, 343–346).

FRANK, JOSEF. Swedish architect, interior-designer, and practical artist, b. 1885 in Baden, Austria. Trained at Vienna Technical College. Professor at Kunstgewerbeschule Vienna 1919–27. Own house furnishing firm Haus und Garten 1925–34. Worked with Svenskt Tenn firm, Stockholm, since 1932, with break 1941–43 in which taught at New School of Social Research, New York. Exhibited as architect and furniture designer Paris 1925; Die Wohnung, Stuttgart, 1928; Paris

Bertel Gardberg

1937; New York 1939. Swedish nationality 1939. Wrote 'Architectur als Symbol' 1930, 'Accidentism' 1958. Litteris et Artibus medal. Represented in Stockholm N.M. (31, 32).

FRIBERG, BERNDT. Swedish ceramics artist, b. 1899. Trained at Höganäs stoneware-works, Technical Craft-School, various workshops in Denmark and Sweden. Since 1934 worked with Gustavsberg. Represented in Stockholm N.M., Gothenburg R.A.C.M., Copenhagen I.A.M., New York Museum of Modern Art, and museums in Oslo, Trondheim, Faenza, Taranto, Sydney, Hamburg, Syracuse U.S.A., Vienna, and Malmö. Exhibited individually and in general exhibitions since 1945: Gold medal MTs 1948, 1951, 1954. Gregor Paulsson trophy 1960. (278).

FRONTH, KARI. Norwegian textile-artist, b. 1934. Trained at State S.C.I.A. Worked as designer of fabric-prints and weaves in Holland. Since 1958 with Plus organisation in Frederikstad. Study tours in England, Greece, Italy, and Sweden. (350, 352).

FRYKLUND, SVEN-ERIK. Swedish furniture-designer and sculptor, b. 1921. Trained at Malmsten's workshop school and Royal Academy of Art sculpture department. Has designed pieces for mass-production, inc. nearly all of the output of Hagafors chair-factory, and has fitted out restaurants. Silver medal from Swedish Handicrafts Organisation. (138).

Sven Arne Gillgren

GALAAEN, KONRAD. Norwegian ceramics artist, b. 1923. Trained at State S.C.I.A. and at Royal Porcelain Works, Copenhagen. With Porsgrund porcelain-works since 1948. Has exhibited in all Norwegian applied-art displays since 1949. Has worked chiefly on modelling for industrial production, but has also recently carried out a series of monumental ceramic reliefs. (178).

GARDBERG, BERTEL. Finnish silversmith, b. 1916. Trained at Helsinki C.I.A. and Goldsmiths' School. Own workshop since 1949. Teacher at C.I.A. 1951–53. Has exhibited frequently in Europe and America, inc. MTs 1954–60 (gold medal 1954, 1957, four silver medals 1960) DS, H 55, WG, FZ, FS. Represented in Stockholm N.M., Gothenburg R.A.C.M., Copenhagen and Trondheim I.A.M.s, and museums in Germany and U.S.A. As designer and silversmith he has been a real pioneer in Finland. His refined craftsmanship and his spell as a teacher have at least awakened interest in modelling in metal. He shows respect and understanding for his material, and his vessels are generally quite objective, undecorated, and functionally well-thought-out. The combination of silver (and brass) with finer woods or leather is typical of his work. Has also modelled cutlery etc. in stainless steel for industry. (327, 343, 344, 368, 374, 400, 401, 405, 408, 410, 411).

GATE, SIMON. Swedish painter and glass-designer, 1883–1945. Trained at Stockholm A.C.S. and Royal Academy of Art: then worked as painter of landscapes, portraits, and decorative work, and book-illustration. With Orrefors glassworks since 1916. Exhibited in Society for Industrial Design's exhibition of furnishings for small homes 1917, and later in many others. Represented in museums and collections all over the world.

GILLGREN, SVEN ARNE. Swedish silver-smith, b. 1913. Trained in Court-jeweller C. G. Hallberg's engraving-shop and at Stockholm A.C.S. Worked with Guld-smedsbolaget, Stockholm since 1937, art-director 1942, and with G. Dahlgren & Co., goldsmiths, Malmö, 1944. Principal teacher in metalcraft at A.C.S. 1955. First prize in 'Hantverket' competitions 1936 and 1957. First prize in International Design Competition for Silver Flat-ware, American Craftsmen's Council, 1960. Represented in Stockholm N.M. and Nordiska Museum, Gothenburg R.A.C.M., Oslo and Trondheim I.A.M.s, Houston Museum of Fine Arts, and many other museums and collections. Has frequently exhibited at home and abroad since 1940. Articles in Swedish and foreign professional Press on questions of design, silver, and jewellery. Many works in silver, e.g. for over 40 Swedish churches, trophies, vessels, cutlery for Swedish embassies. As jewellery designer uses mostly gold and stones, and makes his pieces romantic and placid. (395, 396, 398).

GNISTA, FORSE. Swedish furniture-designer and sculptor, b. 1932. Trained as woodworker at Stockholm City Craft School and in sculpture and interior-design at A.C.S. Society for Industrial Design medal for proficiency and industry 1955. (109).

GRAF, BIRGITTA. Swedish textile- and pattern-designer, b. 1933. Trained at Gothenburg, School of Arts and Design, Otto Sköld school of painting Stockholm, Académie de la Grande Chaumière Paris. Has worked for Elsa Gullberg Ltd. Stockholm since 1955. Fabric-prints in Stockholm N.M. (139).

GRIEGST, ARJE. Danish goldsmith, b. 1938. Trained with Just Andersen Ltd. Has

exhibited at home and abroad, inc. MT 1960, AD. Represented in Copenhagen I.A.M. (360).

GRIMSRUD, RAGNAR. Norwegian ceramics artist, b. 1902. Trained at State S.C.I.A. Own workshop 1925–28. Artist in Gra-veren Ltd. ceramic department 1928–33, with Egersund potteries 1933–34. Chief of Graveren's pottery and ceramics de-partment 1934–46. Buyer and artist at Figgjo faience-works since 1946. Director of Stavanger Applied Art Assoc. since its foundation in 1947. Has exhibited in several countries. Represented in Oslo I.A.M., Helsinki, Sèvres museum. A pio-neer in modern Norwegian ceramics. After having his own small workshop, has now gone over to industry and is today buyer and artistic chief of a large ceramics firm, but still personally makes fresh and surely-formed models. (126, 311).

GRÅSTEN, VIOLA. Swedish textile-artist, b. 1910 in Finland. Swedish nationality 1949. Trained at Helsinki C.I.A. Worked with F.F.H. 1938–44, Elsa Gullberg Ltd. 1945, Nordiska Co.'s textile department Stockholm 1945–56. Art-director and pattern-designer with Mölnlycke Textiles Ltd. Gothenburg since 1956, and free-lance designer for Tidstrand woollen-mills Sågmyra and Kasthall carpet-works. Gold medal Paris 1937, diplôme d'honneur MT 1954, gold medal MTs 1951 and 1957. Gregor Paulsson trophy 1959. Re-presented in Stockholm N.M., Helsinki, Trondheim, and Copenhagen I.A.M.s,

Viola Gråsten

New York Museum of Modern Art. Has exhibited at home and abroad since 1937. She started in the domestic crafts move-ment, and certainly draws much inspi-ration from Finnish folk-art, first in her long-pile rugs and later also in printed fabrics for house-furnishing and clothes. These latter are often bright, sometimes garish and glowing, sometimes on the other hand in a limited range of greys, but always strongly individual. (143, 149, 302).

GULBRANDSEN, INGER. Norwegian fabric-printer, b. 1932. Trained at State S.C.I.A. and in factory and workshop practice in Holland. Study tours in Denmark, Finland, and Sweden. Own workshop for hand-printed fabrics since 1953. Has exhi-bited in all Norwegian applied-art exhi-bitions since 1953. (177–179).

GULLBERG, BENGT-JOHAN. Swedish in-terior-designer, b. 1919. Trained in fabric-printing and weaving, and in furniture-making with Karl Mathsson in Värnamo. Also Royal Institute of Technology and business training. Worked with Elsa Gullberg Ltd. fabrics and furnishings 1945–53. Has worked on construction of standard kitchens, fabrics, and light-fittings. Exhibited Stockholm 1945, 1949; London, Brussels, H 55, and various places in Sweden. (92).

GULLBERG, ELSA. Swedish textile-artist and production-director, b. 1886. Learned weaving at home in Scania. Practised in metal and carpentry. Trained Stockholm A.C.S. while also working in printing. Director of Swedish Society for Industrial Design testing and furniture-design de-partments 1907–17. Director of Society's intermediary bureau 1917–24. Own firm, Elsa Gullberg fabrics and furnishings, 1927, from the direction of which she retired 1955. Trade name on international market Gullberg-Gray, 1950. Has exhib-ited in, and organised, exhibitions at home and abroad since First World War. Represented in Stockholm N.M., Gothen-burg R.A.C.M., New York Metropolitan Museum, V. & A., Copenhagen I.A.M., etc. Has made fabrics for many build-ings in Sweden and elsewhere, inc. Stockholm Concert Hall, Gothenburg Town Hall, Malmö City Theatre, King's

College Chapel Cambridge. Litteris et Artibus medal 1924. (138).

HAGEN, OLE. Danish architect, b. 1913. Trained at Copenhagen Academy of Art building department. Worked in several drawing-offices, inc. those of his father G. B. Hagen and Prof. Palle Suenson. Partnership with father 1937, independent business 1941. Has planned many Copenhagen houses, schools, and hotels, and since 1941 has designed vessels and cutlery for A. Michelsen silverworks. Has exhibited at home and abroad, inc. MTs (Prix d'honneur 1951, 1954), DS, NF, FS, AD. Works bought e.g. by Melbourne National Gallery, Copenhagen and Trondheim I.A.M.s, Gothenburg R.A.C.M. (385).

HALD, ARTHUR. Swedish art-historian, writer, and production-director, b. 1916. Graduate in philosophy. Editor of Swedish Society for Industrial Design's periodicals *Form* 1946–56, *Kontur* 1950–56. Art-director of Gustavsberg works since 1957. Chairman of Swedish Society for Industrial Design council since 1959. Published 1948 in collaboration with Erik Wettergren: *Simon Gate–Edward Hald;* in 1951 in collaboration with Sven Erik Skawonius: *Nyttokonst–Contemporary Swedish Design.*

HALD, DAGNY. Norwegian ceramics artist, b. 1936, wife of Finn Hald. Trained at State S.C.I.A. and Accademia di Belle Arti, Rome, and with Marianne and Lars Thirslund, Denmark. Gold medal, with her husband, Cannes 1957. Generally decorates her husband's stoneware, and with close harmony with his forms produces sensitive and artistic effects. Also has achieved interesting results in glazed reliefs. (258, 259).

HALD, EDWARD. Swedish painter, artist in glass and ceramics, and managing director, b. 1883. Trained as painter at Johan Rohde's school in Copenhagen, at Artists' League school in Stockholm, and with Matisse. From 1917 artist for Orrefors glassworks, managing director 1933–44: for Rørstrand porcelain-works (then in Stockholm) 1917–23, for Karlskrona porcelain-works 1924–33. Represented in Stockholm N.M., Gothen-

Edward Hald

burg R.A.C.M., Småland Museum Växjö, Musée des Arts Décoratifs Paris, V. & A., Oslo and Copenhagen I.A.M.s, New York Metropolitan Museum, Chicago Art Institute, etc. Has frequently exhibited and organised exhibitions at home and abroad. Grand Prix Paris 1925. Hon. member Faculty of Royal Designers for Industry, London: Hon. fellow, Society of Glass Technology, Sheffield. Prince Eugen medal 1945. Hon. Professor 1952. One of the three hon. members of Swedish Society for Industrial Design. An outstanding figure in the development of Swedish applied art. Helped to make Swedish glassware and Orrefors world-famous. (218, 227, 369).

HALD, FINN. Norwegian ceramics artist, b. 1920. Husband of Dagny Hald. Trained at Istituto d'arte per la Ceramica, Faenza, and State S.C.I.A. Own workshop since 1956. The Halds have held several exhibitions of their own, and also exhibited in Belgium, England, France, Sweden, Germany, and Austria. (258, 259).

HALLING, ELSE. Norwegian weaver, b. 1899. Trained at State S.C.I.A. and Frk. Stoltenberg's weaving-school. Worked 3 years in U.S.A. Has for several years run weaving-schools in Trondheim, North Norway, and Oslo. Teacher at State I.S.W. Since 1951 chief of Norsk Billedvev (tapestry) studio, connected with Oslo I.A.M. Has made several large tapestries after cartoons by artists. King's gold

medal of merit. No Norwegian textile artist has done so much to improve colour-schemes and technical quality in tapestry. Her long study of old Norwegian fabrics, and her careful selection of the yarn she uses, together with her determined and consciously artistic industry, have produced a renaissance in this field.

HALVORSEN, ARNE. Norwegian interior-designer, b. 1929. Trained at State S.C.I.A. Worked in Rastad & Relling's drawing-office for 5 years, and also works free-lance. First and second prize in Chamber of Commerce furniture competition 1960. (27, 28).

HANSEN, ROLF. Norwegian ceramics artist, b. 1922. Workshop in Kongsberg since 1947. Represented in V. & A., Whitworth Gallery Manchester, Faenza M.I.C., Norwegian Applied Art Association's permanent collection. Gold medal Cannes 1955. Exhibited MTs 1954, 1960: U.S.A., France, Sweden, Germany. (170, 306).

HASSEL, LIV. Norwegian fabric-printer. Trained at State S.C.I.A. and London Central School of Arts and Crafts. Has worked in small workshops in Norway and England and in Norwegian factories. Own workshop in Oslo since 1950. Represented in Oslo I.A.M. and V. & A. Has exhibited at home and abroad since 1954 and twice independently. (180, 201).

HAUGSTOGA, SIGNE. Norwegian textile artist, b. 1903. Trained at State I.S.W. and further courses in weaving, spinning, and dyeing. Principal teacher at State I.S.W. since 1934. Since 1955 has been in charge of the School's experimental weaving workshop. (171).

HAVE, ELISABETH. Danish weaver, b. 1930. Trained at Copenhagen A.C.S. Own workshop since 1952. Fabric-designer for C. Olesen's Cotil collection since 1960. Exhibited at AD. (162).

HEDBERG, HANS. Swedish ceramics artist, b. 1917. Trained as painter with Kræsten Iversen at Copenhagen Academy of Art and in ceramics with Giuseppe Ballardini at Istituto delle Ceramiche, Faenza.

Poul Henningsen

Own workshop at Biot, A.M., France. Represented in Stockholm N.M., Gothenburg R.A.C.M., New York Museum of Modern Art, Faenza M.I.C. Independent exhibitions since 1953 in Europe and U.S.A. Diplôme d'honneur MT 1954: gold medal Cannes 1955. (284).

HENNINGSEN, POUL. Danish architect, b. 1894. Trained at Technical School and Danish College of Technology, Copenhagen. Since 1920 has worked as independent architect in Copenhagen, where has designed several houses, a factory, part of Tivoli lay-out, and outfitting of two theatres. Correspondent for several newspapers and periodicals (editor of *Kritisk Revy* 1926–28) and author of books on social and cultural topics. Since 1929 has scripted a number of revues for Copenhagen theatres. In 1924 won competition for light fittings for Paris Exhibition 1925. His lampshades won a gold medal, and one first made in 1925 has since–as the 'PH shade'–been produced in various versions by Louis Poulsen & Co. Ltd. Also in the 30's made drawings for steel furniture, pianos, and flutes. As practical artist has frequently exhibited at home and abroad, inc. MTs, FS, AD. The PH-shade has been bought by several museums, inc. Copenhagen and Trondheim I.A.M.s, Malmö Museum, New York Museum of Modern Art. (37, 49, 50).

HERLUFSDATTER, MARIANNE. Danish ceramics artist, painter, and craftsman, b. 1931. Trained as painter at Copenhagen Academy of Art and in Stockholm. Own workshop with husband Lars Thirslund (q.v.) since 1951. Has exhibited as potter at home and abroad, inc. NF, FS. Represented in Copenhagen I.A.M. (317).

HERLØW, ERIK. Danish architect, b. 1913. Trained at Copenhagen Academy of Art school of architecture. Own business 1945, from 1957 in partnership with Tormod Olesen (q.v.). As designer connected with many firms inc. A. Michelsen, I. G. Schwartz & Sons, Danish Bakelite, Philips, Universal Steel Co., Danish Aluminium, Nordiska Co. Stockholm. Art-consultant for Royal Porcelain Manufactory and Aluminia Faience Manufactory. Chief of design department of Copenhagen A.C.S. goldsmiths' school, 1949–52. Since 1957 lecturer and 1958 professor at Copenhagen Academy of Art, in charge of industrial design department. Co-founder of Industrial Design Society 1954. As architect has had charge of construction and fitting out of several buildings inc. stores in Italy and Stockholm and Scandinavian furnishing of FAO building in Rome. Architect for several exhibitions, inc. Danish section of MT 1951, DS, FS. As practical artist has exhibited regularly at home and abroad inc. (in addition to above) NF, AD, MTs (Grand Prix 1951, gold and silver medals 1954, gold medal, with Tormod Olesen, 1957). Represented in several museums inc. Museum of Modern Art and Metropolitan Museum of Art New York, Bergen and Copenhagen I.A.M.s, Stockholm N.M., Gothenburg R.A.C.M. (352, 353, 357, 375, 384, 386, 409).

HETTING, GEORG. Danish ceramics artist, b. 1920. Trained as technical draftsman: self-taught in ceramics. With Herman A. Kähler, Næstved, 1945–49. Painter in a Norwegian pottery 1949–50. Attached to Bing & Grøndahl porcelainworks 1950–60. Own workshop since 1961. Has exhibited at home and abroad inc. MTs, FS, AD. Represented in Copenhagen I.A.M. (318).

HIDLE, JONAS. Norwegian architect, b. 1912. Trained at Norwegian College of Technology. Clerk-of-works 1938–42. With Christiania glassware stores since 1942, specialising in design of light-fittings. Several responsible functions in National Applied Art Federation and its Oslo section. A sensitive designer, who has shown much adaptability in his collaboration with a series of architects. In every case has successfully suited his light-fittings to the building, even when the work required has been of very different kinds, and has never abandoned his own artistic principles. (55, 97, 98).

HILLFON, HERTHA. Swedish ceramics artist, b. 1921. Trained at Stockholm A.C.S. Society for Design's 'Proficiency and Industry' medal 1957. Own workshop at Hägersten, Stockholm, since 1957. Represented in Stockholm N.M., Gothenburg R.A.C.M., Trondheim I.A.M. Has exhibited in Stockholm, Gothenburg, Amsterdam, The Hague, and MT 1960. (281).

HJORTH, PETER. Danish furniture-designer, b. 1928. Trained as furniture craftsman, then at Copenhagen A.C.S. Since 1957 with Philips Ltd. as designer of radio cabinets, television sets, etc. Since 1956 has collaborated with Arne Karlsen (q.v.) in designing a series of furniture types, produced since 1958 by Interna. Has exhibited at home and abroad inc. MT 1960, AD. (48, 76).

HOPEA, SAARA. Finnish silverware designer and ceramics artist, b. 1925. Trained in interior-design at Helsinki C.I.A. Free-lance interior-designer 1946–49. Designed for Taito light-fitting firm. Ceramic artist and assistant to Kaj Franck at Wärtsilä/Arabia 1952–59, since when has designed silverware for Ossian Hopea firm in Borgå. Emigrated to U.S.A. 1960, where works as free-lance silver designer. Special exhibition with Kaj Franck in Helsinki 1953: also exhibited abroad, inc. MTs 1954, 1957 (silver medal for practical pottery), DS, Brussels 1954, H 55, WG, FZ. (238).

HUGHES, ELSE BERNTSEN. Norwegian silver- and gold-designer, b. 1938. Trained at London Central School of Arts and Crafts. Own silver workshop with husband Paul (see below). Has exhibited in Norway, Italy, and Germany. Represented in Oslo I.A.M. and Applied Art Association's permanent collection, Oslo. (364).

HUGHES, PAUL C. Norwegian silversmith, b. 1934. Trained at Mid-Essex School of Art and London Central School of Arts and Crafts. Same exhibitions as wife (see above). (364).

HULL, RUTH VEDDE. Danish fabric-printer, b. 1912. Trained at Copenhagen A.C.S.: own workshop 1935. Fabric designer for Unika Vaev Ltd. Has exhibited at home and abroad, inc. NF, FS, AD. Works bought by Trondheim and Copenhagen I.A.M.s. (152).

HULTÉN, BJÖRN. Swedish interior- and furniture-designer, b. 1928. Trained at Crafts Association School, Gothenburg. Own firm in Gothenburg since 1957. Teacher in furniture- and interior-design at above school since 1959. Exhibited in e.g. Gothenburg cabinetmakers' 'Tercentenary', 1956, Interbau, Berlin, 1957. Has designed furniture for Bofyra, a combine of four Swedish furniture firms. (12).

HVIDT, PETER. Danish furniture-designer, b. 1916. Qualified as cabinet-maker, then trained as furniture-designer at Copenhagen A.C.S. Since 1944 own drawing-office in partnership with O. Mølgaard Nielsen (q.v.). Has designed furniture for several Copenhagen furniture-makers and e.g. for France & Son Ltd., Fritz Hansen Ltd., and Søborg furniture-works. Exhibited frequently at home and abroad inc. MTs, DS, NF, FS, AD. Diplôme d'honneur MTs 1951, 1954. Works bought by Melbourne National Gallery, New York Museum of Modern Art, Copenhagen I.A.M. etc. (40, 41).

HÖGLUND, ERIK. Swedish sculptor and glass-artist, b. 1932. Trained in sculpture at Stockholm A.C.S., then designer at Boda works. Lunning Prize 1957. Represented in Stockholm N.M., Gothenburg R.A.C.M., etc., and Hessisches Landesmuseum, Darmstadt. Besides glass for Boda has also made many sculptural works and compositions in glass. As glass-designer has endeavoured to make new use of ancient techniques such as applied and stamped decoration. Boda can make excellent crystal glass, but he has worked chiefly with brown or grey bubble-glass, to which he gives bluff forms. Cutting, which can be done with mathe-

Erik Höglund

matical precision, he uses for deep-cut, coarse, expressive ornament. Thus, like some of his contemporaries, he is in revolt against the complacent elegance of industrial art and the balanced formalism of industrial design. (221).

HØLAAS, KJELLAUG. Norwegian textile-artist, b. 1906. Trained at State S.C.I.A. Two years with J. Tostrup silversmith firm. Teacher of dyeing and decoration at same school: since 1948 head of department and principal teacher. Has made fabrics for Trondheim Cathedral, Oslo Town Hall, and various assembly-rooms. Consultant to several firms. (116).

ILVESSALO, KIRSTI. Finnish textile-artist, b. 1920. Trained at Helsinki C.I.A. Head of FFH workshop 1947–52. Own workshop in Helsinki since 1947. Art-assistant with Barker-Littoinen Ltd. since 1958. Many prizes in competitions for rugs, fabrics in general, carpets, and silver. Rugs represented in V. & A., Copenhagen and Trondheim I.A.M.s, Stockholm N.M., Amsterdam Stedelijke Museum, Louisiana Museum, Copenhagen. Has frequently exhibited in Europe and America, inc. MTs 1951–60 (gold medal 1951, 1960, Grand Prix 1954), DS, FS, FZ; gold medal at international textile exhibition California 1960. Individual exhibition Copenhagen 1959. Best known for her rugs, in which she combines an individual sense for colour with patterns derived from centuries-old traditions of Finnish folk-art rugs. Dark glowing shades

in red and black are typical of her products. Her inspiration from the best of ancient Finnish design is also apparent in her silver jewellery for Kalevala Koru Ltd., in which she gives a modern version of primitive decorative forms from Finnish Bronze Age finds. She also produces sober and well-thought-out furnishing-fabrics, both for industrial manufacture and to be made in her own workshop. Has collaborated with Alvar Aalto on the interiors of some of his most important buildings, e.g. National Pensions Office and Hall of Culture in Helsinki and Teachers' Training College at Jyväskylä. (183–185, 195, 196).

ISOLA, MAIJA. Finnish textile-designer, b. 1927. Trained at Helsinki C.I.A. Works as painter and fabric-print designer for Printex Ltd. Has exhibited in Europe and U.S.A. inc. DS, MT 1957, Brussels, FS, FZ. (193, 197–199).

JACOBSEN, ARNE. Danish architect, b. 1902. Trained at Copenhagen Academy of Arts architecture department: emeritus professor 1956. Comprehensive work as architect inc. Rødovre Town Hall, Royal Hotel Copenhagen, housing, schools, factories. Has also designed furniture for Fritz Hansen Ltd., silver and stainless steel for A. Michelsen, light-fittings for Louis Poulsen & Co., textiles for Grautex, Aug. Millech, and C. Olesen. Has exhibited regularly at home and abroad, inc. MTs, DS, NF, FS, AD. Grand Prix MT 1957. Works bought by New York Metropolitan Museum of Art, Copenhagen and Trondheim I.A.M.s, Kunstgewerbemuseum Zürich, etc. (44, 90, 91, 157, 159).

JACOBSSON, EMMA. Swedish domestic crafts organiser, b. 1883 in Vienna. Founded and directed Bohus Stickning since 1939. Has exhibited in Sweden and abroad inc. MTs 1951, 1954, 1960. Her assistants have included Vera Bjurström, Anna Lisa Mannheimer-Lunn, Mona Wistrand, Erna Gislev, Kerstin Ohlsson, and Annika Malmström. (146).

JAKHELLN, ELISE. Norwegian textile-artist, b. 1909. Trained at State I.S.W. and Stockholm A.C.S. Before last war ran workshop in Bilbao, Spain. Own workshop since 1948. Teacher in State I.S.W.

Arne Jacobsen

experimental workshop. Has exhibited regularly at home and abroad. (176).

JENSEN, SØREN GEORG. Danish silversmith, b. 1917. Trained as silversmith with father Georg Jensen and at Copenhagen Academy of Art sculpture department. Silver-designer for Georg Jensen Ltd. since 1949. Glass sculptures for Holmegaard glassworks 1959. Has exhibited frequently at home and abroad, inc. MTs (gold medal 1960), DS, NF, FS, AD. Represented in Louisiana Museum, Copenhagen, with three sculptures. (393).

JOHANSSON, GOTTHARD. Swedish art-historian and author, b. 1891. Worked with *Aftonbladet* 1921–29 and *Svenska Dagbladet* since 1930. Society for Industrial Design council 1932–59, chairman 1951–59. One of the three honorary members. An elegant stylist and a critic with a wide audience and great authority which he used to further functionalist ideas, especially in the Press. His most vital contribution was in the controversy over town-planning, architecture, housing, and interior-design. Planned and assisted with important exhibitions; directed the housing research by the Society for Industrial Design and the National League of Architects, published in *Living Habits and Standards* 1958. Also published *Functionalism in Reality*, 1931; *The Future of Functionalism*, 1953, etc.

JOHANSSON, TORSTEN. Danish sculptor, b. 1917 in Sweden. Trained under Prof.

Otte Sköld, Stockholm, at Akademie der bildenden Künste, Munich, and Académie de la Grande Chaumière, Paris. Has designed furniture for the furniture-maker A. J. Iversen and 'Bovirke' etc., textiles for August Millech Ltd. Exhibited practical works at annual exhibitions of Copenhagen Cabinetmakers League, AD, etc. Sculptures bought by New York Museum of Modern Art, Neue Sammlung Munich, Louisiana Museum, National Art Museum and I.A.M., Copenhagen. (82).

JOHANSSON, WILLY. Norwegian glass-artist, b. 1921. Trained at State S.C.I.A. With Hadeland glassworks since 1942. Diplôme d'honneur MT 1954, gold medal MT 1957, silver medal MT 1960. Represented in Oslo, Bergen, and Trondheim I.A.M.s, Landesgewerbemuseum Baden-Württemberg. Has exhibited in all Norwegian applied art exhibitions since the war. (201, 247–250).

JOHANSSON-PAPE, LISA. Finnish lighting-designer, b. 1907. Trained at Helsinki C.I.A. Designed furniture for Kylmäkoski Ltd. 1928–30, for Stockmann Ltd. 1937–49, with light-fittings from 1942. Textile-design for FFH 1932 and 1935–37. First and second prize and diplôme d'honneur (for rugs) Paris 1937: first prize (furniture) New York 1939: silver medals MTs 1951 and 1960, gold 1954, all for lampshades. Has exhibited in Europe and U.S.A. and arranged exhibitions. MTs, DS, H 55, FS, FZ. A versatile lighting-

Willy Johansson

Finn Juhl

expert, who has been entrusted with planning the lighting in restored mediaeval churches in Finland and has designed fittings for new factories, schools, and hospitals. Does excellent work with simple, austere, rational forms in practical modern materials–aluminium, glass, plastic, and perspex–always entirely undecorated. Has made successful experiments with flexible fittings and changing fields of light. (99, 101).

JOHNSEN, ELI MARIE. Norwegian weaver, b. 1926. Trained at State I.S.W. and Stockholm A.C.S. Teaches at former. Has exhibited at home and abroad and won prizes in several Norwegian and Swedish competitions. Did the textile decorations for Gamleby School 1959–60. (122, 126, 174, 175, 177, 204, 351).

JUEL, ANNETTE. Danish weaver, b. 1934. Trained at Copenhagen A.C.S. Exhibited MT 1960. (165).

JUHL, FINN. Danish architect, b. 1912. Trained at Copenhagen Academy of Art architecture department. Head of School of House-furnishing, Frederiksberg, 1945–55. Has designed furniture for Niels Vodder, 'Bovirke', France & Son, etc. Eckersberg medal 1947 for furniture and fittings of Bing & Grøndahl's building, Amagertorv, Copenhagen. Has arranged many exhibition displays at home and abroad, inc. MTs, DS, NF, FS, AD. Works bought by New York Metropolitan Museum of Art and Museum of Modern

Art, Trondheim and Copenhagen I.A.M.'s, etc. (42, 84, 106).

JUNG, DORA. Finnish weaver, b. 1906. Trained at Helsinki C.I.A. Own workshop since 1932, and has done fabric-design for Tampella linen-works, Tammerfors. Several grants inc. American-Scandinavian Foundation 1958. Has exhibited frequently at home and abroad since 1932, inc. MT's 1951–60 (Grand Prix 1951, 1954, 1957), Paris 1937 (gold medal), DS, FS, FZ. Independent exhibitions Stockholm 1948, Helsinki 1957: with Gunnel Nyman, Helsinki 1938, 1947, Gothenburg, Oslo, Berlin, and Trondheim 1948: with Kaj Franck and Bertel Gardberg, Gothenburg 1955, Copenhagen 1956. Represented in Gothenburg R.A.C. M., Trondheim and Copenhagen I.A.M.s, Hessisches Landesmuseum Darmstadt, New York Museum of Modern Art and Cooper Museum. Though she is ready to experiment, her fabrics have such artistic and technical expertise that a flaw would be as unthinkable as a lapse in taste. Her art is unobtrusive, often simple in expression and cautious in the use of effects. It has a quite unusual nobility. Damask technique has its own strict rules, which she has completely mastered both in factory-made lengths and individual tapestries. In different materials she allows the weft to give tapestry a most interesting and varied material character, even a three-dimensional effect. Her colour-schemes are always restrained, and the draftsmanship slightly stylised, of late frequently quite abstract. (123–125, 127, 181, 182, 344, 408).

JUTREM, ARNE JON. Norwegian practical artist and painter, b. 1929. Trained at State S.C.I.A. and at Fernand Léger's academy in Paris. Glass-designer with Hadeland since 1950. Has also designed fabrics, pewter, copper, and ceramics. Has carried out several decorative schemes in England and Norway. Has exhibited regularly at home and abroad since 1950. Gold medal MT 1954. Represented in Trondheim I.A.M. and Corning Museum of Glass, U.S.A. Lunning Prize 1959 and several grants. (200, 202, 244–246).

JUUL CHRISTENSEN, IB. Danish interior-designer, b. 1921. Trained as cabinet-

Dora Jung

Arne Jon Jutrem

maker and at Copenhagen A.C.S. 3 years as cabinetmaker in Danish and Norwegian furniture and furnishing firms. Further training at Odense Technical School. Moved to Norway 1950: own drawing-office since 1951. Several competition prizes. (67).

KAI-LARSEN, SVEN. Swedish furniture-designer, b. 1920. Trained at Västervik Furniture-makers' School and Stockholm A.C.S. Own business in Stockholm since 1953. Has fitted and furnished offices, schools, hospitals, and hotels, inc. Skogshem Institute for Supervisory Training of Swedish Employers' Confederation, Karlskoga College, hotel in Kalix. Has produced for industry e.g. a furniture series capable of combination and intended for offices, waiting-rooms, and public buildings, for Nordiska Co. 1960. (14).

KAIPIAINEN, BIRGER. Finnish ceramic artist, b. 1915. Trained at Helsinki C.I.A. With Arabia 1937–54 and since 1958: with Rörstrand in Sweden 1954–58. Exhibited at MTs (diplôme d'honneur 1951, Grand Prix 1960), DS, FZ. Represented in Helsinki, Copenhagen, and Trondheim I.A.M.s, Stockholm N.M., Malmö Museum, Gothenburg R.A.C.M., Genoa Accademia, Faenza M.I.C., St. Louis City Art Museum. Independent exhibitions in Helsinki, Milan, Malmö, New York, and Gothenburg. His peculiar talent lies decidedly in the decorative and imaginative, and his use of ceramic material shows the sculptor and painter rather than the

thrower and chemist. Previously he liked rich and florid ornament on large pottery surfaces but later turned to working on a series of pottery figures byzantinesque in form and decoration, infinitely varied and with a nostalgic elegance. He has been attracted by various surrealistic motifs which he treats with a subtle play of form. His Grand Prix MT 1960 was for birds made with strings of pottery beads over a steel frame, and he has used this principle much in his recent work.

KARLSEN, ARNE. Danish architect, b. 1927. Trained at Copenhagen Academy of Art. Own business since 1955. Since 1956 has collaborated with Peter Hjorth (q.v.) in designing a series of furniture types produced since 1958 by Interna etc. Has exhibited frequently at home and abroad inc. MT 1960, AD. Has written articles for Danish professional Press and (with Anker Tiedemann) book *Dansk Brugskunst* 1960.

KAUPPI, STEN. Swedish painter and textile-artist, b. 1922. Trained at Stockholm A.C.S. and Royal Academy of Art. Represented in Stockholm N.M. and Gothenburg R.A.C.M. Has exhibited at home and abroad since 1952. Has worked as freelance for Friends of Handicrafts since 1951 and Licium (church fabrics) since 1952. (145).

KAYSER, FREDRIK A. Norwegian interior-designer, b. 1924. Trained at State

Birger Kaipiainen

Kaare Klint

S.C.I.A. Worked for Rastad & Relling, then own drawing-office since 1956. Specialised in furniture for mass-production. Has won several competitions. (65).

KINDT-LARSEN, TOVE and EDVARD. Danish architects, b. 1906, 1901. Trained at Copenhagen Academy of Art building department: in partnership as architects since 1945. Edvard head of Copenhagen A.C.S. 1945–53. Have collaborated in designing furniture, silver, and glass for the following firms: Gustav Bertelsen & Co., Thorald Madsen, France & Son, Sorø chair-works, Kastrup glassworks, Georg Jensen, A. Michelsen. Tove has separately designed industrial fabrics for Gabriel, South Jutland carpet-works, Volkert Bros. Edvard has arranged Copenhagen Cabinetmakers' League annual exhibitions since 1943. The pair have been regularly represented in exhibitions at home and abroad, inc. MTs, DS, NF, FS, AD. Edvard awarded Eckersberg medal 1948. Works bought by Copenhagen I.A.M. and Louisiana Museum, Copenhagen (89).

KJÆRHOLM, POUL. Danish furniture-designer, b. 1929. Trained as cabinetmaker and furniture-designer at Copenhagen A.C.S. Lecturer at Academy of Art furniture and interior department since 1957. Designs pieces for E. Kold Christensen Ltd. Has exhibited regularly in recent years at home and abroad, inc. MTs, NF, FS, AD. Works bought by New York Museum of Modern Art, Trondheim and

Copenhagen I.A.M.s. Grand Prix MT 1957; Lunning Prize 1958, Eckersberg medal 1960. Has had charge of several Danish applied-art displays, inc. at MT 1960 (gold medal). (43, 47).

KLINT, KAARE. Danish architect and designer, 1888–1954. Originally a painter, worked as architect and designer from 1920. Pupil of father, architect P. V. Jensen Klint, and Carl Petersen. Lecturer in furniture at Copenhagen Academy of Art 1924, Professor of Architecture 1944. Did much important work both as furniture-designer and architect: with Ivar Bentsen, converted old Frederiks Hospital in Copenhagen into I.A.M.: finished Grundtvig's Church after father's death, built Bethlehem Church etc. His furniture and fittings inc. Faaborg Museum (with Carl Petersen) 1914–15, Thorvaldsen Museum 1922–25, Danish I.A.M. 1924–54, wedding-room at Copenhagen Town Hall 1932–33. In furniture and fittings worked first with master-cabinet-makers N. M. Rasmussen, Holbæk, and N. C. Jensen Kjær, later mostly with Rud. Rasmussen workshops, which still produces most of his types. Responsible for exhibition in V. & A. 1948 'Danish Art Treasures through the Ages'. Grand Prix Barcelona 1929 and Brussels 1935. Eckersberg medal 1928, C. F. Hansen medal 1954. Even after his death his furniture has continued to be shown at all important Danish exhibitions abroad, inc. DS, NF, FS, AD. Danish I.A.M. held comprehensive memorial exhibition 1956.

Works bought by Stockholm N.M., Copenhagen I.A.M. and Louisiana Museum, Copenhagen etc. (35, 70, 73, 77, 78, 79, 93).

KLINT, VIBEKE. Danish weaver, b. 1927. Trained at Copenhagen A.C.S. by Gerda Henning, and at tapestry school Aubusson and with Jean Lurçat, France. Own workshop (Gerda Henning succrs.) since 1951. Designs industrial fabrics for C. Olesen's Cotil collection. Has exhibited at home and abroad inc. MTs, NF, FS, AD. Made tapestries for Egmont H. Petersen College, Copenhagen, after cartoons by the painter William Scharff 1957, and fabrics for Taarnby Town Hall to her own designs. Works bought by Trondheim and Copenhagen I.A.M.s and Louisiana Art Museum Copenhagen. Lunning Prize 1960. (37, 42, 43, 76, 155).

KNUDTZON, ANNELISE. Norwegian textile-artist, b. 1914. Trained at State S.C.I.A. and weaving-school in Dalarna. Worked with Maija Kansanen: own workshop since 1946. Has assisted with production of woollen curtains and furnishing-fabrics at Røros Tweed since 1958. Specialises in rugs, in collaboration with the painter Knut Rumohr. Has exhibited at home and abroad. (26, 55, 173).

KOCH, MOGENS. Danish architect, b. 1898. Trained at Copenhagen Academy of Art building-school. Study-tours in most of Europe, U.S.A., and Mexico. Own drawing-office 1934. Professor at Academy of Art 1950. Has designed furniture for Rud. Rasmussen workshops, Danish C.W.S., Interna, etc., and fabrics made by his wife Ea Koch (e.g. for Thorvaldsen Museum). Has designed fittings, silver, and fabrics in connection with restorations of Danish churches. Has exhibited at home and abroad, inc. MTs, FS, AD. Eckerberg medal 1938. Works bought by Stockholm N.M. and Copenhagen I.A.M. Has written articles for Danish professional Press and book 'Modern Danish Art-Craftmanship' 1948. (35, 80, 81).

KOPPEL, HENNING. Danish sculptor, b. 1918. Trained at Copenhagen Academy of Art under Prof. Einar Utzon-Frank and at Académie Ranson, Paris. Silver-designer with Georg Jensen since 1945, since then has exhibited in Georg Jensen's and all general exhibitions at home and abroad, inc. MTs (gold medal 1951, 1954, 1957), DS, NF, FS, AD. Lunning Prize 1953. Represented in Copenhagen I.A.M., Melbourne National Gallery, New York Metropolitan Museum of Art, Goldsmiths' Company London, etc. (356, 388, 389).

KORNERUP, ANN-MARI. Danish weaver, b. 1918 in Sweden. Trained at Borås Textile Institute and Stockholm Industrial Art College. Teacher at Society for Promotion of Handicrafts school since 1955. Exhibited at home and abroad, inc. AD. (120).

KORSMO, ARNE. Norwegian architect and artist, b. 1900. Trained at Norwegian College of Technology. Own drawing-office since 1929. Head of State S.C.I.A. 1936–56. Professor at College of Technology since 1956. Mainly designs furniture and silver. Arranged Norwegian section at Paris 1937. Grand Prix MT 1954 for arrangement of Norwegian section.

KORSMO, GRETE. Norwegian silversmith, b. 1917. Trained at State S.C.I.A. and Chicago Institute of Design. Works for J. Tostrup firm, and also designs for others. Grand Prix MT 1954, gold medal MT 1957 and 1960. Lunning Prize 1952. Exhibits regularly at home and abroad. (350, 353–355, 363).

Grete Korsmo

KREBS, NATHALIE. Danish ceramics artist, b. 1895. Trained as civil engineer at Danish College of Technology. With Bing & Grøndahl porcelain-works 1919–29. In 1929 opened stoneware pottery with Gunnar Nylund, which she took over 1930 and named Saxbo. Since then she and her assistants have exhibited stoneware separately and at all important general exhibitions at home and abroad, inc. MT's (gold medal 1957), DS, NF, FS, AD. Saxbo products bought by New York Museum of Modern Art and Metropolitan Museum, Faenza M.I.C., Landesgewerbemuseum Stuttgart, Gemeentemuseum in The Hague, Oslo, Bergen, Copenhagen, and Trondheim I.A.M.s, Stockholm N.M., Gothenburg R.A.C.M., Malmö Art Museum, etc. (268, 269).

KRENCHEL, HERBERT. Danish industrial designer, b. 1922. Trained as civil engineer at Danish College of Technology. Own business since 1953 as designer and producer of industrial art, manufactured at various factories partly on commission. Has exhibited frequently at home and abroad, inc. MTs (gold medal 1954), NF, FS, AD. Represented at Kunst und Gewerbe Museum Hamburg and Landesgewerbe Museum Stuttgart. (52).

KVILSTAD, MAGNE. Norwegian ceramics artist, b. 1925. Trained at Norwegian potteries and at State S.C.I.A. Exhibited Brussels 1958, Sweden 1958, Paris 1958–59, Gmunden Austria 1959, U.S.A., Germany, MT 1960. Teaches modelling of sculpture and ceramics. Own pottery since 1953. (307).

KÄHLER, NILS. Danish ceramics artist, b. 1906. Trained under his father Herman H. C. Kähler in Næstved, where continued to work as artistic assistant till father's death 1940, when took over direction with brother Herman J. Kähler. Has exhibited frequently at home and abroad, inc. NF, FS, AD. Represented in Malmö Museum, Gemeentemuseum in The Hague, Everson Art Museum U.S.A., Copenhagen I.A.M. (273).

KÅGE, WILHELM. Swedish painter and ceramics artist, 1889–1960. Trained as painter at Valand Art School Gothenburg, under Carl Wilhelmsson, Stockholm, and

Johan Rohde, Copenhagen, and at Plakatschule, Munich. Became known as poster-designer. Designer at Gustavsberg works 1917, later art-director. Represented in Stockholm N.M., Gothenburg R.A.C.M., Faenza M.I.C., New York Metropolitan Museum and Museum of Modern Art, Oslo and Copenhagen I.A.M.s, V. & A., etc. Exhibited Stockholm 1917 and thence in all major exhibitions in Sweden and abroad. Retired as director of Gustavsberg 1949, but continued to work there till his death. Grand Prix Paris 1925. (276).

LANDBERG, NILS. Swedish glass-artist, b. 1907. Trained at Gothenburg School of Art and Design and Orrefors engraving school. Artistic assistant at Orrefors since 1936. Has exhibited frequently, inc. Paris 1937, New York 1939, Zürich 1948, 1957, DS, FS, Amsterdam 1959. Gold medal MT 1954 and California State Fair 1956, 1957, 1959, 1960. Represented in Stockholm N.M., Gothenburg R.A.C.M., New York Museum of Modern Art. (220, 228).

LARSEN, EJNER. Danish furniture-designer, b. 1917. Trained as upholsterer and furniture-designer at Copenhagen A.C.S. Own workshop since 1942, partner with Axel Bender Madsen (q.v.) since 1947. Has designed furniture for Willy Beck, Fritz Hansen Ltd., Næstved Furniture-works, etc. Has exhibited frequently, inc. MT's, FS, DS, NF, AD. Works bought by New York Metropolitan Museum of Art, Louisiana Art Museum, Copenhagen. (85).

Nathalie Krebs

Axel Larsson

Marie Gudme Leth

LARSSON, AXEL. Swedish furniture- and interior-designer, b. 1898. Trained Stockholm A.C.S. Worked for Swedish Furniture-works Ltd. in Stockholm and Bodafors 1925–55, when set up own workshop in Stockholm. Has designed several public and private interiors, inc. Gothenburg Concert Hall (with Nils Einar Eriksson), Foreign Office Stockholm. Has also designed many handicraft pieces for Hantverket and mass-production furniture for Swedish Furniture-works. Represented in Stockholm N.M., Nordiska Museum Stockholm, and Gothenburg R.A.C.M. Has often exhibited at home and abroad, inc. Stockholm 1930, Paris 1937, New York 1939, H 55. His contribution to Swedish furniture thus includes both exclusive handicraft pieces and good mass-production which is modern without being extreme. (5, 6, 11).

LEIN, GRETE. Norwegian weaver, Trained at State I.S.W. One year's work for Plus organisation. Has exhibited in Denmark, France, Iceland, Sweden, Germany, and U.S.A. Own workshop for wall decorations and church fabrics. (167, 169, 355).

LETH, MARIE GUDME. Danish fabric-printer, b. 1895. Trained at Copenhagen Industrial Art School for Women and Academy of Art, and Kunstgewerbeschule Frankfurt on Main. Co-fonder of Danish Calico-printing Works 1935 and director to 1940. Own workshop since 1941. In charge of instruction in fabric-printing at Copenhagen A.C.S. 1931–48. Repre-

sented at all major Danish exhibitions at home and abroad, inc. MTs (gold medal 1951), Paris 1937 (gold medal), DS, NF, FS, AD. Works bought by Copenhagen I.A.M. (156).

LIE-JØRGENSEN, THORBJØRN. Norwegian silversmith and painter, 1900–1961. Trained as goldsmith under Henrik Lund, State S.C.I.A., and Academy of Art. Principal teacher in colour-theory and decoration at State S.C.I.A. from 1940. Has made altar plate for churches in Heddal, Ris, Røa, and Notodden, and large representative works. Won competition for table-silver for Oslo Town Hall. Gold medal MT 1954, Munich 1955. Represented in museums in Prague, Oslo, Stockholm, etc. One of the most significant painters in Norway. (402–404).

LINDAAS, ARNE. Norwegian artist, b. 1924. Trained at State S.C.I.A., Royal Porcelain Works, Copenhagen, and subsequent courses in colour, leatherwork, horn-work, plaiting. First prizes in several competitions in different branches of craftwork. Art-director of Norsk Glassverk 1949–51: part-time with Porsgrund since 1952. Teacher of draftsmanship at State I.S.W. 1957, and temporary head of State S.C.I.A. ceramics department 1957–58. Part-time work for Norsk Glassverk since 1960. Has exhibited in many national and local applied-art exhibitions since 1950. Represented in Trondheim I.A.M., Royal Porcelain Works museum, and Applied Art Association's permanent col-

lection, Oslo. Has also worked effectively as painter and draftsman. (172, 174, 175, 251).

LINDBERG, STIG. Swedish artist, principally ceramics: b. 1916. Trained Stockholm A.C.S. and under Prof. Wilhelm Kåge. Employed by Gustavsberg since 1937, art-director 1949–57. Since 1957 head of ceramics department at A.C.S. Independent exhibitions in Europe, Japan, U.S.A. Has exhibited in major Swedish exhibitions at home and abroad since 1939, inc. New York 1939, Copenhagen 1942, Zürich 1948, DS, FS, H 55, Amsterdam 1959, MTs (gold medal 1948, 1957, Grand Prix 1951, 1954). Gold medal California State Fair 1958, 1959. Gregor Paulsson trophy. Represented in Stockholm N.M., Gothenburg R.A.C.M., Copenhagen, Oslo, and Trondheim I.A.M.s, V. & A., New York Museum of Modern Art, and others in Europe, America, Asia, and Australia. His work is principally in ceramics, both productive at Gustavsberg and educational at A.C.S. His creative energy also embraces the modelling of sanitary ware and plastics, enamelling on iron plate, patterns for fabric-prints, excellent posters, playing cards, glassware, television sets, etc. (53, 279, 303, 304).

LINDBLAD, GRETHE. Danish ceramics artist, b. 1926. Trained Copenhagen A.C.S. Workshop with Signe Boesen Northroup 1956–57, then independently. Has exhibited at home and abroad, inc. MTs, FS, AD. (274).

LINDH, RICHARD. Finnish ceramics artist, b. 1929. Trained at school of painting and C.I.A., Helsinki. Own workshop 1951–54; with Arabia works since 1955, chief of industrial art department from 1960. First prize in competition arranged by New York Museum of Contemporary Art, and other prizes in Scandinavian competitions. Represented at above museum and Trondheim I.A.M. Independent exhibition in Finland, and has exhibited in many in Europe and America, inc. MTs 1957, 1960, H 55, FZ.

LINDSTRAND, VICKE (VIKTOR). Swedish glass-artist, b. 1904. Trained in publicity at School of Arts and Design, Gothen-

Thorbjørn Lie-Jørgensen

Stig Lindberg

Vicke Lindstrand

burg. Designer at Orrefors 1928–1940, where designed practical and ornamental glassware and decorative work e.g. lightshades and crucifix for St. John's Church, Gothenburg, windows for Swedish pavilion Paris 1937, fountain for pavilion at New York 1939, printed curtain for Malmö city theatre. Art-director with Upsala-Ekeby 1940–49, then with Kosta glassworks. Represented in Stockholm N.M., Gothenburg R.A.C.M., Småland Museum Växjö, Museé des Arts Décoratifs Paris, New York Metropolitan Museum, etc. Since 1928 has exhibited frequently, sometimes independently: e.g. Stockholm 1930, MTs since 1933, Paris 1937, New York 1939, Paris 1954, H 55, Amsterdam 1959. Glass is his principal material. His creative imagination works intensively in the fleeting burning moment when the glass object is made. He has worked in coloured glass and with completely abstract forms, as well as with well-proportioned and rational tableglass and mosaic.

LIPPE, JENS VON DER. Norwegian ceramics artist, b. 1911. Husband of Margrethe (see below). Trained at State S.C.I.A., Staatliche Keramische Fachschule, Silesia, and Istituto Statale d'Arte per la Ceramica, Faenza. Pottery experience in Denmark and Norway. Own pottery from 1933. Teacher at State S.C.I.A. 1938, chief of ceramics department since 1956. Represented in Oslo I.A.M. and Faenza M.I.C. Has made large ceramic works with his wife, e.g. in Vardø church and

Risør Modern School. Many works in collaboration with sculptors and practical artists. (255).

LIPPE, MARGRETHE VON DER. Norwegian ceramics artist, b. 1913. Trained at Kunstgewerbeschule Vienna, State S.C.I.A., etc. Own pottery since 1939. Represented in Oslo, Trondheim, and Bergen I.A.M.'s. Has carried out large decorative ceramic works, e.g. in ships. (171).

LUND, ALICE. Swedish textile-artist, b. 1900. Trained at Stockholm A.C.S. Own business, Alice Lund Textiles Ltd., since 1936, since 1949 in Hytting, Borlänge. Represented in Stockholm N.M., Gothenburg R.A.C.M., V. & A. Exhibited at Paris 1937, New York 1939, Zürich 1948, 1957, H 55, DS, FS, Amsterdam 1959 and independently. Has made fabrics for churches, public and private offices, ships, and hotels. Has also made models for industrial production by Borås Jacquard-weave Ltd. Gold medal MT 1957, Gregor Paulsson trophy 1961. Since her return from U.S.A., where she lived 1923–30, she has produced much in the way of textiles. They have great qualities and have had much influence on contemporary Swedish production. (114, 134).

LUNDGREN, TYRA. Swedish sculptor, and artist in glass and ceramics, b. 1897. Trained at Stockholm A.C.S. and Royal College of Art. Worked with Arabia in Helsinki and Sèvres at Paris, Riihimäki

glassworks in Finland, and Venini in Venice. Collaborated with Gustavsberg in 1940's. Has made sculptures in highfired stoneware and patterns for fabricprinting. Represented in Stockholm N.M., Gothenburg R.A.C.M., etc. Has exhibited in Stockholm, Helsinki, Milan, Paris, and London independently and in major exhibitions since 1930's, inc. MTs, DS, Amsterdam 1959. Litteris et Artibus medal 1950. Author of 'Clay and Fire' 1946. (294).

LUNDIN, INGEBORG. Swedish glass-artist, b. 1921. Trained at Stockholm A.C.S. Designer at Orrefors since 1947. Represented in Stockholm N.M., Småland Museum at Växjö, etc. Independent exhibition Stockholm 1959, and has taken part since 1948 in general and Orrefors exhibitions: DS, H 55, Zürich 1957, Orrefors travelling exhibition in U.S.A. 1958, FS, Amsterdam 1959, MTs 1957, 1960. Lunning Prize 1954. (222, 223).

LYNGGAARD, FINN. Danish ceramic artist, b. 1930. Trained at Academy of Art painting and ceramic departments, Copenhagen. Own workshop since 1958. Exhibited in several applied-art exhibitions, inc. MT 1960, AD. (319).

LÜTKEN, PER. Danish glass-artist, b. 1916. Trained as painter and draftsman at Copenhagen A.C.S. Some years as freelance designer. With Holmegaard glassworks since 1942. Study tour in Italy

Ingeborg Lundin

Carl Malmsten

1954. Has taken part in Holmegaard's and general exhibitions at home and abroad, inc. MTs, DS, NF, FS, AD. Works bought by many museums inc. Museo Nacional de Arte Decorativo, Buenos Aires, Corning Museum of Glass, Joslyn Art Museum, Omaha, Museum für Kunst und Gewerbe, Hamburg, Neue Sammlung, Munich, Landesgewerbemuseum, Stuttgart, V. & A., Stockholm N.M. (214).

MADSEN, AXEL BENDER. Danish furniture-designer, b. 1916. Trained as furniture-maker, then as designer at Copenhagen A.C.S. and Academy of Art. Since 1947 in partnership with Ejner Larsen. Has designed furniture for Willy Beck, Fritz Hansen Ltd., Næstved Furniture-works, etc. Exhibited at most major exhibitions at home and abroad, inc. MT's, DS, NF, FS, AD. Works bought by New York Metropolitan Museum of Art, Louisiana Art Museum, Copenhagen. See also under Ejner Larsen. (85).

MALMSTEN, CARL. Swedish furniture-designer and teacher, b. 1888. Trained with master-cabinetmaker Per Jönsson, then independently. Founded own selling organisation in Stockholm 1930 and his own workshop-school. Founded Olof School in Stockholm 1928 (of which chief to 1941), Nyckelvik School in Stockholm for handicrafts and folk-art 1945, and Capellagården School for creative work in Vickelby, Öland. First prize 1916 for designs for furniture for Stockholm Town Hall, where he worked to 1923. Fitted out

Stockholm Concert Hall 1924–25. Has exhibited alone or with others since 1916, inc. Stockholm 1917, Gothenburg 1923, Paris 1927, New York 1939, Gothenburg 1956. Represented in Stockholm N.M., Gothenburg R.A.C.M., New York Metropolitan Museum, Chicago Art Institute, etc. Litteris et Artibus medal 1926. Prince Eugen medal 1945. Author of *Beauty and Comfort in the Home* 1923, *A Central Domain* 1944, and *Live in Peace* 1958. He has had a very great influence on Swedish furniture, not least through his comprehensive activity as teacher and propagandist. Has also designed furnishing-fabrics, fabric-prints, and tapestry patterns, all with an unmistakable personal stamp. (1, 2, 29, 30).

MALMSTRÖM, ANNIKA. Swedish textile-designer, b. 1929. Trained at Anders Beckman School, Stockholm. Designs fabric-prints for Mölnlycke Textiles Ltd. and Bohus Stickning, both in Gothenburg. Exhibited in Gothenburg R.A.C.M. 1955 and Copenhagen I.A.M. 1960: represented in former. (146).

MARKELIUS, SVEN. Swedish architect, b. 1889. Trained at Royal Institute of Technology and Royal Academy of Art, Stockholm. Member of Building Administration 1938–44, town-planning director for Stockholm, 1944–54. Has been responsible for many and various buildings, inc. Hälsingborg Concert Hall, Building Union's headquarters and People's House in Stockholm: share in planning UN building in New

York. Assisted with Stockholm Exhibition 1930 and designed Swedish pavilion New York 1939. Co-author of policy-publication *Accept*, 1931.

MARTIN, EDNA. Swedish textile-artist, b. 1908. Trained at Crafts Association school, Gothenburg. Designer at Mölnlycke Textiles Ltd. and with Swedish Domestic Crafts Association, of which latter artistic director 1945-51. Administrative director and artistic chief of Friends of Handicraft, Licium studio, and Sätergläntan weaving colony in Dalarna since 1952. Head of textile department at Stockholm A.C.S. Represented in Stockholm N.M., Gothenburg R.A.C.M., Trondheim I.A.M. Own exhibitions in Gothenburg 1932, Stockholm 1946, Trondheim and Bergen 1958. Exhibited at home and abroad e.g. New York 1939, DS, H 55, FS, Amsterdam 1959. (140, 147).

MATHSSON, BRUNO. Swedish furniture-designer and maker, b. 1907. Trained under his father, Karl Mathsson, in Värnamo, then independently, particularly in study of the seated body. Has attracted international attention by his technical construction of chairs in which the bearing elements are of pressed laminated plywood and the sitting surface of interwoven webbing. This type was first shown in Gothenburg R.A.C.M. 1936, and has since been improved and added to, though he still confines himself to a limited number of types. In 1945–57 he worked on house-structures characterised by large areas of glass and heated floors, used for houses and schools and his own exhibition building in Värnamo. Independent exhibitions, and share in major ones in Europe and U.S.A., inc. Paris 1937, San Francisco and New York 1939, Svensk Form Copenhagen 1946, H 55, DS, Interbau Berlin 1957, FS, Amsterdam 1959, Zürich and Munich 1960. Represented in Stockholm N.M., Gothenburg R.A.C.M., Trondheim and Copenhagen I.A.M.s, New York Museum of Modern Art. Gregor Paulsson trophy 1955. With unusual consistency, he has worked out, developed, and perfected a constructive and aesthetic line in furniture which puts him amongst the best designers of the Forties and Fifties. (3, 4, 33).

MATTSSON, JOHNNY. Swedish woodcarver, b. 1906: self-taught. Since 1941 has worked in Gävle on sculpture, vessels, and utensils in wood. Has made models for wood for Silva Ltd. Stockholm, for glass for Reijmyre glassworks. Made carved doors for Sundsvall Bank in Gävle 1954, font in Forsbacka church and crucifix for Bomhus church 1955. Olof Högberg gold plaque 1957. Represented in Stockholm N.M. and Moderna Museum, Gothenburg R.A.C.M., Bergen and Oslo I.A.M.s, museums in Norrköping, Gävle, and Örebro. Exhibited in Gävle and Stockholm 1952, Gothenburg 1954, DS, MT 1954, Caracas 1954. (108).

MEEDOM BÆCH, GUDRUN. Danish ceramics artist, b. 1915. Trained at Copenhagen A.C.S. Worked with Bing & Grøndahl 1946-53, then in own pottery. Has exhibited frequently at home and abroad, inc. MTs, DS, AD. Represented in Copenhagen I.A.M. and C. L. David Collection. (267).

MELANTON, KAISA. Swedish textile-artist, b. 1920. Trained at Stockholm A.C.S. Own workshop at Viggbyholm. Art-assistant and teacher for Friends of Handicraft since 1952, and has organised industrial production of linen goods and floor-coverings. (113, 418).

METSOVAARA-NYSTRÖM, MARJATTA. Finnish textile-artist, b. 1928. Trained at Helsinki C.I.A. Since 1954 own workshop in Helsinki, Metsovaara Ltd. Has exhibited in Europe, Brazil, and U.S.A., inc. MTs 1957, 1960 (gold medal), FS, FZ. Own exhibitions in Helsinki 1957, 1960, Stockholm 1958, Brussels 1960. She works on a handicraft basis, partly with traditional materials like wool and linen and partly with plastic- and metal-thread, and in her lampshades and wall-coverings also with wood-chips and cane. She prefers to let the fibres of the material keep their natural colour, and the resultant restrained tones give a fine effect in combination with the sheen of the metal.

MEYER, GRETHE. Danish architect, b. 1918. Trained at Copenhagen Academy of Art building department. With State Institute of Building Research 1955-60. Prepared with Børge Mogensen in 1957 *Built-in Cupboards for the Home*. Designed with Ibi Trier Mørch 1959 a glassware series for Kastrup glassworks. Has exhibited frequently at home and abroad, inc. MTs, AD. Represented in Copenhagen I.A.M. (254).

MIDDELBOE, ROLF. Danish fabric-printer and draftsman, b. 1917. Trained at Copenhagen A.C.S. Own workshop since 1941. Designs fabrics for Spindegaarden, Danish Calico-Printing Ltd., Unika Vaev Ltd. Represented in exhibitions at home and abroad inc. MTs, DS, NF, FS, AD. Works bought by New York Museum of Modern Art, V. &. A, Trondheim and Copenhagen I.A.M.s. (158).

MJØS, KÅRE. Norwegian ceramics artist, b. 1920. Trained at Bergen A.C.S., and in Norwegian and Danish potteries. Own pottery since 1951 and teacher at Bergen A.C.S., where now head of ceramics department. Several applied-art exhibitions. Represented in Oslo and Bergen I.A.M.s. Has recently begun producing articles in enamelled copper. (180).

MOGENSEN, BØRGE. Danish furniture-designer, b. 1914. Trained as furniture-maker, then as designer at Copenhagen A.C.S. and Academy of Arts furniture department. Head of Danish C.W.S. furniture design department 1942-50, thence completely independent. Has designed pieces for Erhard Rasmussen, Karl Andersson & Sons Ltd. (Sweden), Fredericia chair- and upholstery-works, C. M.

Madsen, Søborg furniture-works, etc. Represented at all major exhibitions at home and abroad, inc. MTs, DS, NF, FS, AD. Eckersberg medal 1950. Works bought by Copenhagen I.A.M. (37, 45, 46, 48, 74, 151).

MOHR, ANNE-MARIE BACKER. Norwegian ceramics artist, b. 1928. Trained at Crafts Association school in Gothenburg and under Bernard Leach, England. Own workshop since 1952. Has exhibited in France, Italy, Sweden, and Germany. (314).

MOILANEN, HARRY ALEXANDER. Finnish glass-artist, b. 1931. Trained in interior-design at Helsinki C.I.A. and at La Rinascente, Milan. Worked in Antti Nurmesniemi's house-furnishing design-office 1958-59. Employed as glass-artist at Wärtsilä/Notsjö since 1960. MT 1960, FZ.

MOOS, PEDER. Danish furniture-maker, b. 1906. Trained as cabinetmaker, worked as such in France and Switzerland 1925-30. Under Kaare Klint at Academy of Art furniture department 1935-38. Own workshop from 1935. Head of male crafts department at Danish Domestic Crafts School, Kerteminde, since 1956. Represented at Stockholm N.M., Copenhagen and Trondheim I.A.M.s. Has generally exhibited since 1939 in Cabinetmakers' Guild annual exhibitions, and in others at home and abroad inc. DS and AD. (86, 87).

Bruno Mathsson

Børge Mogensen

MORALES-SCHILDT, MONICA. Swedish glass-artist and potter, b. 1908. Trained at Stockholm A.C.S. Assisted Wilhelm Kåge at Gustavsberg 1935–38, with Arabia in Helsinki 1939, assistant and exhibition-arranger with Nordiska Co. in Stockholm 1945–56. Since 1957 artist at Kosta glassworks. Represented in Stockholm N.M. Individual exhibitions at Stockholm 1959, Gothenburg, Stockholm, and New York 1960. (215).

MUNCH-PETERSEN, LISBET. Danish ceramics artist, b. 1909. Trained at Copenhagen A.C.S. In Hans Syberg's pottery, own since 1933 (originally with sister Gertrud Vasegaard, q.v.). Several independent exhibitions, and has frequently exhibited e.g. at MTs, DS, FS, AD. Several works in Copenhagen I.A.M. (277).

MUNTHE, ALF. Swedish painter and textile-artist, b. 1892. Trained at Royal Academy of Art and with Gerhard Munthe, Lysaker, Norway. Ran 'Decorator' firm in Stockholm 1923–29. Collaborated with Friends of Handicrafts 1936–50. Own textile firm Lekattgården, Leksand, since 1951. Did cartoons for embroideries in Scandia Cinema, Stockholm, 1923, and textile decorations of Swedish pavilion in Paris 1925. Al secco paintings, textiles, ironwork, and silver for dayrooms of Caroline Hospital, Stockholm, 1940 (commissioned by Art Council); altar-cloth in double-weave for Skövde crematorium 1947; double-weave for Swedish embassy in Tokio 1959 and Stockholm Record Office 1958. Represented in Stockholm N.M., Gothenburg R.A.C.M., New York Metropolitan Museum, Detroit Museum of Art. Has exhibited independently and in general exhibitions at home and abroad: Grand Prix Paris 1925. Prince Eugen medal 1960. (131).

MUONA, TOINI. Finnish ceramics artist, b. 1904. Trained at Helsinki C.I.A. and under A. W. Finch. With Arabia since 1931. Medals at Barcelona 1929, MTs 1933, 1951, 1954, 1957, Brussels 1935, Paris 1937, Cannes 1955. Also exhibited at DS, H 55, WG, FS, FZ, etc. Other medals and distinctions. Represented in Stockholm N.M., Gothenburg R.A.C.M., Faenza M.I.C., Swedish Royal Collec-

Toini Muona

tions, Zürich Kunstgewerbemuseum, Helsinki and Trondheim I.A.M.s, New York Museum of Modern Art, V. & A., Amsterdam Stedelijke Museum, etc. Her ceramic output seems largely based on intuition, and does not lend itself to strict chemical analysis. Nevertheless, her long experience with wheel and kiln gives her products very high quality. Her forms are both refined and sensitive and robustly powerful. She may be regarded as the classic amongst the surviving active members of the group who have carried on the work of the original Iris pioneers.

MØLGAARD-NIELSEN, ORLA. Danish furniture-designer, b. 1907. Trained as cabinetmaker, then as designer at Copenhagen A.C.S. and Academy of Art. In partnership with Peter Hvidt since 1944. Has designed pieces for Copenhagen mastercabinetmakers and for France & Son Ltd., Fritz Hansen Ltd., and Søborg furniture-works. Represented at all major exhibitions at home and abroad, inc. MTs, DS, NF, FS, AD. Diplôme d'honneur MTs 1951, 1954. Works bought by Melbourne National Gallery, New York Museum of Modern Art, Copenhagen I.A.M., etc. (see also under Hvidt, Peter). (40, 41).

MÖLLER, GRETE. Swedish ceramics artist, b. 1915 in Denmark. Trained at Copenhagen A.C.S. Taught ceramics at Viggbyholm School (Sweden) 1939–43. Married to Tom Möller (see below).

Represented in Stockholm N.M., V. & A., New York Museum of Modern Art. (288).

MØLLER, INGER. Danish silversmith, b. 1886. Trained under Georg Jensen, for whom worked until own workshop 1922. Represented in many exhibitions at home and abroad, inc. Paris 1925 (silver medal) and 1937 (gold medal), New York 1939, MTs, DS, FS, AD. Represented in Newark Museum New Jersey, Stockholm N.M., Copenhagen I.A.M. (381, 382).

MÖLLER, TOM. Swedish ceramics artist, b. 1914. Trained at Edvin Oller's school of painting and Reimanschule, Berlin. Temporarily with Alsterbo glassworks 1959, with Reijmyre glassworks since 1960. Teacher in ceramics at Stockholm A.C.S. 1960. Works in Stockholm N.M. and V. & A. Since 1943 Grete and Tom Möller have had their own workshop in Stockholm, producing chiefly earthenware but also recently salt-glazed stoneware. They have exhibited together since 1947, inc. H 55, MT 1960. (287).

MØRCH, AXEL. Norwegian glass-artist, b. 1927. Trained at State S.C.I.A. and in sculpture at Academy of Art. With Norsk Glassverk, Magnor, since 1955. Represented in exhibitions in France, Germany, and Norway. Silver medal MT 1960. Works bought by Applied Art Association, Oslo. (204, 205, 252).

MØRCH, IBI TRIER. Danish architect, b. 1910. Trained at Copenhagen Academy of Art building school. Has worked in various design-offices in Copenhagen and Stockholm and as free-lance designer, recently in collaboration with Grete Meyer (q.v.). Teacher at Goldsmiths' College 1951–53. Secretary of Industrial Design Society (SIF) 1955–58. Since 1956 scientific and teaching assistant in Academy of Art industrial design department. Represented in several exhibitions at home and abroad inc. MTs (gold medal 1960) DS, NF, FS, AD., and at New York Museum of Modern Art and Copenhagen I.A.M. (254).

NATVIG, FANNY. Norwegian textile-artist, b. 1917. Trained at State I.S.W., Academy of Art, and Hammersmith School of Arts and Crafts, London, and practically in workshops of Elise Jakhelln and Steen

& Strøm. Teacher at State I.S.W. With Norwegian Domestic Crafts Association 1955–57: chief of Domestic Crafts Pattern Centre.

NILSSON, BARBRO, Swedish textile-artist, b. 1899. Trained at Johanna Brunsson's weaving-school, Stockholm, and A.C.S. Taught at former 1918–20, at Nordenfeldt School Gothenburg 1925–27, and A.C.S. 1931–57, after 1947 as head of textile department. Art-director of Märta Måås-Fjetterström Ltd. in Båstad since 1942. Has made various large decorative compositions in tapestry weave, some to her own cartoons, and floor-coverings, drapes, curtains, etc. Represented in Stockholm N.M., Malmö Museum, Gothenburg R.A.C.M., Copenhagen and Trondheim I.A.M.s. Has exhibited since 1945, inc. Stockholm, Gothenburg, Malmö, H 55, DS, FS, Amsterdam 1960. Litteris et Artibus medal 1948, Prince Eugen medal 1954, etc. (130, 132, 217).

NUMMI, YKI. Finnish designer of light-fittings, b. 1925. Trained at Helsinki C.I.A. in decorative painting. Designer of light-fittings for Stockmann Ltd. Helsinki since 1950, head of Schildt & Hallberg's colour-design department since 1958. Prizes in several Finnish competitions. Lampshades in New York Museum of Modern Art. Has exhibited in Europe, Asia, and America, inc. MTs 1954, 1957 (gold medals), DS, FS, H 55, WG, FZ. Several essays and articles on lighting and colour, and on the philosophic principles of design. The versatile Nummi, who declares that he 'has never worked in ceramics but otherwise has tried every form of art-handicraft', is responsible for the colour-schemes of some half-million cubic metres of new interiors each year in public and industrial buildings. This involves furnishing-fabrics, plastics, and floor-materials, and includes a whole new garden city, Western Tapiola. He began work as a colour-expert in collaboration with Lisa Johansson-Pape for ORNO-Stockmann, and is also an independent and ingenious designer of light-fittings– functional pieces in e.g. white glass or white perspex, or aluminium shades with enamel surfaces. He is also a skilful draftsman and designer of silver, floorcoverings, furniture, radio cabinets, etc. (100).

NURMESNIEMI, ANTTI. Finnish furniture-designer, b. 1927. Trained at Helsinki C.I.A. in interior-design. Works as freelance in Helsinki, often as exhibition arranger. Prizes in Finnish furniture- and tapestry-competitions. Silver medal MT 1957 (furniture), Grand Prix MT 1960 (exhibition arrangement). Lunning Prize 1959. Has taken part in many exhibitions abroad, inc. as arranger in Sweden 1956, Germany 1956–57, Athens 1958, MT 1960, and exhibited at DS, WG, FZ. Independent exhibitions Helsinki 1957, Oslo 1960. (19, 20, 332).

NYSTRÖM, TOINI. Finnish textile-artist, b. 1887. Trained at Helsinki C.I.A. With FFH since 1917. First prize in FFH competition for church fabrics 1945. Has exhibited rugs in Europe and at DS, MT 1957. (191).

OLESEN, TORMOD. Danish architect, b. 1930. Trained at Copenhagen Academy of Art building-school. In Erik Herløw's drawing-office from 1953, partner 1956. Has taken part with E.H. in several exhibitions at home and abroad, inc. MTs (gold medal 1957), AD. (see also under Erik Herløw). (409).

PALMGREN, MÅRTEN. Swedish designer and worker in leather, b. 1889. Trained in family firm J. Palmgren Ltd., Stockholm, and at Sattlerschule in Hildesheim. Court saddler and administrative director of firm. Bottle-case in Stockholm N.M. Has exhibited at home and abroad.

PALMQUIST, SVEN. Swedish glass-artist, b. 1906. Trained at Stockholm A.C.S. and Royal Academy of Art, and at Académie Ranson, Paris. Has worked with Orrefors since 1928, from 1936 as designer. Has also designed light-fittings, and done decorative work e.g. windows for Linköping crematorium 1944. Represented in Stockholm N.M., Småland Museum Växjö, and many others in and outside Sweden. Has exhibited independently and e.g. at Paris 1937, New York 1939, FS, Amsterdam 1959, Orrefors travelling exhibitions in U.S.A. 1958, MT's (several distinctions, inc. Grand Prix 1957). (217, 219, 231).

PAULSSON, GREGOR. Swedish art-historian, b. 1889. With Stockholm N.M. 1913–24. Administrative director of Society for Industrial Design 1920–34, chairman of council 1943–50. Professor at Uppsala University 1934–56. General secretary for Stockholm Exhibition 1930. Published *More Beautiful Everyday Things* 1919, *Accept*, 1931 (in collaboration), *Use and Appearance in Objects* 1956 (with Nils Paulsson). An active propagandist in speech and writing for radical movements in architecture and industrial art. One of the three honorary members of Swedish Society for Industrial Design.

PEDERSEN, BENT GABRIELSEN. Danish goldsmith, b. 1928. Trained as apprentice and at Copenhagen A.C.S. Goldsmiths' College. With Hans Hansen Ltd, silversmith, Kolding, since 1953: has also designed for Georg Jensen. Has exhibited at home and abroad, inc. MT 1960 (gold medal), NF, AD. Represented at Copenhagen I.A.M. (376).

PERCY, ARTHUR C:SON. Swedish painter and glass- and ceramics-artist, b. 1886. Trained at Artists' Union school in Stockholm and with Matisse. Designer with Gävle porcelainworks 1923–60 and occasionally with Karlskrona do., both in Upsala-Ekeby combine. Also with Gullaskruf glassworks since 1952. Has also designed fabric-prints for Elsa Gullberg Ltd. Represented in Stockholm N.M., Gothenburg R.A.C.M., etc., Faenza M.I.C., Oslo and Copenhagen I.A.M.s. Independent exhibitions in Gothenburg and Copenhagen 1957. Took part in Paris 1925, Barcelona 1929, Stockholm 1930, Paris 1937, New York 1939, H 55, DS. Diplôme d'honneur Paris 1925 etc. Prince Eugen medal 1959. (2, 290, 291).

PERSSON, SIGURD. Swedish silversmith and designer, b. 1914. Craft training as silversmith with father, Fritiof Persson, Hälsingborg, then at Munich Fachschule and Akademie der bildenden Künste, and at Stockholm A.C.S. Own workshop in Stockholm since 1942 making cutlery, vessels, and jewellery. Has made silver for several Swedish churches. Also designs for industry: stainless steel vessels for 'Silver & Steel', Vingåker, enamelled iron cooking-pots for Kockum ironworks,

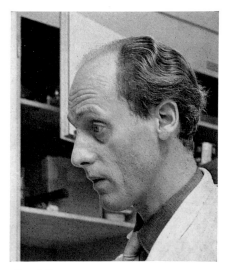

Sigurd Persson

Kallinge, and fitments for SAS planes. Represented in Stockholm N.M., Gothenburg R.A.C.M., Oslo, Trondheim, and Bergen I.A.M.s, Zürich Kunstgewerbemuseum, Stuttgart and Munich dos., New York Museum of Modern Art. Exhibited first at Stockholm 1950, then at DS, Sydney 1954, Pforzheim 1955, H 55, Havana 1956, Stockholm 1957, etc. Diplôme d'honneur MT 1951. Gregor Paulsson trophy. Author of *Modern Swedish Silver* 1951 and articles in the Press. (394, 397, 418).

PERSSON-MELIN, SIGNE. Swedish ceramics artist, b. 1925. Trained with Andersson & Johansson in Höganäs and with Nathalie Krebs in Copenhagen, then Stockholm A.C.S. (ceramics and sculpture) and Copenhagen A.C.S. (ceramics). Own pottery for lightly-fired stoneware in Malmö since 1951. With Anders Österlin carried out wall decoration of Simhall Baths in Malmö and central underground station in Stockholm. With Anders Liljefors decorated People's House and Forestry headquarters in Stockholm. Represented in Stockholm N.M., Gothenburg R.A.C.M., Malmö Museum, etc. Independent exhibitions in Stockholm 1953, Gothenburg and Malmö 1954. Has exhibited at MT, DS, and Amsterdam 1959. Lunning Prize 1958. Her products are of three kinds: household ware such as pots, jugs, and bowls, large decorative chamotte jars, and ornamental plaques. They are decorated sparingly, if at all, with patterns incised or stamped on the surface. (286, 296).

PETTERSEN, SVERRE. Norwegian practical artist, 1884–1958. Trained at State S.C.I.A. Art director at Hadeland glassworks 1927. Made an outstanding contribution in several fields of applied art. Head of State S.C.I.A. No one in Norwegian applied art has shown more talent and versatility, and his work has had great influence.

PLUM, LISE. Danish weaver, b. 1915. Self-taught. Own workshop since 1951. Exhibited at home and abroad, inc. MTs, FS, AD. Works bought by Copenhagen I.A.M. (161).

PLØEN, ERIK. Norwegian ceramics artist, b. 1925. Craft-trained with Schneider and Knutzen. Own workshop. Represented in Faenza M.I.C., Trondheim I.A.M., permanent Applied Art Association collections, Oslo. Has exhibited in Denmark, France, Italy, Germany, U.S.A.: individually in New York. (257, 260).

POULSEN, CHRISTIAN. Danish ceramics artist, b. 1911. Trained at Copenhagen A.C.S., College of Technology, and Royal Porcelain Works. Pottery with Grete Gissemann and Edith Sonne Bruun (q.v.) 1933–34. Own stoneware pottery in Kolding 1935–38. Then studied as sculptor at École des Arts Décoratifs Paris: with Bing & Grøndahl 1939–46. Own pottery since 1946. Taught at House-furnishing School, Copenhagen, 1940–43 and A.C.S. 1951–53. Has exhibited frequently at home and abroad, inc. MTs, FS, AD. Represented in Faenza M.I.C., Zürich Kunstgewerbemuseum, Gemeente Museum in The Hague, Bergen I.A.M., Gothenburg R.A.C.M., Malmö Art Museum, Copenhagen I.A.M. and Louisiana Museum, Copenhagen. (261).

PROCOPÉ, ULLA. Finnish ceramics artist, b. 1921. Trained at Helsinki C.I.A. Designer of practical pottery for Arabia since 1948. Represented in Copenhagen I.A.M. Has exhibited abroad, inc. MT's 1957 (diplôme d'honneur) 1960, FS, WG, FZ. (331, 333).

PRYTZ, JAKOB. Norwegian silversmith, 1886–1962. Trained at State S.C.I.A., Kgl. Zeichenakademie, and Paris. Art director and later proprietor of J. Tostrud

firm. Head of State S.C.I.A. 1914, rector 1945. Co-founder of Applied Art Association, chairman 1920–39. Chairman of National Applied Art Federation 1946–48.

PUOTILA, RITVA. Finnish textile-artist, b. 1935. Trained at Helsinki C.I.A. Works as free-lance, inc. for FFH (rugs) and for Villahtymä, Helsinki (dress-material). First prize in latter's competition for woollens 1960. MT 1960 (gold medal), FZ. (192).

RAASCHOU, DORTE. Danish fabric-printer, b. 1929. Trained at Copenhagen A.C.S. Own workshop since 1951. Designs industrial fabrics for C. Olesen's Cotil collection. Has exhibited at home and abroad inc. MTs, FS, AD. (153).

RAJALIN, BÖRJE. Finnish silversmith, b. 1933. Trained at Helsinki C.I.A. and in craft with Bertel Gardberg, where worked 1953–54 and 1955–57. With Tillander Ltd. 1954–55. Now free-lance. International Design Award, American Institute of Decorators. Has exhibited MT 1960 (gold medal), FS, FZ. Made the bangle given personally by the Finnish President and his wife to Princess Margrethe on her visit to Finland 1958. (371, 372).

RASMUSSEN, FRANKA. Danish weaver, b. 1909. Trained at Kunstgewerbeschule, Frankfurt-on-Main. Lecturer at Copenhagen A.C.S. since 1949. Has made decorative schemes for several Copenhagen theatres, inc. Theatre Royal. Inde-

Signe Persson-Melin

pendent exhibitions in Düsseldorf 1956, Copenhagen 1955, 1960. (163).

RASMUSSEN, PEDER. Danish ceramics artist, b. 1929. Self-taught. Own pottery since 1950. With Bing & Grøndahl since 1959. Has exhibited frequently at home and abroad inc. MTs and AD. Represented in Copenhagen I.A.M. and Louisiana Museum, Copenhagen. (266).

RASTAD, ROLF. Norwegian interior-designer, b. 1916. Training in business and at State S.C.I.A. Own drawing-office with Adolf Relling (q.v.) 1944. Chairman for some years of Interior-designers' Union. This firm has carried out several demanding interiors and also produces models for craft and industrial manufacture. Represented in Oslo and Trondheim I.A.M.s. (61–64, 67).

REIFF, ERIK. Danish ceramics artist, b. 1923. Began as painter and also studied art-history: introduced to ceramics by Axel Brüel (q.v.). Trained with Herman A. Kähler, Næstved, Denmark, in Drøbak, Norway, and at stoneware works in Sèvres. With Bing & Grøndahl 1949–57. Studied in England 1956, inc. with Bernard Leach, Hans Coper, and Lucie Rie. Own workshop since 1957. Has several times exhibited at home and abroad, inc. MTs, AD. Represented in Copenhagen I.A.M. (320).

RELLING, ADOLF. Norwegian interior-designer, b. 1913. Trained at State S.C.I.A.: master-cabinetmaker. Own drawing-office with Rolf Rastad (q.v.) since 1944. (61–64, 67).

RICHTER, MARIANNE. Swedish textile-artist, b. 1916. Trained at craft-school in Hälsingborg and Stockholm A.C.S. Worked with Kronoberg Domestic Crafts, Växjö, 1939–42, with Märta Måås-Fjetterström Ltd. in Båstad from 1942, and with Wahlbeck carpet works in Linköping since 1955. Designed 1952 for MMF pattern for a 200 sq. m. drape for UNESCO council chamber in UN-building, New York. Teacher of textile-design at A.C.S. since 1942. Represented in Stockholm N.M., Malmö Museum, Trondheim I.A.M. Has exhibited textiles since 1945 inc. at DS, FS, H 55, Amsterdam 1960. (11, 137).

Erik Pløen

RING, LOTTA. Finnish textile-artist, b. 1915. Trained at Fredrika Wetterhoff Institute, Tavastehus, and Helsinki C.I.A. With FFH 1949, Tampella Ltd. 1950–53, FFH again from 1956. First prize in Tampella damask competition and Bigelow-Stanford Carpet Co.'s rug competition, 1959 and 1960. Has exhibited in Europe, U.S.A., Japan. (190).

RISLAKKI, EERO. Finnish jewellery artist and industrial designer, b. 1924. Trained Helsinki School of Fine Arts and C.I.A. ceramics department. Designer for Graveren brickworks, Norway, 1950–51, Kalevala Koru, Helsinki, 1951–55. Since 1955 designer for Westerback Ltd. in Helsinki. Own design-office 1959, and teacher of style and composition-design at Helsinki Goldsmiths' School. Has exhibited in Europe and America, inc. MT 1960, DS, FS, FZ. (370).

RODE, AKSEL. Danish art-historian and ceramic artist, b. 1905. Trained in sculpture at Copenhagen Academy of Art, then studied as art-historian. Appointed to Copenhagen State Museum of Art 1941. Lecturer in history of sculpture at Academy of Art since 1948. Art-consultant for Bing & Grøndahl 1945–59, where he devised nearly all the glazes used by Gertrud Vasegaard, Gudrun Bæch, Erik Reiff, and Georg Hetting (q.v.) and Myre Vasegaard. Own pottery from 1959 with Gertrud Vasegaard and her daughter Myra. Comprehensive author in art-history, and articles on Danish

Kyllikki Salmenhaara

ceramics. For representation in museums and exhibitions, see under Gertrud Vasegaard.

ROGNVED, ALF. Norwegian ceramics artist, b. 1924. Trained at Copenhagen A.C.S. Own pottery from 1948 with his wife Kari (q.v.). Teacher at Bergen A.C.S. since 1958. Has exhibited in Europe and America, inc. MT 1960. Works bought by Bergen I.A.M. (177, 305).

ROGNVED, KARI. Norwegian ceramics artist, b. 1925. Trained at State S.C.I.A. and Bergen A.C.S., and practically in a Danish pottery. Own pottery with husband Alf since 1948. This pair work together, and remarks on husband relate also to Kari. (177, 305).

SADOLIN, EBBE. Danish designer, b. 1900. Trained at Copenhagen Academy of Art as painter. Since 1927 with Bing & Grøndahl. Draftsman for Copenhagen dailies since 1935: has illustrated many books. Has exhibited as practical artist frequently at home and abroad, inc. MTs (Grand Prix 1951), DS, AD. Represented in New York Metropolitan and Brooklyn Museums, Württembergisches Museum Stuttgart, Chemnitz Museum, Stockholm N.M., Copenhagen I.A.M., etc. (324).

SALMENHAARA, KYLLIKKI. Finnish ceramics artist, b. 1915. Trained at Helsinki C.I.A. With Arabia from 1947. Has exhibited abroad, inc. MTs (silver medal

Axel Salto

Eystein Sandnes

1951, diplôme d'honneur 1954, Grand Prix 1957, gold medal 1960), DS, H 55, WG, FZ. Represented in Amsterdam Stedelijke Museum, Trondheim I.A.M., etc. Her technical knowledge and instinct for ceramics happily combine to make her a great artist in her chosen field–a hundred-per-cent potter. While she compounds her glazes with the scientific precision which has given her work an unusually homogeneous quality, she is also able to make her products reflect impressions from the Finnish landscape in a way which appears completely instinctive and uncalculated. Her glazes create impressions of birchbark, primaeval mountains, or autumn leaves; and the subtle timeless form she gives her stoneware harmonises, with unfailing certainty, with the surface glaze to make a natural and accomplished ceramic whole.

SALTO, AXEL. Danish painter, draftsman, and ceramic artist, 1889–1961. Trained at Academy of Art, Copenhagen, as painter. Travelled often, especially to Paris and the South of France. Made pottery since 1923, first for Bing & Grøndahl and Nathalie Krebs (q.v.), then for a long period for the Royal Porcelain Manufactory. Designed patterns for bookbinding paper 1934, for printed fabrics made by L. F. Foght 1944. Carried out several decorative commissions in connection with architecture, inc. State Life-Assurance building in Copenhagen. In charge of restoration of Jørgen Sonne's frieze of 1846 on Thorvaldsen Museum,

Copenhagen. Since 1916 has published several books with his own illustrations, and illustrated books and poetry for other authors. Co-founder of periodical *Klingen* 1917. Frequently exhibited independently, and in all major Danish displays inc. MTs (Grand Prix 1951), DS, NF, FS, AD. Represented in Peking, V. & A., Sèvres, Bergen, Trondheim, and Copenhagen I.A.M.s, Stockholm N.M., etc. (71, 263, 264).

SAMPE, ASTRID. Swedish textile-artist and production director, b. 1909. Trained at Stockholm A.C.S. and Royal College of Art London. Worked with Nordiska Co. Stockholm 1936, chief of its newly-founded textile-department 1937. Has worked for Donald Bros. Dundee, Knoll International Textile Section New York, Kasthall carpetworks Kinna, Svängsta Klädesfabrik (floor-coverings), Almedahl-Dalsjöfors (linen), etc. Independent displays at home and abroad and represented at Paris 1937, New York 1939, DS, FS, H 55, Amsterdam 1960. Represented in Stockholm N.M., Gothenburg R.A.C.M., Trondheim I.A.M., V. & A., New York Museum of Modern Art, Walker Art Center Minneapolis. Has assisted with furnishings of seven Swedish embassies. Grand Prix MT 1954. Honorary member of Faculty of Royal Designers for Industry and Royal Society of Arts, London, 1949. Gregor Paulsson trophy 1956. With Vera Diurson published *Textiles Illustrated* 1948. Using Nordiska Co.'s Textile studio as a sounding-board, she has carried on an important

activity as pattern-designer, colour-composer, and production organiser. (112, 115).

SANDNES, EYSTEIN. Norwegian artist specialising in glass and ceramics, b. 1924. Trained at State S.C.I.A. and with practice in ceramic workshop. With Norsk Glassverk 1951, Stavangerflint 1955, Porsgrund 1957. Several first prizes in competitions. Has taken part in all Norwegian applied-art exhibitions at home and abroad since 1952: silver medal MT 1960. (256, 310, 312, 313, 351).

SARPANEVA, TIMO. Finnish glass-artist, designer, and draftsman, b. 1926. Trained as draftsman at Helsinki C.I.A. Glass-artist with Karhula-Iittala since 1950, art-director of Björneborg Cottons since 1955, teacher in fabric composition and printing at C.I.A. 1953–57. Also works for Björneborg Machine-shops with cast-iron household ware and composes rugs for Villahtymä. Lunning Prize 1956. Silver medal MT 1951 (fabrics) Grand Prix 1954 (art-glass) 2 Grands Prix 1957 (art-and useful glass, and for exhibition arrangement) and silver medal (fabrics), gold medal 1960 (glass) and silver (cast-iron ware) 1960. Three first prizes in American Young Scandinavians Exhibition, U.S.A. 1956. In 1958 invited by Brazilian government to arrange Finnish industrial art exhibition and lecture in Rio and São Paulo. Represented in New York Museum of Modern Art, V. & A., Trondheim I.A.M., Amsterdam Stedelijke Museum, Neue Sammlung Munich, Louisiana Copenhagen, Brunswick Design Collection. Has exhibited frequently in Europe and America, inc. MTs 1951–60, H 55, DS, WG, FZ. Independent displays Helsinki 1956, 1960, Copenhagen 1956, Stockholm 1957, New York 1958, London 1958. Designed several Finnish home exhibitions, H 55, Finnish section of MT 1957, and FZ.

His elegant and studied artistry is the result of careful work which leaves nothing to chance. It is typical of him that he first attracted attention with refined compositions in embroidery, before he found his most vital field in art-glass. His draftmanship combines elaborate detail with the sureness of line which one also sees in the contours of his glassware.

Timo Sarpaneva

It is notable that his sense of colour is just as developed as his talent for draftsmanship: he has shown this as colour-consultant for various firms, especially cotton- and woollen-mills. His sureness of taste in material and proportion has brought him work as exhibition-arranger and book-designer. It is typical of developments in Finland that his later activities have brought this sensitive artist into ever closer contact with the making of useful wares such as textile-lengths and cast-iron cooking-pots. (210, 212, 213, 349).

SCHILKIN, MICHAEL. Finnish ceramic artist, 1900–1962. Trained at Helsinki A.C.S. Worked at Arabia since 1936. Represented in Stockholm N.M., Royal Porcelain Works museum, Trondheim I.A.M., Faenza M.I.C., New York Metropolitan Museum, Chicago Art Institute. Has exhibited in Europe and U.S.A., inc. Paris 1937 (gold medal), MTs 1951 (diplôme d'honneur) and 1954 (silver medal), H 55, FZ. He has a special place among Finnish ceramic artists on account of the monumental reliefs with which he has adorned a number of exteriors and interiors in Helsinki and Stockholm, including the façade of the Finnish College of Commerce and of the Arabia works, and the interiors of the Helsinki Town Hall basement and a number of stores. This large format is excellently suited to his powerful and dynamic method of expression, which, with his heavy glazes, also marks his increasingly stylised animal sculptures in stoneware. (348).

SCHOU, AAGE. Norwegian interior-designer, b. 1901. Trained at State S.C.I.A. and Copenhagen Academy of Art and with further study in Munich. In Oslo Town Hall drawing-office 1937–46. Art-director of Norwegian Domestic Crafts Association since 1946. Published *The Book of Furniture* with Eyvind S. Engelstad 1951. Articles in Norwegian and foreign periodicals. Chair in Oslo I.A.M. Has exhibited in various countries. (25, 104).

SCHUMACHER PERCY, ULLA. Swedish textile-artist, b. 1918. Trained at Stockholm A.C.S. Artistic assistant with Stockholm and district Domestic Crafts Association since 1947. Has made embroideries and rugs in her own workshop 'Lintråden', Tullinge, Stockholm. Represented in Stockholm N.M. and Trondheim I.A.M. Individual exhibitions Stockholm 1957, 1960. Has taken part in major exhibitions, inc. FS. (135).

SIIMES, AUNE. Finnish ceramics artist, b. 1909. Trained Helsinki C.I.A. With Arabia since 1932. Has exhibited frequently in Europe, U.S.A., and Canada, inc. MTs 1951–60 (gold medal 1951, 1954), Paris 1937 (silver medal), DS, H 55, WG, FZ. Represented in Stockholm N.M., Faenza M.I.C., Gothenburg R.A.C.M., Trondheim I.A.M., Amsterdam Stedelijke Museum. Porcelain is her favourite material. Previously she also worked in stoneware and chamotte with heavy coloured glazes, but her principal output has been thin-walled bowls and vases with relief patterns of varying transparency in the white, pink, or cobalt-blue porcelain. She has also made jewellery in this material. (336).

SIMBERG-EHRSTRÖM, UHRA BEATA. Finnish textile-artist, b. 1914. Trained at Helsinki C.I.A. Rug-designer for FFH since 1935. Designer of industrial production for Inhemsk Ull (Native Woollens) since 1938, and for Finlayson-Forssa from 1958. Art-consultant for Norna Domestic Crafts 1950–58. Exhibitions inc. Paris 1937 (diploma), MTs (diplôme d'honneur 1954, Grand Prix 1957, gold medal 1960), DS, H 55, FZ. Represented in Copenhagen I.A.M. Several public and private grants. The most outstanding

colorist amongst Finnish weavers, with her own individual colour-scale which gives her products an unusually homogeneous appearance. Her mild and calm colouring is in modest shades of brown, green, grey, and lilac, found equally in her rugs and her industrially-made woollens, scarves, plaids, and shawls. She has also worked on church fabrics and tapestry.

SIMMULSON, MARI. Swedish ceramics artist and painter, b. 1911. Trained at government craft-school in Tallin, Estonia, and Akademie der Bildenden Künste, Munich. Swedish nationality 1952. Designer with Gustavsberg 1945–49, with Ekeby works of Upsala-Ekeby Group since 1949, where works on both useful and decorative earthenware with richly figured decoration and on pure ceramic sculpture. Has carried out decorative commissions for e.g. Upland Bank Enköping branch office and Pharmacia building in Copenhagen. Represented in Stockholm N.M., Tallin Art Museum, Faenza M.I.C., V. & A., Trondheim I.A.M. Has exhibited in Sweden and abroad, inc. MTs 1951 and 1960. (300).

SKAWONIUS, SVEN ERIK. Swedish artist, b. 1908. Trained at Stockholm A.C.S. and Royal Academy of Art. Decoration-painter and costume-designer for Royal Dramatic Theatre in Stockholm to 1946. Designer for industrial firms in glass, ceramics, floor-coverings, fabric-prints, tapestry, posters etc., house-furnishing, silver, and bookbinding. Secretary for exhibitions in Sweden, Denmark, Finland, Holland, Switzerland, and Germany. Has exhibited at home and abroad since 1930: Gold medal MT 1954. Represented in museums in Europe and U.S.A. Administrative director of Swedish Society for Industrial Design 1946–49 and 1957–60. Has written articles for collective works and in the Press at home and abroad. Published with Arthur Hald *Nyttokonst – Contemporary Swedish Design* 1951 and *Household Glass* 1959. Editor of Swedish material in this book. (289).

SKERFE-NILSSON, INGRID. Swedish textile-artist, b. 1918. Trained at Stockholm A.C.S. Worked with Uppsala Domestic Crafts 1945–51, then own textile work-

Alf Sture

Carl-Harry Stålhane

shop and business, Skerfe-Nilsson Konsthantverk-Textilateljé, Uppsala. Took part in H 55, FS, Amsterdam 1959, MT 1960, and had independent exhibition in Stockholm 1959 Has made floor-coverings for various churches. (136, 361).

SONNE BRUUN, EDITH. Danish ceramics artist, b. 1910. Trained at Copenhagen A.C.S. Own workshop with Grete Gissemann and Christian Poulsen (q.v.) 1934–37. After some years absence from ceramics joined Saxbo in 1946, where began an independent production 1951. Since 1952 has taken part in Saxbo's many exhibitions and in general exhibitions at home and abroad, inc MT 1960, DS, NF, FS, AD. Represented in Metropolitan Museum New York, Kunst und Gewerbe Museum Hamburg, Stockholm N.M., and Louisiana Museum Copenhagen. (268).

STEPHENSEN, MAGNUS. Danish architect, b. 1903. Trained at Copenhagen Academy of Art building-school. Own business 1932 after some years in Copenhagen drawing-offices. Has built many dwellings and schools in Copenhagen and also designed furniture, tapestry, silver, stainless steel, porcelain, and earthenware. Collaborated 1943 with Kay Bojesen, 1952 with Georg Jensen Ltd., and since 1956 with Royal Porcelain Manufactory. As artist-designer has taken part in many exhibitions at home and abroad, inc. MTs (2 Grands Prix 1954, 3 gold medals 1951 and 1957), DS, NF, FS, AD. Represented

at several museums inc. New York Metropolitan Museum and Museum of Modern Art, Kunstgewerbemuseum Zürich, Oslo, Bergen, and Trondheim I.A.M.s, Gothenburg R.A.C.M., Copenhagen I.A.M. and Louisiana Museum, Copenhagen. (275, 387, 412).

STILL-MCKINNEY, NANNY. Finnish glass-artist and woodcarver, now living in Belgium, b. 1926. Trained Helsinki C.I.A. With Riihimäen Lasi glassworks from 1949. Has exhibited in Europe, U.S.A., and Brazil, inc. MTs 1954–60 (Diplôme d'honneur for work in wood 1954), DS, H 55, FS, FZ. One of the three in exhibition 'Trois Profils Finlandais', Brussels 1960. (242, 243).

STRINNING, NISSE. Swedish architect and industrial designer, b. 1917. Trained at Royal Institute of Technology Stockholm. Own business in Stockholm since 1948. Exhibited MT 1954 (gold medal), H 55. (7).

STRÖMDAHL, ÅKE. Swedish silversmith and designer, b. 1913. Craft training under father, Court jeweller Hugo Strömdahl, Stockholm, and at A.C.S., Kunstgewerbeschule in Stuttgart, École des Arts Décoratifs in Paris. Master-jeweller and goldsmith. Since 1948 owner and administrative director of Strömdahl firm. Designs church and secular silver, as well as gold and silver jewellery both of exclusive type and in bright everyday ornaments using cut Swedish stones. Also designs

for industry, e.g. plastics for Skaraplast Ltd. Represented in Stockholm N.M. Exhibited in Svensk Form Copenhagen 1942, H 55, DS, FS, Swedish Silver 1953 and Modern Jewellery 1959, both in Stockholm. (358, 390).

STURE, ALF. Norwegian interior-designer, b. 1915. Trained at State S.C.I.A. Designer and apprentice cabinetmaker with Hiorth & Østlyngen 1940–50. Worked independently from 1950, specialising in interiors. Has exhibited at home and abroad. (26, 55, 176, 406).

STÆHR-NIELSEN, EVA. Danish ceramics artist, b. 1911. Trained at Copenhagen A.C.S., after which joined Saxbo, where has since worked with Nathalie Krebs. Study tours in Paris, London, and Italy. For representation in exhibitions and museums see under Nathalie Krebs. (269).

STÅLHANE, CARL-HARRY. Swedish ceramics artist, b. 1920. Trained as painter under Isaac Grünewald in Stockholm and as sculptor under Ossip Zadkine, Académie Colarossi, Paris. Travel in Europe, U.S.A., and Mexico. Since 1939 artist with Rörstrand porcelain-works in Lidköping. Has made painted earthenware, stoneware, and services in felspar-porcelain. Represented in Stockholm N.M., Gothenburg R.A.C.M., Malmö Museum, Copenhagen and Trondheim I.A.M.s, Faenza M.I.C., New York Museum of Modern Art, Syracuse U.S.A. Art Museum, Honolulu and Buenos Aires. Has taken part in Rörstrand exhibitions in Stockholm 1948, Copenhagen 1954, London 1957, and held his own in Stockholm 1951, 1957, 1960. Gothenburg 1946, Malmö 1950, New York 1960. Also MTs (gold medal 1951, diplôme d'honneur 1954), DS, H 55, FS. International Design Award of American Decorators 1960. He has gradually worked out a style of his own, by way of classicist types to very massive and solid stoneware with eruptive glazes. He has also designed striking service-ware and functional restaurant china for Rörstrand's ordinary output. (282, 297).

SVEDBERG, ELIAS. Swedish furniture-designer and organiser, b. 1913. Pupil of Carl Malmsten, and also studied in Europe

Ilmari Tapiovaara

and America. Own business as interior-designer 1935–44, then appointed consultant furniture- and interior-designer with Nordiska Co. in Stockholm and its Nyköping factories: head of furnishing department 1952, sales director 1961. Has arranged interiors and designed both exclusive pieces and mass-produced furniture, e.g. Triva series. Published with Lena Larsson *Home-Furnishing*. Active in the Swedish Society for Industrial Design and in its propaganda work, and has arranged or assisted with many exhibitions.

SVEINSDOTTIR, JULIANA. Icelandic painter and weaver, living in Denmark, b. 1889. Trained as painter at Copenhagen Academy of Art. Represented in exhibitions in Denmark and abroad, inc. MTs (gold medal 1951), DS, FS. Independent exhibitions in Reykyavik 1936, 1949, 1957. Works bought by Gothenburg R.A.C.M. and Copenhagen I.A.M. (121).

SVENSSON, ALF. Swedish furniture-designer, b. 1923. Craft training as cabinetmaker under Johan Svensson and at Gothenburg School of Art and Design. Since 1948 has designed furniture for Ljung Industries Ltd. (DUX) and light-fittings for Bergbom & Co., both in Malmö. Since 1961 own drawing-office with architect Yngvar Sandström. Has exhibited in Gothenburg 1952, H 55, MTs 1954 (gold medal) 1957 (diplôme d'honneur) and 1960, Interbau Berlin 1957, FS. Gold medal at California State Fair in Sacramento 1958. (8).

TAPIOVAARA, ILMARI. Finnish furniture-designer, b. 1914. Trained at Helsinki C.I.A. and in furniture-works in Finland, England, and Sweden, and with Le Corbusier in Paris. Artistic director of Askon Tehtaat Ltd. in Lahtis 1938–41, of Keravan Puuteollisuus Ltd. in Kervo 1941–50. Since 1951 own drawing office with Annikki Tapiovaara. Chief of interior department at C.I.A. 1951–52 and 1953–54, and teacher of industrial design 1954–56. Visiting professor of Product Design at Illinois Institute of Technology 1952–54. UN expert in industrial furniture and design in Paraguay 1958. Has won many competition prizes in Finland, Sweden, and U.S.A. Also prizes for light-fittings, glass, and toys. Has exhibited frequently in Europe and U.S.A., inc. MTs (gold medals 1951, 1954, 1957, 1960), FS, DS, FZ, Museum of Modern Art travelling exhibition 1949–51, and independently in Helsinki, Brussels, and Amsterdam 1947, Chicago 1953, Asuncion 1958. Has done many interiors in schools, offices, industrial premises, etc.

The chairs in wood or steel tubing for which he is best known give striking evidence of his clear constructive thinking. He has also taken an interest in pieces for export, both as regards assembly and stacking, and his solutions to the packaging problem are based on thorough study. He has heavily stressed the necessity for specialisation in export furniture; and within his own special field – small chairs for homes and auditoria – he has made types which can already be called classical. Both his furniture and his interiors have a cool airy structural character. He has explained his attitude to design in a large number of articles and lectures in Finland, Europe, and America. (21–24).

THIRSLUND, LARS. Danish ceramics artist, b.1922. Trained at Copenhagen A.C.S. and Academy of Art school of painting. With Bing & Grøndahl 1945–46, and Søholm Ltd. Rønne 1946–49. Own workshop since 1950 with wife Marianne Herlufsdatter (q.v.). Has exhibited independently and in several Danish applied-art exhibitions at home and abroad, inc. NF, FS, AD. Represented in Copenhagen I.A.M. (315, 316).

THOMMESEN, ANNA. Danish weaver, b. 1908. Self-taught. Took up weaving 1938.

Works bought by State Museum of Art and Copenhagen I.A.M. (154).

TRETTEBERG, RAGNHILD. Norwegian weaver, b. 1904. Trained at State I.S.W. and Friends of Handicraft weaving-school, Stockholm. Member of council and art committee of Norwegian Domestic Crafts Association. Teacher at State I.S.W. since 1931, chief 1958. (122, 126, 174, 204, 351).

TRILLER, ERIK, b. 1898, INGRID, b. 1905. Swedish ceramics artists. Trained at Keramische Werkstatt, Dornburg/Saale and Staatliche Keramische Fachschule, Bunzlau. Own workshop, Tobo Stoneware. Represented in Stockholm N.M. and Nordiska Museum, V. & A., Landesmuseum Stuttgart, and museums in Sèvres, Stoke-on-Trent Prague, Seattle, and Houston. Exhibited independently in Stockholm 1936, 1943, took part in Paris 1937, New York 1939, Stoke-on-Trent, Berlin, Brussels, MT 1960. (280).

TROCK, PAULA. Danish weaver, b. 1889. Trained practically in Denmark, Finland, and Sweden and on study tours in England, Germany, and Italy. Set up Askovhus weaving-school 1928, in charge to 1943. Began production of special yarns in own factory 'Spindegaarden' in Askov 1949. Represented at Paris 1935, Brussels 1952, MTs (gold medal 1960), DS, NF, FS, AD. Works bought by applied-art museums in Denmark, Norway, Switzerland, and U.S.A. (118, 119).

TRÄGÅRDH, GÖTA. Swedish fashion- and pattern-designer and teacher, b. 1904. Trained at Stockholm A.C.S. and Academy of Art. Fashion-designer for Svenska Dagbladet. Head of fashion-department at Anders Beckman School, Stockholm. Artistic director of Stobo Ltd. (screen-printed fabrics) since 1955. Consultant, and arranger of exhibitions and fashion-displays. Designs patterns, clothes, jewellery, etc. Represented in Gothenburg R.A.C.M. and museums in Britain. Has taken part in exhibitions at home and abroad: one of the secretaries for the Swedish Society for Industrial Design Centenary Exhibition in Stockholm 1945 and H 55. Gold medal MT 1951. Gregor Paulsson trophy 1958. (148).

Hans J. Wegner

TUUMI, RAIJA. Finnish ceramics artist, b. 1923. Trained at Helsinki C.I.A. under Elsa Elenius. With Arabia since 1950. Represented in Stedelijk Museum Amsterdam, Trondheim I.A.M., etc., and at exhibitions in Europe, U.S.A., and Canada inc. MTs 1951–60, DS, H 55, WG, FZ. She works mostly with heavy simply-thrown forms in stoneware and chamotte, in which the traces of throwing remain in the coarse outer surface. Her glazes also are crude and uneven, and because of this individual and interesting. The complete simplicity of form characteristic of her bowls and dishes gives her products strength and endows them with an original charm, such as is often said to be typical of Finnish pottery.

TYNELL, HELLIN HELENA. Finnish glass-artist, b. 1918. Trained at Helsinki C.I.A. Designed light-fittings for Taito Ltd. 1943–55, while also working occasionally for Wärtsilä/Arabia as potter. Artist with Riihimäki glassworks since 1945: also since 1957 permanent assistant with firm Nord, New York, for which designs glass light-fittings. Represented in Corning Glass Museum, N.Y., and in many exhibitions, inc. MTs 1954–60, H 55, FZ. (241).

VASEGAARD, GERTRUD. Danish ceramics artist, b. 1913. Trained at Copenhagen A.C.S. 1933–35 workshop in Bornholm with sister Lisbet Munch Petersen (q.v.), then own workshop in same place to 1948. Connected with Bing & Grøndahl 1945–59, then own workshop in Copenhagen with husband Aksel Rode (q.v.) and daughter Myre Vasegaard. Represented in Museum of Art Syracuse N.Y., Trondheim and Copenhagen I.A.M.s, Stockholm N.M., Louisiana Museum Copenhagen; and in exhibitions at home and abroad inc. MTs (gold medal 1957), DS, FS, AD. (262, 321).

VIGELAND, TONE. Norwegian silversmith, b. 1936. Trained at State S.C.I.A. and craft school. Employed by Norway Silver Designs Ltd. 4 prizes in Goldsmiths' League competition. Three works in Applied Art Association permanent collections, Oslo, and represented in Oslo I.A.M. (365, 366).

WALTHER, CONNY. Danish ceramics artist, b. 1931. Trained at Saxbo and Copenhagen A.C.S. Own workshop since 1955. Exhibited art-handicraft at home and abroad, inc. AD. (271).

WANSCHER, OLE. Danish architect, b. 1903. Trained at Academy of Art building-school: succeeded Kaare Klint as professor in Academy's furniture- and interior-department 1955. Has designed furniture for A. J. Iversen, Rud. Rasmussen, France & Son, Fritz Hansen, etc. Represented in exhibitions at home and abroad inc. MTs (gold medal 1960), DS, NF, FS, AD. Works bought by Stockholm N.M., Copenhagen I.A.M. and Louisiana Museum, Copenhagen. Has written many articles for professional press and published several books on the art and history of furniture, inc. *Furniture Types* 1932, *Outline History of Furniture* 1941, *English Furniture c. 1680–1800* 1944, and major work *History of the Art of Furniture* 1946–56. (36, 88).

WECKSTRÖM, BJÖRN. Finnish goldsmith, b. 1935. Trained at Helsinki Goldsmith school. Own workshop Helsinki since 1958, where makes jewellery. Exhibited in Munich 1958, MT 1960, FZ. (367).

WEEKE, KIRSTEN. Danish ceramics artist, b. 1932. Trained at Copenhagen A.C.S., since then with Saxbo. Has exhibited in Saxbo and general exhibitions at home and abroad, inc. MTs, FS, AD. (265).

WEFRING, TUSTA. Danish fabric-printer, b. 1925 in Norway. Trained in workshop and at Copenhagen A.C.S. Own workshop since 1950. Textile-designer for Unika-Vaev Ltd. Exhibited in Denmark and abroad, inc. NF, AD. (160).

WEGGERBY, BIRTE. Danish ceramics artist, b. 1927. Trained at Copenhagen A.C.S. Half-year with Saxbo, then own workshop 1950. Has exhibited independently and in general exhibitions at home and abroad. Represented in Copenhagen I.A.M. and Louisiana Museum, Copenhagen. (272).

WEGNER, HANS J. Danish furniture-designer, b. 1914. Trained as cabinetmaker and then as designer at Copenhagen A.C.S. Taught at A.C.S. 1946–55. Own drawing-office 1948. Has designed furniture for Johannes Hansen, A. P. chairs, Danish C.W.S., Getama Ltd., Carl Hansen & Son, Fritz Hansen, C .M. Madsen furniture-works, Planmøbel Ltd., Ry Møbler Ltd., Andreas Tuck, etc. Represented at all major exhibitions at home and abroad inc. MTs DS, NF, FS, AD. Lunning Prize 1954, Eckersberg medal 1956. Grand Prix MT 1951, gold medal 1954. Royal Designer for Industry, London, 1959. International Design Award of American Institute of Decorators 1961. Works bought by New York Museum of Modern Art and Metropolitan Museum, Melbourne National Gallery, Oslo, Trondheim, and Copenhagen I.A.M.'s, Stockholm N.M., Gothenburg R.A.C.M., Loui-

Tapio Wirkkala

siana Museum Copenhagen, etc. Fitted out conference room in UNESCO headquarters, Paris, 1958. (38, 39, 75, 76).

WESSEL, BIRGIT. Norwegian weaver, b. in Sweden. Trained at Stockholm College of Industrial Art and with Swedish Domestic Crafts and Märta Måås-Fjetterström. Own weaving-room since 1937. Member of Applied Art Association council, Oslo; has made fabrics and rugs for Crown Princess Märtha and royal yacht Norge. Also collaborated with Norwegian textile industry. (170, 256, 308, 354).

WESTMAN, MARIANNE. Swedish ceramics artist and pattern-designer, b. 1928. Trained at Stockholm A.C.S. Designer with Rörstrand porcelain-works since 1950. Pattern-designer for and part-owner of Westmans Textilateljé, Falun, established 1958 (making hand-printed fabrics). Exhibited for Rörstrand Copenhagen 1954, in London 1957, New York 1960. (292, 302).

WETTERGREN, ERIK. Swedish art historian and museum official, 1883–1961. Secretary of Society for Industrial Design 1913–18, chairman 1931–43. Keeper of art-handicraft department in Stockholm N.M. 1918–42, Director 1942–50. Chief of Royal Dramatic Theatre 1928–34. A vital force in Swedish art-handicrafts and industrial art since c. 1910, and his work had a great influence on their inner development and outer appearance. One of the active sponsors of the important exhibition of furnishings for small homes in Stockholm in 1917. Published 1925 *L'Art décoratif moderne en Suède* (also in English).

WIDÉN, SOFIA. Swedish textile artist, 1900–1961. Trained at Stockholm A.C.S. Worked with Licium fabric studios from 1923, head of firm 1930–51. Also had her own firm in Hytting, Borlänge, where made fabrics for many Swedish churches and for Oslo, Helsinki, Copenhagen, Paris, and London. Represented in Stockholm N.M., Gothenburg R.A.C.M., V. & A., etc., and in exhibitions inc. Stockholm 1930, Paris 1937, New York 1939, H 55, DS, FS. Independent exhibitions in Oslo I.A.M. and Stockholm. Gold medal MT 1954. (133).

WILSGAARD, JAN. Swedish industrial designer, b. 1927. Trained at Crafts Association school, Gothenburg, and with Volvo Ltd. Gothenburg, where designed car models. Head of Volvo design department since 1961. Represented at motor-shows in Europe and U.S.A.

WINGE, BENDT. Norwegian interior-designer, b. 1907. Trained as cabinetmaker and at State S.C.I.A. and craft-school in Germany. Own drawing-office since 1945. Consultant to Applied Art Federation 1947–59. After war, in charge of Applied Art Federation's travelling exhibitions in war-damaged areas in Finmark. Arranged Norwegian travelling exhibitions in Sweden 1958–59. Has frequently exhibited at home and abroad. (56–60).

WIRKKALA, TAPIO. Finnish glass-artist, designer, and draftsman, b. 1915. Trained at Helsinki C.I.A. Artistic director of Karhula-Iittala glassworks since 1947, and of C.I.A. 1951–55. Worked with design-firm Raymond Loewy, New York, 1955–56. Has modelled silver for Kultakesus in Helsinki. First and second prize in Finnish bank-note competition 1947, four prizes in postage-stamp competition 1952: 3 Grands Prix MT 1951 (glass, light-fittings, exhibition arrangement): 3 Grands Prix MT 1954 (glass, sculpture, exhibition-arrangement): Grand Prix MT 1960 (lampshades) and gold medal. Lunning Prize 1951. First prize in international competition 'The big store and daily life in 2000 AD' in connection with Brussels 1958. Prize in silver competition arranged by New York Museum of Contemporary Crafts 1960. Represented in New York Museum of Modern Art and Metropolitan Museum, V. & A., Kunstgewerbemuseum Zürich, Stockholm N.M., Copenhagen and Trondheim I.A.M.s. Arranged Finnish exhibitions in Zürich and Gothenburg 1951, Finnish sections MT's 1951–54, travelling exhibitions in Britain (1952) and U.S.A. (1953), Finnish pavilion Brussels 1958. Independent exhibitions Oslo 1952 and (with wife Rut Bryk) travelling ex. in U.S.A., arranged by Smithsonian Institution. Also took part in MTs 1951–60, DS, FS, H 55, WG, FZ.

Wirkkala's name has almost become a symbol of Finnish industrial art in the past decade, partly because of his unusual versatility and partly because he made such an impression at the beginning of the Fifties with his art glass and his original works in plywood. In addition, his seven Grands Prix at three Triennali, Lunning Prize, and many other international distinctions, have made him the best known of all present day Finnish artists. His most masterly work is done in exhibition arrangement, draftsmanship, and glass, in which fields he has many achievements which deserve to be called classic. He is a bold and dynamic artist, and one of the most colourful in Finland.

WIWEN-NILSSON, KARL EDVIN. Swedish silversmith and jeweller, b. 1897. Craft-trained under his father, Court-jeweller Anders Nilsson, Lund, and at Hanau Zeichenakademie and technical school in Copenhagen, practically with Georg Jensen, and finally at Académie de la Grande Chaumière and Académie Colarossi in Paris. Took over father's workshop and business 1928. Represented in Stockholm N.M., Gothenburg R.A.C.M., Malmö Museum, etc. Has made silver for Swedish churches. Exhibited at Gothenburg 1923, Paris 1925, New York 1939, Zürich 1948, H 55, DS, FS, Amsterdam 1959, etc. and in U.S.A. Gold medal Paris 1925. Gregor Paulsson trophy 1955. Swedish Goldsmiths' and Jewellers' Guild gold medal 1956, Prince Eugen medal 1958. (359, 391, 392).

INDEX